ROYAL EDINBURGH

HER SAINTS, KINGS, PROPHETS AND POETS

Margaret Oliphant

SENATE

Royal Edinburgh

First published in 1890 by Macmillan & Co., London

This edition published in 1999 by Senate,
an imprint of Tiger Books International plc,
26A York Street, Twickenham,
Middlesex TW1 3LJ, United Kingdom

ISBN 1 85958 544 2

Printed and bound in the UK by
Cox & Wyman, Reading, England

TO MY OLD FRIEND

ALEXANDER MACMILLAN

CONTENTS

PART I

PAGE

PART II

THE STEWARDS OF SCOTLAND

CHAPTER I

CHAPTER II

CHAPTER III

CHAPTER IV

CHAPTER V

PART III

THE TIME OF THE PROPHETS

CHAPTER I

CHAPTER II

CHAPTER III

CHAPTER IV

PART IV

THE MODERN CITY

CHAPTER I

CHAPTER II

CHAPTER III

LIST OF ILLUSTRATIONS

ROYAL EDINBURGH

QUEEN MARGARET'S CHAPEL, EDINBURGH CASTLE

PART I

MARGARET OF SCOTLAND, ATHELING—

QUEEN AND SAINT

IT is strange yet scarcely difficult to the imagination to realise the first embodiment of what is now Edinburgh in the far distance of the early ages. Neither Pict nor Scot has left any record of what was going on so far south in the days when the king's daughters, primitive princesses with their rude surroundings, were placed for safety in the *castrum puellarum*, the maiden castle, a title in after days proudly (but perhaps not very justly) adapted to the

B

supposed invulnerability of the fortress perched upon its
rock.   Very nearly invulnerable, however, it must have been
in the days before artillery; too much so at least for one
shut-up princess, who complained of her lofty prison as a place
without verdure.   If we may believe, notwithstanding the
protest of that much-deceived antiquary the Laird of Monkbarns, that these fair and forlorn ladies were the first royal
inhabitants of the Castle of Edinburgh, we may imagine
that they watched from their battlements more wistfully
than fearfully, over all the wide plain, what dust might
rise or spears might gleam, or whether any galley
might be visible of reiver or rescuer from the north.   A
little collection of huts or rude forts here and there would
be all that broke the sweeping line of Lothian to the east or
west, and all that width of landscape would lie under the
eyes of the watchers, giving long notice of the approach of
any enemies.   " Out over the Forth I look to the north," the
maidens might sing, looking across to Dunfermline, where
already there was some royal state, or towards the faint
lines of mountains in the distance, over the soft swelling
heights of the Lomonds.   No doubt Edinburgh, Edwines-
burgh, or whatever the antiquaries imagine it to have been,
must have been sadly dull if safe, suspended high upon the
rock, nearer heaven than earth.   It is curious to hear that it
was " without verdure " ; but perhaps the young ladies took no
account of the trees that clothed the precipices below them,
or the greenness that edged the Nor' Loch deep at their
feet, but sighed for the gardens and luxuriance of Dunfermline, where all was green about their windows and the
winding pathways of the dell of Pittendreich would be
pleasant to wander in.   This first romantic aspect of the
Castle of Edinburgh is, however, merely traditional, and the
first real and authentic appearance of the old fortress and
city in history is in the record, at once a sacred legend and a
valuable historical chronicle, of the life of Margaret the
Atheling, the first of several Queen Margarets, the woman
saint and blessed patroness of Scotland, who has bequeathed
not only many benefits and foundations of after good to her

adopted country, but her name—perhaps among Scotswomen still the most common of all Christian names.

No more moving and delightful story was ever written or invented than the history of this saint and Queen. She was the daughter of Edward, called the Outlaw, and of his wife a princess of Hungary, of the race which afterwards produced St. Elizabeth : and the sister of Edgar Atheling, the feeble but rightful heir of the Saxon line, and consequently of the English throne. The family, however, was more foreign than English, having been brought up at the Court of their grandfather, the King of Hungary, one of the most pious and one of the richest Courts in Christendom ; and it was not unnatural that when convinced of the fact that the most legitimate of aspirants had no chance against the force of William, they should prefer to return to the country of their education and birth. It was no doubt a somewhat forlorn party that set out upon this journey, for to lose a throne is seldom a misfortune accepted with equanimity, and several of the beaten and despondent Saxons had joined the royal exiles. Their voyage, however, was an unprosperous one, and after much beating about by winds and storms they were at last driven up the Firth of Forth, where their ship found shelter in the little bay at the narrowing of the Firth, which has since borne the name of St. Margaret's Hope.

Lying here in shelter from all the winds behind the protecting promontory, with perhaps already some humble shrine or hermit's cell upon Inchgarvie or Inchcolm to give them promise of Christian kindness, with the lonely rock of Edinburgh in the distance on one side, and the soft slopes of the Fife coast rising towards the King's palace at Dunfermline on the other, the travellers must have awaited with some anxiety, yet probably much hope, the notice of the barbaric people who came to the beach to stare at their weather-beaten ships, and hurried off to carry the news inland of such unwonted visitors. It is the very spot which is now disturbed and changed by the monstrous cobwebs of iron which bear

PILLAR IN NAVE, DUNFERMLINE ABBEY

the weight of the Forth Bridge and make an end for ever of the Queen's Ferry, which Margaret must have crossed so often, and by which a personage more familiar, Mr. Jonathan Oldbuck, once, as we all know, made his way to the North; but these are modern reflections such as have nothing to do with that primitive morning, fresh no doubt as to-day with sun and dew, when Malcolm's messengers came hurrying down to see what were these intruders, and what their purpose, and whether anything was to be apprehended from a visit apparently so unusual. The eager and curious emissaries had apparently no warrant to board the strangers, but gazed and wondered at the big ship and all its equipments, so unlike their own rude galleys; then hastened back

again with an excited and exciting description of the greatness of the passengers on board and all their splendid array.
Malcolm, cautious yet excited too, sent forth, as we are told
in the *Scotichronicon*, "his wisest councillors" to make further
inquiries. They too were astonished by the splendour of
all they saw, and especially by the mien of a certain lady
among these strangers, "whom, by her incomparable beauty,
and the pleasantness of her jocund speech, I imagined to be
the chief of the family," said the spokesman ; "nor was it
wonderful," adds the chronicler, "that they should believe
her to be the chief who was destined to be Queen of
Scotland and also heir of England." Perhaps it was the
after light of these events that conveyed that high appreciation of Margaret's qualities into the story, for she must
have been quite young, and it is very unlikely that in
presence of her mother, and the brother whom they all considered as the King of England, a young girl, however
gifted, would have taken upon her the chief place.

The report he received, however, had so much effect upon
King Malcolm that he went himself to visit the strangers in
their ship. He was not a mere barbaric prince, to be dazzled
by the sight of these great persons, but no doubt had many a
lingering recollection in his mind of Siward's great house in
Northumberland, where he had taken refuge after his father's
murder. It is curious and bewildering to go back in that
dawn of national life to familiar Shakspearian regions, and
to think that this primitive King who had so much
in him of the savage, along with all his love and gentleness,
was the son of that gracious Duncan who addressed his
hostess like a kingly gentleman though her hospitality was
to be so fatal. King Malcolm came down, no doubt with
such state as he could muster, to see the wandering foreign
princes. He was not unlearned, but knew Latin and the
English tongue, though he could not read, as we are afterwards told. He had already reigned for fourteen years, after
about as long a period of exile, so that he could not now be
in his first youth, although he was still unmarried. He came
down with his suite to the shore amid all the stir of the in-

quiring country folk, gathered about to see this strange thing
—the ship with its unusual equipments, and the group of
noble persons in their fine clothes who were to be seen upon
the deck. The Athelings were carrying back with them to
Hungary all the gifts with which the Emperor, Henry III,
had loaded their father when he went to England, and had
jewels and vessels of gold and many fine things unknown to
the Scots. And Margaret, even though not so prominent·
as the chroniclers say, was evidently by the consent of
all a most gracious and courteous young lady, with
unusual grace and vivacity of speech. The grave middle-
aged King, with his recollections of a society more
advanced than his own, which probably had made him long
for something better than his rude courtiers could supply,
would seem at once to have fallen under the spell of the
wandering princess. She was such a mate as a poor Scots
King, badgered by turbulent clans, could scarcely have
hoped to find—rich and fair and young, and of the best
blood in Christendom. Whether the wooing was as short
as the record we have no means of knowing, but in the
same year, 1070, Margaret was brought with great rejoicing
to Dunfermline, and there married to her King, amid the
general joy.

The royal house at Dunfermline, according to the chronicle,
was surrounded by a dense forest and guarded by immense
cliffs. The latter particular, however, it is difficult to accept,
for the dell in which the ruins of the mediæval palace (a
building much more recent, it is needless to say, than that
of Malcolm) still stand, though picturesque in its acclivities
and precipices, is as far as possible from including any cliffs
that could be called immense. The young Queen made a
great change in the internal arrangements of what was no
doubt a grim stronghold enough, soft as was the country
around. Probably the absence of decoration and ornament
struck her painfully, accustomed as she was to palaces of a
very different kind—for almost the first thing we hear in
the contemporary history written by her confessor Theodoric, afterwards a monk at Durham, is of the work-

DUNFERMLINE ABBEY

shops and rooms for embroidery and all the arts which were
established in Dunfermline, presumably in the palace itself
under Margaret's own eye, for the beautifying of the great
church which she founded there, and also no doubt for her
own house.   Certain women of good birth were judged
worthy to share the Queen's work, and lived with her, it
would seem, in a kind of seclusion, seeing only such
chosen visitors as Margaret brought with her to cheer their
labours, and forswearing all idle talk and frivolity.   The
Queen had such austerity mingled with her graciousness
and such grace with her severity, says her monkish
biographer, loving an antithesis, that all feared and respected
her presence.   " Her life was full of moderation and gentleness, her speech contained the very salt of wisdom ; even
her silence was full of good thoughts."

    This biographer — according to the conscientious and
painstaking investigations of the Bollandist Fathers, who
examine in their careful way all the guarantees and
traditions of the manuscript with a jealousy worthy of the
most enlightened historians—is not Turgot, who is usually
credited with it, but Theodoric, a monk of Durham, who must
have shared with Turgot, at some period of his life, the office of
spiritual director and confidant to the Queen.   It is curious
that both these writers should have passed from the northern
Court to the community at Durham, of which Turgot was prior
and Theodoric a simple brother ; yet not so strange either,
for Durham was largely patronised and enriched by Margaret
and her husband, their kingdom at this period reaching as
far south.   Of Turgot's Life, which was presumably written
in the vernacular, there seems nothing existing ; but that of
Theodoric is very full, and contains many details which set
before us the life of the simple Court, with its many
labours and charities : the King full of reverence and
tender surprise and admiration of all his wife's perfec-
tions ; the young saint herself, sweet and bright in modest
gravity amid a tumultuous world little respectful of women,
full of the excessive charity of the age and of her race, and
of those impulses of decoration and embellishment which were

WEST TOWER, DUNFERMLINE ABBEY

slow to develop among the ruder difficulties of the north. Theodoric himself must have been more or less of an artist, for in speaking of the "golden vases" and ornaments for the altars of her new church which Margaret devised, "I myself carried out the work," he says. These must have been busy days in Malcolm's primitive palace while the workmen were busy with the great cathedral close by, the mason with his mallet, the homely sculptor with his chisel, carving those interlaced and embossed arches which still stand, worn and gray, but little injured, in the wonderful permanency of stone, in the nave of the old Abbey of Dunfermline: while the Queen's rooms opened into the hall

THE NAVE, DUNFERMLINE ABBEY—LOOKING WEST

where her ladies sat over their embroidery, among all
the primitive dyes that art had caught from herbs and
traditional mixtures, on one hand—and on the other into
noisier workshops, where workmen with skilful delicate
hammers were beating out the shining gold and silver
into sacred vessels and symbols of piety. Margaret along
with her stores of more vulgar wealth, and the ingots
which were consecrated to the manufacture of crucifix and
chalice, had brought many holy relics : and no doubt the
cases and shrines in which these were enclosed afforded
models for the new, over which Father Theodoric, with his
monkish cape and cowl laid aside, and his shaven crown
shining in the glow of the furnace, was so busy. What a
pleasant stir of occupation and progress, the best and most
trustworthy evidences of growing civilisation, must have arisen
within the shelter of the woods which framed that centre of
development and new life : the new abbey rising day by
day, a white and splendid reality in the clearing among the
trees; the bells, symbols of peace and pleasantness, sounding
out over the half-savage country ; the chants and songs of
divine worship swelling upward to the skies. Margaret's
royal manufactory of beautiful things, her tapestries and
metal work, her adaptation of all the possibilities of ornament
latent in every primitive community, with the conviction,
always ennobling to art, that by these means of sacred
adornment she and her assistants and coadjutors were serving and pleasing God, no doubt consoled her ardent and
active spirit for the loss of many comforts and graces with
which she must have been familiar. At the same time her
new sphere of influence was boundless, and the means in her
hand of leavening and moulding her new country almost
unlimited—a thing above all others delightful to a woman,
to whom the noiseless and gradual operation of influence is
the chief weapon in the world.

There is nothing, however, in this history more charming
than the description of the relations between the royal pair.
King Malcolm had probably known few graces in life except
those, a step or two in advance of his own, which were to

be found in Northumberland in the house of Earl Siward ; and after the long practical struggle of his reign between the Scots and Celts, who had already so far settled down together as to constitute something which could be called a kingdom, he had no doubt fallen even from that higher plane of civilisation. Such rude state as the presence of a queen even in those primitive days might have procured had been wanting, and all his faculties were probably absorbed in keeping peace between the unruly chieftains, and fostering perhaps here and there the first rising of a little community of burghers, strong enough by union to defend themselves. Uneasy, there can be little doubt, was often the head which bore the circlet of troubled supremacy among all those half-subdued tribes ; and his dwelling in the heart of the " dense forest," amid all the noisy retainers in the hall and jealous nobles in the council chamber, would leave little room for beauty or sweetness of any kind. When the stranger princess suddenly came in like an enchantment, with her lovely looks and "jocund eloquence"—full of smiles and pleasant speech, yet with a dignity which overawed every rude beholder—into these rude and noisy halls, with so many graceful ways and beautiful garments and sparkling jewels, transforming the very chambers with embroidered hangings and all the rare embellishments of a lady's bower, with which no doubt the ship had been provided, and which mediæval princesses, like modern fine ladies, carried about with them —the middle-aged man of war was evidently altogether subdued and enraptured. To see her absorbed in prayer—an exercise which Malcolm had perhaps felt to be the occupa-tion of monks and hermits only—to see her bending over her beautiful book with all its pictures, reading the sacred story there, filled him with awe and a kind of adoration. He could not himself read, which made the wonder all the more ; but though incapable of mastering what was within, he loved to handle and turn over the book from which his beautiful wife derived her wisdom, touching it with his rude hands with caressing touches, and kissing the pages she loved. When he found one manuscript which she particularly esteemed, he " sent for his goldsmith " and had the vellum encased in gold and ornamented with jewels ; then carried it back to her with such fond pleasure as may be easily imagined. Margaret on her part did what she could to secure to her King some of the punctilios of reverential

QUEEN MARGARET'S CAVE

respect due in her knowledge to a monarch. She suggested the formation of a royal guard to protect the King's person and surround him with honour and observance. She filled the palace with her wealth, adorning it in every way, providing fine clothes for the retainers and so enriching the house that the table was served with dishes of gold and silver. And it would seem that the reputation of a new and splendid Court thus suddenly evolved among the northern mists got abroad, and brought merchants with their wares up the Firth, and quickened, if it did not altogether originate, the first feeble current of trade which was the precursor and origin of all our after wealth in Scotland.

This was not all, however, that Margaret did for the commonwealth. If we may trust her biographer, it was she who established that great principle of reform so important in all states, and generally one of the later fruits of civilisation, that the soldiers should be prevented from exacting or putting under requisition the peaceful people about, and that all they had should be honestly paid for, which was the last thing likely to be thought of by a mediæval prince. Altogether Margaret's influence was exerted for the best purposes to induce her husband "to relinquish his barbarous manners and live honestly and civilly," as the chronicler says. It was perhaps not so good an exercise of her power when she opened arguments, apparently through Malcolm as interpreter, with the native clergy of Scotland, the hermits and ecclesiastics of Columba's strain, and the mysterious Culdees of whom we know so little. The one certain fact fully established concerning them being, that they kept Easter at a different date from that appointed by Rome. The King, though no scholar, would seem to have been a linguist in his way, since he spoke both languages, that is the Saxon, and the Celtic or Pictish, again a most difficult question to determine —with a smattering of Latin ; and was thus able to act as Margaret's mouthpiece in her arguments. She found fault with the Celts not only for the date of their Easter, but for their habit of not communicating at that festival. It is very curious to note in their answer the very same reason which has prevailed in later days among all the changes of faith and ceremonial, and is still put forth in Highland parishes as an excuse for the small number of communicants. The Celtic priests and bishops defended their flocks by producing

the words of St. Paul, in which that Apostle says that those
who eat and drink unworthily eat and drink condemnation to
themselves.   So, according to Theodoric, the Celtic party in the
Church answered Margaret, and so would their descendants, the

WEST DOORWAY, DUNFERMLINE ABBEY

"Men" of the Highlands, answer at this day.   The integrity
of the tradition is very remarkable.   On the other hand,
they offended the devout Queen by their neglect of Sunday,
a reproach which cannot be addressed to their descendants.

C

These theological discussions between the fair and learned Queen and the Highland ecclesiastics and anchorites, carried on by means of her chief convert the warrior King, whom love for her had taught to respect and share in her devotion, must have afforded many picturesque and striking scenes, though unfortunately there was no modern observer there to be interested and amused, but only Theodoric standing by, himself very hot upon the atrocity of a miscalculated Easter, and perhaps helping his royal mistress here and there with an argument. Naturally his story is especially full upon the religious side of Margaret's life—her much prayer, her humility and reverence during the services of the Church, an intent and silent listener to all teachings, only a little disposed to rebel now and then when her confessor passed too lightly over her faults. As for her charities, they were boundless. It was not for nothing that the blood of St. Ursula, and that which was to give life to still another saint, Elizabeth of Hungary, was in her veins. It is needless to say that nobody in those days had discovered the evil of indiscriminate almsgiving, which was, on the contrary, considered one of the first of Christian virtues. Margaret was the providence of all the poor around her. Her biographer tells us naïvely, with no sense that the result was not one to be proud of, that the fame of her bounty and kindness brought the poor in crowds to every place where she was. When she went out they crowded round her like children round their mother. When she had distributed everything she had of her own she took garments and other things from her courtiers and attendants to give away, a spoliation to which they consented willingly, knowing that the value of everything thus appropriated would be returned to them— an excellent reason for acquiescence. This " rapine of piety " was so strong in her that she sometimes even appropriated to her poor certain of the gold pieces which it was the King's custom to offer at Easter to the Church— a pious robbery which Malcolm pretended not to perceive until he caught her in the act, when he accused her with a laugh of tender amusement for her rapacity. In all the touches by which the sympathetic priest delineates the union of this pair there is something at once humorous and pathetic in the figure of the King, the rough old warrior, always following with his eyes the angelic saintly figure by his side, all believing, half adoring, and yet not without that gleam of amusement at the woman's absolute unhesitating enthusiasm—an amusement mingled with admiration and respect, but still a smile—a delighted surprise at all her amazing ways, and wonder what she will do next, though everything in his eyes was perfect that she did—such as may still be seen in the eyes of many a world-worn husband looking on at the movements of that directer, more simple, yet more subtle being, and the quick absolutism and certainty of the bright spirit at his side. The gray-bearded old soldier, leader of many a raid and victor in many a struggle, with this new revelation of beauty and purity bursting upon his later life, becomes to us a recognisable and friendly human soul in these glimpses we have of him, unintentional and by the way. Theodoric himself must have liked Malcolm, half-barbarian as he was, and even admired the look of ardent supplication which would come into the King's face, "a great intentness and emotion," such as seemed to him extraordinary in a secular person, and which his wife's beautiful example and the contagion of her piety alone could have developed.

Among Margaret's many duties there was one which throws a very strange light upon the time. Just before her arrival in Scotland, King Malcolm had been carrying fire and sword through Northumberland in one of the many raids over the Border which were the commonplace of the time— if indeed we may speak of the Border at such an unsettled and shifting period when the limits of the kingdoms were so little certain. The issue of this raid was that Scotland, probably meaning for the most part Lothian, the southern portion of the country, was filled with English captives, apportioned as slaves, or servants at least, through the entire population, so that scarcely a house was without one, either male or female. The Queen interested herself particularly

in these captives, as was natural; sometimes paying the
ransom exacted for them, and in all cases defending and
protecting them. Her emissaries went about among them
inquiring into their condition and how they were treated,
visiting them from house to house : and all that Margaret
could do to mitigate the evils of their captivity was done.
Nothing can be more strange than to realise a time when
Northumbrian prisoners of war could be house slaves in
Lothian. No doubt what was true on one side was true on the
other, and Scotch captives had their turn of similar bondage.

In those days the ancient county which her children love
to call the Kingdom of Fife was far more than Edinburgh,
then a mere fortress standing up on an invulnerable rock in
the middle of a fertile plain, the centre of the national life.
Not only was the King's residence at Dunfermline, but the
great Cathedral of St. Andrews was the ecclesiastical
capital, gradually working out that development of Roman
supremacy and regularity which soon swept away all that
was individual in the apostleship of St. Columba and the
faith of his followers. That the King and Queen were
frequently at Edinburgh is evident from the fact that
Margaret had her oratory and chapel on the very apex of
the rock, and had there established a centre of worship and
spiritual life. St. Andrews, however, was the centre of influence,
the shrine to which pilgrims flowed, and the pious Queen, in
her care for every office of religion and eagerness to facilitate
every exercise of piety, gave special thought to the task of
making the way easy and safe towards that holy metropolis.
The Canterbury of the north was divided from the other half
of Malcolm's kingdom by that sea which in these later days,
at much cost of beauty, money, and life, has been bridged
over and shortened—" the sea which divides Lothian from
Scotland " according to the chronicler, " the Scottish Sea "
as it is called by others, the mighty Firth, which to the
rude galleys of the little trading villages along its shores
must have been a sea dangerous and troubled, full of risks
and perils. The Queen, we are told, erected houses of
shelter on either side of this angry strait, and established

what we should call a line of passenger boats to take the
pilgrims over at the expense of the State. One wonders
how much or how little of State policy might mingle in this
pious act, for no doubt the establishment of an easy and
constant means of communication between the wealthy
Lothians and the then centre of national life must have
been of unspeakable use in consolidating a kingdom still
so imperfectly knit together and divided by the formidable
line of the great estuary. It is one drawback of a religious
chronicler that no such motive, large and noble as it might
be, is thought of, since even national advantage counted so
much less than the cultivation of piety. And it is very
likely that Margaret thought of nothing else, and reckoned
a prayer at the shrine of the patron saint as far more important than the intercommunications thus established and
the knowledge of each other thus acquired by the different
parts of a kingdom which still retained the differences
of separate nationalities. A mingled aim, a practical
motive, might not have accomplished half so much ;
but no doubt among Malcolm's men, his greybeards
pondering in council, or perhaps himself thinking of many
things as he protected all his wife's schemes, there was a
dawning perception, along with the undoubted advantages of
piety, of a national use in the quickened intercourse and
securely established communications. If so he would probably blame himself for a mixed motive by the side of
Margaret's pure and absolute heavenly-mindedness, yet take
pleasure in the secondary unacknowledged good all the
same.

Thus their life went on for nearly a quarter of a century
in a course of national development to which everything
contributed, even the love of splendour which Margaret
brought with her, and her artistic tastes, and the rage for
decoration and beautiful surroundings which had then begun
to be so strong an element in national progress. She had
many children in the midst of all these labours and public
interests, seven sons and two daughters, whom she brought
up most carefully in all the perfection of her own faith.

Three of these sons succeeded one after the other to the Scottish throne, and proved the efficacy of her teaching by piety as strong and as liberal as her own. It was in the year 1093 that Margaret's beautiful and touching life came to an end, in great sorrow yet triumph and pious victory over trouble. Before this time, but at a date not indicated in the narrative, she had parted with her friend and biographer Theodoric, probably not very long before her own death, as we are told that she was oppressed by forebodings, or rather premonitions of death and sorrow, of which she spoke to him with tears. When the moment of separation came both penitent and confessor so long united in the closest bonds of sympathy wept sore. "Farewell," said the Queen ; " I shall not live long, but you will live long after me. Remember my soul in your prayers, and take care of my children ; cease not to teach and admonish them, especially when they are raised to great estate." He made the promise with tears, not daring to contradict her by happier auguries, and in this way took his last farewell of the Queen, and never saw her more. He continues his story, however, taking it from the lips of a priest who remained with her during the rest of her life, probably also a Saxon, since he became a monk of St. Cuthbert's on Margaret's death.

The narrative goes on with an account of the declining health of the Queen. For more than six months she had been unable to mount a horse, or sometimes to rise from her bed, and in the midst of this illness the King set forth upon one of his raids into England, on what provocation or with what motive it is difficult to tell, except that the provocation was perpetual and the motive persistent the leading rule of life. His two elder sons accompanied him on this expedition, which for some reason Margaret had opposed, " much dissuading " him from going ; but this time, unfortunately, had not been hearkened to. Probably she set out along with him, on her way to Edinburgh to pass the time of his absence there, which was a place where news could be had more readily than beyond the sea in Fife. The solitary castle, high perched upon its hill, whence messengers could be

seen approaching, or, better still, the King's banners coming
back, was a fitter home for an anxious wife than the palace
over the Firth among its woods. How long she remained
there we are not told, and there are now unhappily no
articulate remains at all of the old stronghold which must
have risen upon that height, with its low massive walls
and rude buildings. The oldest relic in Edinburgh is
that little sanctuary, plain and bare as a shed, deprived
of all external appearance of sanctity, and employed
for vulgar uses for many centuries, which has been
at length discovered by its construction, the small dark
chancel arch and rude ornament, to have been a chapel, and
which there seems no doubt is at least built upon the site
consecrated for Margaret's oratory, if not the very building
itself. It is small enough and primitive enough, with its
little line of toothed ornament, and its minute windows
sending in a subdued light even in the very flush of day, to
be of any antiquity. I believe that even the fortunate
antiquary who had the happiness of discovering it does not
claim for this little chapel the distinction of being the very
building itself which Margaret erected. Yet it must
have been one very similar, identical in form and ornament,
so that the interested spectator may well permit himself
to picture the sick and anxious Queen, worn out with illness and weighed down by sore forebodings, kneeling there
in the faint light before the shadowed altar, trying to derive
such comfort as was possible from the ministrations of the
priests, and following with her prayers her husband and her
boys, so young still and not hardened to war, who might be
falling by the hands perhaps of her own kindred, in the
country which was hers, yet which she scarcely knew. In
the intervals of these anxious prayers, when her failing
strength permitted, how wistfully the Queen and her ladies
must have gazed from the walls far around on every side
to watch for the first appearance of any messenger or herald
of return. From the woods of Dunfermline and its soft
rural landscape, and the new abbey with its sweet singing
and all its magnificence, it must have been a change indeed to

dwell imprisoned so near the sky, within the low, stern rugged walls of the primitive fort, with a few rude houses clinging about it, and the little chapel on the rock, small and dark, as the only representative of the stately arches and ornate services which she loved. But the little chapel is deeply involved in all the later history of Margaret's life.

One day her attendants remarked that she was even more sad than her wont, and questioning her received a reply which must have made them tremble. "Perhaps to-day," she said, "a great evil has fallen upon the Scots, such as has not happened to them for years." Her hearers, however it alarmed them, made as light as they could of this prophetic foreboding, which might be but a deepened impression of the prevailing despondency in her heart. No doubt it was a melancholy night in the fortress, where the women who had husbands or sons or brothers in the distant army would cluster together in the antechamber and watch for the attendants who came and went behind the curtain into the sick chamber where the Queen, visibly sinking day by day, lay sleepless and sad, listening for every sound. Terrors surrounded the castle for the personal safety of its occupants as well as for their brethren in the wars; and no doubt there would be whispers of the King's brother, Donald Bane, and of the watchful, jealous Celtic chiefs all ready to rise with him, should an opportunity occur, and dash the stranger brood from the throne. All these sad prognostications were quickly realised. Next morning brought messengers in fear and distress from the army to say that the King had fallen at Alnwick in Northumberland, and to prove that Margaret's prophecy had been fulfilled at the very time it was spoken. It was November, dark and cheerless both within and without, and the Queen would seem to have been prostrated for a day or two by the sad news: but on the fourth day she rose from her bed and tottered to the little chapel on the rock to hear mass for the last time, and receive the Holy Sacrament in preparation for death. She then returned to her rooms with the pallor of death already on her face, and bidding all around—" me," says the

priest, "and the others who stood by"—to recommend her
to Christ, asked that the black rood should be brought to
her. This was the most holy of all the relics which she
had brought with her to Scotland. It was a case of pure
gold in the form of a cross, ornamented with marvellous

INTERIOR OF QUEEN MARGARET'S CHAPEL, EDINBURGH CASTLE

work, bearing the image of the Saviour curiously carved
in ivory, and enclosing a portion of the true cross (proved to
be so by many miracles). The Queen took it in her hands,
pressed it to her dying breast, and touched with it her eyes
and face. While thus devoutly employed, with her thoughts

diverted from all earthly things, Margaret was brought back
to her sorrow by the sudden entrance of her son Ethelred,
who had returned from the defeated army to carry to his
mother the dreadful news of the death not only of his father
but of his elder brother. The sight of his mother in extremity, almost gone, no doubt confused the poor boy, still
little more than a stripling, and with that weight of disaster
on his head—and he answered to her faltering inquiry at first
that all was well. Margaret adjured him by the holy cross
in her arms to tell her the truth : then when she heard of
the double blow, burst out in an impassioned cry. " I thank
Thee, Lord," she said, " that givest me this agony to bear in
my death hour." Her life had been much blessed ; she had
known few sorrows ; it was as a crown to that pure and
lovelit existence that she had this moment of bitterest anguish
before God gave to His beloved sleep.

While this sad scene was enacting within, the country
was full of tumult and conspiracy without. Donald Bane,
the brother of Malcolm, had no doubt chafed at the Saxon
regime under which the King had fallen, for years, and
struggled against the influences brought in from abroad
in the retinue of the foreigner, as has been done in every
commonwealth in history at one time or another. He
represented the old world, the Celtic rule, the traditions of the
past. Some of the chroniclers indeed assert that Malcolm
was illegitimate and Donald Bane the rightful heir to the crown.
He was, at all events, a pretender kept in subjection while
Malcolm's strong hand held the sceptre, but ready to seize
the first opportunity of revolution. No doubt the news of
the King's death, and of that of his heir, would run like
wildfire through the country ; but it would seem that the
attempt of Donald must have been already organised, since
his siege of Edinburgh, where most of his brother's children
were with their mother, placed there for safety in the King's
absence, had already begun. Upon the death of the Queen,
Donald was not likely to have treated the royal children
who stood in his way with much mercy ; and the state of
affairs was desperate when young Ethelred, the third of her

sons, not yet arrived at man's estate, closed his mother's eyes, and found himself at the head of the weeping family shut up within the castle, surrounded by precipices on every side except that upon which his angry uncle lay with all the forces of the discontented in Scotland at his back, all the lovers of the old regime and enemies of the stranger, and with a fierce contingent from Norway to support his Celtic horde. In the simplicity of the narrative we hear not a word of the troubled councils which must have been held while the boy prince in his sorrow and the sudden dreadful responsibility laid on his young shoulders turned to such wise advisers as might have followed Margaret into the stronghold, and took thought how to save the children and carry off the precious remains of the Queen. The expedient to which they had recourse was one which their assailants evidently thought impossible. That the rock upon which Edinburgh Castle stands should have been considered inaccessible by practical mountaineers like the followers of Donald Bane seems curious : but in those days the art of climbing for pleasure had not been discovered, and it had no place in the methods of warfare. It seemed enough to the assailants to hold the gates and the summit of the eastern slopes, where probably there must already have been some clusters of huts or rough half-fortified dwellings descending from the Castle Hill, foreshadowing a Lawnmarket at least if not yet a Canongate. No one would seem to have thought of the possibility of any descent on the other side from that perpendicular rock.

But despair sharpens the wits, and no doubt after many miserable consultations a desperate expedient was found. Even now nothing but a goat, or a schoolboy, or perhaps a young private fearful of punishment, could find a way down the wonderful curtain of rock which forms the west side of Edinburgh Castle ; and to guide the children and their attendants, a sorrowful little group of mourners, distracted with grief and fear, and Margaret's body in its litter, down those rocks where there was scarcely footing for an alert and experienced climber, must have been one of the most

difficult as it was one of the boldest of undertakings. While
the rebel host raged on the other side, and any traitor might
have brought the enemy round to intercept that slow and
painful descent, it was accomplished safely under cover of
" a great myst," Heaven, as all thought, helping the forlorn
fugitives by that natural shield. Mists are no rare things, as
everybody knows, on these heights. Perhaps it was the well-
known easterly haar, the veil of salt sea fog which Edinburgh
so often wraps round her still, which, blowing up from the
mouth of the Firth, enveloped the travellers and hid them
in its folds of whiteness, impenetrable by the closest watcher,
till they had safely reached the level ground, and stealing
down to the Queen's Ferry escaped to loyal Fife and their
home in Dunfermline. Needless to say that this mist was a
miraculous agency to all the family and servants of the
Queen. To us it adds a touch of local colour, the well-
known symbol of a familiar scene. Edinburgh was then
nothing but a castle upon a rock, and now is one of the
fairest and most celebrated of historical cities ; but still its
perpendicular crags rise inaccessible against the setting sun,
and still the white mist comes sweeping up from the sea.

It is to the credit of the priests that this is the only
miracle that is connected with the name of Margaret, if we
except the pretty legend which tells how a hundred years
later, when her descendants removed the remains of the saint
from the place where they had been deposited to lay them
before the high altar in Dunfermline, the coffin in which
they were placed could not be carried past the humble spot
in which lay, brought back from Northumberland, the bones
of her King. The cortege stopped perforce, the ceremonial
had to be interrupted, for all the force of all the bearers could
not carry even in death the faithful wife from her husband ;
and the only thing it was found that could be done was to
transport Malcolm along with the partner of his life to the
place of honour, to which on his own account that rude
soldier had but little claim. Many saints have had whims
as to the place of their interment, and showed them in a
similar way, but this is all sweetness and tender fidelity

and worthy to be true. The royal pair were carried off
afterwards, stolen away like so much gold or silver, by Philip
of Spain to enrich his gloomy mausoleum-palace, and can be
traced for a long time in one place or another receiving that
strange worship which attaches to the most painful relics of
humanity. But where they now lie, if in the bosom of the
kindly earth or among other dreadful remains in some
sanctuary filled with relics, no one knows.

Margaret had done in her lifetime great things for
Scotland. She had introduced comforts and luxuries of
every kind, and the decorative arts, and a great deal of
actual wealth, into a very poor and distracted country. The
earliest charter which is found in the Scottish archives is one
of Malcolm and Margaret, showing how the time of settlement and established order began in their reign. She had
helped to give the distracted and divided kingdom, made up
of warring sects, that consolidation and steadiness which
enabled it to take its place among recognised nations. She
turned the wavering balance between Celt and Saxon to what
has proved to be the winning side, the side of progress and
advancement. The Donalds and Duncans were swept away
after a brief and bloody interval and were no more possible in
Scotland after her, and the reign of the Anglo-Saxon was
assured. She was apparently the instrument too, though
there is little information on this subject, of drawing the
Church of Scotland into that close union with Rome which
had been already accomplished in England ; a step which, if
it lost some doubtful freedom and independence in ecclesiastical matters, secured still more completely a recognised
place in Catholic Christendom to the northern kingdom.
" The pure Culdee " of whom we know so little did not
survive, any more than did the Celtic kings, her influence
and the transformation she effected. Her life and legend
formed the stepping-stone for Scotland into authentic
history as into a consolidated and independent existence.
The veil of fable and uncertainty cleared away before the
mild shining of her name and story. Like Edinburgh
coming suddenly into sight, as in some old and primitive

picture, high upon its rock, with the slope of the Castle Hill on one side and the precipices round, and the white mist sweeping up from the sea, Scotland itself becomes recognisable and grows into form and order by the light of her peaceful and gracious presence.

And it is something worth noting that this image of purity and excellence was no monkish vision of the purity of the cloister, but that more complete and at the same time more humble ideal of the true wife, mother, and mistress, whose work was in and for the world and the people, not withdrawn to any exceptional refuge or shelter—which has always been most dear to the Anglo-Saxon race. The influence of such an example in a country where manners and morals were equally rudimentary, where the cloister proved often the only refuge for women, and even that not always a safe one—was incalculable, and the protection of a virtuous Court something altogether novel and admirable. The gentlewomen who worked at their tapestry under Margaret's eye, and learned the gentler manners of other Courts and countries of old civilisation by her side, and did their wooing modestly with the sanction of her approval, must have changed the atmosphere of the north in the most wonderful way and quickened every current of national development though the influence was remote and the revolution unperceived. The chroniclers go back with a fond persistence to the story of Margaret and her sons, and the number of her family and the circumstances of her marriage and of her death. Before her there is little but fable ; after her the stream of history flows clear. The story of Macbeth, which is, yet is not, the Shakspearian drama, and accordingly takes quite a curious distinct flow of its own, like a new and imperfect version of something already familiarly known, is the only episode of secular history that has any reality before we come, in the next generation, to herself and her King. The earlier annals of Adamnan, the life of Columba and the records of his sacred isle, belong to those ever-living ever-continuing legends of the saints in which the story of the nations counts for little. But Margaret was fortunately

secular, and though a saint, a great and influential personage
in the front of everything, and also a woman in the fullest
tide of life to whom all human events were happening ; who
lived by love and died of grief, and reigned and rejoiced
and triumphed as well as suffered and prayed.

There followed, however, a terrible moment for that new
Scottish-Saxon royal family, when both their parents were
thus taken from them. Donald Bane set up a brief
authority, restoring the old kingdom and banishing, after
the familiar use and wont of such revolutions, his brother's
children from Scotland. Of these children, however, but
three sons are mentioned : Edgar, Alexander, and David,
who must all have been under age at the time. Ethelred,
who had the dangerous office of conveying his brothers and
sisters along with his mother's body to Dunfermline, died or
was killed immediately after this feat, and was laid with the
King and Queen before the rood altar in Dunfermline ; and
of Edmund, an elder son, we have but a confused account,
Wynton and Fordun both describing him as " a man of
gret wertu," who died in religion, having taken the cowl of a
monk of Cluny ; whereas William of Malmesbury accuses
him of treachery and complicity in the murder of his base-
born brother Duncan. However this might be, he was at
least swept from the succession, in which there is no mention
of him. Malcolm's lawful heirs were thus reduced to the
three boys whom their uncle, Edgar Atheling, had received
in England. But Donald Bane was not long permitted to
enjoy his conquest in peace. Duncan, the illegitimate son
(but this counted for little in those days) of Malcolm, who
was a hostage in England, after his uncle had held the
sovereign power for six months, made a rush upon Scotland
with the help of an English army, and overcame and displaced Donald ; but in his turn was overcome after a reign
of a year and a half, Donald Bane again resuming the power,
which he held for three years more. By this time young
Edgar, Margaret's son, had come to man's estate, and with
the help of the faithful Saxons who still adhered to his
uncle, Edgar Atheling, and encouraged by dreams and

revelations that the crown was to be his, came back to Scotland and succeeded finally in overcoming Donald and securing his inheritance. The period of anarchy and trouble lasted for five years, and no doubt the civilisation and good order which Malcolm and Margaret had toiled to establish were for the moment much disturbed. But after Edgar's succession the interrupted progress was resumed. " He was a man of faire havyng," says old Wynton, and in his time the Saxon race came again to great honour and promotion, at once by his own firm establishment upon the Scottish throne, and by the marriage of his sister Maud to the new King of England, Henry I., which restored the Saxon succession and united right to might in England. Thus after a moment of darkness and downfall the seed of the righteous took root again and prospered, and the children of St. Margaret occupied both thrones. Edgar, like so many of his race, died childless ; but he was peacefully succeeded by his brother Alexander, who, though as much devoted to church-building and good works as the rest of his family, was apparently a more warlike personage, since he was called Alexander the Fierce, an alarming title, and was apparently most prompt and thoroughgoing in crushing rebellion and other little incidents of the age. He was succeeded in his turn by the youngest of Margaret's sons, David, that " sair sanct for the crown," who covered Scotland with ecclesiastical foundations.

> " He illumynyd in his dayes
> His landys wyth kirkis and abbayis ;
> Bishoprychs he fand bot foure or three,
> Bot or he deyd nyne left he."

Among the many other foundations made by King David was the house of the Holy Rood which has been so familiar a name in Scottish history—built low in the valley at the foot of the surrounding hills and that castle in which the Queen died pressing the black rood—her most precious possession—to her dying breast. Whether a recollection of that scene, which might well have impressed itself even on the memory of a child, and of the strange wild funeral procession, with all its associations of grief and terror, which had stumbled down the dangerous rocks in the mist thirty-five years before, was in David's mind, it would be vain to inquire. The black rood of itself, besides these touching and sacred associations, was a relic of almost unequalled sanctity, and well warranted the erection of a holy house for its guardianship and preservation. How far the street, which would be little more than a collection of huts, had crept down the Castle Hill towards the new monastery in the valley there is no evidence to show, but no doubt both the castle and the religious house were soon surrounded by those humble scattered dwellings, and David's charter itself makes it plain that already the borough of Edinburgh was of some importance. Part of the revenues of the monastery were to be derived from the dues and taxes of the town, and it was also endowed with " one half of the tallow, lard, and hides of the beasts slain in Edinburgh," an unsavoury but no doubt valuable gift. The canons of the Abbey of Holyrood, or Holyrood House as it is called from the beginning with a curious particularity, had also permission to build another town between themselves and Edinburgh, which would naturally cluster round the Canons' Gate—the road that led to St. Cuthbert's, at the farther end of the North Loch where every man could say his mass ; or more directly still to the dark little chapel upon the castle rock, made sacred by all its memorials of the blessed Margaret. The nucleus of the future capital is thus plainly apparent between the two great forces of that age, the Church, the great instrument of congregation and civilisation, and the Stronghold, in which at any moment of danger refuge could be taken. It is curious to realise the wild solitude of this historical ridge, with its rude houses coming into being one by one, the low thatched roofs and wattled walls which in the course of time were to give place to buildings so stately. The Canongate would be but a country road lead-ing up towards the strong and gloomy gate which gave entrance to the *enceinte* of the castle—itself like some eagle's nest perched high among the clouds.

D

The line of Margaret went on till her sons held their
Courts and dated their charters from Holyrood House, and
Parliaments were held and laws made in the Castle of Edinburgh, and the scattered huts upon the Castle Hill had grown
into a metropolis.   They were a pious and in many respects
an enlightened race, and they came to great honour and
renown on both sides of the house.   Maud, Margaret's
daughter, became Queen of England, and her grand-daughter
Empress, while Scotland developed and flourished in the
hands of the saintly Queen's sons and their descendants.
There are unfortunate individuals in the most prosperous
races, and Scotland never sustained greater humiliation than
in her attempts to rescue William called the Lion, a sorry
lion for his kingdom, when he allowed himself to be caught
in a trap and made the prisoner of the English king.   But
the children of Malcolm and Margaret retained their character through many generations, and were a Godfearing house,
full of faith and devotion, careful of their people's interests,
and dear to their hearts.   They prospered as the virtuous
and excellent so often do even in this world, and covered
Scotland with endowments — endowments which indeed
proved a snare to the Church on after occasions, but
which at that period were probably the best means in which
money could be invested for the benefit of the people, since
alms and succour and help and teaching in every way came
from the monks in the primitive circumstances of all nations.
They were not only the guardians of learning ; they were
examples in husbandry, in building, in every necessary craft ;
nursing the sick, receiving the stranger, and, as the very
title-deed of their existence, feeding the poor.   In those
uncomplicated times there was no such fear of pauperising
the natives of the soil as holds our hands now, and everything had to be taught to the primitive labourer, who might
have to leave the plough in the middle of the furrow and be
off and away on his lord's commands at any moment, leaving his wife and children to struggle on with the help of the
good fathers who taught the boys, or the gentle sisters who
trained the girls to more delicate work, feeding the widow and

her brood. David and his brothers, and the devout kings who immediately followed, probably did what was best for their agitated kingdom in establishing so many centres of assured and quiet living, succour and peace, even if what was salvation for their age became the danger of another time. Those foundations continued through the whole of the period during which the lineal descendants of Margaret held the throne. Her lineage, it is true, has never died out : but the strain changed with the death of the last Alexander, and another change came over Scotland, not so profound as that which attended the coming of the Saxon princess, yet great and remarkable — the end of an age of construction, of establishment, of knitting together; the beginning of a time disturbed with other questions, with complications of advancing civilisation, nobles and burghers, trade and war.

ARMS OF QUEEN MARGARET OF SCOTLAND
(From the Ceiling of St. Machar's Cathedral, Old Aberdeen)

PART II

THE STEWARDS OF SCOTLAND

CHAPTER I

JAMES I. POET AND LEGISLATOR

THE growth of Edinburgh is difficult to trace through the mists and the tumults of the ages. The perpetual fighting which envelops the Scotland of those days as in the "great stour" or dust, which was Sir Walter Scott's conception of a battle, with gleams of swords and flashes of fire breaking through, offers few breaks through which we can see anything like the tranquil growth of that civic life which requires something of a steady and settled order and authority to give it being. The revolutions which took place in the country brought perpetual vicissitude to the Castle of Edinburgh, and no doubt destroyed and drove from their nests upon the eastern slopes of the rock the settlers who again and again essayed to keep their footing there. When the family of St. Margaret came to a conclusion, and the great historical struggle which succeeded ended in the establishment of Robert Bruce upon the throne, that great victor and statesman destroyed the Castle of Edinburgh with other strongholds, that it might not afford a point of vantage to the English invader or other enemies of the country's peace —a step which would seem to have been premature, though probably, in the great triumph and ascendency in Scotland which his noble character and work had gained, he might have hoped that at least the unanimity of the nation

and its internal peace were secured, and that only an enemy
would attempt to dominate the reconciled and united country.
The castle was, however, built up again and again, re-
established and destroyed, a centre of endless fighting
during the tumultuous reigns that followed, though it is
only on the accession of a new race, a family so deeply connected with the modern history of Great Britain that no
reader can be indifferent to its early appearances, that
Edinburgh begins to become visible as the centre of government, the royal residence from whence laws were issued, and
where the business of the nation was carried on.   Following
what seems to be one of the most wonderful rules of
heredity—a peculiarity considerably opposed to the views
which have been recently current on that subject—Robert
Bruce was too great a man to have a son worthy of him :
and after the trifling and treacherous David the inheritance
of his kingdom came through his daughter to a family
already holding a high place—the Stewards of Scotland,
great hereditary officials, though scarcely so distinguished in
character as in position.   The tradition that their ancestor
Banquo was the companion of Macbeth when the prophecy
was made to him which had so great an effect upon that
chieftain's career, and that to Banquo's descendants was
adjudged the crown which Macbeth had no child to inherit,
is far better known, thanks to Shakspeare, than any fact
of their early history.   It is probably another instance of
that inventive ingenuity of the original chroniclers, which so
cleverly imagined a whole line of fabulous kings, to give
dignity and importance to the " ancient kingdom " thus
carried back to inarticulate prehistoric ages.   In this way
the Stewarts, actually a branch of a well-known Norman
family, were linked to a poetic and visionary past by their
supposed identification with the children of Banquo, with all
the circumstantial details of an elaborate pedigree.   According to the legend, the dignity of Grand Steward of Scotland
was conferred by Malcolm Canmore upon a descendant of
the ancient thane, and the lineage of the family is traced
through all the dim intervening ages with scrupulous minute-

ness. The title of Steward of Scotland was enough, it would
seem, to make other lordships unnecessary, and gradually
developed into that family surname with which we are
now so familiar, which has wrought both Scotland and
England so much woe, yet added so intense an interest
to many chapters of national history. The early Stewards
are present by name in all the great national events : but
have left little characteristic trace upon the records, as of
remarkable individuals. They took the cross in repeated
crusades, carrying their official coat with its chequers, the
brand of the Chief Servitor of the Scottish Court, through the
wars of the Holy Land, till they came finally into the
highest favour and splendour in the days of Bruce, whose
cause, which was also the cause of the independence of Scotland, they maintained. Walter, who then held the office of
Steward, was knighted on the field of Bannockburn. He
was afterwards, as the story goes, sent to receive on the Border,
after peace had been made, various prisoners who had
been detained in England during the war, and among them
Marjory Bruce, the daughter of the patriot-king. It would
be easy to imagine the romance that followed : the young
knight reverently escorting the young princess across the
devastated country, which had not yet had time to recover
its cruel wounds, but yet was all astir with satisfaction and
hope : and how his account of what had happened in Scotland, and, above all, of that memorable field where he had
won from the Bruce's own famous sword the touch of
knighthood, would stir the maiden's heart. A brave young
soldier with great hereditary possessions, and holding so
illustrious an office, there was no reason why he should
despair, however high-placed his affections might be. It
takes a little from the romance to be obliged to acknowledge
that he was already a widower ; but marriages were early
and oft-repeated in those days, and when Marjory Bruce
died her husband was still only about twenty-three. It was
thus that the crown came to the family of the Stewards of
Scotland, the Stewarts of modern times : coming with a
" lass " as her descendant said long afterwards, and likely to

"go with a lass" when it was left to the infant Mary : though this last, with all her misfortunes, was the instrument not of destruction but transformation, and transferred that crown to a more splendid and enlarged dominion.

It was in the reign of Marjory's son, the grandson and namesake of the Bruce, and of his successors, that Edinburgh began to be of importance in the country, slowly becoming visible by means of charters and privileges, and soon by records of Parliaments, laws made, and public acts proceeding from the growing city.   Robert Bruce, though he had destroyed the castle, granted certain liberties and aids to the burghers, both in repression and in favour pursuing the same idea, with an evident desire to substitute the peaceful progress of the town for the dangerous domination of the fortress.   Between that period and the reign of the second Stewart, King Robert III, the castle had already been re-erected and redestroyed more than once.   Its occupation by the English seemed the chief thing dreaded by the Scots, and it was again and again by English hands that the fortifications were restored—such a stronghold and point of defence being evidently of the first importance to invaders, while much less valuable as a means of defence.   In the year 1385 the walls must have encircled a large area upon the summit of the rock, the *enceinte* probably widening, as the arts of architecture and fortification progressed, from the strong and grim eyrie on the edge of the precipice to the wide and noble enclosure, with room for a palace as well as a fortress, into which the great castles of England were growing.   The last erection of these often-cast-down walls was made by Edward III on his raid into Scotland, and probably the royal founder of Windsor Castle had given to the enclosure an amplitude unknown before.   The Scots king most likely had neither the money nor the habits which made a great royal residence desirable, especially in a spot so easily isolated and so open to attack ; but he gave a charter to his burghers of Edinburgh authorising them to build houses within the castle walls, and to pass in and out freely without toll or due—a curious privilege, which must have made the castle a sort of *imperium in imperio*, a town within a town. The little closets of rooms which in a much later and more luxurious age must have sufficed for the royal personages whom fate drove into Edinburgh Castle as a residence, are enough to show how limited were the require-ments in point of space of the royal Scots. The room in which James VI of Scotland was born would scarcely be occupied, save under protest, by a housemaid in our days. But indeed the Castle of Edinburgh was neither adapted nor intended for a royal residence. The abbey in the valley, from which the King could retire on receipt of evil tidings, where the winds were hushed and the air less keen, and gardens and pleasant hillsides accessible, and all the splendour of religious ceremonies within reach, afforded more fit and secure surround-ings even for a primitive court. The Parliament met, however, within the fortress, and the courts of justice would seem to have been held within reach of its shelter. And thither the burghers carried their wealth, and built among the remains of the low huts of an earlier age their straight steep houses, with high-pitched roofs tiled with slabs of stone, rising gray and strong within the *enceinte*, almost as strong and apt to resist whatever missiles were possible as the walls themselves, standing out with straight defiant gables against the northern blue.

King Robert III was a feeble, sickly, and poor-spirited king, and he had a prodigal son of that gay, brilliant, attrac-tive, and impracticable kind which is so well known in fiction and romance, and, alas! also so familiar in common life. David, Duke of Rothesay, was the first in the Scotch records who was ever raised to that rank—nothing above the degree of Earl having been known in the north before the son and brother of the King, the latter by the fatal title of Albany, brought a new degree into the roll of nobility. Young David, all unknowing of the tragic fate before him, was then a daring and reckless youth, held within bounds, as would appear, by the influence of a good and wise mother, and if an anxiety and trouble, at least as yet no disgrace to the throne. He was the contemporary of another madcap prince, far better known to us, of whose pranks we are all more than indulgent, and whose name has the attraction of youth and wit and freedom and boundless humour to the reader still.   David of Scotland has had no one to celebrate his youthful adventures like him whose large and splendid touch has made Prince Hal[1] so fine a representative of all that is careless and gay in prodigal youth, with its noble qualities but half in abeyance, and abounding spirit and humour and reckless fancy making its course of wild adventure comprehensible even to the gravest.   Perhaps the licence of the Stewart blood carried the hapless northern prince into more dangerous adventures than the wild fun of Gadshill and Eastcheap.   And Prince David's future had already been compromised by certain sordid treacheries about his marriage when he first appears in history, without the force of character which changed Prince Hal into a conquering leader and strong sovereign, but with all the chivalrous instincts of a young knight.   He had been appointed at a very early age Lieutenant of the Kingdom to replace his father, it being " well seen and kenned that our lorde the Kyng for sickness of his person may not travail to govern the realm," with full provision of counsellors for his help and guidance ; which argues a certain confidence in his powers. But the cares of internal government were at this point interrupted by the more urgent necessity of repelling an invasion, a danger not unusual, yet naturally of an exciting kind.

On this occasion the invader was Henry IV of England, the father of the other prodigal, whose object is somewhat perplexing, and differs much from the usual raid to which the Scots were so well accustomed.   So far as appears from all the authorities, his invasion was a sort of promenade of defiance or bravado, though it seems unlike the character of that astute prince to have undertaken so gratuitous a demonstration. He penetrated as far as Leith, and lay there for some time threatening, or appearing to threaten, Edinburgh Castle; but all that he seems to have done was to make proclamation by

---

[1] We here take Shakspeare's Prince Hal for granted, as we feel disposed at all times to take the poet's word in defiance of history : though no doubt the historical argument is calculated to throw a chill of doubt upon that gay and brilliant image.

his knights and heralds in every town they passed through, of the old, always renewed, claim of allegiance to the English crown which every generation of Scots had so strenuously and passionately resisted.   The fact that he was allowed to penetrate so far unmolested is as remarkable as that the invasion was an entirely peaceful one and harmed nobody. When Henry pitched his camp at Leith, Albany was within reach with what is called a great army, but did not advance a step to meet the invader—in face of whom, however, young David of Rothesay, and with him many potent personages, retired into Edinburgh Castle with every appearance of expecting a siege there.   But when no sign of any such intention appeared or warlike movement of any kind, nothing but the gleam of Henry's spears, stationary day by day in the same place, and a strange tranquillity, which must have encouraged every kind of wondering rumour and alarm, the young Prince launched forth a challenge to the English king and host to meet him in person with two or three hundred knights on each side, and so to settle the question between them and save the spilling of Christian blood.   Henry, it is said, replied with something of the sarcasm of a grave and middle-aged man to the hasty youth, regretting that Prince David should consider noble blood as less than Christian since he desired the effusion of one and not the other.   The position of the young man shut up within the walls of the fortress in enforced inactivity while the hated Leopards of England fluttered in the fresh breezes from the Firth, and Henry's multitudinous tents shone in the northern sun—an army too great to be encountered by his garrison and noble attendants alone—while dark treason and evil intent in the person of Albany kept the army of Scotland inactive though within reach, was one to justify any such outbreak of impatience.   David must have felt that should the invader press, there was little help to be expected from his uncle, and that he and his faction would look on not without pleasure to see the castle fall and the heir of Scotland taken or slain.   But King Henry's object or meaning is more difficult to divine.   Save for his pro-

clamations, and the quite futile summons to King Robert
to do homage, he seems to have attempted nothing against
the country through which he was thus permitted to march
unmolested.   The little party of knights with their attendant
squires and heralds riding to every market-cross upon the
way, proclaiming to the astonished burghers or angry village
folk the invader's manifesto, scarcely staying long enough to
hear the fierce murmurs that arose—a passing pageant, a
momentary excitement and no more—was a sort of defiant
embassage which might have pleased the fancy of a young
adventurer, but scarcely of a king so wary and experienced ;
and his own stay in the midst of the startled country is
still more inexplicable.   When the monks of Holyrood
sent a mission to him to beg his protection, lying undefended
as they did in the plain, his answer to them was curiously
apologetic.   " Far be it from me," he said, " to be so inhuman as to harm any holy house, especially Holyrood in
which my father found a safe refuge. . . . I am myself half
Scotch by the blood of the Comyns," added the invader.
The account which Boece gives of the expedition altogether
is amusing, and strictly in accord with all that is said by
other historians, though they may not take the same amiable
view.   I quote from the quaint translation of Bellenden.

"A schort time efter King Harry came in Scotland with an army.
Howbeit he did small injury to the people thairof, for he desirit nowt
but his banner to be erected on their walls.   Alwayis he was ane
plesand enneme, and did gret humaniteis to the people in all places of
Scotland where he was lodgit.   Finally he showed to the lords of Scotland that he come in their rialm more by counsel of his nobles than ony
hatred that he bore to Scottes.   Soon efter he returnit without any
further injure in England."

It is very seldom that a Scotch historian is able to desig-
nate an English invader as " a pleasant enemy," and whether
there was some scheme which came to nothing under this
remarkable and harmless raid, or whether it was only the
carrying out of Henry's own policy " to busy giddy minds
with foreign quarrels "

> " Lest rest and lying still might make them look
>   Too near unto my state,"

it is difficult to say.   The nobles pent up in Edinburgh Castle
with the hot-headed young Prince at their head did not know
what to make of the pleasant enemy.   The alarm he had
caused, compelling their own withdrawal into the stronghold,
wrath at the mere sight of him there in the heart of Scotland, the humiliating inaction in which they were kept by a
foe which neither attacked nor withdrew, must have so chafed
the Prince and his companions that the challenge thrown
forth like a bugle from the heights to break this oppressive
silence and bring about the lingering crisis one way or
another must have been a relief to their excitement if nothing
else.   One of the bewildered reasons alleged for the invasion
is that young David had written letters to France in which
he called Bolingbroke a traitor—letters which had fallen
into Henry's hands ; but this is as unlikely to have brought
about the invasion as any other frivolous cause, though no
doubt it might make the young Prince still more eager to
take upon himself the settling of the quarrel.   We have no
reason to suppose that any foreboding of his fate had crossed
the mind of the youth at this period of his career, yet to
watch the army of England lying below, and to know his
uncle Albany close at hand, and to feel himself incapable
—with nothing but a limited garrison at his command
and no doubt the wise Douglas and the other great noblemen holding him back—of meeting the invader except by
some such fantastic chivalrous expedient, must have been
hard enough.

And how strange is the scene, little in accordance with
the habits and traditions of either country : the English
camp all quiet below, as if on a holiday expedition, the
Scots looking on in uneasy expectation, not knowing what
the next moment might bring.   The excitement must
have grown greater from day to day within and without,
while all the inhabitants, both citizens and garrison,
kept anxious watch to detect the first sign of the enemy's
advance.   Henry, we are told, was called away to oppose a
rising in Wales; not indeed that rising which we all know so
well in which Prince Hal, more fortunate than his brother

prodigal, had the means of showing what was in him ; but even the suggestion approaches once more strangely and suggestively the names of the two heirs whose fate was so different—the one almost within sight of a miserable ending, the other with glory and empire before him.   Prince Henry did not apparently come with his father to Scotland, or there might perhaps have been a different ending to the tale, and it would not have needed Harry Hotspur to rouse his namesake from his folly.   There was, alas ! no such noble rival to excite David of Scotland to emulation, and no such happy turning-point before him.   No one, not even a minstrel or romancer, has remembered it in his favour that he once defied the English host for the love of his country and the old never-abandoned cause of Scottish independ- ence.   Already it would seem a prodigal who was a Stewart had less chance than other men.   Whether some feeble fibre in the race had already developed in this early representative of the name, or whether it was the persistent ill-fortune which has always pursued them, making life a continual struggle and death a violent ending, the fatal thread which has run through their history for so many generations comes here into the most tragic prominence, the beginning of a long series of tragedies.   It adds a softening touch to the record of David's unhappy fate that the death of his mother is recorded as one of the great mis- fortunes of his life.   In the same year in which these public incidents occurred the Queen died, carrying with her the chief influence which had restrained her unfortunate son. She was Annabella Drummond, a woman of character and note, much lamented by the people.   And to add to this misfortune she was followed to the grave within a year by the great Earl of Angus, David's father-in-law, and the Bishop of St. Andrews, to whom, as the Primate of Scotland, the young Prince's early instruction had probably been committed, as his loss is noted along with the others as a special disaster.

Thus the rash and foolish youth was left to face the world and all its temptations with no longer any one

whom he feared to grieve or whom he felt himself bound
to obey.　His father, a fretful invalid, had little claim
upon his reverence, and his uncle Albany, the strong man of
the family, was his most dangerous enemy, ever on the
watch to clear out of his path those who stood between him
and the throne : or such at least was the impression which
he left upon the mind of his time.　Thus deprived of all
the guides who had power over him, and of the only parent
whom he could respect, the young Duke of Rothesay, only
twenty-three at most, plunged into all those indulgences
which are so fatally easy to a prince.　It is supposed that
the marriage into which a false policy had driven him was
not the marriage he desired.　But this was a small particular
in those days, as it has proved even in other times less rude.
He ran into every kind of riot and dissipation, which the
councillors appointed to aid him could not check.　After no
doubt many remonstrances and appeals this band of serious
men relinquished the attempt, declaring themselves unable
to persuade the Prince even to any regard for decency :
and the ill-advised and feeble King committed to Albany,
who had been standing by waiting for some such piece of
good fortune, the reformation of his son.　The catastrophe was
not slow to follow.　Rothesay was seized near St. Andrews
on the pretence of stopping a mad enterprise in which he was
engaged, and conveyed to Falkland, where he died in strict
confinement, "of dysentery or others say of hunger" is the
brief and terrible record—blaming no one—of the chroniclers,
on Easter Eve 1401.　It would be vain to attempt to add
anything to the picture of the young unfortunate and his end
which Sir Walter Scott has given.　We can but rescue out of
obscurity the brief moment in which that young life was at the
turning-point and might have changed into something noble.
Had his challenge been accepted, and had he died sword in
hand outside the castle gates for Scotland and her independence, how touching and inspiring would have been the story!
But Fortune never favoured the Stewarts ; they have had
no luck, to use a more homely expression, such as falls to
the lot of other races, and what might have been a legend

of chivalry, the record of a young hero, drops to the horror
of a miserable murder done upon a victim who foils even
the pity he excites—a young debauchee almost as miserable
and wretched as the means by which he died.

There was this relic of generosity and honour about the
unfortunate Prince, even in his fallen state, that he refused
to consent to the assassination of the uncle who found no
difficulty, it would appear, in assassinating him ; thus showing that wayward strain of nobleness among many defects
and miseries which through all their tragic career was to be
found even in the least defensible of his race.

King Robert, who had for some time been retired from
the troubles of the throne, a poor man, infirm in health and
in purpose, virtually deposed in favour of the son who was
Lieutenant or the brother who was Regent of the kingdom,
and from whom all his domestic comfort had been taken as
well as his power, was driven to desperation by this blow.
He had lost his wife and his best counsellors ; he had never
been strong enough to restrain his son, nor resist his brother.
David, his first-born and heir, the gay and handsome
youth who was dazzling and delightful to his father's
eyes even in his worst follies, had been, as no doubt he felt,
delivered over to his worst enemy by that father's own tremulous hand ; and the heartbroken old man in his bereavement
and terror could only think of getting the one boy who
remained to him safe and out of harm's way, perhaps with
the feeling that Albany might once again persuade him to
deliver over this last hope into his hands if he did not take
a decisive step at once.   The boy-prince was at St. Andrews,
pursuing his studies, under the care of the bishop, when his
brother was murdered ; and from thence he was sent, when
the preparations were complete, across the Firth to the Bass,
there to await a ship which should take him to France.
It was a forlorn beginning for the Prince of Scotland to
be thus hastily taken from his books and the calm of a
semi-monastic life and hurried off to that wild rock in the
middle of the waves, probably with his brother's awful
story thrilling in his ears and his terrible uncle within reach,

pushing forward a mock inquiry in Parliament into the causes of Rothesay's death. How easy it would have been for that uncle with the supreme power in his hands to seize the boy who now stood alone between him and the throne ; and with what burning at the heart, of impotent rage and fierce indignation, the little Prince, old enough to know and feel his father's helplessness, his own abandonment, and his brother's terrible end, must have been conveyed away to the sea stronghold among the bitter eastern blasts. James, the first of the name, was not one of the feeble ones of the family. With all the romance and poetry of his race he conjoined a great spirit and a noble intelligence, and even at twelve, in the precocious development of that age of blood, when even a royal stripling had to learn to defend himself and hold his own, he must have had some knowledge why it was that he had to be sent thus clandestinely out of his native country : he, the hope of Scotland, in terror for his life.

The little garrison on the rock and the governor to whom the Prince's safety was confided must have watched with many an anxious vigil among the trading vessels stumbling heavily down the Firth from Leith, for that sail which was to carry their charge, into safety as they thought. Whether there was any navy belonging to the Crown at this period, or whether the King himself possessed some galley that could venture on the voyage to France, we are not told. But no doubt the ship when it arrived bore some sign by which the Prince's guardians, and unfortunately others besides, could recognise it. It could not be in any way a cheerful embarkation. It was in the dark days of Lent, in March, when the north is most severe : and the grey skies and blighting wind would be appropriate to the feelings of the exiles as they put forth from their rock amid the wild beating of the surf, anxiously watched by the defenders of the place, who no doubt had at the same time to keep up a vigilant inspection landward, lest any band of spearmen from Albany should arrive upon the adjacent shore in time to stop the flight. The grey rock, the greyer leaden sea, the whirling

THE BASS ROCK

E

flight of wild sea birds white against the dark horizon, the little boat, kept with difficulty from dashing against the cliffs and rocky boulders, the attendant ship, driven up and down by the waves, and distant Fife, with its low hills in tones of neutral tint upon the horizon—would all increase the sadness of the parting: but no doubt there was a long breath of relief breathed by everybody about when the vessel continued its course, and slowly disappeared down the Firth. Whatever might happen elsewhere, at least the heir was safe.

But this hope soon proved futile. Whether it was some traitorous indication from Albany, or information from another source, or pure hazard, which directed the English ships to this one vessel with its royal freight, it had but rounded the headland of Flamborough when it fell into the hands of the enemy. Palm Sunday 1405 was the date of this event, but it was not till the end of Lent 1423, almost exactly eighteen years after, that James came back. The calamity seemed overwhelming to the nation and to all who were not pledged to Albany throughout Scotland. It was the death-warrant of poor old King Robert in his retirement. He lingered out a weary year in sickness and sorrow, and when the anniversary of his son's loss came round again, died at Rothesay, in Bute, amid the lovely lakes and islets of western Scotland—a scene of natural peace and tranquillity, which, let us hope, shed some little balm upon the heart of the helpless superseded sovereign. Perhaps he loved the place because it had given his title to his murdered boy, the hapless David, so gallant and so gay. There is something more than ordinarily pathetic and touching in the misfortunes of the feeble in an age of iron. As civilisation advances they have means of protecting themselves, but not in a time which is all for the strongest. One son buried, like any peasant's son, ignobly in the Abbey of Lindores: the other in an English prison, at the mercy of the "auld enemy," whom Scotland had again and again resisted to the death: and his kingdom entirely gone from him, in the hands of his arrogant and imperious brother: there was nothing left for poor King Robert but to die.

Thus James became at thirteen, and in an English
castle, the King of Scotland. His prison, however, proved
a noble school instead of an ignoble confinement to his
fine and elevated spirit. The name of Stewart has never
been so splendidly illustrated as by this patriotic and chivalrous Prince. No doubt it is infinitely to the credit of
the English kings, both Henrys, IV and V, that he
received from them all the advantages of education that
could have been given to a prince of their own blood—
advantages by which he profited nobly, acquiring every art
and cultivation that belonged to his rank, besides that divine
art which no education can communicate, and which is
bestowed by what would seem a caprice, were it not divine,
upon prince or ploughman as it pleases God. For above
all his knightly and kingly qualities, his studies in chivalry
and statesmanship, which prepared him to fill the throne of
Scotland as no man save his great ancestor Bruce had yet
filled it, James Stewart was a poet of no mean rank, not
unworthy to be named even in the presence of Chaucer,
and well worthy of the place which he has kept in literature.
We need not enter here into that part of his history which
concerns another locality full of great and princely associations—the noble Castle of Windsor, where the royal youth
first saw and sang the lady of his love, " the fairest and the
sweeteste yonge flour," of whom he has left one of the most
tender and beautiful descriptions that is to be found in all
the course of poetry. It is more to our present purpose
to tell how, amid all the charms of that courtly residence,
so far superior to anything which primitive Scotland could
offer in the way of dignity or luxury, the boy-king remained
faithful to his country, and maintained the independence for
which she had so long struggled. It is said that the one
advantage taken of his captivity and youth was to press the
old oft-repeated arguments concerning the supposed supremacy of England, and the homage due from the kings of
Scotland, upon the boy who bore that title sadly amid the
luxury and splendour of what was still a prison, however
gracious and kind his jailers might be. No circumstances

could have been better suited to impress upon James's mind
the conviction that submission was inevitable : and it would
have been almost more than mortal virtue on the part of his
captors had they not attempted to bring about so advantageous a conviction.   King Henry V, under whom it is
said the attempt was made, had been most generously liberal
to and careful of the boy.   He was a man so brilliant in
reputation and success that a generous youth might well
have been led by enthusiasm into any homage that was
suggested, too happy to feel himself thus linked to so great
a king ; and James was very young, distant from his own
country and all native advisers, his very life as well as his
liberty in the power of those who asked this submission
from him, and the force of circumstances so great that even
his own people might have forgiven, and Holy Church could
scarcely have hesitated to dispense him from keeping, an
obligation entered into under such pressure.   But the royal
youth stood fast, and was not to be moved by any argument.
Boece, whose authority is unfortunately not much to be
depended upon, has a still more distinct and graphic story
of judgment and firmness on the part of the young captive.
He had been, according to this account, taken to France in
the train of King Henry, who after the defeat the English
had sustained near Orleans, chiefly through the valour of
the Scots who had joined the French army, sent for James,
and desired him " to pass to the Scots, and to command
them to return to Scotland.   King Harry promised, gif the
said James brought this matter to good effect, not only to
remit his ransom but to send him to Scotland with great
riches and honour."   James answered courteously, with expressions of goodwill and gratitude for the humanity shown
towards him, but " I marvel not little," he said, " that thou
considerest not how I have no power above the Scots so
long as I am ane private man and holden in captivity."
The chronicler adds : " Then said King Henry, ' Maist
happy people shall they be that happens to get yon noble
man to their prince.' "   It is a pity that we have no more
trustworthy proof of this charming story.

As a matter of fact James attained his freedom only
after the death of Albany, when the resistance or the still
more effectual indifference to his liberation of the man who
alone could profit by his death in prison, or by any unpopular step he might be seduced into making to gain his
freedom, was dead, and had ceased from troubling. It
would perhaps, however, be false to say that his imprisonment had done him nothing but good. So far as education
went this was no doubt the case; but it is possible that in
his subsequent life his reforms were too rapid, too thoroughgoing, too modern, for Scotland. The English sovereigns
were richer, stronger, and more potent : the English commonalty more perfectly developed, and more capable of
affording a strong support to a monarch who stood against
the nobles and their capricious tyranny. James might not
have been the enlightened ruler he was but for his training
in a region of more advanced and cultivated civilisation ;
but had he been less enlightened, more on the level of his
subjects, he might have had a less terrible end and a longer
career.

He returned to Scotland—with the bride of whom he had
made so beautiful a picture, preserving her lovely looks and
curious garments, and even the blaze of the Balas ruby on
her white throat, to be a delight to all the after generations—
in 1423, during Lent ; and on Passion Sunday, which Boece
calls *Care* Sunday, entered Edinburgh, where there was "a
great confluence of people out of all parts of Scotland richt
desirous to see him : for many of them," says the chronicle,
"had never seen him before, or else at least the prent of his
visage was out of their memory." There must indeed have
been but few who could recognise the little prince who had
been stolen away for safety at twelve in the accomplished
man of thirty in all the fulness of his development, a bridegroom, and accustomed to the state and prestige of a
richer Court than anything that Scotland could boast, who
thus came among them full of the highest hopes and purposes, and surrounded by unusual splendour and wealth. It
is true there was the burden behind him of a heavy ransom

to pay, but her English kindred, we may well believe, did not suffer the Lady Jane to appear in her new kingdom without every accessory that became a queen ; and a noble retine of adventurous knights, eager to try their prowess against the countrymen of that great Douglas whose name was still so well known, would swell the train of native nobles who attended the sovereign.   Old Edinburgh comes to light in the glow of this arrival, not indeed with any distinctness of vision, but with something of the aspect of a capital filled to overflowing with a many-coloured and picturesque crowd.   The country folk in their homespun, and all the smaller rank of gentlemen, with their wives in the French hoods which fashion already dictated, thronged the ways and filled every window to see the King come in. It was more like the new setting up of a kingdom, and first invention of that dignity, than a mere return : and eager crowds came from every quarter to see the King, so long a mere name, now suddenly blazing into reality, with all the primitive meaning of the word so much greater and more living than anything that is understood in it now.   The King's Grace ! after the long sway of the Regent, always darkly feared and suspected, and the feeble deputyship full of abuses of his son Murdoch, it was like a new world to have the true Prince come back, the blood of Bruce, the genuine and native King, not to speak of the fair Princess by his side and the quickened life they brought with them. From the gates of the castle where they first alighted, down the long ridge—through the half-grown town within its narrow walls, where a few high houses, first evidences of the growth of the wealthy burgher class, alternated with the low buildings which they were gradually supplanting—through the massive masonry of the Port with its battlements and towers to the country greenness and freshness of the Canons' Gate which led to the great convent of the valley, there could be no finer scene for a pageant.   Holyrood was one of those great monastic establishments in which kings could find a lodgment more luxurious than in their own castles, and though there would scarcely seem as yet to have been any

palace attached to that holy house, it was already a frequent residence of royalty, and with all its amenities of parks
and gardens would be more fit for the reception of a young
queen coming straight from princely Windsor than the
narrow chambers in the castle. Among the many presents
which she is said to have brought with her from England
there is a special mention of fine tapestries for the adornment of her new habitation.

Thus the royal pair took possession of their kingdom,
and of the interest and affection of the lively and eager
crowd for which Edinburgh has always been famous—a
populace more like that of a French town than an English,
though with impulses sometimes leading to tragedy. James
would scarcely seem to have been settled in that part of the
ancient establishment of the abbey which was appropriated
to the lodging of the King, or to have exhausted the thanks-
givings of Easter and the rejoicings of the restoration, when
he set himself to inquire into the state of the country and of
the royal finances, to which he had been so long a stranger.
There was no Civil List in those days nor votes of supply,
and the state of the Crown lands and possessions, "the
King's rents," was doubly important in view of the ransom
yet to be paid, of which only a fourth part had been remitted
as the portion of the Queen. The result of this investigation
was anything but satisfactory. It was found that during
the reign of Albany many of these possessions had been
alienated, made into fiefs, and bestowed upon the leaders
of the faction which supported the Regent. "There was
nothing left to sustain the Crown," says Boece, "except the
customs of burrows. He was naething content of this,"
adds the chronicler with pithy conciseness, "howbeit he
shewed good will (gud vult) for the time." James had
already griefs enough against the family of his cousin
without this startling discovery ; and his "gud vult" would
seem rather to have been the serious self-control of a man
who was biding his time than any pretence of friendliness
with his unfaithful relations and stewards. Amid the early
pageants and festivities it is indeed recorded that he knighted

Walter Stewart among the other candidates for that honour, the flower of the noble youth, a band of twenty-six gentlemen of the best houses in Scotland; but this was probably a step which was inevitable, as it would have been impossible to leave his own nearest relative out of the list until he had finally made up his mind how the family of Albany was to be treated. It is stated that the complaints and grievances of the people brought him to a decision on this point, and helped him to carry out his revenge upon the house which had, in popular belief at least, the guilt of his brother's blood upon it as well as that of his own long confinement. Walter Stewart, whose only other appearance in history is that of a rebellious and undutiful son whom his father was incapable of keeping in subjection, was arrested in Edinburgh Castle about a year after James's restoration, and after an interval of several months his arrest was followed by that of Duke Murdoch and his son Alexander, both of whom were also seized in Edinburgh Castle, where they had probably retired for safety. A few of their retainers arrested with them were speedily liberated, and it became apparent that upon this doomed family alone was King James's wrath directed. They were tried at Stirling, by a court of their peers, under the presidency of the King himself. The offences charged against them were misgovernment and oppression of the people, the greatest of public sins: but it was no less the end of a long tragedy. The younger branch of the race had been engaged in a struggle with the elder for the last two generations at least: and it had been the royal line that had suffered most during that period. Bitterly, in blood and heartbreak and long suppression, they had been weighed down under superior force: but now the time of reprisals had come. As they stood there confronting each other, the stern young King on one side and his kinsmen on the other, with a quarter of a century of wrong between them, the shadow of the young prince at Falkland, and the old father at Rothesay, and the eighteen years of captivity full in the minds of all, what a day of reckoning at

last! It makes the retribution almost more tragic, like the
overwhelming fate of the Greek drama, that the men upon
their trial had nothing to do with these crimes, unless it might
be the last. Murdoch of Albany had not exerted himself to
liberate James, but that was his only evident offence, and his
sons were not instrumental, so far as appears, in any injury to
their royal cousin. The sins of the fathers were to be visited
upon the children. We are told that the two sons, young
men in the flower of their youth, were executed one day,
and their father and maternal grandfather, a very old man,
the Earl of Lennox, whose share in the matter it is difficult
to make out, on the next. Thus James settled summarily
the question between himself and his kinsmen. The house
of Albany ended upon the scaffold, and however just their
doom might have been, there was something appalling in
this swift and sweeping revenge, carried out rigorously without a sign of hesitation by a young king, a happy bridegroom,
an accomplished and gay cavalier.

It must indeed be allowed, notwithstanding his poetry
and his evident love of everything that was lovely and of
good report, that the reign of the first James was a stern
one. Every witness agrees as to his accomplishments, and
that he was the flower of knighthood, of splendour and
courtesy, the most chivalrous, the most daring, the most
graceful and gracious of all his Court : and his genius as a
poet is even more generally acknowledged. The King's
" Quhair " as a poem is quite capable of standing on its own
merits, and needs no additional prestige as the performance of
a king. Had he been but a wandering minstrel Chaucer
would have had no need to be ashamed of his pupil. It
is full of delightful descriptions of nature and love and
youth : the fresh morning as it rises upon the castled heights,
the singing of the birds and fluttering of the leaves, the
impulse of a young heart even in the languor of imprisonment to start up and meet the sun, with all the springs of
new life which at that verdant season come with every new
day—the apparition of the beautiful one suddenly appearing
in the old immemorial garden with all its flowers, herself

the sweetest and the fairest of flowers, all are set before us, with a harmony and music not to be excelled. The young Prince chafing at his imprisonment, dreaming of all the fantastic wonderful things he might do were he free, yet still so full of irrepressible hope that his impatience and his longings are but another form of pleasure, takes shape and identity as distinct as if he had been one of the figures in that famous pilgrimage to Canterbury, which had been part of his training in this delightful art. If James had never reigned at all he would still have lived through all these centuries in the guise in which he stood at his window on that May morning, and suddenly, amid his youthful dreams, beheld the lovely vision of the Lady Jane emerging from under the young spring verdure of the trees. There is a certain window not generally supposed to be that at which the royal captive stood—a window in the Norman Tower of Windsor Castle, now fitly garnished and guarded by sympathetic hands, from which the spectator looking out upon the deep moat-garden underneath in the circle about the old donjon will scarcely be able to withstand the thrill of feeling which attends a poetic scene and incident fully realised. Nothing could be more green, more fresh, more full of romance and association, than this garden where all is youthful as the May, yet old in endless tradition, the garden of the Edwards and Henrys, where Chaucer himself may have thought over his accounts or taken the delightful image of his young squire "synging" who was, "or flouting all the day" from among some group of bright-faced lads in their bravery, where the countess who dropped her garter may have wandered, and the hapless Henry, the mild and puny child who was born there while James was undergoing his far from harsh captivity, played. James Stewart's name, had he been no king, would have been associated with this place, as that of his master in poetry is with the flowery ways of Kent.

Nor was his inspiration derived alone from the well of English undefiled. A still more wonderful gift developed in him when he got home to his native country. Though

the tones of Scotch humour were much less refined, and its
utterances at that early period could be scarcely more than
the jests and unwritten ballads of the populace, yet his
early acquaintance with them must have lingered in the
young Prince's mind, acquiring additional zest from the prepossessions of exile and the longing for home.   And when
the polished singer of the King's " Quhair " found himself
again in his native land he seems to have burst forth with the
most genuine impulse into the broad fun, rustical and natural
and racy of the soil, which perhaps was more congenial
to his Scottish audience.   " Peblis to the Play " and " Christis
Kirk on the Green " are poems full of the very breath of
rural life and the rude yet joyous meetings of the country
folk at kirk and market, which with wonderfully little difference of sentiment and movement also inspired Burns.   He
must have had a mind full of variety and wide human
sympathy almost Shakspearian, who could step from the
musings of Windsor and the beautiful heroine, all romance
and ethereal splendour, to the lasses in their gay kirtles, and
Hob and Raaf with their rustic " daffing," as true to the life
as the Ayrshire clowns of Burns, and all the clumsy yet
genial gambols of the village festival.   It is one of the most
curious and least to be expected transformations of poetic
versatility—for it is even amazing how he could know the
life into which he thus plunged joyous, as if he had been
familiar with it from his childhood.   King James was not
without an object amid all the laughter and the pranks
of his holiday. The King's cheerful ridicule of the
clumsy fellows who could not draw the bow was intended, with a prick of scorn under the laughter, to rouse
up his rustic lieges to emulation, not to be behind the
southern pock-puddings whose deadly arrows were, in every
encounter between Scots and English, the chief danger to
the fighting men of the north. It is curious that this
difference should have existed and continued with such
obstinacy through all these fighting centuries ; the Scotch
spearmen were all but invulnerable in their steady square,
like a rock, but they had little defence against the cloth-yard

shafts of the English bowmen, which neither exhortation
nor ridicule, neither prizes to win nor disaster to fear,
could teach them to adopt. James laboured hard, in
ways more practical than his poems, to introduce this
new arm, but in vain. It was kept up languidly in
holiday contentions, like that of Christis Kirk on the
Green, while his life lasted ; but when his reign was over
and the momentary stimulus withdrawn the bows were all
thrown away.

The King's command of this humorous vein, so dear to
his people, with its trenchant sketches from the life and
somewhat rough jests, is wonderful, when his courtly breeding
and long separation even from such knowledge of rustic
existence as a prince is likely to obtain is considered. And
the many-sided nature which made these humours so
familiar and easy to him is a strange discovery in the midst
of all the tragic circumstances of his life and reign. The
union of the most delicate poetry and romance with
that genial whim and fancy is unusual enough : but it is
still more unusual to find the stern Justiciar, avenger of
blood and redresser of wrong, the reconstructer of a distracted country, capable not only of the broad fun of the
rustic ballad-maker, but of so tolerant and humorous a
view of the humble commons, the underlying masses upon
which society is built. For the first aspect of affairs in
Scotland could not be a cheerful one : although it was rather
with the nobles and gentlemen, the great proprietors of the
country, who had to be summoned to exhibit their charters
and prove their titles, partly no doubt with the view of
discovering what Crown lands had been alienated by the
Albany party, that the King's quarrel was, than with the
humbler subjects of the nation.

Yet there is no doubt, with all these lights and softening
influences of character and genius, that his reign was a stern
one. James had everything to reform in the country to
which he came with so many new ideas and so enlarged a
knowledge of what the internal economy of a nation might be
made. It is rather against the general historical estimate of

the talents and power of the Regent Albany that the new
King should have found, as appears, so much to do for the
reorganisation of the commonwealth—regulating the laws,
appointing courts of justice, inquiring into the titles of property, and in every other way giving consistency and order
to the affairs of Scotland.　However, the lavish grants made
to the great Scots lords and the licence given them to rule
their vassals as they pleased arose not from weakness but
from Albany's deliberate policy of securing a strong party
on his side, a policy exactly opposed to that of James,
whose heart was set on subduing these fierce nobles, and
perhaps of developing the people at large, the nation itself, if
that is not too modern an ambition.　The reign of Law, broken
and disturbed by a hundred storms, but still henceforward
with a statute-book to fall back upon and some fitful
authority at its command, began in Scotland in his day.
There are some curious details in the *Scotichronicon* about
the taxes, now, it would seem, for the first time levied upon
the general mass of the people.　In 1424, the year after
James's return, a tax of twelvepence in the pound was imposed by the Parliament at Perth, for the maintenance of
the King's state and payment of his ransom, upon all goods,
lands, and annual revenues of whatever description, both
spiritual and temporal, which was passed with the consent
of the estates, no doubt under the stimulus of the general
rejoicing at the King's return.　This impost was to last for
two years.　An income tax so general and all-embracing
could scarcely be expected to be popular, but for the first
year it was paid, we are told, with readiness, certain of the
greatest nobles in the kingdom being appointed in their
various districts to the office of collecting.　That the Church
should have taken her share in the payment of this tax says
much for the loyalty of the Scotch priesthood and their unity
with the people at this crisis of the national history.　In the
second year, however, grumblings arose.　It is comprehensible
that a nation unaccustomed to this pressure should respond
to it in a moment of enthusiasm, yet become uneasy under
the repetition when the enthusiasm had probably died away,

especially if a fear arose that it might become permanent.
King James, however, adopted a course not at all usual with
governments when the power to exact has once been placed
in their hands.   When the popular murmur came to his
ears he stopped at once the unpopular demand.   How the
paying of the ransom was carried on, and how the maintenance of the King's state, we need not inquire.   The
Crown lands were no doubt extensive still.   Some years later
another experiment of the same kind was made ; the new
tax, however, being only twopence in the pound, and its
object the payment of expenses of a mission sent to France
to negotiate a marriage between the baby-princess Margaret
and the equally juvenile dauphin—an object which does not
appear to have appealed to the sympathies of the people,
since we are told that it was the cause of immediate
murmurs, the King not only stopped the unpopular tax
but returned the money to those who had paid it—a most
admirable but seldom followed example.

The curious system afterwards employed by all the Scots
kings of tours or " raids " of justice throughout the kingdom seems to have originated in James's energetic reign,
but he carried not only the officers of the law, but occasionally his entire Parliament with him, moving about to the
different centres of Scotland with great impartiality.   Sometimes they met at Edinburgh, in the great Parliament Hall in
the Castle, and made "many good laws if they could have been
kept," says the chronicler ; sometimes at Perth, a favourite
residence of the King ; and on one memorable occasion so
far north as Inverness, where, impatient of continual dis-
quietude in the Highlands, James went to chastise the
caterans and bring them within the reach of law.   This he
did with a severe and unsparing hand, seizing a number of the
most eminent chiefs who had been invited to meet him there,
and executing certain dangerous individuals among them
without mercy.   These summary measures would seem to
have borne immediate fruit in the almost complete subjugation of the Highlands.   But it was hard to reckon with such
a restless element as the clans, and hanging and heading

were very ineffectual measures among people with whom
" another for Hector" was the simplest suggestion of natural
law.

It was after this stern Parliament of Inverness that there
occurred at Edinburgh one of the most curious and picturesque scenes that it is possible to imagine. One of the
chiefs tried at that assize was the greatest and most important of all, the Lord of the Isles, sometimes called Donald
and sometimes Alexander by the chroniclers, who on his
promise to amend his ways, and no longer harbour caterans
or head forays, was, no doubt out of respect for his almost
princely position, set at liberty. But no sooner was the fierce
chieftain set free, " within few days after," says the chronicler,
than he took and burnt the town of Inverness, in which the
Parliament had been held, and showed his impenitence by an
utter abuse of the mercy accorded to him. When, however,
he heard that the King himself with all the forces of the
kingdom was coming against him, Donald hastily disbanded
his men and took refuge in the watery fastnesses of his
islands: and it would seem that he must have felt the tide of
national sentiment to be against him, and his power not equal
to make any stand against all the force of peaceful and law-
abiding Scotland under the energetic new King. The wily
Highlander made his submission in the way which, no doubt,
he thought most likely to disarm authority and gain exemption.
He chose Easter day, the greatest of religious festivals, for his
appearance as a penitent, and in the middle of the service in
the Chapel of Holyrood appeared suddenly, almost without
clothing, and knelt down before the King "where he was
sittand at his orison," praying for grace in the name of Him
who rose from the dead that day. So strange an interruption in the midst of all the glories of the Easter mass throws
a strange and wild light upon the varieties of national life in
Scotland. That half-savage figure, with plaid and weapons
cast aside, defenceless, at the King's mercy, in all the primitive abandonment yet calculation of early patriarchal times ;
while all that the art and culture of a splendid age could do
to give magnificence to the most imposing ceremonial of the

Church surrounded this strange apparition, the incense rising, the music pealing, the Court in all its glory of flashing jewels and splendid stuffs filling the lofty area. Like some wild god of the mists suddenly gleaming through the fragrant smoke between the bishop's white robes and the kneeling King, what a strange interruption to the mass! The King, at the request of the Queen we are told, gave him his life, as the adjuration addressed to him and all the force of the surroundings gave James little choice but to do ; for he could not have offended the sentiment of his people by refusing the boon which was demanded in that Name, however doubtful he might be of the expediency of granting it. " Then the King began to muse," says Boece. He must have been devout indeed to have been able to return to the course of the service with the Islesman before him on his knees, and all that wild half of the kingdom, with its dangerous habits and fierce tribal laws, thus suddenly made visible—a spectre which had often before troubled the King's peace. James had not to learn for the first time that apparent submission from such a suppliant did not necessarily mean any real change, and must have thoroughly felt the hollowness of that histrionic appearance, and all the difficulties which beset his own action in the matter. The conclusion was, that the life of the Lord of the Isles was spared, but he was committed to safe keeping in the strong Castle of Tantallon, with, however, the unfailing consequence, that his brother took the field with all his caterans in his stead.

James reigned in Scotland for thirteen years—a reign full of commotion and movement, by which many in high place were humiliated, the spoils of the feudal tyrants taken from them, and the wrongs of the suffering commonalty redressed, proceedings which procured for the King many enemies among the nobility before the force of popular sentiment was strong enough to balance this opposition by its support. He began in Scotland that struggle which for some time had been going on in England against the power of the nobles, who were still in the north something like a number of petty kings ruling in their own right, making

little account of national laws, and regarding the King with
defiance as almost a hostile power. One of the greatest risks
of such a struggle is that it raises now and then a fiery
spirit stung by the sense of injury and the rage of deprivation into a wild passion of revenge which bursts every
restraint. The Grahams of Strathearn in the north had
fallen specially under the rectifying process of James's new
laws of property : and out of this house there suddenly arose
the tragic figure of an avenger whose brief but terrible career
occupies but a single page in history, yet contains all the
elements of a fatal drama. Sir Robert Graham, of whose
antecedents there is little record, was not the head of the
house, but a younger brother of daring character, and one of
those fanatics of race to whom the glory of their house is a
religion. The first we hear of him is a sudden appearance
in the Parliament of January 1435, when he made a fiery
and violent speech, ending by an impeachment of the King
himself for injustice and robbery. Such an assault would
find little support in the public assembly of the States, in
the awe of the royal presence, and Graham had to escape
for his life, finding means of flight into the Highlands, the
ever - ready refuge for rebels. There he launched wild
threats against James, which the King, probably well accustomed to missiles of the kind, paid little attention to.
The monarch was warned too, we are told, by another
wild apparition, which suddenly appears out of the mists
for this purpose—a Highland witch of the order of those
who drove Macbeth's ambition to frenzy, but whose mission
now was to warn James of the mischief brewing against
him. The King was brave and careless, used to the continual presence of danger, keeping his Christmas merrily
at Perth with all the sports and entertainments with which
it was possible to cheat the gloomy weather, and made little
but additional mirth both of the prophecy and the threats.
Evidently the Court found pleasure in the fair city on the
Tay. They were still lingering there, having taken up their
residence in the monastery of the Black Friars, at the end of
February. In Scotland as elsewhere the great religious

houses seem to have been the best adapted to give hospitality
to kings. It was long after this date before anything that
could be called an independent royal residence was built at
Holyrood itself : for generations the King and Court were
but guests in the stately abbey, which was, like the monastery
of the Black Friars, so convenient and commodious a house
both for entertainment and shelter that its great chambers
became the natural, as they were the most stately and
pleasant, lodging that could be provided for a monarch.

The tragedy that followed is well known. At the end
of a pleasant evening when there had been music—in which
James himself was the first connoisseur in Scotland, inventing,
some say, the national lilt, the rapidly rising and falling
strain which is so full of pathos yet so adaptable to mirth—
"and other honest solaces of grete pleasance and disport,"
the sound of trampling feet and angry voices broke upon the
conventual stillness outside and the cheerful talk of the
friendly group within. The King was taken at a disadvantage, apparently without even a gentleman of his Court
near him, nothing but his wife and her ladies lingering for a
last moment of pleasant conversation before they went to
bed. It is easy to imagine the horror with which the little
party must have listened to the rush of the savage band,
hoping perhaps at first that it was but some tumult in the
street, or affray between the townsfolk and the caterans—
never very far off and often threatening St. John's town—till
the cries and clashing of the arms came nearer, and wild torch-
light flared through the high windows and proved the fatal
object of the raid. The groans of a few easily despatched
sentinels, the absence of any serious opposition or stand
in defence, the horrible discovery of bolts and bars removed
and the King at the mercy of his enemies, must have followed in a few terrible moments. No incident in history
is better known than that piteous attempt of one distracted
girl, a Douglas, born of a heroic race, to bar the door with
her own slim arm, thrusting it through the holdfasts from
which the bolt had been taken away : poor ineffectual bar !
yet enough to gain a moment when moments were so pre-

cious, and while there was still a chance of saving the King.

The narrative of the death struggle, and the distracted attempts to find a place of concealment for the victim, are too heartrending to be repeated here. James fell, it is said, with sixteen wounds in him, hacked almost to pieces, yet facing his murderers so desperately that some of them bore the marks of his dying grip when they were brought to the scaffold to be killed in their turn with every circumstance of horror conceivable some time later. The execution of these miserable traitors, one of them the King's own uncle Athole, took place at Edinburgh for the greater solemnity and terror of the punishment, which was accomplished by every kind of torture. The Queen, too, after the horrible scene of which she had been a witness, and almost more than a witness—for she had thrown herself before her husband and had been wounded in the terrible struggle—gathered her children and fled to Edinburgh Castle to put the little heir of the kingdom, now James II, in security. The hapless child was sadly crowned at Holyrood at six years old, with a hastily adapted ceremonial, the first of many such disastrous rites to come.

The time of James's reign had been one of rising prosperity throughout the realm. Law and order had been established in recognised courts and tribunals, the titles of property had been ascertained and secured, not without loss, no doubt, to many arrogant lords who had seized upon stray land without any lawful title, or on whom it had been illegally bestowed during the Albany reign—but to the general confidence and safety. And the condition of the people had no doubt improved in consequence. It is difficult to form any estimate of what this condition was. All foreign witnesses give testimony of an unpleasing kind, and represent the country as wretched, squalid, and uncivilised : but on the other hand nothing can be more unlike this report than the most valuable and unintentional evidence furnished by King James's own poems, with their tale of village merry-makings and frays which convey no impression of abject

poverty, nor even of that rudest level of life where material
wants are so pressing as to exclude all lighter thoughts.
" On Mayday," says King James, " when everybody is bound
to Peblis to the play,"

> " At Beltane quhan ilke bodie bownis
>   To Peblis to the play,
> To heir the singing and sweit soundis,
>   The solace suth to say.
> Be firth and forest furth they found,
>   They graythit them full gay ;
> God wot that wald they do that stound,
>   For it was thair feist day
>   They said
>   Of Peblis to the Play."

All the lasses of the west, he goes on to tell us, were
up at cockcrow, and no men might rest for the chatter and
the noise of their preparations.   One cried that her curch
was not starched enough, another that a hood was best,
another bewailed herself as " so evil sunburnt " that she was
not fit to be seen.   The young folk stream along " full
bold " with the bagpipes blowing, and every village adding
its contingent, " he before and she before to see which was
most gay."

> " Some said that they were mercat folk,
> Some said the Quene of May
>   Was cumit
>   Of Peblis to the Play."

When they arrive at " the taverne hous " they give orders
that the board be served, and to see that the napery is white,
" for we will dyn and daunce."   At " Christis Kirk on the
Green " there is a similar description, the lasses coming out as
before, " weshen clean," in their new grey kirtles " well prest
with many plaits," with their gloves of doeskin and morocco
shoes.   All these incidental traits, and the atmosphere of
the merry ballads, though both end in a fray, contradict with
vigour the cold and wretched picture given by outsiders of a
country where the people warmed themselves by burning
sulphureous stones dug out of the ground, where the houses

had a cow's hide stretched for a door, and all was squalid
misery and nakedness. There was plenty of fighting going
on it is evident—not a lowland fair without its broken heads
(a habit that according to Sir Walter Scott, no mean authority,
lasted into the nineteenth century)—and much oppression,
the great lords reigning like absolute tyrants in the midst
of subjects without resource or protection ; but the case of
the peasantry notwithstanding all these evils does not seem
to have been a bad one. A certain vigorous capacity of
revival, which history shows us continually as existing on the
broad level of the soil, must have brought them back to rough
ease and comfort, and the freedom of the natural healthful atmosphere which makes itself apparent in transcripts of life so
little likely to be forced or optimistic. In all times and
circumstances there can be little doubt that the amount of
simple enjoyment to be got out of life, especially by the
young, who form at least the half of every community, far
exceeds the elements of wellbeing which outsiders see in it.
And the protection of the Church, the comparative quiet to
be enjoyed on church lands, the charities and succour of the
cloister, must have made an incalculable addition to the
possibilities of existence. Everything in James's reign was
calculated to increase the stability and good order which are
the best guarantees of national life ; even his severities cultivating a sense of security in the weak and a wholesome
consciousness of the necessity of self-restraint in the strong.
For the first time for many generations the nobles were kept
within bounds, and exceptional cruelties became if not
impossible, yet of so certain discovery and punishment that
lesser tyrants at least must have trembled. The law that
might makes right fell into temporary disuse, and a better
law, that of the courts that sat periodically over all the kingdom, and—appealing still more strongly to the imagination—
a king that shut his ears to no petition and interfered with a
strong hand to right the wronged, began a new era for the
commonalty of Scotland. Even the unfavourable description so often quoted of Eneas Silvius, reports the common
people as having "abundance of flesh and fish," no small

ingredient of wellbeing, and records rather a complete absence of luxuries than that want which reduces the vital strength of a nation. The same authority tells of exportations of "hides, wool, salt fish, and pearls," the latter a curious item, although there were as yet no manufactures, and even such necessaries as horse-shoes and every kind of harness had to be imported from Flanders. But the Scots in their farmhouses and cottages made the cloth with which they were clothed, and their "blew caps," the well-known blue bonnet which has lasted to our own days. And they retained the right which, according to her monkish chronicler, St. Margaret had been the first to secure for them — of immunity from all military requisitions, and even, which is a curious contradiction of the supposed tyrannies of the nobles, held an absolute property in their own goods which out of the island of Great Britain no peasantry in the world possessed. The French allies who were in Scotland in the end of the fourteenth century were struck with angry consternation to hear themselves hailed by a set of clodhoppers, and bidden to keep the paths and not trample down the growing corn, and to find that, however willing the Scots men-at-arms might be to harry England when occasion offered, not the greatest lord in the French contingent could carry off a cow or a brace of pullets without compensation. We cannot but think that the country in which the peasant's barnyard was thus defended was at least as forward in the best elements of civilisation as those in which there were hangings of arras and trenchers of silver, but no security for anything in homesteads or workshop which might be coveted by the seigneur.

Edinburgh, as has been said, never seems to have been a favourite habitation of this enlightened and accomplished Prince. Perhaps Queen Jane found the east winds too keen on the heights, or the Abbey of the Holy Rood too low in the valley. The heir was born there it is true, and we have note of various Parliaments and visits, but no settled residence in the capital. One incident is mentioned by the chroniclers which must have afforded a picturesque scene,

HOLYROOD

when the King himself presided, before the gates of Edinburgh Castle,
at a duel between a knight called
Henry Knokkis or Knox (curious
precursor in the dimness of distance
of another of his name!), who had
been accused by an Edinburgh burgess of treasonable
speeches against the King—and his accuser. But who this
accuser was, and by what privilege he was allowed to meet
a gentleman and knight in single combat we have no information. Perhaps he was himself of noble blood, a younger
son, a man before his time, seeking the peaceful profits of
trade instead of those of the marauder, as it has become
the fashion of a later age to do. It is almost impossible not to fancy that there must have been a touch
of the burlesque in this combat, which James himself interfered to stop, separating the combatants. He was very
careless it would seem of treasonable speeches, apt to treat
them lightly, and very probably smiled a little at the zeal

of the citizen who was more jealous of his honour than he
was himself. The platform before the gates would still
make a splendid area for any feat of arms, if the winds did
not interfere before the King and blow the combatants away:
and the old-world crowd with their many colours, the jerkins
slashed and embroidered with the blazon of all the great
families in Scotland, the plumed caps and dazzling helmets
of courtier and knight, the border of blue bonnets outside,
and all the shining array of fair ladies around and behind
the throne, would present a more striking picture than the
best we could do nowadays. Let us hope the sun shone
and warmed the keen clear air, and threw into high relief the
towers and bastions against the northern blue.

Edinburgh by this time had grown into the proportions
of a town. The houses which the citizens had the privilege
of building within the castle precincts would appear to have
been low, to secure the protection of the walls ; and by
certain precautionary regulations for their preservation from
fire it would seem that many of them were still thatched.
The King's residence there, judging from the straitened accom-
modation, which was all that existed in a much more advanced
period, must have been small and poor, though there already
existed a Parliament Hall, in which probably other great
assemblies were held. The city walls were continued along
the crest of the ridge in narrow lines, deflecting a little only
on the south side, where the limits were broken by several
wealthy and well-cultivated enclosures where brotherhoods
were established—White and Black Friars, sons of Augustine
and Dominic, with their great detached houses, their gardens
always an example of husbandry, and chapels filling the air
with pleasant sound of bells. King James had himself
endowed, besides many existing foundations, a monastery
for the Franciscans or Grey Friars, which has always
continued to be one of the chief ecclesiastic centres of
Edinburgh. It was so fine a building, as the story
goes, that the humble-minded Minors declined at first
to take possession of it as being too magnificent for an
Order vowed to poverty ; though as their superior was a

monk from Cologne, sent for by the King on account of his learning and sanctity, and accustomed to the great convents of the Continent, such an objection is curious.　On the south side of the town, at some distance outside the walls, on the platform afterwards occupied by the buildings of the old High School, stood amid its blossoming gardens the Church of St. Mary in the Field, afterwards so fatally known as the Kirk of Field, a great house so extensive and stately that it had already served on several occasions as a royal lodging. St. Giles's, one of the oldest foundations of all, stood among its graves, at the foot of the Castle Hill in the centre of the life of ancient Edinburgh, as it does still.　These clusters of sacred buildings, encircled by their orchards and gardens, made a fringe of verdure, of charity and peace, sanctuaries for the living and resting-places for the dead, round the strong and dark fortifications of the little royal town, which hitherto had held for its life upon that ridge of rock, a dangerous eminence lying full in every invader's way.

EDINBURGH CASTLE FROM THE SOUTH-WEST

CHAPTER II

JAMES II: WITH THE FIERY FACE

IT is clear that the public opinion of Scotland, so far as
there was such a thing in existence, had no sympathy whatever with the murderers of James. The instruments of that
murder were in the first place Highland caterans, with whom

no terms were ever held and against whom every man's
hand was armed. And the leaders who had taken advantage of these wild allies against their natural monarch and
kindred were by the very act put beyond the pale of sympathy. They were executed ferociously and horribly, according to the custom of the time, the burghers of Perth rising
at once in pursuit of them, and the burghers of Edinburgh
looking on with stern satisfaction at their tortures—these
towns feeling profoundly, more perhaps than any other
section of the community, the extraordinary loss they had in
the able and vigorous King, already, like his descendant and
successor, the King of the commons, their stay and encouragement. If there was among the nobility less lamentation over a ruler who spared none of them on account of his
race, and was sternly bent on repressing all abuse of power,
it was silent in the immense and universal horror with which
the event filled Scotland. It would seem probable that the
little heir, only six years old, the only son of King James,
was not with his parents in their Christmas rejoicings at
Perth, but had been left behind at Holyrood, for we are told
that the day after his father's death the poor little wondering child was solemnly but hastily crowned there, the dreadful news having flown to the centre of government. He
was "crownd by the nobilitie," says Pitscottie, the great
nobles who were nearest and within reach having no doubt
rushed to the spot where the heir was, to guard and also
to retain in their own hands the future King. He was proclaimed at once, and the crown, or such substitute for it as
could be laid sudden hands upon, put on his infant head. The
scene is one which recurred again and again in the history
of his race, yet nothing can take from it its touching features. At six years old even the intimation of a father's
death, especially when taking place at a distance, would
make but a transitory impression upon the mind ; yet we
may well imagine the child taken from his toys, wrapped
from head to foot in some royal mantle, with a man's crown
held over his baby head, receiving with large eyes of wonder and fright, easily translated into tears, the sacred oil, the

sceptre which his little fingers could scarcely enclose.   Alas
for the luckless Stewarts! again and again this affecting
ceremony took place before the time of their final promotion which was the precursor of their overthrow.   They were
all kings almost from their cradle—kings ill-omened, entering upon their royalty with infant terror and tears.

When they had crowned the little James, second of the
name, the lords held a convention " to advise whom they
thought most able both for manheid and witt to take the
government of the commonwealth in hand."   They chose
two men for this office, neither of whom was taken from
a very great family, or had, so far as can be known, any
special importance—Sir Alexander Livingstone, described
as Knight of Callender, and Sir William Crichton, Chancellor of Scotland.   Perhaps it was one of the compromises
which are so common when parties are nearly equal in power
which thus placed two personages of secondary importance at
the head of affairs : but any advantage which might have been
secured by this selection was neutralised by the division of
power, which added to all the evils of an interregnum the
perplexity of two centres of government, so that "no man
knew," as says Pitscottie, "whom he should obey."   One of
the Regents reigned in Edinburgh, the other in Stirling—
one had the advantage of holding possession of the King,
the other had the doubtful good of the support of the Queen.
It may be imagined what an extraordinary contrast this was
to the firm and vigilant sway of a monarch in the fulness of
manhood, with all the prestige of his many gifts and
accomplishments, his vigorous and manful character and his
unquestioned right to the government and obedience of the
country.   It had been hard work enough for James I., with
all these advantages, to keep his kingdom well in hand :
and it would not be easy to exaggerate the difficulties now,
with two rival and feeble powers, neither great enough to
overawe nor united enough to hold in check the independent
power of the great houses which vied with each other in the
display of dominion and wealth.   In a very brief time all
the ground gained by King James was lost again.   Every

element of anarchy arose in new force, and if it had been
hard to secure the execution of the laws which would have
been so good had they been kept in the time when their chief
administrator was the King himself, it may be supposed what
was the difficulty now, when, save in a little circuit round
each seat of authority, there was virtually no power at all.
Pitscottie gives a curious and vivid picture of the state of
affairs in this lamentable interval.

" In the mean time many great dissensions rose amongst us, but it
was uncertain who were the movers, or by what occasion the chancellor
exercised such office, further than became him.   He keeped both the
Castle of Edinburgh and also our young King thereintill, who was committed to his keeping by the haill nobilitie and ane great part of the
noble men assisted to his opinion.   Upon the other side, Sir Alexander
Livingstoun bearing the authoritie committed to him by consent of
the nobilitie, as said is, contained another faction, to whose opinion
the Queen mother with many of the nobility very trewly assisted.   So the
principals of both the factions caused proclaime lettres at mercat crosses
and principal villages of the realm that all men should obey conforme to
the aforesaid letters sent forth by them, under the pain of death.   To
the which no man knew to whom he should obey or to whose letters he
should be obedient unto.   And also great trouble appeared in this
realm, because there was no man to defend the burghs, priests, and poor
men and labourers hauntind to their leisum (lawful) business either
private or public.   These men because of these enormities might not
travel for thieves and brigands and such like : all other weak and
decrepit persons who was unable to defend themselves, or yet to get
food and sustentation to themselves, were most cruelly vexed in such
troublous times.   For when any passed to seek redress at the Chancellor
of such injuries and troubles sustained by them, the thieves and
brigands, feigning themselves to be of another faction, would burn
their house and carry their whole goods and gear away before ever they
returned again.   And the same mischief befell those that went to complain to the Governor of the oppression done to them.   Some other
good men moved upon consideration and pitie of their present calamities
tholed (endured) many such injuries, and contained themselves at home
and sought no redresse.   In the midst of these things and troubles, all
things being out of order, Queen-Mother began to find out ane moyane
(a means) how she should diminish the Chancellor's power and augment
the Governor's power, whose authority she assisted."

The position of Queen Jane in the circumstances in
which her husband left her, a woman still young, with a band
of small children, and no authority in the turbulent and

distracted country, is as painful a one as could well be imagined. Her English blood would be against her, and even
her beauty, so celebrated by her chivalrous husband, and
which would no doubt increase the immediate impulse of
suitors, in that much-marrying age, towards the beautiful
widow who was of royal blood to begin with and still bore
the title of Queen. That she seems to have had no protection from her royal kindred is probably explained by the
fact that Henry VI was never very potent or secure upon his
throne, and that the Wars of the Roses were threatening and
demanding the whole attention of the English Government.
Wounded in her efforts to protect her husband by her own
person, seeing him slaughtered before her eyes, there
could not be a more terrible moment in any woman's life,
hard as were the lives of women in that age of violence,
than that which passed over Jane Beaufort's head in the
Blackfriars Monastery amid the blood and tumult of that
fatal night. The chroniclers, occupied by matters more
weighty, have no time to picture the scene that followed that
cruel and horrible murder, when the distracted women who
were its only witnesses, after the tumult and the roar of the
murderers had passed by, were left to wash the wounds and
compose the limbs of the dead King so lately taking his
part in their evening's pastime, and to look to the injuries of
the Queen and the torn and broken arm of Catherine
Douglas, a sufferer of whom history has no further word to say.
The room with its imperfect lights rises before us, the wintry
wind rushing in by those wide-open doors, waving about the
figures on the tapestry till they too seemed to mourn and
lament with wildly tossing arms the horror of the scene—the
cries and clash of arms as the caterans fled, pausing no
doubt to pick up what scattered jewels or rich garments
might lie in their way : and by the wild illumination of a
torch, or the wavering leaping flame of the faggot on the
hearth, the two wounded ladies, each with an anxious group
about her — the Queen, covered with her own and her
husband's blood ; the girl, with her broken wrist, lying near
the threshold which she had defended with all her heroic

might. They were used to exercise the art of healing, to
bind up wounds and bring back consciousness, these hapless
ladies, so constantly the victims of passion and ambition.
But amid all the horrors which they had to witness in their
lives, horrors in which they did not always take the healing
part, there could be none more appalling than this. Neither
then nor now, however, is it at the most terrible moment of
life, when the revolted soul desires it most, that death comes
to free the sufferer. The Queen lived, no doubt, to think of
the forlorn little boy in Holyrood, the five little maidens
who were dependent upon her, and resumed the burden
of life now so strangely different, so dull and blank, so
full of alarms and struggles. Her elder child, the little
Princess Margaret, had been sent to France three or four
years before, at the age of ten, to be the bride of the
Dauphin—a great match for a Scottish princess—and it is
possible that her next sister, Eleanor, who afterwards married
the Duc de Bretagne, had accompanied Margaret—two little
creatures solitary in their great promotion, separated from all
who held them dear. But the four infants who were left
would be burden enough for the mother in her unassured
and unprotected state. It would seem that she was not
permitted to be with her boy, probably because of the
jealousy of the Lords, who would have no female Regent
attempting to reign in the name of her son : but had
fixed her residence in Stirling under the shield of Livingstone, who as Governor of the kingdom ought to have
exercised all the functions of the Regency, and especially
the most weighty one, that of training the King. Crichton,
however, who was Chancellor, had been on the spot when
James II was crowned, and had secured his guardianship
by the might of the strong hand, if no other, removing him
to Edinburgh Castle, where he could be kept safe under
watch and ward. The Queen, who would seem to have
been throughout of Livingstone's faction, and who no doubt
desired to have her son with her, both from affection and
policy, set her wits to discover a " moyane," as the chroniclers
say, of recovering the custody of the boy. The moyane

was simple and primitive enough, and might well have been
pardoned to a mother deprived of her natural rights :
but it shows at the same time the importance attached

INNER BARRIER, EDINBURGH CASTLE

to the possession of the little King, when it was only in
such a way that he could be secured. Queen Jane set
out from Stirling "with a small train" to avert suspicion,
and appeared at the gates of Edinburgh Castle suddenly,

without warning as would seem, asking to be admitted to see
her son.   The Chancellor, wise and wily as he was, would
appear to have acknowledged the naturalness of this request,
and "received her," the chronicler says, "with gladness, and
gave her entrance to visit her young son, and gave command
that whensoever the Queen came to the castle it should be
patent to Her Grace."   Jane entered the castle accordingly,
with many protestations of her desire for peace and anxiety
to prevent dissensions, all which was, no doubt, true enough,
though the chroniclers treat her protestations with little faith,
declaring her to have "very craftilie dissembled" in order to
dispel any suspicion the Chancellor may have entertained.
It would seem that she had not borne any friendship to him
beforehand, and that her show of friendship now required
explanation.   However that might be, she succeeded in
persuading Crichton of her good faith, and was allowed to
have free intercourse with her son and regain her natural
place in his affections.   How long they had been separated
there is no evidence to show, but it could scarcely be
difficult for the mother to recover, even had it fallen into
forgetfulness, the affection of her child.   When she had
remained long enough in the castle to disarm any prejudices
Crichton might entertain of her, and to persuade the little
King to the device which was to secure his freedom, the
Queen informed the Chancellor that she was about to make
a pilgrimage to the famous shrine of Whitekirk, "the white
kirk of Brechin," Pitscottie says, in order to pray for the
repose of the soul of her husband and the prosperity of her
son, and asked permission to carry away two coffers with
her clothes and ornaments, probably things which she had
left in the castle before her widowhood, and that means of
conveyance might be provided for these possessions to Leith,
where she was to embark.   This simple request was easily
granted, and the two coffers carried out of the castle, and
conveyed by "horss" to the ship in which she herself
embarked with her few attendants.   But instead of turning
northward Queen Jane's ship sailed up the Firth, through
the narrow strait at Queensferry, past Borrowstounness,

where the great estuary widens out once more, into the
quiet waters of the Forth, winding through the green country
to Stirling on its hill.   She was " a great pairt of the watter
upward before ever the keepers of the castle could perceive
themselves deceived," says Pitscottie.   As the ship neared
Stirling, the Governor of the kingdom came out of the
castle with all his forces, with great joy and triumph, and
received the King and his mother.   For one of the coffers,
so carefully packed and accounted for, contained no less an
ornament than the little King in person, to whose childish
mind no doubt this mode of transport was a delightful
device and pleasantry.   One can imagine how the Queen's
heart must have throbbed with anxiety while her son lay
hidden in the bed made for him within the heavy chest,
where if air failed, or any varlet made the discovery
prematurely, all her hopes would have come to an end.   She
must have fluttered like a bird over her young about the
receptacle in which her boy lay, and talked with her ladies
over his head to encourage and keep him patient till the
end of the journey was near enough, amid the lingering links
of Forth, to open the lid and set him free.   It is not a
journey that is often made nowadays, but with all the
lights of the morning upon Demayat and his attendant
mountains, and the sun shining upon that rich valley, and
the river at its leisure wending, as if it loved them, through
all the verdant holms and haughs, there is no pleasanter
way of travelling from Edinburgh to Stirling, the two hill-
castles of the Scottish crown.

It would be pleasant to think that Queen Jane meant
something more than the mere bolstering up of one faction
against another in the distracted kingdom by the abduction
of her son.   It is very possible indeed that she did so, and
that to strengthen the hands of the man who was really
Regent-Governor of Scotland, but whose power had been
stolen from his hands by the unscrupulousness of Crichton,
seemed to her a great political object, and the recovery of
the supreme authority, which would seem to have appeared
to all as infallibly linked with the possession of the young

King, of the greatest importance. It is evident it was considered by the general public to be so ; but there is something pitiful in the struggle for the poor boy, over whose small person those fierce factionaries fought, and in whose name, still so innocent and helpless as he was, so many ferocious deeds were done.

No sooner was he secure in Stirling than the Governor called together a convention of his friends, to congratulate each other and praise the wit and skill of " that noble woman, our soverain mother," who had thus set things right. " Whereby I understand," he says piously, " that the wisest man is not at all times the sickerest, nor yet the hardy man happiest," seeing that Crichton, though so great and sagacious and powerful, should be thus deceived and brought to shame. " Be of good comfort therefore," adds this enlightened ruler ; " all the mischief, banishment, troubles, and vexation which the Chancellor thought to have done to us let us do the like to him." He ended this discourse by an intimation that he was about to besiege Edinburgh. " Let us also take up some band of men-of-war, and every man after his power send secret messages to their friends, that they and every one that favours us may convene together quietly in Edinburgh earlie in the morning, so that the Chancellor should not know us to come for the sieging of the castle till we have the siege even belted about the walls ; so ye shall have subject to you all that would have arrogantly oppressed you."

This resolution was agreed to with enthusiasm, the Queen undertaking to provision the army " out of her own garners " ; but the Governor had no sooner " belted the siege about the castle," an expression which renders most graphically the surrounding of the place, than the Chancellor, taken by surprise, prostrated by the loss of the King, and finding it impossible to draw the powerful Earl of Douglas to his aid, made overtures of submission, and begged for a meeting " in the fields before the gates," where, with a few chosen friends on either side, the two great functionaries of the kingdom might come to an agreement between themselves.

By this time there would seem to have begun that pre-ponderating influence of the Douglas family in Scotland which vexed the entire reign of the second James, and prompted two of the most violent and tragic deeds which stain the record of Scottish history. James I. was more general in his attempt at the repression and control of his fierce nobility, and the family most obnoxious to him was evidently that of his uncle, nearest in blood and most dangerous to the security of the reigning race. The Douglas, however, detaches himself in the following genera-tion into a power and place unexampled, and which it took the entire force of Scotland, and all the wavering and un-certain expedients of law, as well as the more decisive action of violence quite lawless, to put down. Whether there was in the pretensions of this great house any aim at the royal authority in their own persons, or ambitious assertion of a rival claim in right of the blood of Bruce, which was as much in their veins as in those of the Stewarts, as some recent historians would make out, it is probably now quite impossible to decide. The chroniclers say nothing of any such intention, nor do the Douglases themselves, who throughout the struggle never hesitated to make submission to the Crown when the course of fortune went against them. The Chancellor had been deeply stung, it is evident, by the answer of Douglas to his appeal, in which the fierce Earl declared that discord between " you twa unhappie tyrants " was the most agreeable thing in the world to him, and that he wished nothing more than that it should continue. Deprived of the sanction given to all his proceedings by the name of the King, outwitted among his wiles, and exposed to the ridicule even of those who had regarded his wisdom with most admiration, Crichton would seem to have turned fiercely upon the common opponent, perhaps with a wise prescience of the evil to come, perhaps only to secure an object of action which might avert danger from himself and bring him once more into command of the source of authority—most likely with both objects together, the higher and lower, as is most general in our mingled nature.

The meeting was held accordingly outside the castle gates,
the Chancellor coming forth in state bearing the keys of the
castle, which were presented, Buchanan says, to the King in
person, who accompanied the expedition, and who restored
the great functionary to his office.   The great keys in the
child's hand, the little treble pipe in which the reappoint-
ment would be made, the tiny figure in the midst of all
these plotters and warriors, gives a touch of pathos to the
many pictorial scenes of an age so rich in the picturesque ;
but the earlier writers say nothing of the little James's
presence.   There was, however, a consultation between the
two Regents, and Douglas's letter was read with such angry
comments as may be supposed.   The Earl's contempt
evidently cut deep, and strongly emphasised the necessity of
dealing authoritatively with such a high-handed rebel against
the appointed rulers.

It would appear, however, that little could be done
against the immediate head of that great house, and the
two rulers, though they had made friends over this common
object, had to await their opportunity, and in the meantime
do their best to maintain order and to get each the chief
power into his own hands.   Crichton found means before
very long to triumph over his adversaries in his turn by
rekidnapping the little King, for whom he laid wait in the
woods about Stirling, where James was permitted precociously
to indulge the passion of his family for hunting.   No doubt
the crafty Chancellor had pleasant inducements to bring
forward to persuade the boy to a renewed escape, for " the
King smiled," say the chroniclers, probably delighted by the
novelty and renewed adventure—the glorious gallop across
country in the dewy morning, a more pleasant prospect than
the previous conveyance in his mother's big chest.   Thus
in a few hours the balance was turned, and it was once
more the Chancellor and not the Governor who could
issue ordinances and make regulations in the name of the
King.

Nothing, however, could be more tedious and trifling in
the record than these struggles over the small person of the

child - king.   But the story quickens when the long-desired occasion arrived, and the two rulers, rivals yet partners in power, found opportunity to strike the blow upon which they had decided, and crush the great family which threatened to dominate Scotland, and which was so contemptuous of their own sway.   The great Earl, Duke of Touraine, almost prince at home, the son of that Douglas whose valour had moved England, and indeed Christendom, to admiration, though he never won a battle—died in the midst of his years, leaving behind him two young sons much under age as the representatives of his name.   It is extra-ordinary to us to realise the place held by youth in those times, when one would suppose a man's strength peculiarly necessary for the holding of an even nominal position.   Mr. Church has just shown in his Life of Henry V how that prince at sixteen led armies and governed provinces ; and it is clear that this was by no means exceptional, and that the right of boys to rule themselves and their possessions was universally acknowledged and permitted.   The young William, Earl of Douglas, is said to have been only about fourteen at his father's death.   He was but eighteen at the time of his execution, and between these dates he appears to have exercised all the rights of independent authority without tutor or guardian.   The position into which he entered at this early age was unequalled in Scotland, in many respects superior to that of the nominal sovereign, who had so many to answer to for every step he took—counsellors and critics more plentiful than courtiers.   The chronicles report all manner of vague arrogancies and presumptions on the part of the new Earl.   He held a veritable court in his castle, very different from the semi-prison which, whether at Edinburgh or Stirling, was all that James of Scotland had for home and throne—and conferred fiefs and knighthood upon his followers as if he had been a reigning prince.   "The Earl of Douglas," says Pitscottie, "being of tender age, was puffed up with new ambition and greater pride nor he was before, as the manner of youth is ; and also prideful tyrants and flatterers that were about him through this occasion spurred him ever to greater tyranny and oppression." The lawless proceedings of the young potentate would seem to have stirred up all the disorderly elements in the kingdom. His own wild Border county grew wilder than ever, without control. Feuds broke out over all the country, in which revenge for injuries or traditionary quarrels were lit up of the strong hope in every man's breast not only of killing his neighbour, but taking possession of his neighbour's lands. The caterans swarmed down once more from the mountains and isles, and every petty tyrant of a robber laird threw off whatever bond of law had been forced upon him in King James's golden days. This sudden access of anarchy was made more terrible by a famine in the country, where not very long before it had been reported that there was fish and flesh for every man. " A great dearth of victualls, pairtly because the labourers of the ground might not sow nor win the corn through the tumults and cumbers of the country," spread everywhere, and the state of the kingdom called the conflicting authorities once more to consultation and some attempt at united action.

The meeting this time was held in St. Giles's, the metropolitan church, then, perhaps, scarcely less new and shining in its decoration than now, though with altars glowing in all the shadowy aisles and the breath of incense mounting to the lofty roof. There would not seem to have been any prejudice as to using a sacred place for such a council, though it might be in the chapter-house or some adjacent building that the barons met. It is to be hoped that they did not go so far as to put into words within the consecrated walls the full force of their intention, even if it had come to be an intention so soon. There was but a small following on either side, that neither party might be alarmed, and many fine speeches were made upon the necessity of concord and mutual aid to repress the common enemy. The Chancellor, having restolen the King, would no doubt be most confident in tone ; but on both sides there were equal professions of devotion to the country, and so many admirable sentiments

expressed, that "all their friends on both sides that stood
about began to extol and love them both, with great thanksgiving that they both regarded the commonwealth so mickle
and preferred the same to all private quarrels and debates."
The decision to which they came was to call a Parliament,
at which aggrieved persons throughout the country might
appear and make their complaints.   The result was a crowd
of woeful complainants, " such as had never been seen before.
There were so many widows, bairns, and infants seeking
redress for their husbands, kin, and friends that were cruelly
slain by wicked murderers, and many for hireling theft and
murder, that it would have pitied any man to have heard
the same."   This clamorous and woeful crowd filled the
courts and narrow square of the castle before the old parlia-
ment-hall with a murmur of misery and wrath, the plaint of
kin and personal injury more sharp than a mere public grief.
The two rulers and their counsellors no doubt listened with
grim satisfaction, feeling their enemy delivered into their
hands, and finding a dreadful advantage in the youth and
recklessness of the victims, who had taken no precaution,
and of whom it was so easy to conclude that they were
"the principal cause of these enormities."   Whether their
determination to sacrifice the young Douglas, and so crush
his house, was formed at once, it is impossible to say.   Perhaps some hope of moulding his youth to their own purpose
may have at first softened the intention of the plotters.   At all
events they sent him complimentary letters, "full of coloured
and pointed words," inviting him to Edinburgh in their joint
names with all the respect that became his rank and importance.   The youth, unthinking in his boyish exaltation of any
possibility of harm to him, accepted the invitation sent to
him to visit the King at Edinburgh, and accompanied by his
brother David, the only other male of his immediate family,
set out magnificently and with full confidence with his gay
train of knights and followers—among whom, no doubt, the
youthful element predominated—towards the capital.   He
was met on the way by Crichton—evidently an accomplished
courtier, and full of all the habits and ways of diplomacy—

who invited the cavalcade to turn aside and rest for a day or
two in Crichton Castle, where everything had been prepared
for their reception. Here amid all the feastings and delights
the great official discoursed to the young noble about the
duties of his rank and the necessity of supporting the King's
government and establishing the authority of law over the
distracted country, sweetening his sermon with protestations
of his high regard for the Douglas name, whose house, kin,
and friends were more dear to him than any in Scotland,
and of affection to the young Earl himself. Perhaps this was
the turning-point, though the young gallant in his heyday
of power and self-confidence was all unconscious of it ;
perhaps he received the advice too lightly, or laughed at the
seriousness of his counsellor. At all events, when the gay
band took horse again and proceeded towards Edinburgh,
suspicion began to steal among the Earl's companions.
Several of them made efforts to restrain their young leader,
begging him at least to send back his young brother David
if he would not himself turn homeward. "But," says the
chronicler, "the nearer that a man be to peril or mischief
he runs more headlong thereto, and has no grace to hear
them that gives him any counsel to eschew the peril."

The only result of these attempts was that the party of boys
spurred on, more gaily, more confidently than ever, with the
deceiver at their side, who had spoken in so wise and fatherly
a tone, giving so much good advice to the heedless lads.
They were welcomed into Edinburgh within the fatal walls
of the castle with every demonstration of respect and delight.
How long the interval was before all this enthusiasm turned
into the stern preparations of murder it seems impossible to
say—it might have been on the first night that the catastrophe happened, for anything the chroniclers tell us. The
followers of Douglas were carefully got away, "skailled out
of the town," sent for lodging outside the castle walls, while
the two young brothers were marshalled, as became their
rank, to table to dine with the King. Whether they suspected
anything, or whether the little James in his helpless innocence
had any knowledge of what was going to happen, it is im-

possible to tell.   The feast proceeded, a royal banquet with

EDINBURGH CASTLE FROM THE VENNEL

"all delicatis that could be procured."   According to a
persistent tradition, the signal of fate was given by the bring-

ing in of a bull's head, which was placed before the young
Earl.   Mr. Burton considers this incident as so picturesque
as to be merely a romantic addition ; but no symbol was
too boldly picturesque for the time.   When this fatal dish
appeared the two young Douglases seem at once to have
perceived their danger.   They started from the table, and
for one despairing moment looked wildly round them for
some way of escape.   The stir and commotion as that tragic
company started to their feet, the vain shout for help, the
clash of arms as the fierce attendants rushed in and seized
the victims, the deadly calm of the two successful conspirators who had planned the whole, and the pale terrified
face of the boy-king, but ten years old, who "grat verie
sore," and vainly appealed to the Chancellor for God's sake
to let them go, make one of the most impressive of historical pictures.   The two hapless boys were dragged out to
the Castle Hill, which amid all its associations has none more
cruel, and there beheaded with the show of a public execution, which made the treachery of the crime still more
apparent ; for it had been only at most a day or two,
perhaps only a few hours, since the Earl and his brother in
all their bravery had been received with every gratulation at
these same gates, the welcome visitors, the chosen guests, of
the King.   The populace would do little but stare in startled
incapacity to interfere at such a scene ; some of them, perhaps, sternly satisfied at the cutting off of the tyrant stock ;
some who must have felt the pity of it, and had compunction
for the young lives cut off so suddenly.   A more cruel
vengeance could not be on the sins of the fathers, for it is
impossible to believe that the Regents did not take advantage
of the youth of these representatives of the famous Douglas
race.   Older and more experienced men would not have
fallen into the snare, or at all events would have retained
the power to sell their lives dear.

If the motives of Livingstone and Crichton were purely
patriotic, it is evident that they committed a blunder as well
as a crime : for instead of two boys rash and ill-advised and
undeveloped, they found themselves in face of a resolute

man who, like the young king of Israel, substituted scorpions for whips, persecuting both of them without mercy, and finally bringing Livingstone at least to destruction.   The first to succeed to William Douglas was his uncle, a man of no particular account, who kept matters quiet enough for a few years ; but when his son, another William, succeeded, the Regents soon became aware that an implacable and powerful enemy, the avenger of his two young kinsmen, but an avenger who showed no rash eagerness and could await time and opportunity, was in their way.   The new Earl married without much ceremony, though with a papal dispensation in consequence of their relationship, the little Maid of Galloway, to whom a great part of the Douglas lands had gone on the death of her brothers, and thus united once more the power and possessions of his name. He was himself a young man, but of full age, no longer a boy, and he would seem to have combined with much of the steady determination to aggrandise and elevate his race which was characteristic of the Douglases, and their in-difference to commonplace laws and other people's rights, an impulsiveness of character, and temptation towards osten-tation and display, which led him at once to submission and to defiance at unexpected moments, and gave an element of uncertainty to his career.   Soon after his succession it would seem to have occurred to him, after some specially unseemly disputes among some of his own followers, that to get himself into harmony with the laws of the realm and gain the friend-ship of the young King would be a good thing to do.   He came accordingly to Stirling where James was, very sick of his governors and their wiles and struggles, and throwing himself at the boy's feet offered himself, his goods and castles, and life itself, for the King's service, " that he might have the licence to wait upon His Majesty but as the soberest courtier in the King's company," and proclaimed himself ready to take any oath that might be offered to him, and to be " as serviceable as any man within the realm."   James, it would seem, was charmed by the noble suitor, and all the glamour of youth and impulse which was in the splendid

young cavalier, far more great and magnificent than all
the Livingstones and Crichtons, who yet came with such
abandon to the foot of the throne to devote himself to its
service. He not only forgave Douglas all his offences, but
placed him at the head of his government, " used him most
familiar of any man," and looked up to him with the half-
adoring admiration which a generous boy so often feels
towards the first man who becomes his hero.

This happened in 1443, when James was but thirteen.
It would be as easy to say that Douglas displaced with a
rush the two more successful governors of the kingdom, and
took their places by storm—and perhaps it would be equally
true : yet it would be vain to ignore James as an actor in
national affairs because of his extreme youth. In an age
when a boy of sixteen leads armies and quells insurrections,
a boy of thirteen, trained amid all the exciting circumstances
which surrounded James Stewart, might well have made a
definite choice and acted with full royal intention, perhaps
not strong enough to be carried out by its own impulse, yet
giving a real sanction and force to the power which an elder
and stronger man was in a position to wield. We have no
such means of forming an idea of the character and personality of the second James as we have of his father. No
voice of his sounds in immortal accents to commemorate his
loves or his sadness. He appears first passively in the hands
of conspirators who played him in his childhood one against
the other, a poor little royal pawn in the big game which
was so bloody and so tortuous. His young memory must
have been full of scares and of guileful expedients, each
party and individual about him trying to circumvent the
other. Never was child brought up among wilder chances.
The bewildering horror of his father's death, the sudden
melancholy coronation, and all the nobles in their sounding
steel kneeling at his baby feet, which would be followed in
his experience by no expansion or indulgence, but by the
confinement of the castle ; the terrible loneliness of an imprisoned child, broken after a while by the sudden appearance
of his mother, and that merry but alarming jest of his

conveyance in the great chest, half stifled in the folds of her embroideries and cloth of gold.   Then another flight, and renewed stately confinement among his old surroundings, monotony broken by sudden excitements and the babble in his ears of uncomprehended politics, from which, however, his mind, sharpened by the royal sense that these mysterious affairs were really his own, would no doubt come to find meaning at a far earlier age than could be possible under other circumstances.   And then that terrible scene, most appalling of all, when he had to look on and see the two lads, not so much older than himself, young gallants, so brave and fine, to whom the boy's heart would draw in spite of all he might have heard against them, so much nearer to himself than either governor or chancellor, those two noble Douglases, suddenly changed under his eyes from gay and welcome guests to horrified victims, with all the tragic passion of the betrayed and lost in their young eyes.   Such a scene above all must have done much to mature the intelligence of a boy full like all his race of spirit and independence, and compelled to look on at so much which he could not stop or remedy. Thus passive and helpless, yet with the fiction of supremacy in his name, we see the boy only by glimpses through the tumultuous crowd about him with all their struggles for power, until suddenly he flashes forth into the foreground, the chief figure in a scene more violent and terrible still than any that had preceded it, taking up in his own person the perpetual and unending struggle, and striking for himself the decisive blow.   There is no act so well known in James's life as that of the second Douglas murder, which gives a sinister repetition, always doubly impressive, to the previous tragedy.   And yet between the two what fluctuations of feeling, what changes of policy, how many long exasperations, ineffectual pardons, convictions unwillingly formed, must have been gone through.   That he was both just and gentle we have every possible proof, not only from the unanimous consent of the chronicles, but from the manner in which, over and over again, he forgives and condones the oft-repeated offences of his friend.   And there could be few more interesting psychological studies than to trace how, from the sentiments of love and admiration he once entertained for Douglas, he was wrought to such indignation and wrath as to yield to the weird fascination of that precedent which must have been so burnt in upon his childish memory, and to repeat the tragedy which within the recollection of all men had marked the Castle of Edinburgh with so unfavourable a stain.

We are still far from that, however, in the bright days when Douglas was Lieutenant-Governor of the kingdom, and the men who had murdered his kinsmen were making what struggle they could against his enmity, which pursued them to the destruction of one family and the frequent hurt and injury of the other. How Livingstone and his household escaped from time to time but were finally brought to ruin, how Crichton wriggled back into favour after every over-throw, sometimes besieged in his castle for months together, sometimes entrusted with the highest and most honourable missions, it would be vain to tell in detail. James would seem to have yielded to the inspiration of his new prime minister for a period of years, until his mind had fully developed, and he became conscious, as his father had been, of the dangers which arose to the common weal from the lawless sway of the great nobles, their continual feuds among themselves, and the reckless independence of each great man's following, whose only care was to please their lord, with little regard either for the King and Parliament or the laws they made. During this period his mother died, though there is little reason to suppose that she had any power or influence in his council, or that her loss was material to him. She had married a second time, another James Stewart called the Black Knight of Lorne, and had taken a considerable part in the political struggles of the time always with a little surrounding of her own, and a natural hope in every change that it might bring her son back to her. It is grievous that with so fair a beginning, in all the glow of poetry and love, this lady should have dropped into the position of a foiled conspirator, undergoing even the indignity of imprisonment at the hands of the Regents whom she sometimes aided and sometimes crossed in their arrangements. But a royal widow fallen from her high estate, a queen-mother whose influence was feared and discouraged, and every attempt at interference sternly repressed, would need to have been of a more powerful character than appears in any of her actions to make head against her antagonists. She died in Dunbar in 1446, of grief, it is said, for the death of her husband, who had been banished from the kingdom in consequence of some hasty words against the power of the Douglas, of whom however, even while he was still in disgrace, Sir James Stewart had been a supporter. Thus ended in grief and humiliation the life which first came into sight of the world in the garden of the great donjon at Windsor some quarter of a century before, amid all the splendour of English wealth and greatness, and all the sweet surroundings of an English May.

James was married in 1450, when he had attained his twentieth year, to Mary of Gueldres, about whom during her married life the historians find nothing to say except that the King awarded pardon to various delinquents at the request of the Queen—an entirely appropriate and becoming office. No doubt his marriage, so distinct as a mark of maturity and independence, did something towards emancipating James from the Douglas influence ; and it is quite probable that the selection of Sir William Crichton to negotiate the marriage and bring home the bride may indicate a lessening supremacy of favour towards Douglas in the mind of his young sovereign. Pitscottie records a speech made to the Earl and his brothers by the King, when he received and feasted them after their return from a successful passage of arms with the English on the Border, in which James points out the advantage of a settled rule and lawful authority, and impresses upon them the necessity of punishing robbers and reivers among their own followers, and seeing justice done to the poor, as well as distinguishing themselves by feats of war. By this time the Douglases had once more become a most formidable faction. The

H

head of the house had so successfully worked for his family
that he was on many occasions surrounded by a band of
earls and barons of his own blood, his brothers having in
succession, by means of rich marriages or other means of
aggrandisement, attained the same rank as himself, and,
though not invariably, acting as his lieutenants and supporters, while his faction was indefinitely increased by the
followers of these cadets of his house, all of them now
important personages in the kingdom. It was perhaps the
swelling pride and exaltation of a man who had all Scotland
at his command, and felt himself to have reached the very
pinnacle of greatness, which suggested the singular expedition to France and Rome upon which Douglas set forth, in
the mere wantonness of ostentation and pride, according to
the opinion of all the chroniclers, to spread his own fame
throughout the world, and show the noble train and bravery
of every kind with which a Scottish lord could travel. It
was an incautious step for such a man to take, leaving
behind him so many enemies ; but he would seem to have
been too confident in his own power over the King, and in
his greatness and good fortune, to fear anything. No sooner
was he gone, however, than all the pent-up grievances, the complaints of years during which he had wielded almost supreme
power in Scotland, burst forth. The King, left for the first
time to himself and to the many directors who were glad to
school him upon this subject, was startled out of his youthful
ease by the tale of wrong and oppression which was set
before him. No doubt Sir William Crichton would not be far
from James's ear, nor the representatives of his colleague,
whom Douglas had pursued to the death. The state of
affairs disclosed was so alarming that John Douglas, Lord
Balvenie, the brother of the Earl, who was left his procurator
and representative in his absence, was hastily summoned to
Court to answer for his chief. Balvenie, very unwilling to
risk any inquisition, held back, until he was seized and
brought before the King. His explanations were so little
satisfactory, that he was ordered at once to put order in the
matter, and to " restore to every man his own : " a com-

mand which he received respectfully, but as soon as he got free ignored altogether, keeping fast hold of the ill-gotten possessions, and hoping, no doubt, that the momentary indignation would blow over, and all go on as before. James, however, was too much roused to be trifled with. When he saw that no effect was given to his orders he took the matter into his own hands. The Earl of Orkney with a small following was first sent with the King's commission to do justice and redress wrongs : but when James found his ambassador insulted and repulsed, he took the field himself, first making proclamation to all the retainers of the Douglas to yield to authority on pain of being declared rebels. Arrived in Galloway, he rode through the whole district, seizing all the fortified places, the narrow peel-houses of the Border, every nest of robbers that lay in his way, and, according to one account, razed to the ground the Castle of Douglas itself, and placed a garrison of royal troops in that of Lochmaben, the two chief strongholds of the house. But James's mission was not only to destroy but to restore. He divided the lands thus taken from the House of Douglas, according to Pitscottie, "among their creditors and complainers, till they were satisfied of all things taen from them, whereof the misdoers were convict." This, however, must only have applied, one would suppose, to the small losses of the populace, the lifted cows and harried lands of one small proprietor and another. "The King," adds the same authority, "notwithstanding of this rebellion, was not the more cruel in punishing thereof nor he was at the beginning : " while Buchanan tells us that his clemency and moderation were applauded even by his enemies.

This is throughout the opinion which we find of James. He was capable of being moved to sudden violent indignation and hasty action, as was too distinctly demonstrated afterwards ; but the hasty outburst once over came back at once without rancour to his natural benignity, always merciful, slow to anger, ready to hear whatever the accused might have to say for himself, and to pardon as long as pardon was possible. Notwithstanding the rebellious and

audacious contempt of all authority but their own shown by
the Douglas party, notwithstanding the standing danger of
their insolent power, their promises so often broken, their
frequent submissions and actual defiance, his aim in all his
dealings with them was rather to do justice to the oppressed
than to punish the guilty. His genial temper, and that
belief in his kind which is always so ingratiating a quality,
is proved by the account Major gives of his life on those
military expeditions which from this time forth occupied so
much of his time. He lived with his soldiers as an equal, that
historian tells us, eating as they did, without the precaution
of a taster, which Major thinks highly imprudent, but which
would naturally bind to the frank and generous monarch the
confidence and regard of his fellow-soldiers, and the captains
with whom he shared the sometimes scanty provisions of the
campaign.

News of these strange events was conveyed to Douglas, now
in England on his return from the pilgrimage of pride and
ostentation to which, though it was professedly for the Papal
jubilee, no one attempts to give a religious character. He
was returning at his leisure, lingering on his way, not without
suspicion of secret treaties with the English in support of
the party of York, though all the prepossessions of Scotland
and King James were on the other side : but hurried home
on hearing the news, and was politic enough to make immediate submission as soon as he became aware of the
seriousness of the crisis, promising everything that could
be demanded of him in the way of obedience and respect of
" the King's peace." Once more he was fully and freely
pardoned, his lands, with some small diminution, restored,
and the King's confidence given back to him with a too
magnanimous completeness. In the Parliament held in
Edinburgh in June 1451 he was present, and received back
his charters in full amity and kindness, to the great satisfaction and pleasure of " all gud Scottis men." Later in the
year, in his capacity of Warden of the Marshes, he was
employed to assuage the endless quarrels of the Border, but
during his negotiations for this purpose secretly renewed his

mysterious and treacherous dealings with England, of which there is no very clear account, but which was of all others the kind of treachery most obnoxious to his countrymen. So far as would appear, James obtained some hint of these clandestine proceedings, and was very angry, " highly commoved," as was natural : on hearing which Douglas appeared once more to ask pardon, with apparently an inexhaustible confidence in the clemency of the young man whom he had guided so long. But the idea of some " quyet draucht betwixt him and the King of Ingland," some secret understanding with the old enemy, was more serious still than domestic rebellion, and though he pardoned at the " great request " of the Queen and nobles, the King did not again restore so doubtful a representative to the great offices he had held. There would seem to have been a pause of consternation on the part of Douglas when he found for the first time the charm of his friendship and every petition for pardon ineffectual. To attribute the change to old Crichton, who had recovered much of his former influence and was again Chancellor, was easy, and the Earl who had but the other day sworn the King's peace with all, set an ambush for his old opponent, and would have succeeded in killing him but for Crichton's son, " ane young valiant man," who overcame the bravos, and housed his father safely in his Castle of Crichton. Douglas himself was afterwards almost surprised in Edinburgh by Crichton's followers, and saved himself only by a hurried departure not unlike a flight.

This disappointment, and the loss of the King's favour, and the apparent solidity of his rivals in their place, half maddened the great noble, little accustomed to yield to any contradiction. He had been up to this time, save in so far as his private feuds and covetousness were concerned, on the side of lawful authority ; the King's man so long as the King was his man, and did not interfere with the growth of his wealth and greatness. But now he would seem to have given up hope of recovering his hold upon his sovereign, and turned his eyes elsewhere for support. The Earl of Crawford in the north country, and the Lord of the Isles who was also

Earl of Ross in the west, were as powerful and as intractable
as Douglas himself, and more often in open rebellion than in
amity with the King, a constant danger and disturbance of
all good order and law. Douglas in his anger made an
alliance with these two, by which all bound themselves to
resent and avenge any injury offered to either. It was
probably an expedient of rage and despair—the desire of
doing what was most baneful and insolent to his former
friends, such as happens often when a breach occurs—as much
as a political act; but it is evident that in every way
Douglas was on the eve of open treachery, no longer disposed
to keep any terms with the royal master whose patience had
been exhausted at last. It required, however, a crowning
outrage to arouse once more James's much-forgiving spirit.

Among the gentlemen of Galloway, the most of whom
rode with Douglas and supported him in all his high-handed
proceedings, too near neighbours to venture upon independence, were a few who preferred to hold the other side, that
of law and justice and the authority of the King. Among
them was "one called Maclelan, who was tutor of Bombie
for the time, and sister's son to Sir Patrick Gray, principal
servitor to the King, and captain of his guard." The refusal
of this man to serve in the rebellious host under the Earl
was immediately punished by Douglas, who assailed his
house and carried him off prisoner. The story reads like a
romance, which, however, is no reason for receiving it with
discredit. A more doubtful circumstance is that it is
asserted to have happened in Douglas Castle, which had
been very recently destroyed by James, and which was
besides at a great distance from Edinburgh. I hazard
a conjecture whether it may have happened in the Castle of
Abercorn, since it must have been impossible for Douglas in
Galloway to pursue Sir Patrick to the very gates of Edinburgh.
Wherever the incident may have occurred, the story is, that
Sir Patrick Gray, the uncle of the prisoner, hastened to the
King with the story of his nephew's danger, and was at once
sent off by James with "a sweit letter of supplication," praying
the Earl to deliver over the unfortunate gentleman to the

messenger for love of the King. The Earl was at dinner
when, "bloody with spurring, fiery red with haste," Sir
Patrick arrived at the castle, where the drawbridge was lifted
and the doors closed. "The Earle caused incontinent draw
the boards, and rose and met the said Sir Patrick with
great reverence and humilitie, because he was the King's
principal servant and familiar to His Grace." I tell the rest
of the tale in the words of Pitscottie :—

"He inquired at the said Patrick if he had dined, who answered that
he had not. Then the Earle said there was 'no talk to be had betwixt
ane full and ane fasting ; therefore ye shall dine, and we shall talke
together at length.'

"In this meane tyme Sir Patrick Gray sat down to his dinner, and the
Earle treatted him and made him goode cheare, whereof Sir Patrick was
well contented, believing all things to succeed well thereafter. But the
Earle of Douglas on the other pairt took a suspicion and conjecture
what Sir Patrick Gray's commission was, and dreading the desyne thereof
should be for his friend, the tutor of Bombie ; therefore in the meane
time when they were at the dinner, talking of merry matters, the Earle
caused quietly take forth the tutor of Bombie out of prison, and have
him to the greene and there strooke off his head and took the samine
away from him, and syne covered a fair cloth on his bodie that nothing
might be seene of that treasonable act that was done.

"In this meane time when dinner was done Sir Patrick Gray presented
the King's writing unto the Earle, who reverently received it and considered the effect thereof. He gave great thanks to Sir Patrick Gray,
saying he was beholden to him that brought so familiar an writing
from his Prince to him, considering how it stood betwixt them at that
time : and as to the desire and supplication, it should be thankfullie
granted to the King, and the rather for Sir Patrick's sake ; and took
him by the hand and led him furth to the greene where the gentleman
was lying dead, and shew him the manner, and said, 'Sir Patrick, you
are come a litle too late ; but yonder is your sister's son lying, but he
wants the head ; take his body and do with it what you will.' Sir
Patrick answered again with ane sore heart, and said, 'My Lord, ye
have taken from him his head, dispone upon the body as ye please ;' and
with that called for his horse and leapt thereon. And when he was on
horseback he said to the Earle on this manner, 'My Lord, an I live ye
shall be rewarded for your labour that ye have used at this time,
according to your demerits.' At this saying the Earle was highly
offended and cryed for horse. Sir Patrick seeing the Earle's fury
spurred his horse, but he was chased neare to Edinburgh before they
left him, and had it not been his leid horse was so tryed and goode
he had been taken."

The scene that ensued when James, awaiting in Edinburgh the return of his messenger, without a doubt we may
suppose of the obedience of Douglas the friend of his youth,
the often-pardoned, owing so much to his clemency and
friendship—saw Sir Patrick arrive breathless and haggard,
scarcely escaping, though the King's messenger, with his life,
and heard his story—the insolent contempt, the brutal jest,
the cruel murder—is one that might well mark the turning-
point even in a mind so magnanimous. The King had not
been entirely without signs of inheriting his father's firmness
and promptitude ; but his gentleness of disposition, and
strong inclination towards kindness and peace, had in
general carried the day over his sterner qualities. He had
shown both sides of his character when he pardoned Douglas
and accepted his promises of reformation on his return, but
cut him off from public service and closed all the doors of
advancement against him. The defiance now addressed to
him, the scorn of his letters and request, so audaciously
shown, raised a sudden storm of indignation in his breast.
Whether his future action was based on the decision of his
council to which he submitted, sanctioning on his own part
the treachery by which alone Douglas could be beguiled
within his reach, as the chroniclers, to whom such a device
was quite justifiable, tell us ; or whether when he issued his
safe-conduct he still hoped to be able to convince the Earl
of his folly in resisting, and to bring him to a real and
effectual change of mind, no one can now tell. But James
was so little addicted to treachery, so fair, tolerant and
merciful, that we may well give him the benefit of the
doubt, and believe that it was with the intention of making
another effort to bring Douglas back to his right mind and
allegiance that the King invited him to Stirling, where it was
strange indeed that with all his enormities on his conscience
Douglas ventured to come, whatever were the safe-conducts
given. " Some sayes he got the great seale thereunto before
he would grant to come to the King," says the chronicle.
The fact that he did come however, after all that had
passed, says much for his confidence in King James and in

his own power over him, for Douglas must have been very well aware that safe-conducts and royal promises were but broken reeds to trust to.

When he arrived in Stirling, whatever lowering looks he might see around him—and it is scarcely possible to believe that Sir Patrick Gray for one could have entirely cleared his countenance of every recollection of their last meeting, of the men-at-arms thundering at his heels, and his nephew's body headless on the greensward—Douglas found no change in the King, who received and banqueted him " very royally," thinking if it were possible " with good deeds to withdraw him from his attempt that he purposed to do." After supper the King took his rebellious subject aside, into another room opening from that in which they had supped, and which is still exhibited in Stirling Castle to the curious stranger, and once more reasoned with him on his conduct. No private matter would seem to have been introduced, the treasonable league which the Earl had made with Craw-ford and Ross, rebels against the lawful authority of the kingdom, being the subject on which James put forth all his strength of argument.   Douglas, Pitscottie tells us, answered " verrie proudlie," and the argument grew hot between the two men, of whom one had always hitherto been the con-queror in every such passage of arms.   It was probably this long habit of prevailing that made the proud Earl so obstinate, since to submit in words had never heretofore been difficult to him.   At last the dispute came to a climax, in the distinct refusal of Douglas to give up his traitor-allies.   " He said he myt not nor wald not," says a brief contemporary record. " Then the King said, 'False traitor, if you will not, I sall,' and stert sodunly till him with ane knyf."   " And they said," adds this chronicle with grim significance, " that Patrick Gray straik him next the King with ane pole ax on the hed."   The other companions crowded round, giving each his stroke.   And thus within a short space of years the second Earl of Douglas was killed in a royal castle, while under a royal safe-conduct, at a climax of hopeless discord and antagonism from which there seemed no issue.   The exasperation of the King, the dead-lock of all authority, the absolutely impracticable point at which the two almost equal powers had arrived, account for, though they do not excuse, such a breach of faith. I prefer to believe that James had at least no decided purpose in his mind, but hoped in his own power to induce Douglas to relinquish these alliances which were incompatible with his allegiance ; but that the sudden exasperation with which he became convinced of his own powerlessness to move him brought about in a moment the fatal issue (with who knows what sudden wild stimulus of recollection from the murder of which he had been a witness in his childhood ?) which statesmen less impulsive had already determined upon as necessary, though probably not in this sudden way.

The " Schort Memorial of the Scottis Cronikles," called the Auchinleck Chronicle, gives a brief but striking account of the proceedings that followed. Earl Douglas's retainers and kinsmen would seem to have been struck dumb by the event, and probably fled in horror and dismay ; but it was not till long after, when the King had left Stirling, that the younger brothers returned, on St. Patrick's Day in Lent, bringing with them the safe-conduct with all its seals, which they exhibited at the cross and dragged through the streets tied to a horse's tail, with many wild and fierce words against the King and all that were with him, ending by spoiling and burning the town. As James was no longer in it, however, nor apparently any one who could resist them, this was a cheap and unsatisfactory vengeance.

Some months after, in the summer of 1452, a Parliament was held at Edinburgh, in which the three Estates passed a declaration that no safe - conduct had been given on that fatal occasion — a declaration which it is evident no one believed, and which probably was justified by some quibble which saved the consciences of those who asserted it. The new Earl, James Douglas, was summoned to appear at this Parliament, but answered by a letter under his seal and that of his brother, which was secretly affixed to the door of the Parliament House, " declynand from the King, saying that

ST. ANTHONY'S CHAPEL AND ST. MARGARET'S LOCH

they held not of him, nor would hold with him, with many other slanderous words, calling them traitors that were his secret council." Some say it was upon the church doors that this defiance was attached. In any case it must have produced a wonderful hum and commotion through the town, where already no doubt the slaying of the Douglas had been discussed from every point of view—at the cross, and among the groups at the street corners, where there would be many adherents of the Douglas, and many citizens ready to discuss the new event and all its possible consequences. The Parliament was followed by a general muster upon the Burrowmuir, where the barons and their men gathered, with all their spears and steel caps glistening in the June sunshine, with an apparent intention of pursuing the race to its stronghold and making an end of it. The raid, which was led by the King in person, with an army of some thirty thousand men, accomplished little however, doing more mischief than good the chronicle says, treading down the new corn, and spoiling the country "right fellonly," notwithstanding the King's presence. The result, at all events, was complete submission on the part of the new Earl, accompanied by a promise to bear no enmity, a promise often made but altogether impossible in the fifteenth century to mortal flesh and blood.

It was scarcely possible however, short of a moral miracle, that such a thing could happen as the abandonment of the entire policy of the house of Douglas at a moment when their minds were embittered by so great a tragedy. The new Earl was not a mere soldier, still less a courtier, but a man of some culture, originally intended, it is said, for the Church, though this does not seem to have withheld him from taking part in the tumults of the time. Nor did it restrain him from marrying his brother's widow, the hapless Maid of Galloway, whose share of the Douglas lands made her indispensable to her two warlike cousins, though it seems uncertain whether either of the two marriages, which necessitated two dispensations from the Pope, was anything but nominal. After his submission

James Douglas was employed as his brother had been in the arrangement of terms of truce with England, which was too great a temptation for him, and led to further treasonable negotiations. He would seem also to have renewed his brother's alliances with the rebels of the north : and in a very brief period the nominal peace and doubtful vows were all thrown to the winds, and this time there seems to have been no question of partial rebellion, but every indication that a civil war, rending the entire country in two, was about to break forth. Douglas had the strong backing of England behind him, the support of the Highland hordes always ready to be poured upon the peaceful country, and many great lords in his immediate train. He had raised an army of, it is said, forty thousand men, an enormous army for Scotland, and it was evident that the struggle was one of life and death.

At this moment it would seem that King James for the first time lost heart. He had been fighting during all the beginning of the year 1455, reducing the west and south, the Douglas country, to subjection and desolation. But when he found himself menaced by an army as great as anything he could muster, with the angry north in the background and clouds of half-savage warriors on the horizon, the King's heart sank. He is said to have left Edinburgh in disgust and depression, and taken ship at Leith for St. Andrews, to seek counsel from the best and most trustworthy of his advisers, a man whose noble presence appears in the distracted history with such a calm and sagacious steadfastness that we can well understand the agitated King's sudden impulse towards him at this painful period of his career. Bishop Kennedy had himself suffered from the lawlessness of the Douglas retainers : and he too had royal blood in his veins. He occupied one of the highest positions in the Church, and his wisdom and strength had made him one of the most prominent statesmen in the kingdom. James arrived hastily, according to the chronicle, unexpected, and with many signs of distress and anxiety. He betrayed to the Bishop his weariness of the ever-renewed struggle, and of the falsehood and treachery which, even if victorious, were all he had to encounter, the failure of every pledge and promise, the faith sworn one day which failed him the next, and the deep discouragement with all things round him which had taken possession of his mind. The wise prelate heard this confession of heart-sickness and despondency, and with a fatherly familiarity bade the young King sit down to meat, which he much wanted, while he himself went to his oratory to pray for enlightenment. That James thought no less than to throw up the struggle and retire from his kingdom, is what the old writers say. But when, with his bosom lightened by utterance of his trouble, and his courage a little restored by food and rest, the Bishop came back to him with a cheerful countenance from his prayers, the King took heart again. Kennedy produced to him the old image of the sheaf of arrows which, bound together, were not to be broken, but one by one could easily be snapt asunder, and advised him to make proclamation of a free pardon to all who would throw down their arms and make submission, and to march at once against the rebel host with full confidence of victory. Inspired by this advice, and by the companionship of the Bishop who went with him, the King set out to meet the rebels, though with an army inferior in number to theirs. Douglas, from some unexplained reason, wavered and hesitated, taking no active step, and gave Bishop Kennedy time to put his own suggestion in practice in respect to his nephew Lord Hamilton— who was one of Douglas's chief supporters—sending secret messengers to him to urge him to submission. Hamilton no doubt had already perceived signs of wavering purpose and insecurity in the heterogeneous host, in which were many whose hearts failed them at sight of the King's banners— men who were apt to rebellion without being wound up to the extreme point of civil war : but he had " ane kyndlie love to Earl Douglas " as well as a regard for his own honour, and would not lightly desert his friend. While thus uncertain he appealed to Douglas to know what he meant to do, warning him that the longer he hesitated, the less would be the forces at his disposal. Douglas replied haughtily that if he were tired of waiting he might go when he pleased—an indiscreet answer, which decided Hamilton to withdraw and throw himself upon the King's promised mercy. The same night he went over to the royal army, carrying with him so many that "on the morn thereafter the Earl Douglas had not ane hunder men by his own household," the whole host having melted away. Never was a greater risk for a monarchy nor a more easy and bloodless escape. The Earl fled to the depths of his own country and thence to England, where he lived long a pensioned dependant, after all his greatness and ambition, to reappear in history only like a ghost after many silent years.

Amid all these bewildering and bitter struggles, in which much misery was no doubt involved, it is recorded of the King that he never lost his humane character, and that even in the devastations he was forced to sanction or command, the cruel reprisals carried out over all the south of Scotland, his severity was always tempered with mercy. "He was not so much feared as a king as loved like a father," says Major. This luminous trait appears through all the darkness of the vexed and furious time. The King was always ready to pardon at a word, to believe in the vows and receive the submission of the fiercest rebels. One curious evidence of the confidence felt in him was shown by the widow of the murdered Earl, Margaret Douglas, the Maid of Galloway, a woman doubly injured in every relation—the sister of the young Earl murdered at Edinburgh, married by his successor in order to reunite the Douglas patrimony, a great portion of which went to her as her brother's heir— and again forced into another and unlawful marriage by her husband's brother, immediately upon his death, for the same end. James received this fugitive kindly, restored to her part of the lands of her family, and finally married her— thus freeing her from the lawless bond into which she had been driven—to his own step-brother, John, Earl of Atholl, "the Black Knight of Lorne's son ;" upon hearing of which another fugitive of a similar description appeared upon the scene.

" When the Earl of Ross's wyff understood the King to be some pairt favourable to all that sought his grace she fled also under his protection to eschew the cruel tyranny of her husband, which she dreaded sometyme before.   The King called to remembrance that this woman was married not by her own counsel to Donald of the Isles (the Earl of Ross).   He gave her also sufficient lands and living whereon she might live according to her estate.

.   The case of women, and especially heiresses, in that lawless age must have been miserable indeed.   Bandied about from one marriage to another, forced to accept such security as a more or less powerful lord could give, and when he was killed to fall victim to the next who could seize upon her, or to whom she should be allotted by feudal suzerain or chieftain, the mere name of a king who did not disdain a woman's plaint, but had compassion and help to give, must have conveyed hope to many an unhappy lady bound to a repugnant life.   James would seem to have been the only man who recognised the misery to which such unconsidered items in the wild and tumultuous course of affairs might be driven.

Thus King James and Scotland with him were delivered from the greatest and most dangerous of the powerful houses that held the country in fear.   Shortly after he conquered, partly by arms, partly by the strain of a universal impulse, which seemed to rouse the barons to a better way, those great allies in the north who held the key of the Highlands, the Earl of Crawford and the Earl of Ross, so that at last something of a common rule and common sentiment began to move the country.   It is almost needless to say that James took advantage of this temporary unity and enthusiasm in order to invade England—a thing without which no Scots King could be said to be happy.   The negotiations by which he was at once stimulated and hindered—among others by ambassadors from the Duke of York to ask his help against Henry VI, with orders to arrest his army on their way—are too complicated to be entered upon ; but at last the Scots forces set out and, after various successes, James found himself before Roxburgh, a town and castle which had remained in the hands of the English from the time when the Earl of March deserted his country for England in the

I

reign of Robert III. The town was soon taken, but the
castle, in which there was a brave garrison, stood out manfully. This invasion of the Borders, and opportunity of
striking a blow at the " auld enemy," was evidently an act
of the highest policy while yet the surgings of civil war
were not entirely quieted, and a diversion of ideas as well
as new opportunities of spoil were peculiarly necessary.
Its first excellent result was that Donald of the
Isles, the Earl of Ross and terror of the north
country, whose submission had been but provisionally
accepted, and depended upon some evidence of real
desire for the interest of the common .weal, suddenly
appeared with " ane great armie of men, all armed in the
Highland fashion," and claimed the vanguard, the place of
honour, and to be allowed to take upon him " the first press
and dint of the battell." James received this unexpected
auxiliary with " great humanitie," but prudently provided,
before accepting his offer, which apparently, however, was
made in all good faith, that Donald should " stent his
pavilliones a little by himself," until full counsel had been
taken on the subject. The army was also joined by " a
great company of stout and chosen men," under the Earl of
Huntly, whose coming " made the King so blyth that he
commanded to charge all the guns and give the castle ane new
volie." James would seem throughout to have felt the greatest
interest in the extraordinary new arm of artillery which had
made a revolution in warfare. He pursued siege after siege
with a zeal in which something of the ardour of a military
enthusiast and scientific inquirer mingled with the necessities
of the struggle in which he was engaged. The " Schort
Cronikle," already quoted, describes him as lingering over
the siege of Abercorn, " striking mony of the towers down
with the gret gun, the whilk a Franche man shot richt wele,
and failed na shot within a fathom where it was charged him
to hit." And when, in the exultation of his heart to see
each new accession of force come in, he ordered " a new
volie " against the stout outstanding walls, the excitement
of the discharge, the eagerness of an adept to watch the

MONS MEG

effect, no doubt made this dangerous expression of satisfaction a real demonstration of pleasure.

King James had attained at this time a success which probably a few years before his warmest imagination could not have aspired to. He had brought into subjection the great families which had almost contested his throne with him. Douglas, the highest and most near himself, had been swept clean out of his way. The fiercest rebel of all, the head of the Highland caterans, with his wild host in all their savage array, was by his side, ready to charge under his orders. The country, drained of its most lawless elements, was beginning to breathe again, to sow its fields and rebuild its homesteads. Instead of the horrors of civil war his soldiers were now engaged in the most legitimate of all enterprises—the attempt to recover from England an alienated possession. Everything was bright before him, the hope of a great reign, the promise of prosperity and honour and peace.

It is almost a commonplace of human experience that in such moments the blow of fate is near at hand. The big guns which were a comparatively new wonder, full of interest in their unaccustomed operation, were still a danger as well as a prodigy, and James would seem to have forgotten the precautions that were considered necessary in presence of an armament still only partially understood. The historian assumes, as every human observer is apt to do in face of such a calamity, a tone of blame. "This Prince," says the chronicle with a shrill tone of exasperation in the record of the catastrophe, "more curious than became the majestie of a king, did stand hard by when the artilliarie was discharging." And in a moment all the labours and struggles, and the hope of the redeemed kingdom and all the prosperity that was to come, were at an end. One can imagine the sudden dismay in the group around him, the rush of his attendants, his own feeble command to keep silence when some cry of horror rose from the pale-faced circle. His thigh had been broken, "dung in two," by the explosion of the gun, "by which he was struken to the ground, and died hastilie thereafter," with no time to say more than to order silence, lest the army should be discouraged and the siege prove in vain.

So ended the troublous reign of the second James, involved in strife and warfare from his childhood, vexed by the treacheries and struggles over him of his dearest friends, full of violence alien to his mind and temper, which yet was justified by his example at the most critical moment of his life. He made his way through continual contention, intrigue, and blood, for which he was not to blame, to such a settlement of national affairs as might have consolidated Scotland and made her great—by patience and firmness and courage, and conspicuously by mercy, notwithstanding one crime. And when the helm was in his hands, and a fair future before him, fell, not ignominiously indeed, yet uselessly, a noble life thrown away, leaving once more chaos behind him. He was only twenty-nine when the thunderbolt thus falling from a clear sky destroyed all the hopes of Scotland ; yet had reigned long, for twenty-three years of trouble, tumult, and distress.

CHAPTER III

JAMES III: THE MAN OF PEACE

AGAIN the noises cease save for a wail of lamentation over the dead. The operations of war are suspended, the dark ranks of the army stand aside, and every trumpet and fatal cannon is silent while once more a woman and a child come into the foreground of the historic scene. Once more, the most pathetic figure surely in history, a little startled boy clinging to his mother—not afraid indeed of the array of war to which he has been accustomed all his life, and perhaps with an instinct in him of childish majesty, the consciousness which so soon develops even in an infant mind, of unquestioned rank, but surrounded by the atmosphere of horror and affright in which he has been taken from among his playthings—stands forth to be hastily enveloped in the robes so pitifully over-large of the dead monarch. The lords, we are told, sent for the Prince in the first sensation of the catastrophe, and had him crowned at Kelso, feeling the necessity of that central name at least, round which to rally. They were not always respectful of the real King when they had him, yet the divinity which hedged the title, however helpless the head round which it shone, was felt to be indispensable to the unity and strength of the kingdom. Mary of Gueldres in her sudden widowhood would seem to have behaved with great dignity and spirit at this critical moment. She is said to have insisted that the siege should not be abandoned, but that her husband's death might at least accomplish what his heart had been set upon ; and the army after a moment of despondency was so "incouraged" by the coming of the Prince "that they forgot the death of his father and past manfullie to the hous, and wan the same, and justified the captaine theroff, and kest it down to the ground that it should not be any impediment to them hereafter." The execution of the captain seems a hard measure unless he was a traitor to the Scottish crown ; but no doubt the conflict became more bitter from the terrible cost of the victory.

Once more accordingly the kingdom was thrown into the chaos which in those days attended a long minority, the struggle for power, the relaxation of order, and all the evils that follow when one firm hand full of purpose drops the reins which half a dozen conflicting competitors scramble for. There was not, at first at least, anything of the foolish anarchy which drove Scotland into confusion during the childhood of James II, and opened the way to so many subsequent disasters, for Bishop Kennedy, the dead King's chief counsellor and support and a man universally trusted, was in the front of affairs, influencing if not originating all that was done : and to him, almost as a matter of course, the education of the little heir was at once confided. But Mary of Gueldres was a woman of resolution and force, and did not give up without a struggle her pretensions to the regency. Buchanan relates a scene which, according to his history, took place in Edinburgh on the occasion of the first Parliament after James's death. The Queen had established herself in the castle while Kennedy was in Holyrood, probably with his little pupil, but there is no mention made of James. On the second day of the Parliament Mary appeared suddenly in what would seem to have been, according to modern phraseology, "a packed house," her own partisans having no doubt been warned to be present by the action of some energetic "whip," and was, then and there, by a hasty Act, carried through at one sitting, appointed guardian and Regent, after which summary success she returned with great pomp to her apartments, though with what hope of having really attained

a tenable position it is impossible to say.   When the news
was carried to Holyrood, Bishop Kennedy in his turn

THE CANONGATE TOLBOOTH

appeared before the Estates, which had been thus taken by
surprise.   It is evident that the populace of Edinburgh was
excited by what had occurred—Mary's partisans no doubt

rejoicing, while the people in general, always jealous of a foreigner and never very respectful of a woman, surged through the great line of street towards the castle with all the fury of a popular tumult.   The High Street of Edinburgh was not unaccustomed to sudden encounters, clashing of swords between two passing lords, each with fierce followers, and all the risks of sudden brawls when neither would concede the "crown of the causeway."   But the townsfolk seldom did more than look on, with perhaps an ill-concealed satisfaction in the wounds inflicted by their natural opponents upon each other.   On this occasion, however, the tumult was a popular one, involving the interests of the citizens ; and it is difficult to believe that the inclinations of the townsfolk would not rather lean towards the Queen, a woman of wealth and stately surroundings, likely to entertain princes and great personages and to fill Edinburgh with the splendour of a Court, than to the prelate, although his tastes also were magnificent, whose metropolis was not Edinburgh but St. Andrews, and who might consider frugality and sobriety the best qualities for the Court of a minor.   At all events the crowd had risen and was ripe for tumult, when Bishop Kennedy persuaded them to pause, and reminded them of the mutual forbearance and patience and quiet which was above all necessary at such a troublous time.   Other prelates would seem to have been in his train, for we are told it was the intercessions and explanations of "the bishops" which prevented the tumult from rising into a fight. The parties would seem to have been so strong, and so evenly divided, that the question was finally solved by a compromise, Parliament appointing a counsel of guardians, two on each side : Seaton and Boyd for the Queen; John Kennedy, brother of the Bishop, and the Earl of Orkney, for the others—an experiment which was no more successful than in the previous minority.

The Queen-mother had soon, however, something to occupy her leisure in the visit, if visit it can be called, of Henry VI and his Queen and household, fugitives before the victorious party of York, who had sought refuge from the

Scots, and lodging for a thousand attendants—a request which
was granted, and the convent of the Greyfriars allotted to them
as their residence.   The Queen at the Castle would thus
be a near neighbour of the royal fugitives, and it is interesting to think of the meeting, the sympathy and mutual con-
dolences of the two women.   Margaret, the fervid Provençal,
with her passionate sense of wrong and restless energy, and
the hopeless task she had of maintaining and inspiring to
play his part with any dignity her too patient and gentle
king ; and Mary, the fair and placid Fleming, stung too in
her pride and affections by the refusal of the regency, and
her subordination to those riotous and unmannerly lords and
the proud Bishop who had got the affairs of Scotland in his
hand.   The two Queens might have had some previous
acquaintance with each other, at a time when both had
fairer hopes ; at all events they amused themselves sadly, as
they sat and talked together, with fancies such as please
women, of making a marriage between the little Edward, the
future victim of Tewkesbury, then a child at his mother's
knee, and the little Princess of Scotland who played beside
him, in the good days when all these troubles should be past,
and Henry or his son after him should have regained the
English crown.   One follows with regretful interest the noble
figure of Margaret, under the guise in which that sworn Lancastrian Shakspeare has disclosed it to us, before her sweeter
mood had disappeared under the pressure of fate, and when
not curses but hopes came from her mouth in her young
motherhood, and every recovery and restoration, and happy
marriage and royal state, were possible for her boy.   Mary
too had been cut off in the middle of her greatness.   They
were two Queens discrowned, two fair heads veiled with misfortune, though nothing irremediable had as yet happened,
nothing that should make the future a desert though the
present might be dark ; ready to live again in their children,
and make premature treaties over the little blonde heads at
their knee.   So natural a scene comes in strangely to the
records of violence and misery.   Nothing more tragic could
be than the fate of Margaret ; and the splendour and hap-

piness had been very shortlived in Mary's experience, soon
quenched in sudden destruction ; but to see the two young
mothers planning over the heads of the little ones how the
two kingdoms were to be united, and happiness come back
in a future that was never to be, while they sat together in
brief companionship in those strait rooms of Edinburgh
Castle, which were so narrow and so poor for a queen's
habitation, or within the precincts of the Greyfriars, looking
out upon the peaceful Pentlands and the soft hills of Braid,
is like the recurring melody in a piece of stormy music, the
bit of light in a tempestuous picture.   It teaches us to perceive that, however the firmament of a kingdom may be torn
with storms, there are everywhere about, even in queens'
chambers, scenes of tenderness and peace.

Mary died in her own foundation of Trinity College
Hospital — the beautiful church of which was demolished
within living memory—three years after her husband, while
her children were still very young : and thus all further
struggles about the regency were ended.   She does not seem
indeed ever to have repeated her one stand for power. Bishop
Kennedy, we may well believe, was not a man with whom there
would be easy fighting.   His sway procured a little respite
for Scotland in the ordinary miseries of her career.   The
Douglases were safely out of the way and ended, and there was
a truce of fifteen years with England which kept danger from
that side at arm's length—not, the chroniclers assure us, from
any additional love between the two countries, but because
" the Inglish had warres within themselves daylie, stryvand
for the crown."   Kennedy lived some years after the Queen,
guiding all the affairs of the kingdom so wisely that " the
commounweill flourished greatly."   He was a Churchman of
the noblest kind, full of care for the spiritual interests of his
diocese as well as for the secular affairs which were placed
in his hands.   " He caused all persones (parsons) and vicars
to remain at their paroche kirks," says Pitscottie, " for the
instruction and edifying of their flocks : and caused them
preach the Word of God to the people and visit them that
were sick ; and also the said Bishope visited every kirk within

the diocese four times in the year, and preached to the said parochin himself the Word of God, and inquired of them if they were dewly instructed by their parson and vicar, and if the poor were sustained and the youth brought up and learned according to the order that was taine in the house of God."

With all this, and many other gifts beside, among which are noted the knowledge he had of the "civil laws, having practised in the same," and his experience and sagacity in all public affairs—he was a scholar and loved all the arts. "He founded," says Pitscottie, "ane triumphant college in Sanct Androis, called Sanct Salvatore's College, wherein he made his lear (library) very curiouslie and coastlie ; and also he biggit ane ship, called the Bishop's Barge, and when all three were complete, to wit, the college, the lear, and the barge, he knew not which of the three was the costliest ; for it was reckoned for the time by honest men of consideration that the least of the three cost him ten thousand pound sterling." Major gives the same high character of the great Bishop, declaring that there were but two things in him which did not merit approval—the fact that he held a priory (but only one, that of Pittenweem) *in commendam*, "and the sumptuositie of his sepulchre." That sepulchre, half destroyed—after having remained a thing of beauty for three hundred years—by ignorant and foolish hands in the end of the eighteenth century, may still be seen in the chapel of his college at St. Andrews, the only existing memorial of the time when all Scotland was governed from that stormy headland to the great advantage of the commonwealth. It is difficult to make out from the different records whether the young King remained in the Bishop's keeping so long as he lived, which was but until James had attained the age of thirteen, or whether the usual struggle between the two sets of guardians appointed by Parliament, the Boyds and Kennedies, had begun before the Bishop's death. It may be imagined, however, that the evident advantages to the boy of Bishop Kennedy's care would outweigh any formal appointment ; although at the same time the idea suggests itself whether in the perversity of human nature this training was not in itself partly the cause of James's weaknesses and errors. He would learn at St. Andrews not only what was best in the learning of the time, but as much of the arts as were known in Scotland, and especially that noble art of architecture, which has been the passion of so many princes. And no doubt he would see the advancement of professors of these arts, of men skilful and cunning in design and decoration, the builders, the sculptors, and the musicians, whose place in the great cathedral could never be unimportant. A Churchman could promote and honour such public servants in the little commonwealth of his cathedral town with greater freedom than might be done elsewhere ; and James, a studious and feeble boy, not wise enough to see that the example of his great teacher was here inappropriate and out of place, learned this lesson but too well. The King grew up "a man that loved solitariness and desired never to hear of warre, but delighted more in musick and politie and building nor he did in the government of his realm." It would seem that he was also fond of money, which indeed was very necessary to the carrying out of his pursuits. It is difficult to estimate justly the position of a king of such a temperament in such circumstances, whether he is to be blamed for abandoning the national policy and tradition, or whether he was not rather conscientiously trying to carry out his stewardry of his kingdom in a better way when he withheld his countenance from the perpetual wars of the Border, and addressed himself to the construction of noble halls and chapels and the patronage of the arts. He was at least so far in advance of his time, still concerned with the rudest interests of practical life as to be universally misunderstood : and he had the further misfortune of sharing the unpopularity of the favourites with whom he surrounded himself, as almost every monarch has done who has promoted men of inferior position to the high places of the State.

James's supineness, over-refinement, and love of peaceful occupations were made the more remarkable from the contrast with two manly and chivalrous brothers, the Dukes of Mar

and Albany, of fine person and energetic tastes, interested in
all the operations of war, fond of fine horses and gallant doings,
and coming up to all the popular expectations of what was
becoming in a prince.   Nothing is more difficult to make out at
any time than the real motives and meaning of family discords:
and this is still more the case in an age not yet enlightened by
the clear light of history.   The chroniclers, especially Boece,
have much doubt thrown upon them by more serious historians,
who quote them and build upon them nevertheless, having
really no better evidence to go upon.   The report of these
witnesses is that James had been warned by witches, in whom
he believed, and by one Andrew the Fleming, an astrologer,
that his chief danger arose from his own family, and that
"the lion should be devoured by his whelps."   Pitscottie's
account, however, indicates a conspiracy between Cochrane
and the Homes, whom Albany had mortally offended, as the
cause at once of these prophecies and the King's alarm.
The only thing clear is that he was afraid of his brothers, and
considered their existence a danger to his life.   It would
appear that he had already begun to surround himself with
those favourites to whom was attributed every evil thing in his
reign, when this poison was first instilled into his mind : and the
blame was attributed rightly or wrongly to Cochrane, the chief
of his " minions," who very probably felt it to be to his interest
to detach from James's side the manly and gallant brothers
who were naturally his nearest counsellors and champions.

There is very little that is authentic known of the men
whom James III thus elevated to the steps of his throne.
Cochrane was an architect probably, though called a mason
in his earlier career, and had no doubt been employed
on some of the buildings in which the King delighted,
being " verrie ingenious " and " cunning in that craft."
Perhaps, however, to make the royal favour for a mere
craftsman more respectable, according to the notions of
the time, it is added in a popular story that the favourite
was a man of great strength and stature, whose prowess in
some brawl attracted the admiration of the timid monarch,
to whom a man who was a tall fellow of his hands, as well

as a person of similar tastes to himself, might well be a special object of approval. A musician, William Roger, an Englishman, whose voice had charmed the King—a weakness which at least was not ignoble, and was shared by various other members of his race—was the second of James's favourites : and there were others still less important —one the King's tailor,—a band of persons of no condition, who surrounded him no doubt with flattery and adulation, since their promotion and maintenance were entirely dependent on his pleasure. King Louis XI was at that time upon the throne of France, a powerful prince whose little privy council was composed of equally mean men, and perhaps some reflection from the Court of the old ally of Scotland made young James believe that this was the best and wisest thing for a King to do. Louis was also a believer in astrologers, witches, and all the prophecies and omens in which they dealt. To copy him was not a high ambition, but he was in his way a great king, and it is conceivable that the feeble monarch of Scotland, never roused to the height of his father's or grandfather's example, took a little satisfaction in copying what he could from Louis. The example of Oliver le Dain might make him think that he showed his superiority by preferring his tailor, a man devoted to his service, to Albany or Angus. And if Louis trembled at the predictions of his Eastern sage, what more natural than that James should quake when the stars revealed a danger which every spaewife confirmed? No doubt he would know well the story of the mysterious spaewife who, had her advice been taken, might have saved James I. from his murderers. It is rarely that there is not a certain cruelty involved in selfish cowardice. In a sudden panic the mildest-seeming creature will trample down furiously any weaker being who stands in the way of his own safety, and James was ready for any atrocity when he was convinced that his brothers were a danger to his life and crown. The youngest, the handsome and gallant Mar, was killed by one treachery or another ; and Alexander of Albany, the inheritor of that ill-omened title, was laid up in prison to be safe out of his brother's way.

We find ourselves entirely in the regions of romance in this unfortunate reign.   Sir Walter Scott has painted for us the uncomfortable Court of Louis with his barber and his prophet, and Dumas has reproduced almost the identical story in his *Vingt Ans Après*, of the Duke of Albany's escape from Edinburgh.   There could scarcely be a more curious scene.   Strangely enough James himself was resident in the castle when his brother was a prisoner there.   One would have thought that so near a neighbourhood would have seemed dangerous to the alarmed monarch, but perhaps he thought, on the other hand, that watch and ward would be kept more effectually under his own eyes.   Mar had died in the Canongate, perhaps in the Tolbooth there, according to tradition in a bath, where he was bled to death, probably in order that a pretence of illness or accident might be alleged ; and Edinburgh, no doubt, was full of dark whispers of this strange end of one prince, and the danger of the other, shut up within the castle walls where the King's minions had full sway, and any night might witness a second dark deed.   Prince Alexander's friends must have been busy and eager without, while he was not so strictly under bar and bolt inside that he could not make merry with the castle officials now and then, and cheat an evening with pleasant talk and a glass of good wine with a young captain of the guard.   One day there came to him an intimation of the arrival of a ship at Leith with wine from France, accompanied by some private token that there was more in this announcement than met the ear.   Albany accordingly sent a trusted servant to order two flasks of the wine, in one of which, contained in a tube of wax, was enclosed a letter, in the other a rope by which to descend the castle walls.   The whole story is exactly as Dumas tells the escape of the Duc de Beaufort, though whether the romancer could have seen the old records of Scotland, or if his legend is sanctioned by the authentic history of France, I am unable to tell. Alexander, like the prince in the novel, invited the Captain of the guard to sup with him to try the new wine—an invitation gladly accepted.   After supper

the Captain "passed to the King's chamber to see
what was doing, who was then lodged in the castle,"
probably to get the word for the night.   It is curious to
think of the unconscious officer, so little aware of what was
about to befall, going from the chamber of the captive to
that of the King, where the little Court would be assembled
at their music or their "tables," or where perhaps James was
taking counsel over the leafage of a capital or the spring of
an arch—and thence returning when all the rounds were
made, the great gates barred and bolted, the sentries set,
to the Prince in his prison, who was a finer companion still.
Alexander plied the unsuspecting Captain with his wine,
spiced or perhaps drugged to make it act the sooner, and
along with him a warder or two who were in constant
attendance upon the royal prisoner.   A prince to drink with
such carles !   " The fire was hett, and the wyne was strong " :
and the united influence of the spiced drink and the hot
room soon overcame the revellers, all but Alexander and
his trusty man, who had taken care to refrain.   In Dumas
the gaoler was but gagged and bound : but in Scotland life
went for little, and some of the authorities say that when
the Prince saw the drunkards in his power, "he lap from
the board and strak the captane with ane whinger and slew
him, and also stiked other two with his own hand."   He had
been informed that he was to die the next day if he did
not escape that night, which was some excuse for him.[1]
When the men were thus disposed of, in one way or another,
the Prince and his servant, "his chamber chyld," stole out
with the rope to "a quiet place" on the wall.   Coming out
into the dark freshness and stillness of the night after that
stifling and horrible room, seeing the stars once more and
the distant glimmer of the sea, and feeling freedom at hand,
it was little they would reck of the gaolers, always an obnoxious class.   One would imagine that it must have been

---

[1] Buchanan's account is not so bloodthirsty : he represents Alexander as entertaining his guests with stories of his restoration to favour, and approaching deliverance, and dismissing them in all mirth and friendliness though heavy with wine :
so that his guards having incontinently fallen asleep at their posts he was able to
make his escape.

on the most precipitous side of the castle rock where there were few sentinels and the exit was easy, though the descent terrible. The faithful servant tried the rope first but found it too short, and fell, breaking his thigh. With what feelings Alexander must have stolen back to get his sheets with which to lengthen the rope, pushing through the smoke, almost despairing to get off in safety! One is relieved to hear that he took his crippled attendant on his back and carried him, some say to a safe place—or, as others say, all the way across country to where the ship rocked at the pier of Leith. They must have got down to some dark spot on the northern slopes, where there would be no city watchman or late passer-by to give the alarm, and all would be clear and still before them to the water's edge—though a long, weary, and darkling way.

"But on the morne when the watchman perceived that the towis were hinging over the walls, then ran they to seek the Captane to show him the matter and manner, but he was not in his own chamber. Then they passed to the Duke's chamber and found the door open and ane dead man lying in the chamber door and the captane and the rest burning in the fire, which was very dollorous to them ; and when they missed the Duke of Albanie and his chamber chyld, they ran speedilie and shewed the King how the matter had happened. But he would not give it credence till he passed himself and saw the matter."

These events happened in 1479, when Albany escaped to France, where he remained for some years. Up to this period all that is said of him has been favourable. His treatment by his brother was undeserved, and there is no sign of either treachery or rebellion in him in these early years. But when he had languished for a long time in France—perhaps, notwithstanding a first favourable reception, sooner or later eating the exile's bitter bread—exasperation and despair must have so wrought in him that he began to traffic with the "auld enemy" of England, and even put his hand to a base treaty, by which his brother was to be dethroned and he himself succeed to the kingdom by grace of the English king—a stipulation which Albany must have well known would damn him for ever with his countrymen.

In the meantime James had begun to breathe again in the relief he felt to be freed of the presence of both his brothers. He " passed through all Scotland at his pleasure, in peace and rest," says the chronicler.   But it was not long that a king of Scotland could be left in this repose.   The usual trouble on the Borders had begun again as soon as Edward IV was secure upon his throne, and the English king had even sent his ships as far as the Firth of Forth, where he burnt villages and spoiled the coast under the very eyes of James. Though he would so much rather have been left in quiet to complete his beautiful new buildings at Stirling and arrange the choir in his new chapel, where there was a double supply of musicians that the King might never want this pleasure, yet the sufferings of the people and the angry impulse of the discontented nobles were more than James could resist, and he set forth reluctantly towards the Border to declare war. He had become more and more shut up within his little circle of favourites after the death and disappearance of his brothers, and Cochrane had gradually acquired a more and more complete sway over the mind of his master and the affairs of the realm.   The favourite had been guilty of all those extravagances which constitute the Nemesis of upstarts. He had trafficked in patronage and promotion, he had debased the currency, and he was supposed to influence the King to everything least honourable and advantageous to the country. Last injury of all, he had either asked from the King or accepted from him—at least, permitted himself to be tricked out in the name of Mar, the title of the young prince whose death he was believed to have brought about.   The lords of Scotland had already remonstrated with the King on various occasions as to the unworthy favourites who usurped their place around his throne : and their exasperation seems to have risen to a height beyond bearing when they found " the mason," as Cochrane is called, with his new liveries and extravagance of personal finery, at the head of the army which was raised to avenge the English invasion, and in the closest confidence of the King.   When they had got as far as Lauder the great lords, who were left out

of all James's private councils, assembled in a council
of their own in the parish church to talk over their
grievances, and to consult what could be done to reform
this intolerable abuse and to bring back the King to the
right way. Some, it would appear, went so far as to
meditate deposition, declaring that James was no longer fit
to be their King, having renounced their counsel and advice,
banished one brother and slain another, and "maid up
fallowes, maissones, to be lords and earls in the place of
noblemen." The result of the meeting, however, was that
milder counsels prevailed so far as James was concerned :
" They concluded that the King should be taine softlie without
harm of his bodie, and conveyed to the Castle of Edinburgh
with certain gentlemen," while Cochrane and the rest were
seized and hanged over Lauder Brig.

The question, however, remained, Who should be so bold
as to take the first step and lay hands upon the favourite ?
It was now that Lord Gray, one of the conspirators, told,
with that humour which comes in so grimly in many dark
historic scenes, the story of the mice and the cat—how the
mice conspired to save themselves by attaching a bell to
the cat to warn them of her movements—until the terrible
question arose which among them should attach to the neck
of the enemy this instrument of safety. One can imagine the
grave barons with half a smile looking at each other
consciously, in acknowledgment of a risk which it needed a
brave man to run. Angus, the head of the existing branch
of the Douglas family, who had already risen into much of
the power and importance of his forfeited kinsman, answered
with equally grim brevity " I'se bell the cat." But while he
spoke, the general enemy, mad with arrogance and self-confidence, and not believing in any power or boldness which could
stop him in his career, forestalled the necessity. He came to
the kirk, where no doubt he had heard there was some un-
authorised assembly, arrayed in black velvet with bands of
white, the livery he had chosen, a great gold chain round his
neck, a hunting horn slung about him adorned with gold and
jewels, and probably a marvel of mediæval art—and "rushed

rudlie at the kirk door." The hum of fierce satisfaction which arose when the keeper of the door challenged the applicant for admission, and the answer, "The Earl of Mar," rang into the silence in which each man had been holding his breath, may be imagined. It was Archibald Bell-the-Cat, ever hereafter known by that name, who advanced to meet the swaggering intruder in all his pride of privilege and place, but with a welcome very different from that which the favourite expected, who had come, no doubt, to break up the whisperings of the conspirators and assert his own authority. Angus pulled the gold chain from Cochrane's neck, and said "a rop would sett him better," while another Douglas standing by snatched at the horn. Cochrane, astonished but not yet convinced that any real opposition was intended, asked between offence and alarm, perhaps beginning to doubt the sombre excited assembly, "My lords, is it jest or earnest?" It would seem that the grim and terrible event of the execution "over the Bridge of Lauder," though why this special locality was chosen we are not told, followed with an awful rapidity. The chief offender had fallen into the hands of the conspirators with such unhoped-for ease that they evidently felt no time was to be lost.

"Notwithstanding the lords held him quiet while they caused certain armed men pass to the King's pavilion, and two or three wyse men with them, and gave the King fair and pleasant words, till they had laid hands on all his servants, and took them and hanged them over the Bridge of Lauder before the King's eyes, and brought in the King himself to the council. Thereafter incontinent they brought out Cochrane and his hands bound with ane tow, behind his back, who desired them to take ane of his own pavilion tows [cords] which were of silk and bind his hands, for he thought shame to be bound with ane hemp tow lyk ane thiefe. The lords answered and said, 'He was worse than a thiefe, he was ane traitour and deserved no better.'"

The last despairing bravado of the condemned man desiring that his hands might be bound with a silken cord at least, the horror and wrath of the pale King, helpless, looking on, forced into the assembly of the lords to witness their pitiless vengeance, are painfully tragical and terrible. All James's favourite attendants, the friends of his retired leisure and sharers in the occupations he loved, were thus executed before his eyes—all but a certain young Ramsay, who was at least a gentleman, and who, to save his life, leapt up behind his master upon the horse which the King was compelled to mount to see the dreadful deed accomplished. Ramsay's life was spared, not to the advantage of Scotland as became afterwards apparent.

The historical student will not fail to note how close in almost every particular is this grim incident to the catastrophe of Piers Gaveston in England in a previous age.

The state of affairs in Scotland after this extraordinary event was more extraordinary still, if possible. James was conveyed to Edinburgh,

"with certain lords in companie with him that took hold on him and keeped him in the said castle and served and honoured him as ane prince ought to be in all things: for he was not put there as a prisoner, but for the maintaining of the commonweill: gave him leave to use all his directions, gifts, and casualties at his pleasure. For nothing was derogat from him by reason of his authority, and all letters was given and proclamations made and printed in his name lykas they were before at his inputting, nor no regent nor governour was chosen at that time, but every lord within his own bounds was sworn to minister justice and to punish theft and slaughter within themselves, or else to bring the doers of the same to the King's justice at Edinburgh."

" Thus there was peace and rest in the country the space of three-quarters of a year," says Pitscottie. This, however, is a mistake, for the time of the King's retirement was only three or four months, from St. Magdalene's Day to Michaelmas. Short or long, it was one of the most curious moments of interregnum that history knows. James was conveyed back to Edinburgh with every show of respect, attended by the triumphant lords, who despised his milder virtues, his preferences and tastes, not one of whom could manage either pencil or lute, who cared for none of these things—while his strained eyes could still see nothing but the vision against the daylight, the impromptu gibbet of the high-arched bridge over the Border stream, where his familiar friends had been strung up with every sign of infamy. He had to contain within himself the rage, the shame, the grief and loneliness of his heart, and endure as he best could the exultation which his captors would scarcely attempt to conceal. The historians tell us little or nothing of the Queen, Margaret of Denmark, to whom James had been married for several years, and who had brought with her the full allegiance of the isles, the Hebrides, which up to that time had paid a tribute to the Scandinavian kingdom, and Orkney and Shetland which were the Queen's portion. Whether he found any comfort in her and in his children, when he was thus brought back to them to the castle, which would seem to have been their favourite residence, we are not told. At all events the shame of such a return, and of the captivity which was veiled by so many ironical appearances of freedom, must have been grievous to him, even as reflected in the eyes of his foreign wife, or the wondering questions on his sudden return of his baby son.

How this strange state of things was brought to an end it is difficult to tell, for the story is confused and troublesome. According to Pitscottie, James's private friends advised him first to take counsel with the Earl of Douglas, the long forfeited and banished Earl, represented as being then imprisoned in Edinburgh, which is clearly apocryphal : and afterwards with the Duke of Albany, to whom Pitscottie is throughout very favourable, making no mention of his undoubted treachery. For whatever may be the actual truth of all the curious and confused movements that were going on, it appears to be beyond doubt that Albany—though he had lately visited the English Court and formed a treasonable bargain with Edward IV to dethrone James, and to be himself made King in dependence upon England —now acted like a true brother. His first use of his alliance with Edward seems to have been for the advantage of the sovereign whom he intended to displace, a curious paradox of which we can offer no explanation. In this magnanimous act he had the support of the English who had engaged to help him, as the documents prove, in so different an enterprise : all which is very bewildering. Accompanied by the Duke of Gloucester and a small army, he suddenly appeared in Edinburgh to deliver the royal prisoner. There would seem to have been no fighting of any kind, nor any attempt on the part of Albany to dethrone his brother—nothing, indeed, but what would appear the most magnanimous action on his part, were not those secret treaties in existence bearing a silent testimony against him. When the lords heard of the coming of this expedition, which occurred in August 1482 (Albany having escaped in 1479, three years before), they "drew themselves together to ane council," apparently to watch the proceedings of the invaders.

> "Soon therafter compeired the Duke of Albanie and the Duke of Gloucester within the town of Edinburgh, with the number of ane thousand gentlemen, and entered within the Tolbooth thereof before the lords of Scotland, who were sitting at ane council at that time, and there very reverently saluted the Duke of Albanie, reverenced him and welcomed him home, and required of him what was his petition. He answered, 'I desire the King's grace, my brother, to be put to libertie,' which was granted to him incontinent. But the Chancellor answered and said, 'My lord, we will grant you your desires; but as to that man that is with you, we know him not, nor yet will we grant nothing to his desire.'"

This speech, which breathes that undying defiance of English interference which was the very inspiration of Scotland, is too characteristic not to be genuine. "That man" was Richard, afterwards Richard III, "Crookback Richard," the bitter and powerful hunchback of Shakspeare, whom other authorities have endeavoured in vain to persuade us to regard in a more favourable light. Whatever he might be in other aspects, in Scotland he was merely Albany's companion, silently aiding in what seems a most legitimate and honourable mission. The only way the historians can find of reconciling this strangely virtuous and exemplary behaviour with the secret engagements between Albany and England is by the conjecture that the lords of Scotland were so evidently indisposed to favour Albany, and there was so little feeling shown towards him by any part of the population, that the treason was silently abandoned, and in the hopelessness of playing a treasonable

part he played a magnanimous one, with the utmost grace
and semblance of sincerity ; which is a bewildering conclusion.   In any case he was the deliverer of his brother.
It would seem to be the fact, however, that James's deliverance **was** much aided by the attitude of the burghers of
Edinburgh, who were, as so often, on the King's side—and
to whom the character of a patron of the arts, and promoter
of so many persons of their own class into his friendship,
would naturally be as great a recommendation as it was an
offence to the others.   Their action at this period excited
the King's gratitude so much that he conferred upon the
city a special charter, securing the independence of their
municipal government, as well as their right to levy customs
in the port of Leith, and also, it is said, a sign of these
privileges, in the shape of the standard called the Blue
Blanket, which still remains in the possession of the Edinburgh guilds, with liberty to display it for their king, country,
and city rights, when occasion calls.

The two Dukes of Albany and Gloucester marched
together to the castle, preceded by heralds, to claim the
King from the officials who had him in charge.   One
can imagine the mingled relief and humiliation of James
when delivered from that stronghold by the brother who
had escaped from it by night, within a few hours of
the time when he had been ordered for execution, and
who in the meantime had been an exile.   There is no
reason to suppose that he was aware of the secret understanding with England to which his brother had set his seal,
so that there was nothing to lessen the intensity of the coals
of fire thus heaped upon his head.   No doubt all Edinburgh
was in the streets to watch that strange sight, as the King
rode from the castle gates, past the great Church of St. Giles,
and down the long line of the Canongate to Holyrood,
making his emancipation visible to all.   Apparently he
had not left the castle since he was brought into it in
shame and misery after the fatal episode at Lauder.   One
wonders how he looked upon the crowd which no doubt
would throng after him with acclamations—whether thankfully

and cheerfully in the pleasure of release, or with a revengeful
sense of how little he owed to their easy applauses. It is
said that Albany rode behind him on the same horse as an
exhibition of amity. It is very probable that James would
find bitterness in that too, as another humiliation.

The King was no sooner free than he made it evident
that he had not forgiven the humiliation and shame to
which he had been subjected. He imprisoned in their
turn a number of the lords who had been foremost in
the death of Cochrane, and would have "justified" them we
are told, but for the interference of Angus—now too great
apparently for James to touch—and Albany. For some
time after the latter remained with his brother, fulfilling the
functions of chief counsellor and Prime Minister. But
whether he displayed his ambition and evil intentions, or the
old jealousy and terrors of James got the upper hand as the
lords again became suspicious of him, it is difficult to tell
At all events Albany was forced to escape once more for his
life, and again took refuge in France, where either now or
previously, for the chronology is difficult to follow, he had
made a great marriage. Here he disappears altogether from
Scottish history, and not long after from life, having been
killed by accident in a tournament. Had Albany been the
elder instead of the younger brother it seems very probable
that a dark chapter might have been left out of the history
of Scotland, and a third patriotic and energetic King carried
on the traditions of the first and second James.

But it was scarcely to be looked for that, after all the
dissensions between the King and the lords, everything
should settle into harmony again. James is said to have
removed to Stirling from Edinburgh, which no doubt had
acquired painful associations to him from the time of his
enforced residence there—and to have resumed or completed the buildings in which he had taken so much pleasure
—especially the great hall of Stirling Castle, with all its
grotesque and curious ornamentation, which seems to prove
that Scotland was still much behind in refinement, though
with a barbaric inspiration of her own. Whether the

renewed tumults began by the appropriation of certain
Church lands hitherto in the power of the Homes, for the
endowment of the King's new chapel, it is difficult to tell, a
similar reason having been already alleged for disturbances
in which the Duke of Albany was the antagonist of that
powerful family ; at all events a very small matter was
enough to awake again all the old rancours.   The malcontents headed by the same men who had already inflicted
so much suffering and shame upon the King began to draw
together in alarming numbers.   Roused from among his
more congenial occupations by this renewed commotion,
James sent a herald to ask the reason of their assembling :
but the herald was disrespectfully treated and his letters
torn in pieces, an insult which seems to have convinced the
King that the strongest measures of defence were necessary.
He is said to have strongly fortified Stirling, where Prince
James, the heir of the kingdom, now a boy of fifteen or
sixteen, was.   Perhaps the King was suspicious of the boy,
perhaps his old terrors as to the danger to his life which was
to arise from his own family had returned to him : for the
restrictions under which young James was left were exceedingly severe and arbitrary.   No man was to be allowed to
enter the castle, great or small, till the King's return, nor
was the Prince to be allowed to pass the gates "to no
game, nor to meet with no man."   Pitscottie says that
Edinburgh Castle was also strengthened, and the King's
treasury placed in it and all his valuables laid up there.
When these precautions were taken James embarked "in ane
ship of Captane Woode's "—probably the most legitimate
way in which he could have travelled, the vessel being that of
the Admiral, Andrew Wood, the greatest sailor in Scotland—
and went to Fife, from whence he marched to the north,
calling the nobles of the northern counties round him, and
gathering an army with which to oppose the greater lords
and lairds who awaited him on the other side of the Firth
of Forth.   James's unusual energy must have equally roused
and alarmed the rebels, against whom the royal name was
as a strong tower.   That such men as Angus and the other

great nobles of Scotland, who had reduced their King to a
puppet with such entire success, should now feel it necessary
to get possession of Prince James in order to confer dignity
on their proceedings seems very strange ; but perhaps when
rebellion comes to the dignity of a pitched battle its flags
and pretensions are of more importance than when it can so
order matters as to put on an appearance of acting in the
King's own interests, as at Lauder.   And how far the Prince
might be an independent actor in this troubled drama there is
no evidence to show.   He had arrived at an age when youths
in these early-maturing days acted for themselves ; even in
our own a lad of sixteen would scarcely allow his name to be
employed against his father without some protest, and could
not be treated as a child in a conflict so momentous.   Therefore it is scarcely possible to imagine that the Prince was
entirely guiltless.   And the spectator cannot but enter with
warmth into the feelings of the King when he discovered
what had been done, and that his heir was in the enemy's
camp, giving substance and reason to their rebellion.

There is a curious story told of how Lord Lindsay
of the Byres, a fierce and grim baron of Fife, presented
on the very eve of the battle " a great grey courser " to the
King, assuring him that were he ever in extremity that
horse would carry him, " either to fly or to follow," better
than any horse in Scotland, " if well sitten "—a present which
James accepted, and which comes in as part of the parapher-
nalia of fate.   On the morning of the day of battle the King
mounted this horse, and " rade to ane hill head to see the
manner of the cuming " of his enemies against him.   He
saw the host defiling " in three battells," with six thousand
men in each, their spears shining, their banners waving, Homes
and Hepburns in the front, with Merse and Teviotdale and
all the forces of the Border, and the men of Lothian in the rear :
while in the main body rose the ensigns of all the great lords
who had already beaten and humbled him—Bell-the-Cat
and the other barons who had hanged his friends before his
eyes—but now bearing his own royal standard, with his son
among them, the bitterest thought of all.   James sat upon

his fleet horse, presented to him the night before with such
an ominous recommendation, and saw his enemies bearing
down upon him—his enemies and his son. " Then," says
the chronicler, " he remembered the words which the witch
had spoken to him many days before, that he should be
suddenly destroyed and put down by the nearest of his kin."
For this he had allowed the murder of young Mar and driven
Alexander of Albany into exile ; but who can wonder if in
his stricken soul he now perceived or imagined that no man
can cheat the Fates ? His own son, his boy ! Some nobler
poignancy of anguish than the mere sick despair and panic of
the coward must surely have been in his mind as he realised
this last and crowning horror. The profound moral discouragement of a man caught in the toils, and for whom no
escape was possible ; the sickening sense of betrayal ; the
wide country before him, in which there might still be found
some peaceful refuge far from these distractions and contradictions of men ; the whirl of the dreadful yet beautiful
sight, companies marching and ever marching, spears and
helmets shining, banners waving, and all against him—a man
who had never any pleasure in the pomp and circumstance
of war. Who can wonder as these hurrying thoughts overwhelmed his mind, and the fleet courser pawed the turf, and
the wild sweet air blew free in his face, inviting him to
escape, to flee, to find somewhere comfort and peace—that
such a man should have yielded to the mad impulse, and in
an access of despair, longing for the wings of a dove that
he might flee away and be at rest, have turned from the
rising tumult and fled ?

Of all the ironies of Fate there could be none more bitter
than that which drove the hapless fugitive, in growing
consciousness of shame, like a straw before the wind, across
the famous field of Bannockburn. What an association to be
connected with that victorious name ! He had aimed at Stirling, but wild with despair and panic and misery missed the
way. As the gray courser entered the village of Bannockburn
at full flight a woman drawing water let fall her " pig " or
earthen pot in affright, and startled the horse ; and the King

" being evill sitten " (having a bad seat) fell from his saddle before the door of the mill.   The sight of this strange cavalier in his splendid armour, covered with foam and dust, borne to the earth like a log by the weight of his armour, appalled the simple people, who dragged him inside the mill and covered him where he lay with some rough horsecloth, not knowing what to do.   When he had come to himself James implored the wondering people to fetch him a priest before he died.   " Who are you ? " they asked, standing over him. What a world of time had passed in that wild ride ! how many ages since the dying fugitive lying on the dusty floor and covered with the miller's rug was James Stewart, at the head of a gallant army !   " This morning," he said, with a bitter comprehension of all that had passed since then, " I was your King."   The miller's wife ran forth to her door calling for a priest, and some one who was passing by answered her call ; but whether he was really a priest, or only one of the stragglers of the rebel army, seems uncertain.   He came into the mill, hearing no doubt the cries of the astonished couple that it was the King, and kneeling down recognised the fallen monarch ; but instead of hearing his confession, drew a knife and stabbed him three or four times in the breast.   Thus miserably ended James Stewart, the third of the name.

Of all the tragical conclusions to which his family had come this was the most deplorable, as his life had been the least satisfactory.   Whether there was more than weakness to be alleged against him it is now impossible to tell ; and whether his favourite companions and occupations proved a spirit touched to finer issues than those about him, or showed only, as his barons thought, a preference for low company and paltry pursuits of peace.   But howsoever his patronage of the arts, the buildings he has left to Scotland, or the tradition of the music and gentle pleasures which he loved, may justify him to the reader, it is at least clear that his stewardry of his kingdom was a miserable failure, and his life a loss and harm to his country. Instead of promoting the much-interrupted progress of her development, so far as his individual influence went, he arrested and hindered it.   And, difficult as the position of affairs had been when he succeeded at seven years old to his father's uncompleted labours, the situation which he left behind him, the country torn in two, one half of his subjects in arms against the other, his son's name opposed to his own, and every national benefit postponed to the settlement of this quarrel, was ten times more difficult and terrible. He was the first of his name whose influence was all unfavourable to the progress of the nation, not only by evil fortune, but by the disasters of a mind not sufficient for the weight and burden of his time.   He thus died ignominiously, in the month of June 1488, having reigned twenty-eight years and lived thirty-five—a short lifetime for so much trouble and general misfortune.

ARMS OF JAMES IV OF SCOTLAND
(From King's College Chapel, Old Aberdeen)

CHAPTER IV

JAMES IV: THE KNIGHT-ERRANT

THE graver records of the nation pause at the point to which
we have arrived. The tale leaves both battlefield and
counsel chamber, though there is an inevitable something of
both in the chronicle as there is something of daily bread in
the most festive day. But it is not with these grave details
that the historian occupies himself. The most serious page
takes a glow from the story it has to tell, the weighty
matters of national life and development stand aside, and it
is a knight of romance who stands forth to occupy the field.
The story of James, the fourth of the name, is one of those
passages of veritable history in which there is scarcely anything that might not be borrowed from a tale of chivalry.
It is pure romance from beginning to end.

Of the character and personality of the boy whose education was carried on under strict surveillance at Stirling we
know nothing whatever, until he suddenly appears before
us in the enemy's camp, whether with his own consent or not,
or how much, if with his own consent, with any knowledge
of what he was about, it is difficult to tell.   His mother
had died while he was still a child, and probably for the last
few years of his much disturbed life James III had but little
attention to spare for his son.   If there is any truth in a
curious story told by Pitscottie of a search on board Sir
Andrew Wood's ship for the murdered King, while yet the
fact of his death was unknown, and the Prince's wistful
address to the great sailor, "Sir, are ye my father?" we
might suppose that the boy had been banished altogether
from his father's presence.   But perhaps this is too slender
a foundation to build upon.   There can be no doubt, however, that after the battle, little honourable to either side,
and lost by the King's party almost before begun, from
which he fled in a panic so ignominious and fatal, there
was a moment of great perplexity and dismay, when King
James's fate remained a mystery, and the rebel nobles with
the boy-prince among them knew not what to do or to say,
in the doubt whether he was dead or alive, whether he might
not reappear at any moment with a host from the Highlands
or from France, or even England, at his back.   When they
had fully realised their unsatisfactory victory they marched
to Edinburgh, with the Prince always among them and a
chill horror about them, unaware what way to look for news
of the King.   The rush of the people to watch their return
with their drooping banners and faces full of consternation,
and wonder at the unaccustomed sight of the young Prince
which yet was not exciting enough to counterbalance the
anxiety, the wonder, the perpetual question what had
become of the King—must have been as a menace the more
to the perplexed leaders, who knew that a fierce mob might
surge up into warfare at any moment, or a rally from the
castle cut off their discouraged and weary troops.   Where
was the King?   Had he perhaps got before them to

Edinburgh? was he there on that height, misty with smoke
and sunshine, turning against them the great gun which had
been forged for use against the Douglas : or ready to appear
from over the Firth terrible with a new army ; or in the ships,
most likely of all, with the great admiral who lay there watching, ready to carry off a royal fugitive or bring back strange
allies to revenge the scorn that had been done to the King?
The lords decided to take their dispirited and broken array to
Leith instead of going to Holyrood, and there collected together
to hold a council of war.   Among the confused reports brought
to them of what one man and another had seen or heard was
one, more likely than the rest, of boats which had been seen
to steal down Forth and make for the *Yellow Carvel* lying in
the estuary, with apparently wounded men on board.   They
sent accordingly to summon Sir Andrew Wood to their
presence.   The sailor probably cared nothing about politics
any further than that he held for the King—and furious with
the lords who had withstood His Majesty declined to come
unless hostages were sent for his safety.   When this was
accorded, the old sea-lion, the first admiral of Scotland, came
gruffly from his ships to answer their questions.   Whether
there was any resemblance between the two men, as he stood
with his cloak wrapped round him defiant before the rebel
lords, or if the Prince had, as is possible, been so long absent
from his father that the vague outline of a man enveloped
and muffled deceived him, it is impossible to say.   But there
is a tone of penetrating reality in the " Sir, are ye my
father?" of the troubled boy, perhaps only then aroused to
a full comprehension of his position and the sense that he
was himself guiltily involved in the proceedings which had
brought some mysterious and unknown fate upon the King.
It is difficult to see why, accepting from Pitscottie all the
rest of this affecting narrative, the modern historian should
cut out this as unworthy of belief, " Who answered," continues the chronicler, " with tears falling from his eyes,"

" ' Sir, I am not your father, but I was a servand to your father, and
sall be to his authoritie till I die, and ane enemy to them that was the
occasion of his doon-putting.'   The lords inquired of Captain Wood if

he knew of the King or where he was. He answered he knew nothing of the King nor where he was. Then they speired what they were that came out of the field and passed into his ships. He answered : ' It was I and my brother, who were ready to have waired our lives with the King in his defence.' Then they said, ' He is not in your ships?' who answered again, ' He is not in my ship, but would to God he were in my ship safelie, I should defend him and keep him skaithless frae all the treasonable creatures who has murdered him, for I think to see the day when they shall be hanged and quartered for their demerites.' "

The lords would fain have silenced this rude sailor, but having given hostages for his safe return were obliged to let him go. There could not be a more vivid picture of their perplexity and trouble. They proceeded to Edinburgh after this rebuff, coming in, we may well believe, with little sound of trumpet or sign of welcome, and with many a threatening countenance among the crowds that gazed wistfully upon the boy in their midst, who, if the King were really dead, was the King—another James. There might be old men about watching from the foot of the Canongate the silent cortege trooping along the valley to Holyrood — men who remembered with all the force of boyish recollection how the assassins of James I. had been dragged and tormented through Edinburgh streets, and might wonder and whisper inquiries to their sons whether such a horrible sight might be coming again, and what part that pale boy had in the dreadful deed ? It was but fifty years since that catastrophe, and already two long minorities had paralysed the progress of Scotland. How the crowding people must have eyed him as he rode along, the slim stripling, so young, so helpless, in the midst of all these bearded men ! What part did he have in it ? Was his father done to death by his orders ? Was he consenting at least to what was done ? Was he aware of all that was to follow that hurried ride with the lords, into which he had been beguiled or persuaded ? James III had to some degree favoured Edinburgh, where, notwithstanding his long captivity in the Castle, he had found defenders and friends. And there must have been many in the crowd who took part with the unfortunate monarch, so mysteriously gone out of their midst, and who looked with horror upon the boy who had something at least to do with the ruin and death of his father. It was a sombre entry upon the future dwelling to which this young James was to bring so much splendour and rejoicing.

How these doubts were cleared up and certainty attained we have no sure way of knowing. Pitscottie's story is that when the false priest murdered the King, he took up the body on his back and carried it away, "but no man knew what he did with him or where he buried him." Other authorities speak of a funeral service in the Abbey of Cambuskenneth on the banks of the Forth—a great religious establishment, of which one dark grey tower alone remains upon the green meadows by the winding river; and there is mention afterwards of a bloody shirt carried about on the point of a lance to excite the indignant Northmen to rebellion. But notwithstanding these facts no one ventures to say that James's body was found or buried. Masses for the dead were sung, and every religious honour paid; but so far as anything is told us, these rites might have been performed around an empty bier. At last however, in some way, a dolorous certainty, which must by many have been felt as a relief, was attained, and the young King was crowned in Edinburgh in the summer of 1488, some weeks after his father's death. At the same time a Parliament was called, and the Castle of Edinburgh, which all this time seems to have kept its gates closed and rendered no submission, was summoned by the herald to yield, "which was obediently done at the King's command," says the chronicle. There was evidently no thought of rebellion or of resisting the lawful sovereign, so soon as it was certain which he was. The procession of the herald, perhaps the Lord Lyon himself, with all his pursuivants, up the long street to sound the trumpets outside the castle gates and demand submission, must have brightened the waiting and wondering city with the certainty of the new reign. But the bravery and fine colours of such a procession, though made doubly effective by the background of noble houses and all

the lofty gables and great churches in the crowded picturesque
centre at the foot of the Castle Hill, were not then as now
strange to the "grey metropolis of the North." No country
in Christendom would seem to have so changed under the
influence of the Reformation as Scotland. The absence of
pageant and ceremonial, the discouragement of display, the
suppression of the picturesque in action, in the midst of one
of the most picturesque scenes in the world, are all of modern
growth. In the fifteenth century, and especially in the reign
that was now begun, the town ran over with bright colour
and splendid spectacle. When the lists were formed upon
the breezy platform, overlooking the fair plains of Lothian,
the great Firth, and the surrounding circle of hills, at the
castle gate—how brilliant must have been both scene and
setting, the living picture and the wonderful frame, and how
every window would be crowded to see the hundred little
processions of knights to the jousts and ladies to the
tribunes, and the King and Queen riding with all their fine
attendants "up the toun" all the way from Holyrood! Nor
would the curiosity be much less when, coming in from the
country, with every kind of quaint surrounding, the great
nobles with their glittering retinue, the lairds each with a
little posse of stout men-at-arms, as many as he could
muster, the burgesses from the towns, the clergy from
all the great centres of the Church on mules and soft-
pacing palfreys, would gather for the meetings of Parliament. It scarcely wanted a knight-errant like the fourth
James, with his chivalrous tastes and devices, to fill the
noble town with brightness, for all these fine sights were
familiar to Edinburgh. But the brightest day was now
to come.

The Parliament which assembled in all the emotion of that
curious crisis, while still the wonder and dismay of the King's
tragic disappearance were in the air, was a strange one. It
was evidently convened with the intention of shielding the
party which had taken arms against James III, while
making a cunning attempt to throw the blame on those
who had stood by him : these natural sentiments being

OLD HOUSE IN LAWNMARKET

combined with the deter-
mination, most expedient
in the circumstances, to
reconcile all by punishing
none. The young King
and the power now exer-
cised in his name were
in the hands of the lords
who had headed the re-
bellion, Angus, Home, Bothwell, and the rest; and while
their own safety was naturally their first consideration, they
had evidently no desire to stir up troublesome questions
even for the fierce joy of condemning their opponents. At
one or other of the early Parliaments in this reign, either
that first held by way of smoothing over matters and pre-

paring such an account of all that had happened as might
be promulgated by foreign ambassadors to their respective
Courts—or one which followed the easy settlement of an
attempt at rebellion already referred to, when the Lord
of Forbes carried a bloody shirt, supposed to be that
of King James, through the streets of Aberdeen, and raised
a quickly-quelled insurrection—there occurs the trial of
Sir David Lindsay, one of the most quaint narratives of
a *cause célèbre* ever written. The chronicler, whom we
may quote at some length—and whose living and graphic
narrative none even of those orthodox historians who
pretend to hold lightly the ever-delightful Pitscottie,
upon whom at the same time they rely as their chief
authority, attempt to question in this case—was himself
a Lindsay, and specially concerned for the honour of his
name. The defendant was Lindsay of the Byres, one of the
chief of James III's supporters, he who had given the King
that ominous gift of a fleet courser on the eve of the
battle. When he appeared at the bar of the house so to
speak — before Parliament — the following "dittay" or
indictment was made against him :—

"Lord David Lindsay of the Byres compeir for the cruel coming
against the King at Bannokburne with his father, and in giving him
counsall to have devored his sone, the King's grace, here present: and
to that effect gave him ane sword and ane hors to fortify him against
his sone: what is your answer heirunto?"

A more curious reversal of the facts of the case could not
be, and the idea that James the actual monarch could be a
rebel against his own son, then simply the heir to the crown,
is bewildering in its grave defiance of all reason. There is
not much wonder that Lindsay, "ane rasch man, and of rud
language, albeit he was stout and hardy in the field and
exercised in war," burst forth upon the assembled knights and
lords, upbraiding them with bringing the Prince into their
murderous designs against the King. The effect of his speech
on the assembly would seem to have been considerable, and it
is very apparent that the party in power had no desire to
make any fight, for the Chancellor anxiously excused Lindsay

to the King as " ane man of the old world, that cannot answer
formallie nor get speech reverentlie in your Grace's presence." This roused the brother of the culprit, a certain
Mr. Patrick Lindsay, otherwise described as a Churchman, who was by no means content to see the head
of his house thus described, nor yet that Lord Lindsay
should come " in the King's will," thus accepting forfeiture or any other penalties that might be pronounced
against him. Accordingly he interfered in the following
remarkable way :—

"To that effect he stamped on his brother's foot to latt him understand that he was not content with the decree which the Chancellour pro-
poned to him. But this stamp of Mr. Patrick's was so heavy upon his
brother's foot, who had ane sair toe which was painful to him, wherefore
he looked to him and said, ' Ye were over pert to stampe upon my foot ;
were you out of the King's presence I would overtake you upon the
mouth.' Mr. Patrick, hearing the vain words of his brother, pled on his
knees before the King and the Justice, and made his petition to them in
this manner : ' Sir, if it will please your Grace and your honorabill
counsall, I desire of your Grace, for His cause that is Judge of all, that
your Grace will give me leave this day to speak for my brother, for I see
there is no man of law that dare speak for him for fear of your Grace ;
and although he and I has not been at ane this mony yeires, yet my
heart may not suffer me to see the native house whereof I am descended
to perish !' So the King and the Justice gave him leave to speak for
his brother. Then the said Mr. Patrick raise off his knees, and was
very blythe that he had obtained that license with the King's favour.
So he began very reverentlie to speak in this manner, saying to the whole
lords of Parliament, and to the rest of them that were accusers of his
brother at that time, with the rest of the lords that were in the summons
of forfaltrie, according to their dittay, saying : ' I beseech you all, my
lords, that be here present, for His sake that will give sentence and
judgment on us all at the last day, that ye will remember now instantly
is your time . . . therefore now do all ye would be done to in the
administration of justice to your neighbours and brethren, who are accused
of their lives and heritages this day, whose judgment stands in your
hands. Therefore beware in time, and open not the door that ye may not
steik.' Be this Mr. Patrick had ended his speeches, the Chancellour
bid him say something in defence of his brother, and to answer to the
points of the summons made and raised upon his brother and the rest of
the lords and barons. Then Mr. Patrick answered again and said : ' If
it please the King's grace, and your honours that are here present, I say
the King should not sit in judgment against his lords and barons,
because he has made his oath of fidelity when he received the crown of

Scotland that he should not come in judgment against his lords and barons in no action where he is partie himself. But here His Grace is both partie, and was at the committing of the crime himself, therefore he ought not, neither by the law of God nor of man, to sit in judgment at this time ; wherefore we desire him, in the name of God, to rise and depart out of judgment, till the matter be further discussed conform to justice.'"

This bold request apparently commended itself to the Parliament, for we hear that the Chancellor and lords considered it reasonable, and the King was accordingly desired "to rise up and pass into the inner tolbooth, which," adds Pitscottie, "was very unpleasant to him for the time, being ane young prince sittand upon his royall seat to be raised by his subjects." Mr. Patrick so pressed his advantage after this strange incident, and the argument of the young King's presence and complicity in all that had happened was so unanswerable, added to some inaccuracy in the indictment, of which the keen priest made the most, that the summons was withdrawn, and Lindsay along with all the other barons of his party would seem to have shared in the general amnesty, as probably was the intention of all parties from the beginning. For the victors, who were victors by a chance, were not powerful enough to carry matters with a high hand, and their opponents, though overcome, were too strong to be despised. It was better for all to gather round the new King, who had no evil antecedents nor anything to prevent a new beginning of the most hopeful kind. The scene ends with characteristic liveliness. "The lord David Lindsay was so blyth at his brother's sayings that he burst forth saying to him, 'Verrilie, brother, ye have fine pyet words. I should not have trowed, by St. Amarie, that you had sic words'"—an amusing tribute of half-scornful gratitude from the soldier to the Churchman whose pyet or magpie words were so wonderfully efficacious, yet so despicable in themselves, to change the fate of a gentleman! It is grievous to find that the King was so displeased at Mr. Patrick and his boldness that he sent him off to the Ross of Bute, and kept him imprisoned in that solitary yet beautiful region for a whole year.

Notwithstanding, however, this little failure of respect to

ST. ANTHONY'S
CHAPEL

the sovereign, and the dismal uncertainty and anxiety in which his reign began, there seemed to be nothing but the happiest prospects opening before the young King. Out of the miserable struggle which brought him to the throne, he himself, most probably only awakened to the meaning of it after all was over, brought a lifelong remorse which he never threw off, and which was increased by the melancholy services of commemoration and expiation, the masses for his father's soul and solemn funeral ceremonials whether real or nominal, at all of which the youth would have to be present with a sore and swelling heart. We are told that he went and unburthened himself to the Dean of the Chapel Royal in Stirling, his father's favourite church, which James III had built and endowed, arranging the services and music with special personal care. The Dean received his confession with kindness seeing him so penitent, and gave him "good counsel and comfort," and remained his friend and spiritual adviser as he grew into manhood ; but we are not told whether it was by his ordinance as a penance and constant reminder of his sin, or by a voluntary mortification of his own, that James assumed the iron belt which he wore always round him "and eikit it from time to time," that is, increased its size and weight as long as he lived. This sensibility, which formed part of his chivalrous and generous character, the noble, sweet, and lovable nature which conquered all hearts, at once subdued and silenced his many critics, and furnished them with a reproach which spite and ill-will could bring up against him when occasion occurred. But the enemies were few and the lovers many who surrounded the young Prince when the contentions of the crisis were once over, and the warring factions conciliated by general condemnations in principle which hurt nobody so long as they were not accompanied by confiscations or deprivations. Such clemency in so young a king was a marvel to all, the chroniclers say, though indeed there could be little question of clemency on James's part in a mutual hushing-up, which was evidently dictated by every circumstance of the time and the only source of mutual safety.

When, however, he had arrived at man's estate, and makes a recognisable and individual appearance upon the stage of history, the picture of him is one of the most attractive ever made, the happiest and brightest chapter in the tragic story of the Stewarts. Youth with that touch of extravagance which becomes it, that genial wildness which all are so ready to pardon, and an adventurous disposition, careless of personal safety, gave a charm the more to the magnificent young King, handsome, noble, brave, and full of universal

friendliness and sympathy, who comes forth smiling in the
face of fate, ready to turn back every gloomy augury and
bring in another golden age. Pitscottie's description is full
of warmth and vivid reality :—

"In this mean time was good peace and rest in Scotland and great
love betwixt the King and all his subjects, and was well loved by them
all : for he was verrie noble, and though the vice of covetousness rang
over meikle in his father it rang not in himself : nor yet pykthankis nor
cowards should be authorised in his companie, nor yet advanced ; neither
used he the council but of his lords, whereby he won the hearts of the
whole nobilitie ; so that he could ride out through any part of the realme,
him alone, unknowing that he was King ; and would lie in poor men's
houses as he had been ane travellour through the country, and would
require of them where he lodged, where the King was, and what ane
man he was, and how he used himself towards his subjects, and what
they spoke of him through the countrie. And they would answer him
as they thought good, so by this doing the King heard the common bruit
of himself. This Prince was wondrous hardie and diligent in execution
of justice, and loved nothing so well as able men and horses ; therefore
at sundry times he would cause make proclamations through the land to
all and sundry his lords and barons who were able for justing and
tourney to come to Edinburgh to him, and there to exercise themselves
for his pleasure, some to run with the spear, some to fight with the
battle-axe, some with the two-handed sword, and some with the bow,
and other exercises. By this means the King brought the realm to great
manhood and honour : that the fame of his justing and tourney spread
through all Europe, which caused many errant knights to come out of
other parts to Scotland to seek justing, because they heard of the kinglie
fame of the Prince of Scotland. But few or none of them passed away
unmatched, and ofttimes overthrown."

The town to which, under this young and gallant Prince,
the stream of chivalry flowed, was yet more picturesque than
the still and always "romantic town" of which every Scotsman is proud. The Nor' Loch reflected the steep rocks of the
castle and the high crown of walls and turrets that sur-
mounted them, with nothing but fields and greenery, here and
there diversified by a village and fortified mansion between
it and the sea. The walls, which followed the irregularities of
the rocky ridge, as far as the beginning of the Canongate, were
closed across the High Street by the picturesque port and
gateway of the Nether Bow, the boundary in that direction
of the town, shutting in all its busy life, its markets, its

crowding citizens, its shops and churches.   On the south at
the foot of the hill, the burghers' suburb, where the merchants,
lawyers, and even some of the nobles had their houses
and gardens, lay outside the walls in the sunshine, protected
only by the soft summits of the Braid and Pentland hills :
what is now the Cowgate, not a savoury quarter, being then
the South Side, the flowery and sheltered faubourg in which
all who could afford the freedom of a country residence
while still close to the town, expanded into larger life, as the
wealthy tradesfolk of all ages, and persons bound to a
centre of occupation and duty, always love to do.   Towards
the east, and gradually becoming as important and busy as
the High Street itself, though outside the series of towers
which guarded the city gate, lay the long line of the Court
suburb, the lofty and noble Canongate descending towards
the abbey and palace, where all that was splendid in Scotland
congregated around the gay and gallant King.   Outside the
Netherbow Port, striking out in opposite directions, was the
road which led to the seaport of Leith and that which took
its name from the great Kirk of Field, St. Mary's Wynd, a
pleasant walk along the outside of the fortifications to the
great monastery on its plateau, with the Pleasance, a name
suggestive of all freshness and greenery and rural pleasure,
at its feet.   Inside the town, between the castle gates
and those of the city, were the crowded habitations of a
mediæval town, the only place where business could be
carried on in safety, or rich wares exhibited, or money passed
from hand to hand.   The Lawnmarket or Linen Market
would be the chief centre of sale and merchandise, and there,
no doubt, the booths before the lower stories, with all their
merchandise displayed, and the salesmen seated at the head
of the few deep steps which led into the cavernous depths
within, would be full of fine dresses and jewellery, and the
gold and silver which, some one complains, was worn away
by the fine workmanship, which was then more prized than
solid weight.   The cloth of gold and silver, the fine satins
and velvets, the embroidery, more exquisite than anything
we have time or patience for now—embroidery of gold

thread which we hear of, an uncomfortable sort of luxury, even upon the linen of great personages—would there be put forth and inspected by gallants in all their fine array, or by

OLD HOUSES AT HEAD OF WEST BOW

the ladies in their veils, half or wholly muffled from public inspection. Even the cheaper booths that adorned the West Bow or smaller wynds, where the country women bought their kirtles of red or green when they brought their produce to the market, would show more gay colours under their shade in a season than we with our soberer taste in years ; and the town ladies, in their hoods and silk gowns, which were permitted even in more primitive times to the possessors of so much a year, must have been of themselves a fair sight in all their ornaments, less veiled and muffled from profane view than more high-born dames and demoiselles. No doubt it would be a favourite walk with all to pass the port and see what was doing among the great people down yonder at Holyrood, or watch a gay band of French knights arriving from Leith with their pennons displayed, full of some challenge lately given by the knights of Scotland, or eager to maintain on their own account the beauty of their ladies and the strength of their spears against all comers. Edinburgh can never have been so amusing, never so gay and bright, as in these fine times ; though, no doubt, there was always the risk of a rush together of two parties of gallants, a mêlée after the old mode of Clear the Causeway, a hurried shutting of shops and pulling forth of halberds. For the younger population, at least, no doubt these risks were almost the best part of the play.

Thus Edinburgh breasted its ridge of rock—a fair sight across all the green country ; its sentinel mountain crouching eastward between the metropolis and the sea, its suburbs growing and expanding ; this full of the fine people of the Court, that of the quiet wealth and enjoyment which made no extravagant demonstration. It had never been so prosperous, never so much the centre of all that was splendid in the kingdom, as in the reign of the fourth James—the knight of romance, the gayest and brightest representative of the House of Stewart, though unable to defend himself from the tragic fate which awaited every sovereign of his name.

Among the finest sights seen in Edinburgh must have been those which occurred very early in his reign, when the great Admiral, Sir Andrew Wood, he who had met so proudly the inquisition of the lords, came from sea with his prisoners and his spoils. Wood had not pleased the reigning party by his rough fidelity to the dead King, but they could not induce the other sea captains, by any promise of reward or advancement, to attack and punish, as was their desire, the greatest sailor in Scotland.   And when an English expedition began to vex the Scottish coasts, there was no one but Wood to encounter and defeat them, which he did on two different occasions, bringing the captains of the rover vessels—probably only half authorised by the astute King Henry VII, who had evidently no desire to attack Scotland, but who had to permit a raid from time to time as the most popular thing to do—as prisoners to the courteous King, who though he "thanked Sir Andrew Wood greatly and rewarded him richlie for his labours and great proof of his manhood," yet "propined (gave presents to) the English captain richlie and all his men and sent them all safelie home, their ships and all their furnishing, because they had shown themselves so stout and hardie warriours." "So he sent them all back to the King of England," says the chronicler, with full enjoyment of James's magnanimous brag and of thus having the better of "the auld enemy" both in prowess and in courtesy, "to let him understand he had as manlie men in Scotland as he had in England ; therefore desired him to send no more of his captains in time coming."   England was obliged to accept, it appeared, this bravado of the Scots, having no excuse for repeating the experiment, but was "discontented" and little pleased to be overcome both in courtesy and in arms.

A more serious matter than this encounter at sea, which was really more a trial of strength than anything else, was the purely chivalric enterprise of James in taking up the cause of Perkin Warbeck, the supposed Duke of York, who imposed upon all Europe for a time, and on nobody so much as the King of Scotland.   This adventurer, who was given out as the younger son of Edward IV escaped by the relenting of the murderers when his elder brother was killed in the Tower, was by unanimous consent of all history a youth of person and manners quite equal to his pretensions, playing his part of royal prince with a grace and sincerity which nobody could resist.   The

grave Pinkerton, so sarcastically superior to all fables, writing
at the end of the eighteenth century, had evidently not even
then made up his mind how to accept this remarkable
personage, but speaks of him as "this unfortunate prince or
pretender," and of James as "sensible of the truth of his
report or misled by appearance," with an evident leaning to
the side of the hero who played so bold a game. The
young adventurer came to James with the most illustrious of
guarantees. He brought letters from Charles VIII of France,
and from the Emperor Maximilian, and was followed by a
train of gallant Frenchmen and by everything that was
princelike, gracious, and splendid. So completely was he
received and believed at the Scottish Court that when
there arose a mutual love, as the story goes, between him
and the Lady Catherine Gordon, daughter of the Earl of
Huntly, one of the most powerful peers in Scotland, and
at the same time of royal blood, a cousin of the King, the
marriage seems to have been accepted as a most fit and even
splendid alliance. No greater pledge of belief could have
been given than this. The King of Scots threw himself into
the effort of establishing the supposed prince's claims as if
they had been his own. Curious negotiations were entered
into as to what the pretender should do if, by the help of
Scotland, he was placed upon the English throne. He was
to cede Berwick, that always-coveted morsel which had
to change its allegiance from generation to generation as
the balance between the nations rose and fell—and pay a
certain sum towards defraying the expenses of the expedition,
a bargain to which Perkin, playing his part much better
than any king of the theatre ever did before, demurred,
insisting upon easier terms—as he afterwards remonstrated
when James harried the Borders, declaring that he would
rather resign all hopes of the crown than secure it at the
expense of the blood and goods of his people. A pretended prince who thus spoke might well be credited as far
as faith could go. The story of this strange enterprise is
chiefly told in the letters to Henry VII of England of Sir
John Ramsay, the same who had been saved by James III

when the rest of his favourites were killed, and who had more or less thriven since, though in evil ways, occupying a position at the Court of James IV whom he hated, and acting as spy on his actions, which were all reported to the English Court. Ramsay gives the English Government full information of all that his sovereign is about to do on behalf of the fengit (feigned) boy, and especially of the invasion of England which he is about to undertake "against the minds of near the whole number of his barons and people. Notwithstanding," Ramsay says, "this simple wilfulness cannot be removed out of the King's mind for nae persuasion or mean. I trust verrilie," adds the traitor, "that, God will, he be punished by your mean for the cruel consent of the murder of his father."

Curiously enough Pitscottie, the most graphic and circumstantial of historians, says nothing whatever of this most romantic episode. Why he should have left it out, for it is impossible that it could have been unknown to him, we are unable to imagine ; but so it is. Buchanan however enters fully into the tale. The wisest of James's counsellors, he tells us, were disposed to have nothing to do with this spurious young prince coming out of the unknown with his claim to be the rightful King of England ; but many more were in his favour, specially with the reflection that the moment of England's difficulties was always one of advantage for the Scots. An army was accordingly raised, with which James marched into England, carrying Perkin with him with a train of about fourteen hundred followers, and hopes that the country would rise to greet and acknowledge their lost prince. But it is evident that the Northumbrians looked on without any response, and saw in the expedition but one of the many raids which they were always so ready to return on their side when occasion offered. The pretender, on whose behalf all this was done, shrank, it would appear, from the devastation, and with something like the generous compunction of a prince protested that he would rather lose the crown than gain it so—a protest which James must have thought a piece of affectation, for he replied with a jeer that his companion

was too solicitous for the welfare of a country which would
neither acknowledge him as prince nor receive him as citizen.
Perkin must have begun to tire the patience of the finest
gentleman in Christendom before James would have made
such a contemptuous retort. He returned with the King,
however, when this unsuccessful expedition—the only use of
which was that it proved to James the fruitlessness of fighting
on behalf of a pretender who had no hold upon the people
over whom he claimed to reign—came to an end. It was
followed by some slight reprisals on the part of the English,
and after an interval by an embassy to make peace. Henry
VII would seem to have been at all times most unwilling
to have Scotland for an enemy, notwithstanding the strange
motive suggested to him by the traitor Ramsay. " Sir,"
writes this false Scot, " King Edward had never fully the
perfect love of his people till he had war with Scotland ;
and he made sic good diligence and provision therein that
to this hour he is lovit ; and your Grace may as well
have as gude a tyme as he had." But the cunning old
potentate at Westminster was not moved even by this
argument. Instead of following the instructions of the
virulent spy whose hatred of his native king and country
reaches the height of passion, he sent a wise emissary,
moderate like himself, the Bishop of Durham, to inquire into
the reasons of the attack.

And Edinburgh must have had another great sensational
spectacle in the arrival not only of the English commissioners, but of such a great foreign personage as the
Spanish envoy, one of the greatest grandees of the most
splendid of continental kingdoms, who had come to England
to negotiate the marriage of Catherine of Arragon with
the Prince of Wales, and who continued his journey to
Scotland with letters of amity from his sovereigns for James,
and with the object of assisting in the peacemaking between
the two Kings. Henry required James to give up the pretender into his hands—a thing which of course it was not
consistent with honour to do—but it was evident that
the King of Scots had already in his own mind given up

the adventurer's cause. And after the negotiations had been concluded and peace made between England and Scotland, Perkin and his beautiful young wife and his train of followers set sail from Scotland in a little flotilla of three ships, intending it is said to go to Ireland, where he had been well received before coming to the Court of James The imagination follows with irrestrainable pity the forlorn voyage of this youthful band of adventurers : the young husband trained to all the manners and ways of thinking of a prince, however little reality there might be in his claims ; the young wife, mild and fair, the White Rose as she was called, with the best blood of Scotland in her veins ; the few noble followers, knights, and a lady or two who shared their fortunes, setting out vaguely to sea, not knowing where to go, with the world before them where to choose. When they got to Ireland Prince Perkin heard of an insurrection in Cornwall, and hastened to put himself at the head of it, placing his wife for security in the quaint fortress, among the waters, of St. Michael's Mount. But the insurrection came to nothing, and " the unfortunate prince or adventurer " was taken prisoner. He was pardoned it is said, but making a wild attempt at insurrection again, was this time tried and executed. His White Rose, most forlorn of ladies, was taken by King Henry from her refuge at the end of the world, placed in charge of the Queen, and never left the English Court again. There is no record that she and her husband were ever allowed to meet. So ends one of the saddest and most romantic of historical episodes.

This story takes up a large part of the early reign of James, who no doubt saw his error at the last, but in the beginning threw himself into Perkin's fortunes with characteristic impetuosity, and thought nothing too good, not even his own fair kinswoman, for the rescued prince. It was an error, however, that James shared with many high and mighty potentates who gave their imprimatur at first to the adventurer's cause. But even for the most genuine prince, when only a pretender, the greatest sovereigns are but poor supporters in the long run. James had a hundred things to

do to make him forget that unfortunate adventure of Perkin.
It was in the year 1497 that this incident ended so far as
the Scottish Court was concerned, and James returned to
the natural course of his affairs, not without occasional
tumults on the Border, but with no serious fighting anywhere for a course of pleasant years. The old traditional
strife between the King and the nobles no longer tore the
kingdom asunder. Perhaps the first great event of his
life, the waking up of his boyish conscience to find himself in the camp of a faction pitted against his own
father, influenced him throughout everything, and made
the duty of conciliation and union seem the first and most
necessary ; perhaps it was but the natural revulsion from
those methods which his father had adopted to his hurt
and downfall ; or perhaps James's chivalrous temper, his love
of magnificence and gaiety, made him feel doubly the advantage of courtiers who should be great nobles and his peers,
not dependants made splendid by his bounty. At all events
the King lived as no Stewart had yet lived, surrounded by
all without exception who were most noble in the land,
encouraging them to vie with him in splendour, in noble
exercises and pastimes, and almost, it may be imagined—with
a change of method, working by good example and genial
comradeship what his predecessors had vainly tried to do by
fire and sword—tempting them to emulate him also in preserving internal peace and a certain reign of justice throughout the country. There was no lack of barons in the Court
of James. Angus and Home and Huntly, who had pursued
his father to the death and placed himself upon the throne,
were not turned into subservient courtiers by his gallantry
and charm : but neither was there any one of these proud
lords in the ascendant, or any withdrawn and sullen in his
castle, taking no share in what was going on. The machinery
of the State worked as it had never done before. There
were few Parliaments, and not very much law-making.
Enough laws had been made under his predecessors, " if they
had but been kept," to form an ideal nation ; the thing to do
now was to charm, to persuade, to lead both populace and

nobility into respecting them.   It would be vain to imagine
that this high purpose was always in James's mind, or that
his splendour and gaieties were part of a plan for the better
regulation of the kingdom.   But that he was not without a
wise policy in following his own character and impulses, and
that the spontaneous good-fellowship and sympathy which
his frank, genial, and easy nature called forth everywhere
were not of admirable effect in the welding together of the
nation, it would be unjust to say.   If he had not the sterner
nobility of purpose which made the first of his name conceive
and partially carry into effect the ideal reign of justice which
was the first want of his kingdom, he had yet a noble
ambition for Scotland to make her honoured and feared and
famous, and the success with which he seems to have carried
out this object of his life for many years was great.   He
made the little northern kingdom known for a centre of
chivalry, courtesy, courage, and, what was more wonderful,
magnificence, as it had never been before.   He penetrated
that country with traditions and associations of himself in
the character always attractive to the imagination, of that
prince of good fellows, the wandering stranger, who came
in unknown and sought the hospitality of farmer or ploughman, and made the humble board ring with wit and jest,
and who thereafter was discovered by sudden gift, or grace,
or unexpected justice, to be the King :—

" He took a bugle from his side, and blew both loud and shrill,
    And four and twenty belted knights came trooping owre the hill ; "

" Then he took out his little knife, let a' his duddies fa',
    And he was the brawest gentleman that was among them a'."

The goodman of Ballangeich,[1] the jovial and delightful
Gaberlunzie, the hero of many a homely ballad and adventure, some perhaps a trifle over free, yet none involving any
tragic treachery or betrayal, James was the playfellow of

[1] This name and assumed character is generally supposed to belong to James V :
but all the accompanying circumstances seem to point so much more to what is
recorded of James IV, that I venture to attribute them to him.   If it is an error
there is this, at least, to be said in favour of it, that the story is as applicable to
one as to the other monarch.

his people, the Haroun al Raschid of Scotch history. "By
this doing the King heard the common brute (bruit) of himself." Thus he won not only the confidence of the nobles
but the genial sympathy and kindness of the poor. A
minstrel, a poet too in his way, a man curious about all
handicrafts, famous in all exercises, "ane singular good
chirurgian, so that there was none of that profession if they
had any dangerous case in hand but would have craved his
advice"—he had every gift that was most likely to commend
him to the people, who were proud of a king so unlike other
kings, the friend of all. And nothing could exceed the
activity of the young monarch, always occupied for the glory
of Scotland whatever he was doing. It was he who built the
great ship, the *Michael*, which was the greatest wonder ever
seen in the northern seas ; a ship which took all the timber
in Fife to build her (the windswept Kingdom of Fife has
never recovered that deprivation) besides a great deal from
Norway, with three hundred mariners to work her, and
carrying "ane thousand men of warre" within those solid
sides, which, all wooden as they were, could resist cannon shot.
"This ship lay in the road, and the King took great pleasure
every day to come down and see her," and would dine and
sup in her, and show his lords all her order and provisions.
No doubt there were many curious parties from Edinburgh
who followed the King to see that new wonder, and that
groups would gather on the ramparts of the castle to point
out on the shining Firth the great and lofty vessel, rising like
another castle out of the depths. James had also the other
splendid taste, which his unfortunate father had shared, of
building, and set in order the castle at Falkland in the heart
of the green and wealthy Fife—where there was great hunting
and coursing, and perhaps as yet not much high farming
in those days—and continued the adornments of Stirling,
already so richly if rudely decorated in the previous reign.

But Edinburgh was the centre of all the feasting and
splendour which distinguished his time. The lists were
set before the castle gates, on that lofty and breezy plateau
where all the winds blow. Sometimes there were bands of

foreign chivalry breaking lances with the high Scottish nobles according to all the stately laws of that mimic war ; sometimes warriors of other conditions, fighting Borderers or Highlanders, would meet for an encounter of arms, ending in deadly earnest, which was not discouraged, as we are told with grim humour, since it was a gain to the realm to be disembarrassed of these champions at any cost, and the best way was that they should kill each other amicably and have no rancour against Justiciar or King.   Among the foreign guests who visited James was Bernard Stuart of Aubigny, Monsieur Derbine, as Pitscottie calls him, the representative of a branch of the royal race which had settled in France, whom James received, his kinsman being an old man, with even more than his usual grace, making him the judge in all feats of chivalry " at justing and tourney, and calling him father of warres, because he was well practised in the same."   Another of the visitors, Don Pedro d'Ayala, the Spanish grandee who helped to conduct the quarrel over Perkin Warbeck to a great issue, wrote to his royal master a description of King James, which is highly interesting, and full of unconscious prophecy.   The Spaniard describes the young monarch at twenty-five as one of the most accomplished and gallant of cavaliers, speaking Latin (very well), French, German, Flemish, Italian, and Spanish ; a good Christian and Catholic, hearing two masses every morning ; fond of priests—a somewhat singular quality unless such jovial priests and boon-companions as Dunbar, the poet-friar, were the subject of this preference ; though perhaps the seriousness which mingled with his jollity, the band of iron under his silken vest, led him to seek by times the charm of graver company, the mild and learned Gavin Douglas and other scholars in the monasteries, where thought and learning had found refuge.   The following details, which are highly characteristic, bring him before us with singular felicity, and, as afterwards turned out, with a curious foreseeing of those points in him which brought about his tragical end.

" Rarely even in joking a word escapes him which is not the truth. He prides himself much upon it, and says it does not seem to him well

for kings to swear their treaties as they do now. The oath of a king
should be his royal word as was the case in bygone ages. He is
courageous even more than a king should be. I have seen him even
undertake most dangerous things in the late wars. I sometimes clung
to his skirts and succeeded in keeping him back. On such occasions
he does not take the least care of himself. He is not a good captain,
because he begins to fight before he has given his orders. He said to
me that his subjects serve him with their persons and goods, in just or
unjust quarrels, exactly as he likes; and that therefore he does not
think it right to begin any warlike undertaking without being himself the
first in danger. His deeds are as good as his words. For this reason,
and because he is a very humane prince, he is much loved."

The perfect reason yet profound unreasonableness of this
quality in James, so fatally proved in his after history, is
very finely discriminated by the writer, who evidently had
come under the spell of a most attractive personality in this
young sovereign, so natural and manful, so generous and
true. That James should acknowledge the penalty of the
fatal power he had to draw a whole nation into his quarrel,
just or unjust, by risking himself the first, is so entirely just
according to every rule of personal honour, yet so wildly
foolish according to all higher policy; exposing that very
nation to evils so much greater than the worst battle.
Flodden was still far off in the darkness of the unknown,
but had this description been written after that catastrophe,
it could not more clearly have disclosed the motives and
magnanimity but tragic unwisdom of this prince of romance.

The Spaniard adds much praise of James's temperance,
a virtue indifferently practised by his subjects, and of his
morality, which is still more remarkable. The amours and
intrigues of his youth, Don Pedro informs his king, this
young hero had entirely renounced, "or so at least it is
believed," partly "from fear of God, and partly from fear of
scandal," which latter "is thought very much of here"—a
curious touch, which would seem to indicate a magnificent
indifference to public opinion, not shared by the little
northern Court, in the haughtier circles of Madrid. The
picture is perhaps a little flattered; and it is hard to
imagine how James could have picked up so many languages
in the course of what some writers call a neglected educa-

BAKEHOUSE CLOSE

tion, confined to Scotland alone ; but perhaps his father's fondness for clever artificers and musicians may have made him familiar in his childhood with foreign dependants, more amusing to a quick-witted boy than the familiar varlets who had no tongue but " braid Scots." " The King speaks besides," says Ayala, " the language of the savages who live in some parts of Scotland and in the islands " ; clearly in every sense of the word a man of endless accomplishments and personal note, quite beyond the ordinary of kings.

At no time, according to unanimous testimony, had Scotland attained so high a position of national wealth, comfort, and prosperity. The wild Highlands had been more or less subdued by the forfeiture of the traditionary Lord of the Isles, and the final subjection of that lawless region, nominally at least, to the King's authority, and with every precaution for the extension of justice and order to its farthest limits. A navy had suddenly sprung into being, signalising itself in its very birth by brilliant achievements and consisting of vessels few indeed, but of exceptional size and splendour, as great for their time as the great Italian ironclads are for this, and like them springing from something of the bravado as well as for the real uses of a rapidly growing power. And there had been peace, save for that little passage of arms on account of Perkin Warbeck, throughout all the reign of James—peace to which the warlike Scots seem to have accustomed themselves very pleasantly, notwithstanding that on the one side of the Border as on the other there was nothing so popular as war between the neighbour nations ; but the exploits of Sir Andrew Wood with his *Yellow Carvel*, and the *Great Michael* lying there proudly on the Firth, ready to sweep the seas, afforded compensation for the postponement of other struggles.

It was in these circumstances that the negotiations for James's marriage with the little Margaret, Princess Royal of England, and in every way, as it turned out, a true Tudor, though then but an undeveloped child, took place. The gallant young King, then seven or eight and twenty, in the

plenitude of his manhood, was not anxious for the bride of
ten persistently offered to him by her royal father ; and the
negotiations lagged, and seemed to have gone on *à plusieurs
reprises* for several years.   But at length by the persistent
efforts of Henry VII, who saw all the advantages of the
union, and no doubt also of councillors on the Scots side,
who felt that the continued prosperity of the country was
best secured by peace, it was brought about in 1504, when
James must have been just over thirty and Margaret was
twelve—a very childish bride, but probably precocious, and
not too simple or ignorant, as belonged to her violent
Tudor blood.   He " was married with her solemnedlie by
the advice of the nobilitie of England and Scotland, and
gatt great summes of money with her : and promise of peace
and unity made and ordained to stand between the two
realms," says Pitscottie.   The great sums, however, seem
problematical, as the dower of Margaret was not a very
large one, and the sacrifices made for her were considerable
—the town of Berwick being given up to England as one
preliminary step.   The event, however, was one of incalculable importance to both nations, securing as it did the
eventual consolidation in one of the realm of Great Britain,
though nobody as yet foresaw that great consequence
that might follow.   Along with the marriage treaty was
made one of perpetual peace between England and Scotland
—a treaty indeed not worth the paper it was written upon,
yet probably giving comfort to some sanguine spirits.
Had the prudent old monarch remained on the throne
of England as long as James ruled in Scotland it might
indeed never have been broken ; but Henry was already
old, and his son as hot-headed as the cousin and traditionary adversary now turned into a brother.   Margaret
was conveyed into Scotland with the utmost pomp, and
Edinburgh roused itself and put on decorations like a bride
to receive the little maiden, so strangely young to be the
centre of all these rejoicings : her lofty houses covered with
flutterings of tapestries and banners and every kind of gay
decoration, and her windows filled with bright faces, coifs,

and veils, and embroideries of gold that shone in the sun.
The dress worn by James, as he carried his young bride
into Edinburgh seated on horseback behind him, is fully
described for the benefit of after ages. He wore a jacket
of cloth of gold bordered with purple velvet, over a doublet
of purple satin, showing at the neck the collar of a shirt
embroidered with pearls and gold, with scarlet hose to
complete the resplendent costume. At his marriage he wore
a jacket of crimson satin over a doublet of cloth of gold,
with the same scarlet hose, and a gown of white damask
brocaded with gold over all. No doubt the ladies were
not behind in this contest of brave apparel. Grey Edinburgh, accustomed this long time to the dull tones of
modern habiliments, sparkled and shone in those days of
finery and splendour. The streets were meant for such fine
shows ; its stairheads and strong deep doorways to relieve
the glories of sweet colour, plumes, and jewels. When
the lists were set on the summit of the hill, the gates thrown
up, the garrison in their steel caps and breastplates lining
the bars, and perhaps the King himself tilting in the mêlée,
while all the ladies were throned in their galleries like banks
of flowers, what a magnificent spectacle! The half-empty
streets below still humming with groups of gazers not able
to squeeze among the throngs about the bars, but waiting
the return of the splendid procession : and more and more
banners and tapestries and guards of honour shining through
the wide open gates of the port all the way down to Holyrood. There was nothing but holiday-making and pleasure
while the feasting lasted and the bridal board was yet spread.

While this heyday of life lasted and all was bright
around and about the chivalrous James, there was a
certain suitor of his Court, a merry and reckless priest, more
daring in words and admixtures of the sacred and the profane
than any mere layman would venture to be, whose familiar
and often repeated addresses to the King afford us many
glimpses into the royal surroundings and ways of living, as
also many pictures of the noisy and cheerful mediæval town
which was the centre of pleasures, of wit and gay con-

versation, and all that was delightful in Scotland. Dunbar's
title of fame is not so light as this. He was one of the
greatest of the followers of Chaucer, a master of melody, in
some points scarcely inferior to the master himself whose
praise he celebrates as

> " Of oure Inglisch all the light
> Surmounting every tong terrestrial
> Alls far as Mayis morrow dois mydnyght."

But it is unnecessary here to discuss the " Thrissil and
the Rois," the fine music of the epithalamium with which he
celebrated the coming of Margaret Tudor into Scotland, or
the more visionary splendour of the " Golden Targe." The
poet himself was not so dignified or harmonious as his verse.
He possessed the large open-air relish of life, the broad
humour, sometimes verging on coarseness, which from the
time of James I. to that of Burns has been so singularly
characteristic of Scots poetry : and found no scene of contemporary life too humble or too ludicrous for his genius—
thus his more familiar poems are better for our purpose than
his loftier productions, and show us the life and fashion of
his town and time better than anything else can do. This
is one, for example, in which he upbraids " the merchantis of
renown " for allowing " Edinburgh their nobil town " to
remain in the state in which he describes it :—

> " May nane pass through your principall gates
> For stink of haddocks and of skates,
> For cryin' of carlines and debates,
> For fensome flytings of defame.
> > Think ye not shame
> Before strangers of all estates
> That sic dishonour hurt your name ?

> ' Your stinkand schule that standis dirk
> Halds the light from your Parroche Kirk,
> Your forestairs makis your houses mirk
> Like na country but here at hame
> > Think ye not shame,
> Sa little policie to work
> In hurt and sklander of your name ?

> " At your hie Croce, where gold and silk
> Should be, there is but curds and milk,
> And at your Tron but cokill and wilk,
> Pansches, puddings, of Jok and Jame.
>   Think ye not shame
> Sin as the world sayis that ilk
> In hurt and sklander of your name ?"

Thus old Edinburgh rises before us, beautiful and brave as she is no longer, yet thronged about the Netherbow Port, and up towards the Tron, the weighing-place and centre of city life, with fishwives and their stalls, with rough booths for the sale of rougher food, and with country lasses singing curds and whey, as they still did when Allan Ramsay nearly four hundred years after succeeded Dunbar as laureate of Edinburgh. Notwithstanding, however, these defects the Scottish capital continued to be the home of all delights to the poet-priest. When his King was absent at Stirling, Dunbar in the pity of his heart sang an (exceedingly profane) litany for the exile that he might be brought back, prefacing it by the following compassionate strain :—

> " We that are here in Hevinis glory
> To you that are in Purgatory
> Commendis us on our hairtly wyiss,
> I mean we folk in Paradyis,
> In Edinburgh with all merriness
> To you in Strivilling in distress,
> Where neither pleasance nor delyt is,
> For pity thus ane Apostle wrytis.

> " O ye Heremeitis and Hankersaidillis
> That takis your penance at your tabillis,
> And eitis nocht meit restorative
> Nor drinkis no wyne comfortative
> Bot aill, and that is thyn and small,
> With few courses into your hall ;
> But (without) company of lordis or knights
> Or any other goodly wightis,
> Solitar walkand your allone
> Seeing no thing but stok and stone,
> Out of your powerfull Purgatory
> To bring you to the bliss of glory
> Of Edinburgh the merry toun,

> We sall begin ane cairfull soun,
> And Dirige devout and meik
> The Lord of bliss doing besiek
> You to delyvre out of your noy
> And bring you soon to Edinburgh joy,
> For to be merry among us,
> And so the Dirige begynis thus."

Many are the poet's addresses to the King in happier circumstances when James is at home and in full enjoyment of these joys of Edinburgh.   His prayers for a benefice are sometimes grave and sometimes comic, but never-failing. He describes solicitors (or suitors) at Court, all pushing their fortune, "Some singis, some dancis, some tells storyis." Some try to make friends by their devotion, some have their private advocates in the King's chamber, some flatter, some play the fool—

> " My simpleness among the lave
> Wist of na way so God me save,
> But with ane humble cheer and face
> Referris me to the Kyngis grace,
> Methinks his gracious countenance
> In ryches is my sufficence."

Not always so patient, however, he jogs James's memory with a hundred remedies.   " God gif ye war Johne Thomsounis man !" he cries with rueful glee through a lively set of verses—

> " For war it so than weill were me
> Bot (without) benefice I wald not be ;
> My hard fortune war endit then
>   God gif ye war Johne Thomsounis man !"

John Thomson's man was, according to the popular saying, a man who did as his wife told him ; and Dunbar was strong in the Queen's favour.   Therefore happy had been his fate had James been of this character.   We cannot, however, follow the poet through all his pleadings and witty appeals and remonstrances, until at last in despairing jest he commends " the gray horse Auld Dunbar " to his Majesty, and draws or seems to draw at last a consolatory reply, which is thus recorded at the end of the poem under the title of " Responsio Regis."

> " Efter our writtingis, Treasurer
>   Tak in this gray horse, Auld Dunbar,
>   Which in my aucht with service trew
>   In lyart changit is his heu.
>   Gar house him now against this Yuill
>   And busk him like ane Bischoppis muill,
>   For with my hand I have indorst
>   To pay whatever his trappouris cost."

Whether this response was really from James's hand or was but another wile of the eager suitor it is impossible to tell : but he did eventually have a pension granted him of twenty pounds Scots a year, until such time as a benefice of at least fifty pounds should fall to him ; so that he was kept in hope. After this Dunbar tunes forth a song of welcome to " his ain Lord Thesaurair," in which terror at this functionary's inopportune absence—since quarterday we may suppose—is lost in gratulations over his return. " Welcome," he cries—

> " Welcome my benefice and my rent
>   And all the lyflett to me lent,
>   Welcome my pension most preclair,
>   Welcome my awin Lord Thesaurair."

Thus the reckless and jolly priest carols.   A little while after he has received his money he sings " to the Lordes of the King's Chacker," or Exchequer—

> " I cannot tell you how it is spendit,
>   But weel I wat that it is ended."

These peculiarities, however, it need not be said do not belong entirely to the sixteenth century.   The reader will find a great deal of beautiful poetry among the works of Dunbar.   These lighter verses serve our purpose in showing once more how perennial has been this vein of humorous criticism, and frank fun and satire, in Scotland, in all ages, and in throwing also a broad and amusing gleam of light upon Edinburgh in the early fifteen hundreds, the gayest and most splendid moment perhaps of her long history.

All these splendours, however, were hard to keep up, and though Edinburgh and Scotland throve, the King's finances after a while seem to have begun to fail, and there was great talk of a pilgrimage to the Holy Land—it is supposed by the historians as a measure of securing that the King might not have the uncomfortable alternative of cutting short his splendours at home. This purpose, if it was gravely entertained at all, and not one of the proposals of change with which, when need comes, the impecunious of all classes and ages amuse themselves to put off actual retrenchment, never came to anything. And very soon there arose complications of various natures which threw all Christendom into an uproar. Henry VIII, young, arrogant, and hotheaded, succeeded his prudent father in England, and the treaty with the Scots which made, or seemed to make, England safe on the Borders, gave the English greater freedom in dealing with the other hereditary foe on the opposite side of the Channel ; while France on her side began to use all possible efforts to draw from the English alliance the faithful Scots, who had always been the means of a possible diversion, always ready to carry fire and flame across the Border, and call back the warring English to look after their own affairs. James, with perhaps his head slightly turned by his own magnificence and the prosperity that had attended him since the beginning of his career, seemed to have imagined that he was important enough to play the part of peacemaker among the nations of Europe. And there are many embassies recorded of a bustling bishop, Andrew Forman, who seems for some time to have pervaded Christendom, now at Rome, now at Paris, now in London, with various confused negotiations. It was a learned age, and the King himself, as has been seen, had very respectable pretensions in this way ; but that there was another side to the picture, and that notwithstanding the translator of Virgil, the three Universities now established in Scotland, and many men of science and knowledge both in

the priesthood and out of it, there remained a strong body
of ignorance and rudeness, even among the dignified clergy
of the time, the following story, which Pitscottie tells with
much humour of Bishop Forman, James's chosen diplomatist,
will show.

"This bishop made ane banquet to the Pope and all his cardinals in
one of the Pope's own palaces, and when they were all set according to
their custom, that he who ought (owned) the house for the time should
say the grace, and he was not ane good scholar, nor had not good Latin,
but begane ruchlie in the Scottise fashione, saying Benedicite, believing
that they should have said Dominus, but they answered Deus in the
Italian fashioun, which put the bishop by his intendment (beyond his
understanding), that he wist not well how to proceed fordward but
happened in good Scottis in this manner, saying, what they understood
not, 'The devil I give you all false cardinals to, in nomine Patris, Filii,
et Spiritus Sancti, Amen.' Then all the bishop's men leuch, and all the
cardinals themselves; and the Pope inquired whereat they leuch, and
the bishop showed that he was not ane good clerk, and that the cardinals
had put him by his text and intendment, therefore he gave them all to the
devil in good Scottis, whereat the Pope himself leuch verrie earnestlie."

This did not prevent his Holiness, probably delighted with
such a racy visitor, from making Forman Legate of Scotland ;
and it is to be feared that the meddling diplomatist with
his want of education, was perhaps a better example of the
clergy of Scotland, who about this time began to be the mark
of all assailants as illiterate, greedy, vicious, and rapacious,
than such a gentle soul as the other poet of the age, afterwards bishop of Dunkeld, the one mild and tranquil possessor
of the great Douglas name.

The imbroglio of events into which it is unnecessary for
us to enter grew more and more complicated year by year,
until at length it came to be a struggle between France and
England for the ally who could be of most assistance to
the one in the special way of injuring the other, and whom it
was of the first advantage to both to secure. James was bound
by the treaty of permanent peace which he had made at his
marriage, and by that marriage itself, and no doubt the strong
inclination of his wife, to England ; but he was bound to
France by a traditionary bond of a much stronger kind, by
the memory of long friendship and alliance, and the per-

sistent policy of his kingdom and race. The question was
modified besides by other circumstances. England was, as
she had but too often been, but never before in James's experience—harsh, overbearing, and unresponsive: while France,
as was also her wont, was tender, flattering, and pertinacious.
Henry refused or delayed to pay Queen Margaret a legacy
of jewels and plate left to her by her father, and at the same
time protected certain Borderers who had murdered a Scottish
knight, and defended them against justice and James, while
still summoning him to keep his word and treaty in respect
to England; while on the other hand not only the King but
the Queen of France appealed to James, he as to an ancient
ally, she as to her sworn knight, to break that artificial
alliance with his haughty brother-in-law. It may well have
been that James in his own private soul had no more desire
for such a tremendous step than the nobles who struggled
to the last against it. But he had *les défauts de ses qualités*
in a high degree. He was nothing if not a knight of romance.
And though, as the poet has said—

> " His own Queen Margaret, who in Lithgow's bower
>   All silent sat, and wept the weary hour,"

might be more to him than the politic Anne of France, or
any fair lady in his route, it was not in him, a paladin of
chivalry, the finest of fine gentlemen, the knight-errant of
Christendom, to withstand a lady's appeal. Perhaps, besides,
he was weary of his inaction, the only prince in Europe
who was not inevitably involved in the fray; weary of
holding tourneys and building ships (some of which had
been lately taken by the English, turning the tables upon
him) and keeping quiet, indulging in the inglorious arts of
peace, while everybody else was taking the field. And
Henry was arrogant and exasperating, so that even his own
sister was at the end of her brief Tudor patience; and
Louis was flattering, caressing, eloquent. When that last
embassage of chivalry came with the ring from Anne's own
finger, and the charge to ride three miles on English ground
for her honour, it was the climax of many arguments. " He

loves war," the Spaniard had said.   " War is profitable to him
and to the country "—a curious and pregnant saying.   James
would seem to have struggled at least a little against all
the impulses which were pushing him forward to his doom.

WHITE HORSE CLOSE

He promised a fleet to his lady in France for her aid—a
fleet foolishly if not treacherously handled by Arran, and
altogether diverted from its intended end ; finally, that
having failed, James flung away all precaution and yielded

to the tide of many influences which was carrying him
away.

It is needless to tell over again the tale that everybody
knows : how both heaven and hell were stirred by this ill-
omened undertaking ; how an aged saint, venerable and
stately, suddenly appeared out of the crowd when the King
was at his prayers in the Cathedral of Linlithgow, with a
message from on high ; and how when James had gone
back to Holyrood, the High Street of Edinburgh resounded
in the dead of night with trumpet note and herald's call
from the grim Hades of mediæval imagination, summoning
by name a long list of the Scottish nobility, of whom one
man defied the portent and refused the call and was
saved. James paid no heed to these warnings, whether
supernatural or otherwise, or perhaps was too far committed
to give any heed to them, carried away by the wild and
fatal stream which had caught his feet, with something of
that extraordinary impetus of natural tendency long restrained
which acts with tenfold force when at last yielded to.   It
is unnecessary either to tell the story of all the foolish fatal
lingerings upon the ill-omened way: trifling with treacherous
ladies for whom he cared nothing, cartels from Surrey ; the
abandonment of a strong position, lest it should give him an
advantage, in ever greater and greater folly of chivalry: the
refusal to attack, or let his artillery attack, till his foes were
all safely over the bridge : all exhibitions of high honour
gone mad with the intoxication of fate.   The Spaniard's
letter comes back in full significance as we watch with aching
hearts the fatal fray.   " He said to me that his subjects
serve him with their persons and goods, in just or unjust
quarrels, exactly as he wishes, and that therefore he does
not think it right to begin any warlike undertaking without
being himself the first in danger."   The knight-errant kept
his *consigne* of honour to the last.   He betrayed his people to
the most utter defeat they had ever encountered, but he was
himself the first victim.

Thus died the only Stewart king who ever seemed to have
a fair prospect of escaping the fate of his unfortunate race.

The worm in his conscience, the iron belt round his body, were perhaps only symptoms of a susceptible nature, of remorse which was excessive for the bewildered acquiescence in rebellion of an unawakened mind and an irresponsible age. And his life, if soiled by errors which were then and are now but lightly thought of in a prince, was in all public matters noble, honourable, and enlightened, with always the advantage of his country for its aim, even in the midst of the natural gaieties and extravagances of a happy temper and exuberant energy. He was extravagant, light-hearted, a lover of magnificence and display, all of which things, in the face of the political economist, sometimes prove themselves excellent for a country when the moment comes to press it forward into the ranks of high civilisation out of a ruder and more primitive development. The nobility with which his father struggled to the death he held in a leash of silk or of gold, often making them the instruments of the justice which they had so long resisted. There was peace in his time such as had never before been in Scotland, and redress of grievances, and extinction or suppression of mortal feuds and intestine struggles. It is sometimes given to a man in all light-heartedness, in what seems the spontaneous way of his own impulses and pleasures, to do what is best for his surroundings and his time, without any apparent strain of self-sacrifice or gravity of duty. James Stewart, the fourth of his name, was one of these happy and beautiful natures : and though his life was one of almost unbroken prosperity and brightness, yet no man can say that his stewardry was not nobly held, and to the benefit of his kingdom and people. But not for this was the doom to pass by. The brightness and the prosperity came to an end in a sudden folly, infatuation, and madness, which belonged to him as his sunny nature did and his generosity of heart. And it was no evil chance, but the principle of his life, as we have seen, that in the calamity into which he drew his people he himself should be the first to fall.

CHAPTER V

THE course of Scottish history during the fifteenth and beginning of the sixteenth century is like that of a ship on a long voyage, full of vicissitudes and adventures. The little barque amid all the wild commotions of the sea, sometimes driven before the wind, sometimes stripped of every rag of canvas, sometimes beating helpless in the trough of the waves, rights herself when the storm is over, repairs her masts, re-strings her cordage, puts forth again sail after sail ; and with a sure hand at the helm and a moderate breeze in her canvas, rises white and strong against the blueness of sea and sky, triumphant over all the assaults of external nature, animated by human will and courage, the most indomitable of all created things, and affording perhaps the best example of the survival and unconquerable power of these masters of the world : till again there arises in the heavens another hurricane, furious, ungovernable, rousing the sea to madness, striking once more the canvas from the yards, the masts from the deck, and leaving a mere hulk at the mercy of the waves which rush on her and over her with the wild rage of beasts of prey. Again and again these storms overtook the vessel of the State in Scotland, returning after every period of calm, after every recovery of authority, as wild, as tumultuous, as destructive as ever. Again and again they were overcome, the power of resistance restored, the equilibrium regained, only to fall once more into the raging of the elements. Each successive king,

SALISBURY CRAGS

with perhaps one exception, had seized the helm as soon as
his hand was fit for the strain, or even before it was strong
enough for that office, and had gallantly brought the ship
round and re-established the reign of a rational will and a
certain unity of command over all the forces of the storms ;
but when he fell, left the helpless vessel again to be balloted
about by all the winds of Fate.

This was the case almost more wildly than ever when
the fourth James Stewart died at Flodden.   The heir, the
helpless infant prince, was not two years old, and the flower
of Scotland had been slain with their king.   The mature
warriors and statesmen, the wise counsellors, the men to
whom the country might have looked in such an interregnum, were all gone.   There remained only Churchmen and
boys in the devastated country, a passionate English queen
of Tudor blood, and no settled centre of government or
reorganised power.   Such lords as were left assembled
hastily for that pathetic oft-repeated ceremony, the crowning
of the child, taken out of his cradle to have the fatal circlet
put upon his head—and committed some sort of regency,
such as it was, to the Queen.   And after a moment in
which the country was paralysed with woe and every house
full of mourning, Scotland plunged once more into the angry
waves, among the lions of ever-recurring anarchy and strife.

Nothing in all this turbulent and terrible history has ever
been so tragic as Flodden.   The nation which had lost the
very flower and strength of its fighting men, its defenders
and champions, the families which had lost their chiefs, their
breadwinners—often father and son together, the master and
his heir—were struck dumb with dismay and anguish.   It
was only a long time after, when despair had sunk into a
softened recollection, that it was possible even to breathe
forth that wail over the Flowers of the Forest which all
Scotland knows.   In the first shock of such an appalling
event there is no place for elegy.   There was a broken cry
of anguish throughout the country, echoed from castle and
cottage, where the poor women clung together, mistress and
maid equal in the flood of common loss : and there was at

the same time a strained and terrible rallying of all the poor
defenders left, the old men and rusty arms, those of every
house upon the Border and every town upon the road who
had been left behind, to meet as well as they could the no
doubt inevitable march of the conquering English army,
which everybody felt sure must follow. When the news
reached Edinburgh the magistrates of the town put forth a
proclamation calling upon the inhabitants to prepare for
the defence of the capital, and forbidding the women—a
most significant and heartrending order, perhaps unique
in public documents—to spread dismay through the streets
by their crying and lamentations. The condition into
which the community must have fallen when this became a
public danger it is unnecessary to remark upon. The wail
that sounded through all the country must have risen to a
passionate pitch in those crowded streets, where the gates
were closed and all the defences set, and nothing looked for
but the approach of the victorious English with swords still
dripping with Scottish blood. While Edinburgh waited
breathless for this possible attack an extension of the existing wall was begun to defend the southern suburb, then
semi-rural, containing the country-houses of the wealthy
burghers and lawyers, the great convent of the Greyfriars,
that of St. Mary in the Field, and many other monastic
houses. This additional wall greatly increased the breadth
of the *enceinte*, which now included a considerable space of
embowered and luxuriant fields on the south side. It was
called the Flodden Wall, and kept the memory of that great
catastrophe and disaster before the minds of the citizens
for many a day.

But for some reason or other the English army which
had cut Scotland to pieces at Flodden went no farther.
The victory was no doubt a very costly one, and perhaps
Henry VIII did not wish to drive the kingdom of which
his sister would now be Regent to extremity, or do
anything more to increase the desperate hostility of a
country which was capable of giving him so much trouble.
At all events Surrey's army was disbanded, and Scotland

was left to resume her struggle within herself: which proved
the wildest and most miserable turmoil and anarchy which
her troubled records had yet known.

It would be at once hopeless and unnecessary to enter
into any sketch of the endless tumults of this time of distress. There was a momentary lull in which, though all the
old personal feuds arose again, the poor little King and his
mother were left undisturbed—she in possession of a regency
more or less nominal, and in a state of health which must
have subdued her activities, for her second son was not
born till several months after her husband's death. But this
child was only a few months old when Margaret, young,
beautiful, impassioned, and impetuous, compromised her
position by a sudden marriage with the young Earl of
Angus—still almost a boy, and with nothing but his good
looks to recommend him—an event which at once aroused
all sleeping enmities and precipitated the usual struggle for
the possession of the infant king. I will attempt nothing
but an indication of one or two scenes in Edinburgh which
took place during this struggle. Undeterred by the evil
associations which surrounded that name, the Scottish lords
bethought themselves of the French Duke of Albany, the
nearest member of the royal family, the son of that duke
who had been the terror of James III, who had conspired
with England, and who finally had established himself in
France and died there. His son was a French subject, the
son of a French mother, inheriting through her great estates
in France and a position which was little inferior in dignity,
and much superior in comfort, to that of the harassed monarch of a most turbulent kingdom. But he was James
Stewart, the nearest in blood to the crown, and his name
seems, temporarily at least, to have united all parties, even
the Queen, though his presence was fatal to her claims of
regency, receiving him with courtesy and an apparent welcome.
He had not been many months, however, in Scotland before,
with the sanction of his council, he claimed from Margaret
the possession of the King and his brother—sending four
peers, appointed guardians, to the castle, to receive the

children. It was in July 1515, two years after Flodden, when no doubt Edinburgh had regained that common cheerfulness and bustle of a great town which is so little interrupted even by the gravest public events. The deputation with their attendants proceeded from the Canongate, where they had been sitting in assembly, through the Netherbow Port and the bustling crowded High Street, to the castle, no doubt gathering with them on their way all the eager crowd which could free itself from shop or booth, all the passers-by in the streets, a continually-increasing throng. Who the four lords were we are not told. The whole incident is recorded in a letter of Lord Dacre to the English Council. No doubt he had his information either from the Queen herself or from members of her household. Of the four men chosen by Albany the Queen was at liberty to reject one, and no doubt they were men of weight and gravity, probably not unworthy of the trust.

It is not difficult to realise the flying rumour which would go like the wind before them announcing their errand, and how windows and doorways and stairheads would fill with eager spectators, and all the moving population would press up the hill after them to see what was to be seen. The high houses full on every story of eager heads thrust forth, relieving with unintentional yet lively decoration the many-windowed fronts, the shopkeepers crowding at their doors or seizing cap and halberd to follow, the hum and excitement of the roused town, surround the envoys like the background of a picture. Most probably they went on foot, the distance being so short, preceded by glittering herald and pursuivant—perhaps David Lindsay, who can tell? still too young to wear the Lion of Scotland on his tabard, but keen and curious to see this scene—he who had seen the envoy of heaven in Linlithgow Church and so many other wonderful things. The crowd surged upwards, keeping a respectful space in the midst for the lords with their train, and filled with colour and movement and the murmuring of numbers that great square before the castle gates which had held the same excited throng so often. And before the

heralds could summon the wardens or demand entrance in the
name of the Regent, the great gates rolled back, and all who
were near enough to see gazed in amazement at such a group
in the gateway as must have filled many eyes with tears,
and which gave at once the most astonishing climax to that
wonderful picture.   There Margaret stood, a young woman
of twenty-five, not a noble type of beauty, perhaps, but with
the fresh and florid Tudor good looks, and no doubt the
imperious Tudor port imposing to the crowd, with her child
in his little cloak and plumed bonnet, four years old, holding her hand.   Among her little troop of attendants, the
ladies of her subdued Court, and the cluster of cavaliers who
surrounded her young husband, there might well be another
name of gentler fame—the then Provost of St. Giles, Gawin
Douglas, poet and statesman, who was her counsellor and the
negotiator of her many troubled affairs.   But in this emergency it was the Queen herself who bade the startled lords
stand and deliver their message.   They stepped forward in
some confusion, one would guess, not having calculated upon
this sudden encounter with such an unexpected champion,
difficult to silence—not only a queen with all the prestige
both real and sentimental which surrounds such a position,
but also a mother whose children were threatened.   When
they had finished their explanation, the crowd looking on, no
doubt impatient of the pause and of the voices that could
not reach their ears, Margaret stepped back and bade her
attendants quickly to let down the portcullis.   They must
have been stationed ready with the intention, and no doubt
the lords had no attendants with them who could have
hindered any such step or forced an entrance.   While the
people looked on wondering, the iron bars came crashing
down, and in a moment the Queen and her child were safe
though visible within.   Then Margaret addressed through
that iron trellis the astonished deputation.   She told them
that she was the guardian of the castle, enfeoffed in it by
her royal husband, and not minded to yield it to any
man, but that she respected the Parliament and country,
and would take six days to consider the demand made

to her. The lords left outside had no alternative but to turn and go back, not we may be sure without a chorus of commentaries from the lively crowd, ever quick to note the discomfiture of its masters, and delighted with such a novel sensation : though the grave burghers would shake their heads at the boldness of the Englishwoman who had so confronted the Scots lords in their own city.

The Queen transferred herself and her children to Stirling before the six days had expired, but, as might be supposed, her little triumph was short-lived. Her boyish husband had already shown signs of deserting her, and probably enough her fancy for him was as short-lived as those other ephemeral and still more tragical passions which her brother had scarcely yet begun to indulge. The excuse which the Regent and his council put forth for taking the infant King from his mother was partly her second marriage, and partly a supposed plan for carrying off the two children to England, which did actually exist, King Henry being, as a matter of fact, their nearest of kin and most powerful possible guardian, though one who would have been vehemently rejected by all Scotland : while on the other hand the little James was as yet the most likely heir to the English crown. But this scheme had been opposed both by the Queen herself—whose statement that had she been a woman of humble condition she might have taken her children in her arms and gone unknown to her brother, but that, being a queen, she could not move anywhere without observation, is full of homely and natural dignity—and by Gawin Douglas, who repeats the same objection. Margaret, however, did not long continue to identify herself with the Douglases. The conduct of Angus gave her full reason for offence, if, perhaps, she was not altogether guiltless on her side ; and they were in a state of absolute estrangement when the calling of a Parliament early in the year 1520 brought Angus to Edinburgh, where with his party he had been sometimes master and sometimes proscribed man in the

innumerable variations of politics or rather of personal
quarrels and intrigues. Albany had by this time returned to France without however resigning his regency,
and authority was more or less represented by the Earl of
Arran, who was at the head of the opposite faction. The
party of Arran were in possession of Edinburgh and of
the little King, now eight years old, who was in the
castle under charge of the peers who had been appointed his
guardians, when Angus reappeared. Queen Margaret amid
all these tumults, finding little encouragement from her
brother, who was much more intent on securing a party in
Scotland than on consulting her wishes, had also chosen
to reside near her boy in the comparative safety of that
stronghold. Accordingly when Earl Angus came to attend
the Parliament he was confronted by his adversaries in
possession of the town and of the castle, with his wife,
the most violent adversary of all, in the fortress shut
up from his access or approach. He was accompanied,
Pitscottie tells us, "with all his kin and friends to the
number of five hundred spears, weill accompanied and
arrayed." But the city was hostile, and perhaps something
in the sombre air of all about awakened the suspicions of
the Douglases, especially as the gates were hastily shut
behind them and more than usual precautions taken.
Awakened thus to a sense of alarm, the threatened party
sent scouts out into the streets during the night, to find
out what mischief was brewing. While the humbler spies
pursued their inquiries by wynd and changehouse, Maister
Gawin Douglas, the bishop, went out to see what he could
discover of the real state of affairs—if it was true that the
westland lords had held a secret meeting and resolved that
Angus should not leave Edinburgh now that he had put
himself in their power—and "if he could find any gude way
betwixt the two parties." In pursuance of this anxious quest
he went in search of Archbishop James Beatoun, his brother
of St. Andrews, whom he found in the church of the Black
Friars, assisting, it is to be presumed, at some evening
service.

O

"The said Mr. Gawin desired him to take some pains to labour betwixt this two parties which was at ane sharp point, and meaning little less than that the bishop had most part the wyte (blame) thereof. But the bishop assured him again with ane oath, chopping on his breast, saying, ' By my conscience, my lord, I know not the matter.' But when Mr. Gawin heard the bishop's purgation, and chopping on his breast, and perceived the plates of his jack clattering, he thought the bishop deceaved him, so Mr. Gawin said to him, ' My lord, your conscience is not good, for I hear it clattering.' "

After all these advertisements—the bishop's secret coat of mail, the angry discussion between two Hamiltons in the very presence of Arran the head of the house, when he was himself willing to grant licence to Angus " to speak with the Queen's Grace and thereafter depart out of the town "—and all the lesser evidences of danger and conspiracy, the Earl and his band prepared themselves for the worst. " This young lord haisted him to his armour, and caused his friends and servants to do the same, and went right peartlie to the gate, and stood above the Nether Bow in arrayed battle." The other party, when they were made aware that the Douglases were standing on their defence, came rushing together from kirk and market, hastily assembling without discipline or order, to find the little mail-clad line arranged in the strongest way against the background of the houses, where, no doubt, every shopkeeper had rushed to his bolts and bars, and every door clanged to in view of the sudden tumult. Sir Walter has given us in *The Abbot* a glimpse more picturesque and graphic than any we can attempt, of the sudden scuffle in the street between two passing groups, the armed attendants more dangerous and less prudent than their masters, whose strife as to which was to hold the centre of the street was enough to produce at once an encounter of arms ending in blood, and death for some of the band. The struggle known by the name of " Clear the Causeway " was more important, yet of a similar kind. Angus and his five hundred spears—in reality a much greater number since each spear was accompanied by certain men-at-arms—had much the advantage of the other party, hurriedly roused from their occupations, who had expected

to make an easy end of the Douglases, thus betrayed
into a sort of ambush in a hostile city, where no man

REID'S CLOSE, CANONGATE

would lift a hand to help them. But the tables were
completely turned upon the Hamiltons and their supporters, when rushing "out of their lodging rudlie to the

gait in ane furious rage," the peaceable driven forward by
the taunts of the others, they found Angus and his spears in
full array of battle.   "When the Earl of Angus saw them
coming, and perceaved Sir Patrick Hamilton foremost, and
with him the Maister of Montgomerie, and saw them in sic
ane furie, he knew well there was nothing but fighting, and
cryed to his men to save Sir Patrick Hamilton if they might ;
but he came so far before the rest that he was slain hastilie,
and with him the Maister of Montgomerie, with sundry other
gentlemen, to the number of twelve score and twelve persons."
The end of the fray, which was "foughten very hardilie on
both sides ane long space," was that Arran's men were
driven down the side of the hill through the narrow wynds
that led from the High Street towards the wall, and thence
made their way out through some postern, or perhaps at the
gate near the Well-house Tower, where the little well of St.
Margaret now bubbles up unconsidered, and so across the
Nor' Loch, by boat or ford.   Bishop Beatoun, he whose
conscience clattered beneath his robes, fled again to the
Blackfriars Church, where Mr. Gawin had found him on
the previous evening prepared for mischief, and took
refuge there behind the altar, where he was pursued and
"his rockit rivin aff him, and had been slain," but that
Gawin Douglas, following the pursuers, perhaps with a sar-
castic satisfaction in setting forth the virtues of a peaceful
robe over the warlike covering that invited as well as preserved
from danger, interposed, saying, "It was shame to put hand
on ane consecreat bishop."   The encounter of these two
priests by evening and morning, the supercilious refusal of
the mail-clad bishop to interfere, and pretence of ignorance—
and, as one may imagine, the watch over him from afar of
his brother of Dunkeld with the full intention of peaceful
yet effective reprisals, throw a light of grim humour upon
the warlike scene.   Maister Gawin had no mail-coat, and
would not fight ; but he must have kept an eye upon his
natural foe through the fray, and it would be strange if he
had not some pleasure in perceiving the rochet, which
Beatoun must have donned hastily to save himself, pulled

over his head by rude hands in scorn of the priestly pretence—and some satisfaction in interposing to preserve the "consecreat bishop," whose behaviour was so little saintly.

"Thereafter the Earl of Angus passed to the castle and spoke with the Queen at his pleasure," says Pitscottie. It could not be a very gracious or affectionate interview. For Margaret and her husband had long before come to a complete breach, and the greatest desire in her mind was to divorce the young man whom she had married so hastily, who had treated her, indeed, with little consideration, and whom she had come to hate with a bitterness only possible to husbands and wives ill paired.

After this the young King passed from hand to hand, from one guardian or captor to another, according to the custom of his predecessors, with many troubled vicissitudes in his life : but it is pleasant to believe that though the story leaves a painful impression as of a distracted childhood, continually dragged about and harassed between contending forces, yet that persistent placidity of nature which plants flowers upon the very edge of the fiercest precipices interposed to secure for little James as for other children the nursery calm, the infant happiness which is the right of childhood. No more delightful picture of tender infancy, the babbling of the first baby words, the sweet exigence and endless requirements of a child, was ever made than that which Sir David Lindsay, the future Lyon King, whom Sir Walter Scott in *gaieté de cœur* (that he should ever be wrong!) introduces in full panoply of heraldic splendour before Flodden, but who was but a youth in the new James's baby days, gives in his "Epistle to the King's Grace," dedicatory to one of his poems. We will venture, though with compunction, once more as we have already done, to modernise the spelling as far as possible, so as to present no difficulty to the reader in the understanding of these delightful verses.

> " When thou was young I bore thee in mine arme
>   Full tenderlie till thou began to gang,
> And in thy bed oft happit thee full warme ;
>   With lute in hand then sweetly to thee sang.
>   Sometime in dancing wondrously I flang,
> And sometime playing farces on the floor,
> And sometime on mine office taking cure.

> " And sometime like a fiend transfigurate,
>   And sometime like the grisly ghost of Gye,
> In divers forms oft times disfigurate,
>   And sometime dissagyist full pleasantly.
>   So since thy birth I have continually
> Been occupied and aye to thy pleasoure,
> And sometime Server, Coppon, and Carvoure."

In another poem he adds, upon the same subject, returning to the pleasant memory, the following happy description :—

> " How, as a chapman bears his pack,
> I bore thy Grace upon my back,
> And sometime stridling on my neck,
> Dancing with many a bend and beck.
> The first syllables that thou didst moote
> Was ' *Pa, Da Lyn* ' upon the lute.
> And aye when thou camest from the school
> Then I behoved to play the fool."

" Play, Davy Lindsay : " the touch of nature brings the
water to one's eyes. Davy Lindsay had yet to play many
a spring before King James, and some that were not gay.
But the gentle stripling with the infant on his shoulder, the
pertinacity of the little babbling cry, the " homely springs "
played offhand that it was pity to hear, but which the lad
enjoyed almost as much in laughing at their dashing in-
correctness as the baby who knew only that it was a pleasant
sound—how bright and vivid is the picture ! Thus while
the lords and his mother stormed over him, the little King,
perhaps in those small state-rooms in well-defended Edinburgh, perhaps in the sunshine at Holyrood with his poet,
had pleasant days.

James was already a growing boy when the last and
worst of the tyrannies which oppressed his youth began.

When the disastrous episode of Albany was well over the Douglases again made one last desperate struggle for the supreme power.   Angus it would seem was not discouraged by the change in the Queen from love to hate, nor even by the efforts which she had begun to make to divorce and shake him off, and it is evident that he must have secured the liking of the little King, to whom in the close intimacy of the family as his mother's husband he must have been known from earliest childhood.   The Earl was handsome and young, one of the finest cavaliers of the Court, and probably was kind to the infant who could not contradict or cross him, and whose favour it was so expedient to secure.   It costs a young man little to make himself adored by a boy to whom he seems the incarnation of manly strength and splendour.   And there is every appearance that James accepted Angus's rule at first with pleasure, no doubt looking up to him as a guide in the manly exercises which could be pursued in his following with more spirit and zeal than in the Queen's surroundings.   The great power of the Douglases, which it took so much bloodshed to break down, and which James II had spent all his life in contending with, extinguished in one branch of the family, seemed now to have developed in another with increased and extended force.   Angus was as great, as potent, as universally feared as the Earls of Douglas had ever been ; and almost as lawless, filling the country with his exactions and those of his dependants.   He had attained this triumph after many drawbacks and downfalls and against the strongest opponents, and Scotland was overawed by the terror of that well-known name.   It was scarcely to be supposed, however, that the young King, precociously aware of all the dangers of his position, could remain subject willingly as he grew up to the sway of a vassal of the Crown however great.   There must have been private counsellors ever ready to whisper that Douglas was nothing save by the King's authority, and that James's favour alone could keep him in his usurped place.   A few months after he had attained the age of sixteen, the boy over whom everybody had intrigued and plotted all his life long, who had been torn from one side to another since ever he could remember, and whom a Douglas had but recently threatened, at a moment of alarm, that rather than render him up they would tear him in two, took at last the matter into his own hands. Whether the suggestion was his own, or had in some way been breathed into his mind, there is no evidence ; but it is clear that he had good reason to be very tired of his subjection. He had already attempted, we are told, several means of getting free of bondage, but had only succeeded in causing the destruction of various lords to whom he had appealed. All his friends had been alienated from him. His mother was powerless to help, and indeed on her own account in such evil case that she is said to have wandered over the country in disguise, friendless and out of favour with all. She had hastened into a third foolish marriage as soon as she had obtained her divorce from Angus, and thus lost all her supporters and champions. His uncle, Henry VIII, was more closely bound to Angus, who was strongly in the interest of England as against France, than to any other Scot, and the young King was thus surrounded by influences hostile to his freedom.

There are moments, however, when the most vigilant watch relaxes, and it so happened that Angus left his young prisoner on one occasion at the Castle of Falkland, the hunting seat of the Scots kings, to all appearance fully occupied with hunting and hawking and thinking of nothing more important, in the charge of Archibald Douglas, the Earl's uncle, George his brother, and a certain James Douglas of Parkhead, who was the captain of the guard. When Angus had been gone a day or two, the elder of these guardians asked leave of the King, according to the formula, to go to Dundee upon personal business of his own ; and George Douglas rode off to St. Andrews to see the bishop on a question of taxes, leaving only the captain and his hundred guardsmen to be accounted for. Who can doubt that young James was well used to all devices for deceiving his gaolers, he who had been held by so many ? There was nothing in his present expedient which could have offended the

most tender conscience. He desired that preparations might
be made for a great hunting, calling upon "the laird of
Ferme, forester of the park of Falkland, and chamberlain of
Fife," to warn everybody about and call all the surrounding
gentlemen "that had speedie
dogs" to hunt with him,
appointing the meeting
next morning at seven
o'clock, "for he was
determined to slay ane
deare or two for his pleasure." Pitscottie is very
particular in his description,
and places the economy of
the little castle before us,
among its woods—with its
simplicity, its precautions,
the homeliness of the household.   The King desired to
have "his disjeuner" at
four in the morning, and
bade James Douglas "gang
the sooner to his bed that
night that he might rise the
sooner in the morning," and
after he had supped, called
for a drink and drank to
Douglas, saying that they
should see good hunting
on the morn, and warning
him not to be late; from
which it may be guessed
that Captain James was
not fond of early hours.

DOORWAY, SIR A. AITCHESON'S HOUSE

The captain saw as he thought the King go to bed, and
having set the watch, and arranged everything for the night,
went to bed himself, as the boy had laughingly bidden him
to do.   As soon as all was quiet, eluding the watch without

apparent difficulty, the King, attended only by " Jockie Hart, a yeoman of the stable," and another "secret servant," escaped in the stillness of the night into the freedom of the sleeping country. It is said by one authority to have been in June that this evasion was made, but in June there is scarcely any night at all in Scotland, and the brief darkness could scarcely have served as a screen for the fugitives ; probably it was earlier in the year, when the night was more to be calculated upon. One can imagine the breathless excitement and delight of the long ride, with the fresh breeze in his face, and one of the richest valleys in Scotland coming softly into sight in the mists of the morning, as the young King full of spirit, ambition, and all the rising impulses of manhood, left behind him the gentle shadow of the Lomond hills, and swept round the base of the Ochils towards the castle, high-standing on its rock, where freedom and his crown and all the privileges of royal life and independence were awaiting him. He reached Stirling in the breaking of the day, and galloping across the bridge, caused its gates to be closed after him, that no pursuer might cross the river ; and was received with great rejoicing in the castle, where everything had been prepared for his coming, and where the captain, having let down the portcullis and made all secure, "laid the King in his bed, because he had ridden all that night." Probably there was no moment in the life of the young monarch, who had fallen upon such troubled times, more sweet than this when, after the wild excitement of the long night's riding, he closed his young eyes, at an hour so unaccustomed, in the clear radiance of the morning, feeling his life now free before him, as light and fair and unfettered as the rising day. But Pitscottie must continue the tale in his own admirable way. He says :—

"We will lat him sleep in his bed, and return to George Douglas, who came home to Falkland at eleven hours at night, and required at the porters what the King was doing, who answered that he was in his own chamber sleeping, who was to rise tymous to the hunting, and right so said the watchmen. George hearing this went to his bed, till on the morn that the sun rose. Then came Patrick Carmichael, baillie of Abernethie, and knocked at George Douglas's chamber door, and inquired of him what the King was doing. George answered that he was not waked as yet in his own chamber. The baillie answered, 'Ye are deceaved; he is along the bridge of Stirling this night.' Then George Douglas gat up hastilie and went to the porters and watchmen and inquired for the King, who still answered that he was sleeping in his own chamber. Then George Douglas came to the King's chamber door and found it locked, and dang it up, but found no man in it. Then he cryed, 'Fye, treason, the King is gone!'"

The confusion and dismay of the household were great. Some said that the King had gone to Bambriefe "to visit a gentlewoman," which explanation was received with relief, the question of morality being of small consequence in comparison. George Douglas immediately leaped on his horse to ascertain if this were true, but had not ridden more than two miles when he met the Earl of Rothes, who told him the King was not there. By this time the other Douglas who had gone to Dundee had returned also, and a hurried council was held what to do. Angus himself was immediately summoned from Tantallon by an express, "ane haistie post," and instantly answering, set out with his uncle and brother, and rode to Stirling with some forlorn hope it would appear of recovering their empire over the King. But James had already gathered counsellors round him, and was himself too strongly determined to maintain his liberty to allow any approach. The road to Stirling would no doubt be full of scouts, to give warning of what the discomfited but powerful family meant to do, and as soon as their approach was known a herald was sent to the town cross to proclaim by sound of trumpet a royal decree that neither Angus nor his companions should approach within six miles of where the King was under pain of death. It is curious to mark how in a moment the great power of the Douglases and their high courage collapsed in face of this proclamation. They paused on their hasty ride, and held another hasty council, and though some among them were for pressing forward and seizing once more the malapert boy who defied them, the Earl himself and his brother decided to obey the proclamation and withdraw. They fell back upon Linlithgow, where they paused a day or two, hoping perhaps for better news. But by this time the other nobles were crowding round the King. Huntly, Argyle, Athole, Glencairn, Monteith, and Rothes, with a still larger company of barons, hastened to Stirling to protect and aid with their counsel the liberated prince. Archbishop Beatoun, the wily Churchman, who had done all he could to overthrow Angus,—who had been for a moment so worsted in the conflict that he skulked about his own Fife moors in the disguise of a shepherd, but who had lately made friends with the dominant family and entertained the King and his guardians together, calling them "to his pasche (Easter) at St. Andrews,"—and who had no doubt known of the momentous night journey, and probably detained George Douglas late that evening to make it more sure, had also joined the King.

With this powerful escort James proceeded to Edinburgh, where for some time the lords around him kept watch night and day, keeping their little army of attendants under arms in case of any attack on the part of Angus. One night, we are told, James himself in full armour took the command of the guard, more probably, however, from a boyish desire to feel himself at the head of his defenders than for any other reason: and even his bedchamber was shared, after an unpleasant fashion of the time, by the bastard of Arran, "James Hamilton, that bloody butcherer," as Pitscottie calls him, who had precipitated the fray of "Clear the Causeway" and was Angus's most inveterate enemy. These extraordinary precautions, however, seem to have been unnecessary. The Douglases would appear to have accepted their defeat as complete, and to have been entirely cowed by it. Another proclamation was put forth on the arrival of the King in Edinburgh commanding all true subjects to refrain from intercourse of any kind with Angus, his brother, and uncle, not to receive them or succour them or hold any communication with them on peril of being considered sharers in their crime—in short, a sort of interdict after the papal fashion. The impromptu council sat for two days in the upper chamber of the Tolbooth, which was the recognised Parliament House, chiefly, it would seem, to hear

the King's indictment against the family of Douglas.   James
set forth all his grievances, his subjection to the will of
Angus, his separation from his own friends, the appearance
he had been made to assume of enmity to his real
champions, and vowed at the end, says Pitscottie, in the
fervour of his indignation and resentment, that Scotland
should not hold them both.   He would receive nothing but
support in that assembly where all had suffered from the
supremacy of Angus, and where the too powerful race had
no friends.   The council appointed anew all the high officers of
State, whose posts had been appropriated by the Douglases,
and sent an envoy to England to announce that the government of Scotland was henceforward in the King's own hands.
It was also ordained that a Parliament should be called in
the month of September, to confirm in a more decorous
and regular way the decisions of the present hasty assembly.

When Parliament met these questions were accordingly
discussed over again, with confirmation of what had been
already done.   It was decided that Angus should be
summoned before them to answer for his misdeeds, under the
penalty if he did not appear of being "put to the horn and
banished during the King's will."   Angus was not so rash as
to trust himself within the power of his enemies, as his
kinsmen of the house of Douglas had already done on two
fatal occasions : and as neither he nor his retainers put in an
appearance, they were accordingly attainted, their lands forfeited to the Crown, their name put under the public ban,
their great castle of Tantallon seized, and themselves proclaimed through all the country as traitors whom no man
should receive or succour.

The complete downfall which overtook this great house
after the young King's abandonment of it is very remarkable,
and shows how important was the royal position, notwithstanding the manner in which it had been *exploité*, and the
mere nominal power of its actual possessor.   The house of
Angus crumbled into the dust as soon as their young prisoner
escaped their hands.   They took refuge in England, where
they vainly attempted on various occasions to negotiate for

their return, but with no success. The name continued
obnoxious to James during his whole life. Sir Walter has
done his best to rehabilitate that name in the noble Douglas
of *The Lady of the Lake*, who has been identified with
Archibald of Kilspindie, "the uncle of the banished Earl,"
the story of whose appearance at the games at Stirling is
said to have some foundation of reality. But the historians
of the house, who alone mention this, state the facts in a very
different way.

Thus the Angus branch of the Douglas family fell, as
the Earls of Douglas had fallen, and for a generation there
was little heard of it save in mutterings of treason in
moments of difficulty, which never came to much—until in
the following reign the indomitable race rose again in
another branch and under another name, and furnished in
the Regent Morton one of the strongest as well as the most
questionable figures of a deeply disturbed time. Never was
a race more difficult to subdue.

The escape of James from Falkland took place between
Easter and June in the year 1527. In 1528, the Douglases
being clean swept out of the country, the young King went
on a professed hunting expedition to the Borders, where,
besides innumerable deer, its ostensible reason, his ride
through the southern district carried punishment and death
to many a Border reiver and especially to the famous John or
Johnnie Armstrong, the Laird of Kilnokie, and chief or at least
best-known representative of his name. Whether it was wise
policy to hang the reiver who was the terror of the Borders,
yet "never molested no Scottis man," it is not necessary
to decide. He was a scourge to the English, of whom it was
said that there was none from the Scottish Border to
Newcastle who did not "pay ane tribute to be free of his
cumber." Johnnie Armstrong had the folly to come into the
King's presence with such a train, his men so completely
armed and so many in number, as to compete with royal
magnificence, not very great in Scotland in those days.
'What wants yon knave that a king should have?" said the
young James, who had certainly had enough of such power-

ful subjects : and he would not listen to either excuse or
explanation from the Borderer, whose defiance as he was
led to his execution, and the wail of his wild followers
after him, sounds still in the stirring strains of song and
ballad.   No doubt it was justice that James did—but justice
somewhat stern and out of time.

The young Court now blazing out into full splendour, with
a legitimate head and every prospect of prosperity, became
again the resort of foreign chivalry and magnificent envoys,
among them a legate from the Pope to assure the allegiance
of James to the Holy See, which his uncle of England had
deserted.   Henry at the same time did not neglect by
constant messengers and vague promises, now of the hand of
the Princess Mary, now of an English dukedom, to secure
his nephew to his side.   After that princess, whom her father
tried his utmost to put out of the succession by divorcing
her mother, James was the next heir, and Henry did not
forget that possibility.   The hand of the young princess
had already been several times offered to the Scots King
without any certainty either in the proposal or its acceptance.   One cannot help wondering what might have been
the issue had that unhappy Mary, to whom history has
given so grim a nickname, been thus wedded in early youth
to a gracious and gallant Stewart.   In all history there
occurs by times a gleam like this of possible deliverance
from fate, an opening by which the subjects of tragedy
might have secured an escape had they but known.   One
wonders had she thus escaped the wrongs and bitterness of
her early career whether Mary would have got free from
those traces of blood and madness which have left so
dark a shadow upon her name : or whether, in the conflict
that was to follow, her fierce Tudor passion would have
embittered every strife.   It is wonderful to think that
she might have been the mother of that other Mary so
different yet still more sadly fated, who in that case never
could have been the Mary Stewart she was.   We are led to
something like a *reductio ad absurdum* by such speculations,
very vain yet always attractive as they are.   James was

eager to marry at the earliest possible moment, and all would have welcomed the marriage with his kinswoman.

In this respect, however, as in almost every other, Scotland was now at a turning-point of the utmost importance in her career. For the first time her politics had begun to be troubled by the possibility of an alliance with England more strong and lasting than the brief periods of truce which had hitherto existed between two nations whose principle and tradition were those of enmity. A perpetual peace had indeed been sworn and signed at the time of the marriage of Margaret Tudor with James IV, but how little lasting that had been is amply demonstrated by the fact that no such crushing defeat had ever been inflicted upon Scotland as that of Flodden, in which the King and the great part of his nobles perished. Perhaps it was the germ of the design to attract the lesser country into the arms of the greater by friendship rather than to set her desperately at bay against all peaceful influences, which had prevented the successful army from taking advantage of the victory ; but certainly through all the distracted period of James's minority efforts had been made by constant envoys to acquire a share in the councils of the country, such as had hitherto been considered the right of France, who was the old and faithful ally as England was "the auld enemy" of the Scots. The alliance with France had been taken for granted on all sides. That Scotland should harass England in every war between that country and her continental neighbour was a foregone conclusion, and it was something still more sure, a proverb on the English side, that when France was to be assailed the right thing was to begin with Scotland. The position of Henry as brother of the Scottish Queen, and the nearest relative of James, who, under circumstances not at all unlikely to occur, might be his heir, gave the English king now a natural right to interfere ; and it is conceivable that had this right been exercised more wisely it might have led to fortunate issues. But unhappily King Henry had associated his influence with that of Angus, taking the part of his sister's discarded husband with great determination, and apparently without any sympathy in those changes in Margaret's affections which so much resembled his own. Angus was to Scotland the representative of the English alliance, and as everything connected with Angus had now become hateful to James, it followed that his uncle's desire to obtain an influence over him, which was not accompanied by any substantial marks of kindness towards himself, did not meet with much success: though it might have been otherwise had the vaguely-proposed marriage been carried out. But one can scarcely be sorry that the noble and graceful James should have escaped such an alliance.

Other and still more serious matters were now, however, surging upwards in both England and Scotland, which doubled the silent struggle between the old ally and the new. On the side of France was the old religion, the Church which at this period was the strongest of the Estates of Scotland, richer than any of the others, and possessing almost all the political ability of the time: on the side of England a new, scarcely recognised, but powerful influence, which was soon to attain almost complete mastery in Scotland and shatter that Church to pieces. In the beginning of James's reign this new power was but beginning to swell in the silent bosom of the country, showing here and there in a trial for heresy and in the startling fires of execution which cut off the first martyrs for the reformed faith. But there is no evidence to show that James, a young man full of affairs much more absorbing than religious controversy, with more confidence, politically at least, in the Church than in any other power of his realm, had ever been awakened to the importance of the struggle. The smoke of those fires which blew over all Scotland in potent fumes from St. Andrews, on the further side of the Firth; and from Edinburgh, where on the Castle Hill in the intervals of the tiltings and tourneys, the Vicar of Dollar, for example, of whose examination we have a most vivid and admirable report, full of picturesque simplicity, not without humour even in the midst of the tragedy, was burnt—along with several gentlemen of his county: does not seem to have reached the young King, absorbed in some project of State, or busy with new laws and regulations, or inspecting the portraits of the great ladies among whom he had to choose his bride. There is a curious story communicated in a letter of one of the English envoys of the period of his conversation with a Scotch gentleman, in which we find a description of James listening to a play represented before the Court at the feast of the Epiphany, 1540, in the Castle of Linlithgow. This play is believed to have been Sir David Lindsay's *Satire on the Three Estates*, one of the most effective attacks upon the corruptions of the Church which had ever been made, and setting forth the exactions of the priests from the peasantry and the poor at every event of their lives, as well as the wealth and wickedness of the monastic communities, of which Scotland was full, and which had long been the recognised object of popular satire and objurgation. The performance would seem to have had as great an effect upon the young King as had the play in *Hamlet* upon the majesty of Denmark. James turned to Beatoun (the Cardinal, nephew and successor of Archbishop James) the Chancellor in indignant remonstrance. Were these things so? and if they were, would not the bishops and other powerful ecclesiastics join to repress them? Let them do so at once, cried the sovereign : or if not he should send half a dozen of the proudest of them to King Henry to be dealt with after his methods. Even Churchmen had occasionally to brook such threats from an excited prince. Beatoun answered with courtier-like submission that a word from the King was enough, upon which James, not wont to confine himself to words, and strong in the success with which he had overcome one of his Estates, the lords, now so quiet under his hand, replied that he would not spare many words for such an issue. This characteristic scene is very interesting. But probably when the memory of what he had heard faded from the busy King, and the tumult of public events gained possession again of his ear and mind, he forgot the sudden impression, or contented himself with the thought that Beatoun and the

LINLITHGOW PALACE

bishops must put order in their own affairs. Pitscottie tells us in respect to a projected visit to England, vaguely thought of and planned several years before this time, that " the wicked bishops of Scotland would not thole " a meeting between James and Henry. " For the bishops feared that if the King had met with King Henry that he would have moved him to casten down the abbeys, and to have altered the religion as the King of England had done before. Therefore the bishops bade him to bide at home, and gave him three thousand pounds of yearly rent out of their benefices." It is to be feared that history has no evidence of this voluntary munificence, but James found the ecclesiastical possessions in Scotland very useful for the purposes of taxation, and in this respect did not permit Beatoun to have his own way.

When the young King was in his twenty-fourth year he found himself able—many previous negotiations on the subject having come to nothing—to pay a visit to the Continent in his own person in order to secure a wife. It is a greater testimony to the personal power and vigour of James than any mere details could give that, within eight years of the time when, a boy of sixteen, he had escaped from the power of the Douglas, it should be possible for him to leave, after all the wild anarchy of his minority, a pacificated and orderly kingdom behind him, in the care of a Council of Regency, while he went forth upon a mission so important to himself. He had altogether extinguished and expelled the house of Douglas ; he had subdued and repressed other turbulent lords, and convinced them that his authority was neither to be neutralised nor made light of ; he had settled and calmed the Border by the most decisive means ; and he was now free to show himself in the society of kings, and win his princess, and see the world. He had been already the object of many overtures from contemporary Powers. The Emperor and the Pope had both sent him envoys and conciliated his friendship ; and in the imperial house itself as well as in many others of the highest rank there had been ladies proposed to share his crown. The one more immediately in view when he set out on his journey was a daughter of the

Duke of Vendôme. The defeat of Charles V before Marseilles took place almost simultaneously with James's arrival, and the Scotch chroniclers do not lose the opportunity of asserting that it was the coming of the King of Scots with a supposed army of twenty thousand men to the succour of France which was the reason of the Emperor's precipitate withdrawal. Pitscottie narrates, with more evident truthfulness, how the Frenchmen on the Norman coast were alarmed by the ships, fearing it to be an enemy which hove in sight, " for there were many strangers in his companie, so that he appeared ane great army." But the sight of the red lion of Scotland changed their alarms into joy, and they welcomed the Scots King and party, "at the New Haven beside Diep," with much rejoicing. He would seem to have pushed across France to the Court of Vendôme without pausing to pay his respects to the King at Paris ; and we find his movements recorded in a romantic tale, which is neither contradicted nor supported by other authorities, but likely enough to a romantic young prince upon a love-quest. According to this description James did not assume his proper character, but appeared only as one among the many knights, who probably represented themselves, to make his feint successful, as merely a party of cavaliers seeking adventure and the exercises of chivalry. He intended thus to see, while himself unknown, " the gentlewoman who sould have been his spouse, thinking to spy her pulchritud and behaviour unkenned by her."

"Notwithstanding this fair ladie took suspition that the King of Scotland should be in the companie, wherefore she passed to her coffer and took out his picture, which she had gotten out of Scotland by ane secret moyane, and as soon as she looked to the picture it made her know the King of Scotland incontinent where he stood among the rest of his companie, and past peartlie to him, and took him by the hand, and said, ' Sir, ye stand over far aside ; therefore, if it please your Grace, you may show yourself to my father or me, and confer and pass the time ane while.' "

Perhaps it was injudicious of the fair ladie to be so " peart." At all events, after much feasting, " nothing but merriness and banquetting and great cheer and lovelie communing betwixt the King's grace and the fair ladies, with great musick and playing on instruments, and all other kinds of pastime for the fields," as well as " jousting and running of great horses," the ungrateful James " thought it expedient to speak nothing of marriage at that time, till he had spoken with the King of France, considering," adds the chronicler, who perhaps sees an excuse to be necessary, " he was within his realm he would show him his mind and have his counsel thereto before he concluded the matter." Pitscottie thus saves the feelings of the lady of whom other historians say curtly that she did not please the King. But when the Scottish band reached the Court, though it was then in mourning for the Dauphin, recently dead, King James was received with open arms.   The King of France, sick and sad for the loss of his son, was in the country at a hunting seat, and when James was suddenly introduced at the door of his chamber as " the King of Scotland, sire, come to comfort you," the arrival evidently made the best possible impression.   The sorrowful father declared, as he embraced the young stranger, that it was as if another son had been given him from heaven ; and after a little interval the royal party, increased by James's Scottish train, moved on to another palace.   We may be allowed to imagine that the Queen and her ladies came out to meet them, as the first sight which James appears to have had of his future bride was while she was " ryding in ane chariot, because she was sickly, and might not ryd upon hors."   Magdalen, too, saw him as he rode to meet the fair cavalcade in her father's company, who looked so much happier and brighter from the encounter with this gallant young prince.   The poor girl was already stricken for death, and had but a few months to live ; but it is very likely that her malady was that fatal but deceitful one which leaves a more delicate beauty to its victims, and gives feverish brightness to the eyes and colour to the cheek.   A tender creature, full of poetry and imagination, and most likely all unconscious of the fate that hung over her, she loved the gallant cavalier from the first moment of seeing him, and touched the heart of James by that fragile beauty and by the affection that shone in her soft eyes. It was a marriage that no one approved, for her days were known to be numbered. But perhaps some faint hope that happiness, that potent physician, might arrest disease, as it has been known to do, prevailed both with the anxious father and the young man beloved, in whom tender pity and gratitude replaced a warmer senti- ment. At all events the marriage took place in Paris, in the noble church of Notre Dame, in the beginning of the year 1537. The King, we are told, sent to Scotland to invite a number of other noblemen and gentlemen to attend his wedding, which was performed with the greatest pomp and splendour. Not until May did the young couple set out for their home, and then they were laden with gifts, two ships being presented to them, a number of splendid horses fully caparisoned, and quantities of valuable tapestries, cloth of silver and gold, and jewels of every description. Perhaps the long delay was intended to make the journey more safe for the poor young Queen. The voyage from Dieppe to Leith lasted five days, and the bridal party was accompanied by an escort of " fiftie ships of Scottismen, Frenchmen, and strangers." " When the Queen was come upon Scottis eard, she bowed her down to the same, and kissed the mould thereof, and thanked God that her husband and she were come safe through the seas." There could not be a more tender or attractive picture. How full of poetry and soft passion must the gentle creature have been who thus took possession of the land beloved for her young husband's sake ! The Scottish eard indeed was all that she was to have of that inheritance, for in little more than a month the gentle Magdalen was dead. She was laid in the chapel of the palace which was to have been her home, with "ane dolorous lamentation ; for triumph and merriness were all turned into dirges and soul-masses, which were very lamentable to behold."

This sad story is crowned by Pitscottie with a brief note of the death of the Duc de Vendôme's daughter, " who took sick displeasure at the King of Scotland's marriage that she deceased immediately thereafter ; whereat the King of Scot- land was highly displeased, thinking that he was the occasion

of that gentlewoman's death." Other historians say that this
tragical conclusion did not occur, but that the Princess of Vendôme was married on the same day as James. Pitscottie's
is the more romantic ending, and rounds the pathetic tale.

After such a mournful and ineffectual attempt at married
life all the negotiations had to be begun over again, and
James was at last married, to the general satisfaction, to
Mary of Guise, a woman, as it turned out, of many fine and
noble qualities, to which but indifferent justice was ever
done. It was before this event, however, and immediately
after the death of the Queen, that a curious and tragical incident happened, which furnished another strange scene to the
many associations of Edinburgh. This was the execution of
Lady Glamis upon the Castle Hill for witchcraft and secret
attempts upon the life of the King by means of magic or of
poison. No one seems to know what these attempts were.
Pitscottie gives this extraordinary event a short paragraph.
The grave Pinkerton fills a page or two with an apology
or defence of James for permitting such an act. But we are
not told what was the evidence, or how the sovereign's life
was threatened. The supposed culprit was however—and
the fact is significant—the only member of the family of
Angus left in Scotland, the sister of the Earl. Once more
the Castle Hill was covered with an awed or excited crowd,
not unaccustomed to that sight, for the heretics had burnt
there not long before, but at once more and less moved
than usual, for the victim was a woman fair and dignified,
such a sufferer as always calls forth the pity of the spectators,
but her crime witchcraft, a thing held in universal horror,
and with which there would be no sympathisers. Few, if
any, in that crowd would be so advanced in sentiment as to
regard the cruel exhibition with the horrified contempt of
modern times. The throng that lined that great platform
would have no doubt that it was right to burn a witch
wherever she was found ; and the beauty of the woman
and the grandeur of her race would give a pang the more
of painful satisfaction in her destruction. But it is strange
that thus a last blow should have been aimed at that

family, once so great and strong, which James's resentment
had pursued to the end. A little while before, Archibald
Douglas of Kilspindie had thrown himself upon James's
mercy—the only member of the Douglas family who can be
in any way identified with the noble Douglas of *The Lady of
the Lake*.

> " 'Tis James of Douglas, by St. Serle,
>   The uncle of the banished Earl."

But Archibald of Kilspindie did not meet the same
forgiveness with which his prototype in the poem was
received. He was sent back into banishment unforgiven,
the King's word having been passed to forgive no one
condemned by the law. Perhaps the same stern fidelity to
a stern promise was the reason why Lady Glamis was allowed
to go to the stake unrescued. But we speculate in vain on
subjects so veiled in ignorance and uncertainty. Perhaps
his counsellors acted on their own authority in respect to a
crime the reprobation and horror of which were universal, and
did not disturb the King in the first shock of his mourning.
In the same week the fair and fragile Magdalen of France
was carried to her burial, and Lady Glamis was burned at
the other extremity of Edinburgh. Perhaps it was supposed
that something in the incantations of the one had a fatal
influence upon the young existence of the other. At all
events these two sensations fell to the populace of Edinburgh
and all the strangers who were constantly passing through
her gates, at the same time. Life in those days was full of
pictorial circumstances which do not belong to ours. One is
inclined to wonder sometimes whether the many additional
comforts we possess make up for that perpetual movement
in the air, the excitement, the communication of new
ideas, the strange sights both pleasant and terrible. The
burning of a witch or a heretic is perhaps too tremendous a
sensation to be desired by the most heroic spectator ; but the
perpetual drama going on thus before the eyes of all the
world, and giving to the poorest an absolute share in every
new and strange thing, must have added a reality to national
life which no newspapers can give. That the people remain

always eager for this share in historical events, the crowds
that never weary of gazing at passing princes, the innumerable audience of the picture papers, the endless reproduction
of every insignificant public event, from a procession of alder-
men to the simplest day's journey of a royal personage,
abundantly testify.   In the days of the Jameses few of the
crowd could read, and still fewer had the chance of reading.
A ballad flying from voice to voice across the country, sung
at the ingle-neuk, repeated from one to another in the little
crowd at a " stairhead," in which the grossest humorous view
was the best adapted for the people, represented popular
literature.   But most things that went on were visible to the
crowding population.   They saw the foreign visitors, the
ambassadors, the knights, each with his distinguishable crest,
who came to meet in encounter of arms the knights of the
Scottish Court.   All that went on they had their share in,
and a kind of acquaintance with every notability.   The
public events were a species of large emblazoned history
which he who ran could read.

These ballads above referred to came to singular note,
however, in one of the many discussions between England
and Scotland which were carried on by means of the frequent
envoys sent to James from his uncle.   The Borders, it
appears, were full of this flying literature sent forth by
unknown writers, and spread probably by, here and there,
a wandering friar, more glad of a merry rhyme than dis-
concerted by a satire against his own cloth, or with still
more relish dispersing over the countryside reports of King
Henry's amours and divorces, and of the plundering of
abbeys and profane assumption of sacred rights by a monarch
who was so far from sanctified.   Popular prophecies of how
a new believing king should be raised up to disconcert the
heretics, and on the northern side of the Border of the speedy
elevation of James to the throne of England, and final victorious triumph of the Scottish side, flew from village to
village, exciting at last the alarm of Henry and his council,
who made formal complaint of them at the Scottish Court,
drawing from James a promise that if any of his subjects

should be found to be the authors of such productions they should suffer death for it—a heavy penalty for literary transgression. In Scotland farther north it was another kind of ballad which was said and sung, or whispered under the breath with many a peal of rude laughter, the Satires of "Davy Lindsay" and many a lesser poet—ludicrous stories of erring priests and friars, indecent but humorous, with lamentable tales of dues exacted and widows robbed, and all the sins of the Church, the proud bishop and his lemans, the avaricious priest and his exactions, the confessors who bullied a dying penitent into gifts which injured his family, and all the well-worn scandals by which in every time of reformation the coarser imagination of the populace is stirred. If James himself was startled into an angry demand how such things could be after he had witnessed the performance of David Lindsay's play, which was trimmed into comparative decency for courtly ears, it may be supposed what was the effect of that and still broader assaults, upon the unchastened imagination of the people. The Reformation progressed by great strides by such rude yet able help as well as by the purer methods of religion. The priests, however, do not seem to have made war on the balladmakers, as the great King of England would have had his nephew do. Buchanan, indeed, whose classic weapons had been brought into this literary crusade, and who also had his fling at the Franciscans as well as his coarser and more popular brethren, was imprisoned for a time, and had to withdraw from his country, but the poets of the people, far more effective, would seem to have escaped.

All this, however, probably seemed of but little importance to James in comparison with the greater affairs of the kingdom of which his hands were full. When the episode of his marriages was over, and still more important an heir secured, he returned to that imperial track in which he had acquitted himself so well. All would seem to have been in order in the centre of the kingdom; the Borders were as quiet as it was possible for the Borders to be; and only the remote Highlands and islands remained still insubordinate,

in merely nominal subjection to the laws of the kingdom.
James, we are told, had long intended to make one of the
royal raids so familiar to Scottish history among his doubtful
subjects of these parts, and accordingly an expedition was
very carefully prepared, twelve ships equipped both for
comfort and for war, with every device known to the time
for provisioning them and keeping them in full efficiency.
We are told that the English authorities looking on, were
exceedingly suspicious of this voyage, not knowing whither
such preparations might tend, while all Scotland watched the
setting out of the expedition almost as much in the dark as
to its motive, and full of wonder as to where the King could
be going.   Bonfires were blazing on all the hilltops in rejoicing
for the birth of a prince when James took his way with his
fleet down the Firth.   Pinkerton, who ought to have known
better, talks of "the acclamations of numerous spectators on
the adjacent hills and shores" as if the great estuary had
been a little river.   It might well be that both in Fife and
Lothian there were eager lookers-on, as soon as it was seen
that the fleet was in motion, to see the ships pass : but
their acclaims must have been loud indeed to carry from
Leith to Kinghorn.   The King sailed early in June 1540
towards the north.   Many a yacht and pleasure ship still
follows the same route round the Scottish coast towards the
wild attractions of the islands.

> " Merrily, merrily, bounds the bark,
>   She bounds before the gale,
> The mountain breeze from Ben-na-darch
>   Is joyous in her sail.
> With fluttering sound like laughter hoarse
>   The cords and canvas strain,
> The waves divided by her force
> In rippling eddies chased her course
>   As if they laughed again."

But it was on no pleasure voyage that James had set out.
He had in his twelve ships two thousand armed men, led by
the most trusted lords of Scotland, and his mission was to
reduce to order the clans who knew so little what a king's
dignity was, or the restraints of law, or the pursuits of

industry. No stand would seem to have been anywhere made against him. Many of the chiefs of the more turbulent tribes were brought off to the ships, not so much as prisoners in consequence of their own misdoings, but as hostages for their clans : and the startled isles, overawed by the sight of the King and his great ships, and by the more generous motive of anxiety for their own chieftains in pledge for them, calmed down out of their wild ways, and ceased from troubling in a manner unprecedented in their turbulent history.

An incidental consequence of this voyage sounds oddly modern, as if it might have been a transcript from the most recent records. James perceived, or more probably had his attention directed to the fact, that the fishermen of the north were much molested by fishing vessels from Holland, Flanders, and the Scandinavian coasts, who interfered with their fishing, sometimes even thrusting them by violence of arms out of their own waters. The King accordingly detached one or two of his vessels under the command of Maxwell, his admiral, to inquire into these high-handed proceedings, with the result that one of the foreign fisher pirate-ships was seized and brought to Leith to answer for their misdoings. There they were reprimanded and bound over to better behaviour, then dismissed without further penalty. How little effectual, however, this treatment was, is exemplified by the fact that the self-same offence continues to be repeated until this very day.

There would seem to have been a little pause of calm and comfort in James's life after this victorious expedition. Clouds already bigger than a man's hand were forming on his horizon ; the country had begun to be agitated throughout its depths with the rising forces of the reform, and the priests who had always surrounded James were hurrying on in the truculence of terror to sterner and sterner enactments against heretics : while he, probably even yet but moderately interested, thinking of other things, and though adding to the new laws which he was persuaded to originate in this sense, conditions to the effect that corresponding reforms were to be wrought in the behaviour of the priesthood,

—had not entered at all into the fierce current of theological strife. He followed the faith in which he had been bred, revolted rather than attracted by the proceedings and pretensions of his uncle of England, willing that the bishops, who probably knew best, and who were, as he complained to the English ambassador, the only men of sense and ability near him, should have their own way in their own concerns ; but for himself much more intent on the temporal welfare of his kingdom than on its belief, or the waves of opinion which might blow over it. He had just been very successful in what no doubt seemed to him an enterprise much more kingly and important—the subjugation of the islands. He was happy and prosperous in his private life, his Queen having performed the high duty expected of her in providing the kingdom with an heir, indeed with two sons, to make, as appeared, assurance doubly sure; and though the burning of a heretic was not a pleasant circumstance, Beatoun and the rest of the brotherhood were too clever and helpful as men of the world to be easily dispensed with. James had, there can be no doubt, much reason to be discontented and dissatisfied, as almost all his predecessors had been, with the nobility of his kingdom. Apart from some of those young companions-in-arms who were delightful in the camp and field but useless in the council chamber, his state of mind would seem to have resembled more the modern mood which is represented by the word "bored" than any other more dignified expression. The priests might be fierce (as indeed were the lords, still more) but they were able, and knew something of the necessities of government. The barons disgusted him with their petty jealousies, their want of instruction, their incapacity for any broad or statesmanlike view, and there would seem little doubt that he dispensed with their services as much as possible, and turned to those persons who comprehended him with a natural movement which unfortunately, however, is never fortunate in a king. Something of the severance between himself and those who were nearest to him in rank, which had ruined his grandfather, showed itself as he advanced towards the gravity of manhood:

and the fatal name of favourite began to be attached to one
man at least in the Court, who would seem to have understood better than the others the ways and intentions of
James.   But in the meantime the clouds were only gathering;
the darkness had not begun.   A year or two before, the
King had given to the legal faculty of Scotland a form and
constitution which it has retained to this day.   He had
instituted the Court of Session, the " Feifteen," the law lords
in their grave if short-lived dignity.   He had begun to build
and repair and decorate at Holyrood and Linlithgow.   " He
sent to Denmark," says Pitscottie, " and brought home great
horss and meares and put them in parks that their offspring
might be gotten to sustein the warres when need was.   Also
he sent and furnished the country with all kinds of craftsmen
such as Frenchmen, Spaniards, and Dutchmen, which ever
was the first of their profession that could be had."   He
went even so far in his desire to develop the natural wealth
of his kingdom that he brought over certain German wise
men to see if gold could be found in the mines, of which
there has always been a tradition, as probably in most
countries.   All these pacific enterprises occupied James's
time and helped on the prosperity of the country.   But evil
times were close at hand.

One of the first indications that the dreadful round of
misfortune was about to begin was the sudden denunciation
of James Hamilton, the bastard of Arran, as a conspirator
against the King, an event which Pitscottie narrates as
happening in the year 1541.   He had been a favourite of
the King in his youth, and a great champion against the
Douglas faction, and it was indeed his intemperate and imprudent rage which determined the fight called Clear the
Causeway, and wrought much harm to his own party.   He
had been high in favour for a time, probably on the ground
of his enmity to the house of Angus, then had fallen into
discredit, but had lately been employed in certain public
offices, and if we may trust Pitscottie, had been put into
some such position by the priests as that which Saul of
Tarsus held in the service of the persecuting ecclesiastics of

Jerusalem.   At all events his sudden accusation as plotting against the King's life, and especially as doing so in the interests of the Douglases, was evidently as startling and extraordinary to the great officials to whom the communication was made as it would be to the reader who has heard of this personage only as the infuriated opponent of Angus and his party.   No credence seems to have been given to the story at first, though it was told by another Hamilton, a cousin of the culprit.   As this happened, however, in the King's absence from Edinburgh, the lords thought it a wise precaution to secure Sir James, and, according to Pitscottie, proceeded in their own dignified persons — the Lord Treasurer, Secretary, and "Mr. Household," preceded by Lyon King-of-Arms—to his lodging in Edinburgh, whence they conveyed him to the castle.   Such arrestations would probably cause but little excitement, only a momentary rush and gazing of the crowd as the group with its little band of attendants and defenders passed upward along the High Street, the herald's tabard alone betraying its character. Sir James Hamilton, however, was very well known and little loved, and small would be the sympathy in the looks of the citizens, and many the stern nods and whispers of satisfaction that vengeance had seized him at length.   The King, like his representatives, was astonished by the accusation, but when he heard of the terrible "dittay" which had been brought against Hamilton "he came suddenly out of Falkland, where His Grace was for the time, and brought the said Sir James out of the castle to the Tolbooth, and gave him fair assize of the lords and barons, who convicted him of sundry points of treason ; and thereafter he was headed and quartered, and his lands annexed to the Crown."

It is a curious question, which however none of the historians think of asking, whether there could be any connection between the scheme, if any, for which the Lady Glamis suffered, and this wholly unexpected outbreak of murderous intention on the part of Hamilton.   The Hamiltons and Douglases were sworn enemies, yet greater wonders have been seen than the union of two feudal foes to compass the destruction of the enemy of both. Angus and his brothers banished, but little forgetful of all that had happened, and trusting in the favour of King Henry, were soon to show themselves at the head of expeditions hostile to Scotland across the Border. Were these two sudden disclosures of unexpected treachery the manifestations of a deep-laid plot which might have further developments—if with the bastard of Arran also perhaps in still more unlikely quarters? It is but a conjecture, yet it is one that might seem justified by two isolated events so extraordinary, and by the state of discouragement and misery into which James seems soon to have fallen. Pitscottie relates that the King "took ane great suspition of his nobles, thinking that either ane or other of them would deceive him"; and then there began to appear to him "visions in his bed." He thought he saw Sir James Hamilton, fierce and vengeful, appearing to him in the darkness with a drawn sword, with which he cut off the King's right arm. Next time the cruel spectre appeared it upbraided him with an unjust sentence and struck off the other arm: "Now therefore thou sall want both thy armes, and sall remain in sorrow ane while, and then I will come and stryk thy head from thee," said the angry ghost. Whatever may be the reader's opinion about the reality of these visions, there can be little doubt that they show deep depression in the mind of James to whom they came. He woke out of his sleep in great excitement and terror, and told his attendants what he had dreamed, who were very "discontent of his visioun, thinking that they would hear hastily tidings of the same."

"On the morning word came to the King that the prince was very sick and like to die. When the King heard thereof he hasted to Sanct Andros, but, or he could come there the prince was depairted, whereat the King was verrie sad and dolorous. Notwithstanding immediately thereafter the post came out of Stirling to the King showing him that his second son, the Duke of Albany, could not live; and or the King could be in Stirling he was depairted. Whose departures were both within fortie-eight hours, which caused great lamentations to be in Scotland and in especial by the Queen, their mother. But the Queen comforted the King, saying they were young enough, and God would send them more succession."

There is no suggestion, such as might have been natural enough at that age, of poison or foul play in the death of the two infants—nothing but misfortune and fatality and the dark shadows closing over a life hitherto so bright.   James was the last of his name : the childless Albany in France, whom Scotland did not love, was the only man surviving of his kindred, and it is not wonderful if the King's heart failed him in such a catastrophe, or if he thought himself doomed of heaven.   When this great domestic affliction came to him he was on the eve of a breach with England, brought about not only by the usual mutual aggravations upon the Border, but by other matters of graver importance.   King Henry had made many efforts to draw the Scottish King to his side.   He had discoursed to him himself by letter, he had sent him not only ambassadors but preachers, he had done everything that could be done to detach the young monarch from the band of sovereigns who were against England, and the allegiance of the Pope.   Latterly the correspondence had become very eager and passionate on Henry's side.   He had repeatedly invited his nephew to visit him, and many negotiations had passed between them on the subject.   The project was so far advanced that Henry came to York to meet James, and waited there for nearly a week for his arrival.   But there was great reluctance on the Scottish side to risk their King so far on the other side of the Border.   They had suggested Newcastle as a more safe place of meeting, but this had been rejected on the part of the English king.   Finally, Henry left York in great resentment, which was aggravated by a defeat upon the Border.   Pitscottie tells us that he sent a herald to James declaring that he considered the truce between them broken ; that "he should take such order with him as he took with his father before him ; for he had yet that same wand to ding him with that dang his father ; that is to say, the Duke of Norfolk living that strak the field of Flodden, who slew his father with many of the nobles of Scotland." The King of Scotland thought, the chronicler adds, that these were " uncouth and sharp words "—an opinion in which

the reader will agree. But whether Pitscottie is verbally
correct or not it is very evident that Henry did not
hesitate to rate his nephew in exceedingly sharp and
discourteous terms, as for instance bidding him not to make
a brute of himself by listening to the priests who would lead
any man by the nose who gave them credence. The
negotiations altogether were carried on from the English
side in a very arrogant manner as comported with Henry's
character, made all the more overbearing towards James by
their relationship, which gave him a certain natural title to
bully his sister's son.

 And everything in Scotland was now tending to the
miseries of a divided council and a nation rent asunder by
internal differences. The new opinions were making
further progress day by day, the priests becoming more
fierce in their attempts to crush by violence the force of the
Reformation — attempts which in their very cruelty and
ferocity betrayed a certain growing despair. When Norfolk
came to Scotland from Henry—an ill-omened messenger if
what is said above of Henry's threat was true—the Scottish
gentlemen sought him secretly with confessions of their
altered faith ; and the ambassador made the startling report
to Henry that James's own mind was in so wavering and
uncertain a state that if the priests did not drive him into
war during the current summer he would confiscate the possessions of the Church before the year was out. But Norfolk's
mission, which was in itself a threat, and the presence of
the Douglases over the Border, who had never ceased to be
upheld by Henry, and whose secret machinations, of which
Lady Glamis and James Hamilton had been victims, were
now about to culminate in open mischief, all contributed
to exasperate the mind of James. That he was not supported
as his father had been by the nobility, who alone had the
power of giving effect to his call for a general armament, is
evident from the first. His priestly counsellors could support him by the imposts which he made freely upon the
revenues of the Church, not always without complaint on
their part : but they were of comparatively little influence in

bringing together the hosts who had to do the fighting ; and from the first the nobility,—half of which or more was leavened with Reformation doctrines and felt that their best support was in England—while the whole, almost without exception, resented the prominence of the Church in the national councils, hating and scorning her interference in secular and especially in warlike matters, as is the case in every age,—showed itself hostile.   After various incursions on the part of England, made with much bravado and considerable damage, one of which was headed by Angus and his brother George Douglas (this latter, however, being promptly punished and defeated on the spot by the brave Borderers), James made the usual call for a general assembly of forces on the Boroughmuir : but he had advanced only a little way on his march to the Borders when he was stopped by the declaration of the lords that they would only act on the defensive, and would on no account go out of Scotland.   The fathers of these same lords had followed James IV, though with the strongest disapproval, to the fatal field of Flodden, their loyalty triumphing over their judgment : but the sons on either side had no such bond between them.   James disbanded in disgust the reluctant host, which considered less the honour of Scotland than their own safety ; but got together afterwards a smaller army under the leadership of Lord Maxwell, with which to try over again the old issue.   Pitscottie's account of the discussions and dissensions, and of all the scorns which subdued James's spirit, is very graphic.   Norfolk had led a great body of men into Scotland, who though not advancing very far had done great harm burning and ravaging ; but, checked by a smaller force, which held him back without giving battle, had finally retired across the Border, where James was very anxious to have followed him.

"The King's mind was very ardent on battel on English ground, which when the lords perceived they passed again to the council, and concluded that they would not follow the Duke of Norfolk at that time for the King's pleasure, because they said that it was not grounded upon no good cause or reasone, and that he was ane better priests' king nor he was theirs, and used more of priests' counsel nor theirs. Therefore they had the less will to fight with him, and said it was more meritoriously done to hang all such as gave counsel to the King to break his promises to the King of England, whereof they perceived great inconvenients to befall. When they had thus concluded, and the King being advertised thereof, the King departed with his familiar servants to Edinburgh ; but the army and council remained still at Lauder."

It was a fatal spot for such a controversy, the spot where, two generations before, the favourite friends and counsellors of James III, whether guilty or not guilty—who can say ?—were hanged over the bridge as an example to all common men who should pretend to serve a king whose peers and the nobles of his realm were shut out from the first of his favour. James V had in his train some familiar servants, confidants of his many public undertakings, who were not of noble blood or, at least, of distinguished rank, and his angry withdrawal might well be explained by his determination to save them, if indeed any explanation beyond his vexed and miserable sense of humiliation and desertion were necessary to account for it. He left the lords, whom he would seem to have had no longer either the means or the heart to confront, saying in his rage and shame that he would " either make them fight or flee, or else Scotland should not keep him and them both," and returned to Edinburgh sick at heart to his Queen, who was not in very good health to cheer him—passing, no doubt, with a deepened sense of humiliation through the crowds which would throng about for news, and to whom the spectacle of their King thus returning discomfited was no pleasant sight : if it were not, perhaps, that many among them had now begun to think all failures and disappointments were so many proofs of the displeasure of heaven against one who would not take upon him the office of reformer.

When James heard soon after that his rebellious lords had disbanded their host, he collected a smaller army to revenge the ravages of Norfolk, issuing, according to Pitscottie, a proclamation bidding all who loved him be ready within twenty-four hours " to follow the King wherever he pleased to pass " ; but even this new levy was little subordi-

nate. After it had penetrated a little way into England a
fatal mistake arose—an idea that Oliver Sinclair, the King's
"minion," whom he had sent to read a manifesto to the
army, had been appointed its general—upon which the new
bands, disgusted in their turn, fell into a forced retreat, and
getting involved in the broken ground of Solway Moss were
there pursued and surrounded by the English, miserably
defeated and put to flight. "There was but ane small
number slain in the field," says Pitscottie, "to wit, there was
slain on both sides but twenty-four, whereof was nine Scottish-
men and fifteen Englishmen"; a very great number, however, were taken prisoners, many of the gentlemen, it is
suggested, preferring captivity to the encounter of the King
after such an inexcusable catastrophe. We are not told why
it was that James had not himself taken the command of his
army. He does not even seem to have accompanied it,
perhaps fearing that personal opposition which was an insult
to a king in those days.

"When these news came to the King of Scotland where he was for
the time, how his lords were taken and had in England, and his army
defaitt, he grew wondrous dollorous and pensive, seeing no good success
to chance him over his enemies. Then he began to remord his conscience, and thought his misgovernance towards God had the wyte therof
and was the principal cause of his misfortune; calling to mind how he
had broken his promise to his uncle the King of England, and had lost
the hearts of his nobles throw evil counsel and false flattery of his
bishops, and those private counsellors and his courtiers, not regarding
his wyse lords' counsels.

"He passed to Edinburgh," adds the chronicler, "and
there remained eight days with great dollour and lamentation for the tinsell (loss) of his lieges and shame to himself."
Discouragement beyond the reach of mortal help or hope
seemed to have taken hold of the unfortunate King. He
saw himself alone, no one standing by him, his nobles
hostile, his people indifferent; he had vowed that Scotland
should not be broad enough to hold both them and him,
but he had no power to carry out this angry threat. His
life had been threatened in mysterious ways; he had lost
his children, his confidence in himself and his fortunes;

last and worst of all, he was dishonoured in the eyes of the
world. His army had refused to advance, his soldiers to
fight. He was the King, but able to give effect to none of
a king's wishes—neither to punish his enemies nor to carry
out his promises. He who had done so much for his realm
could do no more. He who had ridden the Border further
and swifter than any man-at-arms to carry the terror of
justice and the sway of law—who had daunted the dauntless
Highlands and held the fiercest chiefs in check—who had
been courted by pope and emperor, and admired and feasted
at the splendid Courts of France—he who had been the
King of the Commons, the idol of the people—was now cast
down and miserable, the most shamed and helpless of
kings.

There seems no reason why James should have so entirely
lost heart. There had already been moments in his life
when he had suffered sore discouragement and overthrow,
yet never had been overcome. But now it is clear he felt
himself at the end of his resources. How could he ever hold
up his head again? a man who could not keep his own
kingdom from invasion, or avenge himself upon his enemies!
After he had lingered a little in Edinburgh, where the Queen
was now near the moment which should give another heir to
Scotland, he left the capital—perhaps to save her at such a
time from the sight and the contagion of his despair—and
crossed the Firth to Falkland, a place so associated with
stirring passages in his career. But there his sickness of
heart turned to illness of body; he became so "vehement
sick" that his life was despaired of; he was "very near
strangled to death by extreme melancholie." One hope
remained, that the Queen might restore some confidence to
his failing strength and mind by an heir to the crown,
another James, for whom it might be worth while to live.
James sent for some of his friends, "certain of his lords,
both spiritual and temporal," to help him to bear this time
of suspense, and advise him what might yet be done to
set matters right, who surrounded him, as may be imagined,
very anxiously, fearing the issue.

FALKLAND PALACE

" By this the post came out of Linlithgow showing the King good tidings that the Queen was delivered. The King inquired whether it was man or woman. The messenger said it was ane fair dochter. The King answered and said, ' Farewell ! it came with ane lass, and it will pass with ane lass,' and so commended himself to Almighty God, and spoke little from thereforth, but turned his back to his lords and his face to the wall."

Even at this bitter moment, however, the dying Prince was not left alone with his last disappointment. Cardinal Beatoun, whose influence had been so inauspicious in his life, pressed forward, " seeing him begin to fail of his strength and natural speech," and thrust upon him a paper for his signature, " wherein the Cardinal had writ what he pleased for his own particular weill," evidently with some directions about the regency, that ordeal which Scotland, unhappily, had now again to go through. When James had put his dying hand to this authority, wrested from him in his last weakness, a faint light of peace seems to have fallen across his deathbed.

" As I have shown you, he turned him upon his back, and looked and beheld his lords around about, and gave ane little lauchter, syne kissed his hand and gave it to all his lords about him, and thereafter held up his hands to God and yielded the spirit."

There are many pathetic death scenes in history, but few more touching. His father, after a splendid and prosperous life, had fallen " in the lost battle, borne down by the flying ; " he, after a career almost as chivalrous and splendid and full of noble work for his country, in a still more forlorn overthrow ; his hopes all gone from him, his strength broken in his youth. Nothing, it would seem, could save these princes, so noble and so unfortunate. It was enough to bear the name of James Stewart to be weighed down by cruel Fate. But before his spirit shook off the mortal coil a ray of peace had shot through the clouds ; he looked upon the anxious faces of his friends, some of whom at least must surely have been true friends, bound to him by comradeship and brotherhood, with that low laugh which is one of the most touching expressions of weakened and failing humanity—love and kindness in it, and a certain pleasure to see them round him ; and yet to be free of it all—the heavy kingship, the hopes that ever failed, the friends that so rarely were true. The lips that touched that cold hand which he kissed before he gave to them must have trembled, perhaps with compunction, let us hope with some vow of fidelity to his memory and trust.

Thus died the last of the five Jameses—the last in one sense of that unfortunate but gallant line. A life more swept by storms, more rent asunder by conflicting passions and influences, more tragic still and passionate than theirs, was to part them from the singularly changed, modified, and modernised successors who, with a difference, were to wear yet drop this ancient crown. The Stewarts after Mary are no longer like those that went before. James's dying words came in some curious fashion true, though not as he thought. It came with a lass and it went with a lass that ancient crown. When another James reached the throne Scotland was no more as it had been.

It may seem a fantastic chronology to end here the records of the Stewards of Scotland: but it is I think justified by this change, which altered altogether the character of the history and the circumstances of the monarchs. Henceforward new agencies, new powers, were at work in the little proud and self-contained kingdom, which had maintained its independence and individuality so long. Torn asunder by rival influences, by intrigues incessant and profound, by that struggle between the old and the new which was never more desperate than in her bosom, and which, being a religious change chiefly, was one of life and death : and with a monarch no longer native, but of foreign training and thoughts, even if she had not been a woman and half a Tudor, the little ship of State, the gallant little nation, plunged amid waves and billows, not unfamiliar, indeed, but fiercer and wilder than ever before, with winds so much increased in force as they raged over wider seas.

The Stewards of Scotland here ended their special trust and gave in their account. No race was ever more unfor-

tunate, but I think we may say that none more nobly
endeavoured to discharge that high commission.   With one
exception, and that doubtful—for a man may be weak and
may not be brave without being a bad man or even king—
every bearer of this fated name laboured with courage and
constancy at the great work of elevating his country.
"Another for Hector!" cried the Highland warrior when his
young chief was in danger, and all the world has read the
story with moistened eyes.   Another for Scotland! had been
the cry of the house of Stewart throughout more than a
century.   As one man fell he handed the sword to another ;
to an infant hand trained amid feuds and anarchy, but always
clasping, as soon as it had force enough, the royal weapon
with royal courage and meaning.   None of the Jameses
lived beyond the earliest chapter of middle age ; all of them
succeeded in early youth, most of them in childhood ; and,
with but that uncertain exception of James III, every one of
them was actuated by a noble patriotism, and did his *devoir*
manfully for the improvement and development of his
country.   They were noble gentlemen one and all: the
bigotry, the egotism, the obstinacy of the later Stewarts were
not in them.   Knights and paladins of an age of romance,
they were also stern executors of justice, bold innovators,
with eyes ever open to every expedient of progress and prosperity.   Their faults were those faults of a light heart and
genial temperament, which are the most easily understood
and pardoned.   Under their sway their country and their
little capital came to be known over Christendom as not
unworthy to hold place among the reigning kingdoms and
cities through which the stream of chivalry flowed.   They
invented the trade, the shipping, the laws and civic order of
Scotland.   Among her heroes there are none more worthy
of everlasting remembrance.   They fulfilled their stewardry
with a unity of purpose and a steadfastness of aim which,
when we take into account the continually recurring lapses
of long minorities, is one of the wonders of the time.   Edinburgh grew under their sway from an angry village, lying
between a fierce castle and a rich monastery, little dis-

tinguished above its peers, less favoured than Stirling, less wealthy than the town of St. John, to one of the most noted of cities, picturesque and splendid, full of noble houses, the centre of national life and government.   And it is curious to record that no one of the monarchs who brought it such nobility and fame left any sadness of death to the associations of Edinburgh.   They lived and were wedded and filled with the brightness of their happier moments the town which afforded so beautiful a scene for all rejoicings : they died on the field of battle or in other places in conflict or violence or despair.   But Edinburgh only retains the brighter memories, the triumphal processions, the bridal finery, the jousts and the feasts, the Parliaments and proclamations of laws and high alliances.   The reigns of the Jameses contain the history of her rise, her splendour, her climax of beauty and stateliness, without any association of downfall or decay.

PART III

THE TIME OF THE PROPHETS

CHAPTER I

UNDER THE QUEEN REGENT

THERE is perhaps among the many historical personages attached by close association to Edinburgh no one so living, so vigorous, so present, as the great figure of the Reformer and Prophet, who once filled the air with echoes of his vehement and impassioned oratory, who led both Lords and Commons, and mated with princes on more than equal terms, the headstrong, powerful, passionate Preacher, who was at once the leading spirit of his time and its most vigorous chronicler. To fill the circle of association, he alone, of all the animated groups who withstood or who followed him, has left us not only a number of books which disclose his mind with all its powers and imperfections, but the very dwelling in which he passed at least the latter part of his life, intact and authentic, a memorial more striking and attractive than any "storied urn or animated bust." Nor are even the associations of burial wanting; for though it is no longer within the solemn enclosure of a churchyard, and there is no certainty that the stone which is supposed to mark the position of the Reformer's grave is historically exact, it is yet sure enough that near by, within reach of the doors of his ancient church, beneath the pavement trodden by so many feet, his remains repose in the centre of the life of the Scottish capital, a position more appropriate than any other that could be imagined. Thus by life and by death this singular and most evident and unmistakable man, still alive in every lineament, is connected with the city in which his life was passed, and in the history of which he can never be forgotten. There may be doubts about other localities, and it may be difficult to identify the houses which have been inhabited and the floors that have been trod by other distinguished personages. Crowding footsteps of the poor have obliterated the record in many a noble house abandoned by history; even the fated steps of the Queen save in one bloodstained closet have left but little authentic trace. But Knox is still present with all the force of an indestructible individuality—in the existing life of the country which took so strong an impression from him, and in the absolutely personal facts of the church in which he preached, the house in which he lived, the stone under which he lies.

To estimate the share he had in the foundations of that modern Scotland which has so increased and thriven since his day, is perhaps more hard now than it was even eighty years ago, when his biography was written by Dr. M'Crie to the great interest and enthusiasm of the country. The laws of historical judgment are subject to perpetual change, and the general estimate of the great personages of the past has undergone various modifications since that time. Perhaps even the Church is less sure of her share in the record, less certain of the doom once so unhesitatingly denounced against "the Paip that Pagan fu' of pride"; less confident of her own superiority to all other developments of Christianity. The least enlightened are no longer able to feel with a good conscience, as our best-instructed fathers did, that an important part of religious liberty was freedom to curse and pull down every tenet other than their own. No belief has been more obstinate or is more time-honoured: but in theory at least it has been much subdued in recent times, so that few of us are able to hold by our own side with the perfect confidence which once we felt. And in these changing views, and in the impulse towards a greater catholicity of feeling

which has sprung up in Scotland, the influence of that uncompromising teacher to whom reform was everything, who
had no prepossession in favour of what was old and venerable, but desired with all the fervour of his fiery soul to make
everything new, has doubtless waned, save to that sacred
simplicity of ignorance which forms no judgment.   But
nothing can obliterate the person and strenuous being of
John Knox, or make him a less interesting figure on the
crowded and tragic stage of that epoch which he dominated
and chronicled.   And nothing can unlink the associations
which make him ever present and living in Edinburgh, which
was the capital and centre of his kingdom as much as of any
king who ever breathed.

John Knox was in every sense of the words a son of the
soil, yet came of a not unknown family, " kent folk " of East
Lothian : if not lairds of any great heritage, yet possessing
lands and living sufficient to entitle them to consideration.
They were able to give him the best education of the time,
which he completed at the University of Glasgow under the
teaching of Major or Mair, the same whom George Buchanan
accompanied to France ; so that both these great men, as well
as various nobles and ecclesiastics of the time, were his fellow-
students, trained under the same influence.   Whether Knox
followed Major to St. Andrews as Buchanan followed him to
Paris is not known ; but he would seem to have lectured
on philosophy in St. Andrews at the beginning of his career.
It might be that he was himself present, and heard some of
the bold and familiar addresses of the wandering friars, the
first rude champions of Reform, whose protest against the
wickedness of the bishops and the extortions of the clergy
he quotes with so much enjoyment of their rough humour,
in the beginning of his history ; or even might have witnessed
the lighted pile and felt across his face the breath of that
" reek " which carried spiritual contagion with it, as it flew
upon the keen breeze from the sea over that little centre of
life, full of scholars and wits, and keen cynical spectators
little likely to be convinced by any such means.   It is
curious to hear of Major for instance, one of the Sorbonne,

. R

a doctor of Paris and man of the world, as present at all those proceedings, listening to Friar William's denunciation of the priests, to which he gave his assent as "a doctrine that might weill be defended, for it contayned no heresye"—and in very different circumstances to the sermons of Rough, addressed to the slayers of the Cardinal, and to the calling of Knox himself, a crisis of popular emotion and vehement feeling. Such a man as Major, a son of the Renaissance, no Reformer nor careful of any of these things, must have looked on with strange feelings at all the revolutions accomplished before him, the rude jests and songs, the half-jocular broadly humorous assaults, the cry of heresy, the horror of the burnings, the deadly earnest of both preacher and people after Beatoun's well-deserved but terrible end which cut all compromises short. One wonders what thoughts were going on in the mind of the old scholar who kept his place in his stall as well when mass was sung as when every trace of that "idolatrous sacrifice" had been trodden under foot. Would it be more or less the same to him whatever they preached, those wild religionists, who tore each other in pieces? did he look on with a secret smile at the turmoil they made, as if it mattered which was uppermost, with a natural horror at the fierce flames of the human sacrifice, yet consent in his mind that if they could so stamp the heresy out which would otherwise destroy them, the bishops were only logical to do it? while on the other side there was not much in point of natural justice to be said against Norman Leslie and his men who slew the Cardinal. Such spectators there must have been in no small number, affording a curious rim and edge of observers to all that the more active and violent might do or say. But these lookers-on have said nothing on the subject, or their mild voices have been lost in the clangour of actors vehement and earnest. It has been reserved for our age to bring these dispassionate or, as we are apt to think, cynical observers into the front rank.

The first scene in which John Knox comes prominently into sight of the world occurs in the midst of that small but urgent and much-agitated society on the fierce little headland by the sea, in the great and noble cathedral which for most of the intervening time has been nothing but ruins. We must in imagination rebuild these lofty walls, throw up again the noble piers and clustered pillars, and see the townsfolk streaming in—a crowd more picturesque in garb than any Scots assembly nowadays, with its provost and councillors in their municipal finery : and the grave representatives of the colleges filing in to their stalls—very grave now, we may well believe, with many a look at the group of gentry, among whom were half a dozen men whose hands were stained with the blood of the Cardinal. No doubt to these spectators, beyond even the great volume of sound which pealed upward from that vast company, in some popular hymn or ancient war-cry of a psalm, the stir of the languid besieging army outside, and the guns of the French Fleet, already on its way to avenge Beatoun and crush this nest of heretics out, sounded ominous in the background. Among the congregation was a dark, vehement man, full of repressed fervour and energy, with two or three lads by his side, of whom he had charge—strange tutor ! flames of zeal and earnestness burning in his deep-set eyes ; the mark of the tonsure (if it was ever there, which is a doubtful question) obliterated by long disuse ; a man known by the congregation as a zealous instructor of youth, catechising his boys publicly of afternoons in the cathedral, vacant then of the many services, the vespers and benedictions, of the superseded faith.

Knox's gifts and qualities were already well known ; he had been a devoted friend and follower of Wishart, the martyr whose memory was still fresh in the minds of all men ; and these public examinations of the three boys, and the expositions he addressed to them, but which many of mature age also gathered to hear, had given the many competent judges then assembled in the beleaguered city a practical knowledge of his gifts and endowments. And Rough, who filled the post of preacher in St. Andrews, was not a man of learning, and in consequence would seem to have been troubled by disputatious members of the priesthood, eager, not unnaturally, to defend their own tenets, and with all the authorities at their fingers' ends. In this strait John Knox was entreated to accept the charge of the congregation, but in vain. Perhaps the memory of Wishart's charge to him, "Return to your bairns," was still in his ears ; perhaps the reluctance and hesitation of a man who felt himself incompetent for so great a responsibility—though it is strange to associate any idea of shrinking from responsibility with such a dauntless spirit, and he was by this time a man of forty-two, with a matured mind and some experience of life. At all events he "utterlie refused" : he "would not run where God had not called him." This being so, there was no alternative but to take him by surprise and force him into the position which all desired him to assume. And this was the step which was accordingly taken by the assembly of the Reformers in St. Andrews, an assembly in which were many well-known and distinguished men, so illustrious a councillor as Sir David Lindsay, the poet and Lyon-King of Scotland, being one of the gentlemen and commoners who decided upon this dramatic and picturesque call.

They were all met to the preaching upon a certain day, the date of which is not given, but which was presumably in the summer of 1547, Knox having arrived with his pupils in St. Andrews in the Easter of that year. The principal persons present were aware of what was coming, and probably the mass of the congregation knew that some event more than ordinary was preparing, which would quicken the eagerness of their attention. The sermon was upon the right of the congregation to the services of "any man in whom they espied the gifts of God," and the risk on his part of refusing their call. Mair, sitting by in his doctor's gown, though he had committed himself to no religious heresy, had discoursed much to his students upon the rights of the people as the source of power—a doctrine, indeed, which Knox did not hold in that naked form, though most probably he had been influenced by these teachings towards the still more tremendous form of doctrine which sets forth the

voice of the Christian people as representing the voice of
God. And no doubt up to this point he gave his adhesion
to the words of the preacher. But when Rough had reached
the crown of his argument he suddenly turned to where
Knox sat and addressed him individually, while the people
held their breath.

"Brother," he said, "ye shall not be offended albeit that
I speak unto you that which I have in charge even from all
those that are here present : which is this. In the name of
God and of His Son Jesus Christ, and in the name of those
that presently call you by my mouth, I charge you that ye
refuse not this holy vocation, but that as you tender the
glory of God, the increase of Christ His kingdom, the edifi-
cation of your brethren, and the comfort of me, whom ye
understand well enough to be oppressed by the multitude of
labours, that you take upon you the public office and charge
of preaching even as ye look to avoid God's heavy displeasure and desire that He shall multiply His grace with
you." And in the end he said to those present, "Was not
this your charge to me ? and do ye not approve this vocation ? " They answered, "It was, and we approve it."
" Whereat the said John, abashed, burst forth in most abundant tears and withdrew himself to his chamber."

It would be difficult to find a more striking scene. Any
sudden incident of an individual character thus occurring in
a public assembly calls forth a thrill of interest, and gives
at once to the most disconnected crowd a pictorial unity.
The interest and excitement in those roused and eager eyes,
the crowd all turned towards the astonished subject of this
appeal, the soft young faces making a little circle round him,
half terrified, half flattered by the sudden consciousness that
all eyes were turned towards them, would make a fine theme
for a historical painter. And "the said John, abashed,"
finding no refuge in the great excitement and surprise of the
moment, he so stern and so strong, but in tears ! It was
thus that the ministry of the great Reformer began.

It is unnecessary to follow in detail a career so well
known. Every particular of it, and even the sermons with

all their heads, may be found in the *Historie of the Reforma-tion in Scotland*, which yields in interest, in picturesqueness and the most living and graphic power of narrative, to none of the primitive chronicles. No professional word-painter has ever put a dramatic scene, a contention, a battle, such as those which were everyday occurrences in Scotland at that time, upon paper with more pictorial force, or with half the fervour of life and reality. The writer goes through all the gamut of popular passion. He exults sometimes fiercely, laughs sometimes coarsely, throws in "a merry jest," which is often grim with savage humour ; but throughout all is always real, always genuine, writing not impartially, but with the strong conviction and sentiment of a man elucidating matters in which he has been himself a prominent actor. The arguments of his adversaries when he enters upon a public controversy are unaccountably feeble, which perhaps may be explained by the fact that the friars were not much accustomed to controversy, perhaps by the natural bias of a controversialist to lessen the force of his antagonists' argu-ments ; and he does not pretend to contemplate his adver-saries, either spiritual or political, with any tolerance, or permit any possibility that they too might perhaps mean well and have a righteous intention, even though it was entirely opposed to that of John Knox : such ideas had no currency in his day. That Mary of Guise might really mean and wish to avoid bloodshed, to strike no blow that was not inevitable, to keep the breach from being widened by actual civil war ; and that the policy of temporising as long as that was possible was anything but wicked wiles and intentions of betrayal, was an idea which he would seem to have been incapable of conceiving. This is a drawback perhaps common to every struggle so important and funda-mental as was the strife which began to rage in Scotland. Had we a history compiled by the spectators to whom we have referred it would probably, unless nature gave them an exceptional keenness of vision, be wanting in those qualities of animation and force which he who is confident of having every good influence on his side, and nothing but the powers of evil against him, is likely to possess. Major indeed was a historian, but he did not meddle with the history of his own time ; and Buchanan, while separated from the reader by the bonds and cerements of his Latin, and therefore shut out from a popular audience, is as great a partisan as Knox.

The little garrison of St. Andrews was taken, as everybody knows, by the French, and carried away to prison and the galleys ; but no blood was shed to avenge the blood of Beatoun, a point which ought to be put to their credit. John Knox suffered all these misfortunes with a steadfast soul, still declaring to all who surrounded him, in the extremity of suffering, hardship, and sickness, that he should again preach in that church of St. Andrews from which he had been taken. This is the first of the many prophecies completely verified afterwards with which he is credited. He escaped after about three years of captivity and misery in France, during which he would seem to have been actually employed in the galleys, and came to England, where it is to be supposed the story of his influence and power with the Scotch Reformers had preceded him, otherwise the advancement to which he reached, and which might have been greater but for his dissatisfaction with the imperfectly Reformed Church there, and the bondage of ceremonials and traditions still left in it, would have been still more extraordinary. He was one of the chaplains to the boy-king Edward, for whom he had the amiable prejudice common to those who secure the favour of very young princes, expecting from him everything that was great and good. At the death of the young King, however, Knox removed hurriedly to the Continent with many others, knowing that under the reign of Mary there would be little acceptance for men of his views. During his stay in England he had met with a pair of ladies who were henceforward to be very closely connected with his life—Marjory Bowes, his future wife, and to all appearance still more important, her mother, Mrs. Bowes, to whom, contrary to the ordinary idea of that relationship, he seems to have given much regard and affection, notwithstanding that she was a melancholy woman, depressed and despondent, sometimes overwhelmed with religious terrors, and requiring continued support and encouragement in the faith. One cannot help feeling a sort of compassion for the silent Marjory, of whom nothing is ever heard, between her solemn lover of fifty and her sad mother. But she is voiceless, and though there are letters of religious counsel addressed to her under the title of "weill belovit sister," there is not among them all, so strange is the abstract effect of religious exhortation thus applied, one gleam of anything like individual character, or which can throw any light upon what she was ; which, considering the marked individuality of the writer, is curious exceedingly. We must hope that on other occasions, notwithstanding his mature years, there were letters calculated to give more satisfaction to a young woman than these expositions and addresses.

For the next two years Knox, now it is evident universally known wherever the Reformation had penetrated, filled the place of minister to a congregation of exiles assembled at Geneva, most of them refugees from England, who had fled, as he himself had done, at the accession of Mary. But his heart was in his own land, where in the meantime the progress of the new Reformed faith was arrested, and silence and discouragement had fallen over the country. The leaders were dispersed or destroyed, the preachers silenced, and there was no one to gather together the many groups of believers all over the country in whose hearts the seed had sprung up strongly, but who as yet had made no public profession. In 1555 Knox suddenly reappeared in Scotland, brought thither at once by urgent letters and by the eagerness of his own heart. When he arrived in Edinburgh he found that many who "had a zeal to godliness" still attended mass, probably finding it more difficult to break the continual habit of their lives than the bonds of doctrine— and that the outer structure of the Church remained much as it had been, without any such shattering and falling asunder as had taken place in regions more advanced. That this arose from no want of zeal was proved as soon as the preacher appeared : for his arrival was no sooner known than the house in which he had alighted from his journey was filled by a stream of inquirers, whom he "began to exhort secretly." One night he was called to supper with the Laird of Dun, the well-known John Erskine, who was one of the most earnest of the Reforming party, and in the grave company he found there—among whom were one or two ministers and the young but already promising and eminent William Maitland of Lethington—the question was fully discussed, Was it lawful to conform while holding a faith not only different but hostile? was it permissible to bow down in the house of Rimmon? To this Knox answered No, with all the uncompromising and stern sincerity of his soul. "Nowise was it lawful." The question was very fully defended from the other point of view. "Nothing was omitted that might make for the temporiser"; even the example of Paul, who went up into the Temple to pay his vow by the advice of the Apostle James, which step, however, Knox pronounced at once, notwithstanding his absolute reverence for Holy Writ, to have been wrong, and not of God—a mistake of both the Apostles, and manifestly bringing no blessing with it. His bold and assured argument cut the ground from under the feet of the hesitating Reformers, to whom no doubt it was very difficult thus to break away from all the traditions of their lives.

This scene throws a strange and in some respects new light upon the more human side of the great movement. It is easier perhaps to us who are acquainted with all that followed to understand the fiery zeal which flamed against every accessory of what they conceived to be idolatry—the saintly image, which was nothing but a painted board, and the "round clipped god" upon the altar, which was blasphemously asserted to be the very Lord Himself—than to remember that these men had also many links of use and wont, of attachment and habit, to the churches in which they had been christened, and the position, with all its needs and simple duties, to which they had been born. To see them standing there for a moment reluctant, with the tremendous breach that must be made in life gaping before them, and the sense of universal disruption and tearing asunder which must follow, is to me more touching than the stern conviction which never pauses nor fears. They were so thoroughly convinced, however, of the necessity which he reasoned out with such remorseless logic, that Erskine first, and after him many gentlemen through Scotland, craved the help of the preacher to put the crown upon their convictions, and spread in their halls and private chambers, no church being attainable, what was now for the first time called the Table of the Lord. Knox went to Dun in Forfarshire across the great firths of Forth and Tay, and to Calder, the house of Sir James Sandilands, afterwards Lord Torphichen, in Lothian, where many gathered to hear him. But it would seem to have been in the West, always the most strenuous in doctrine, that he first celebrated the new rite, the holy feast as yet unknown in Scotland. During the eventful winter of 1555-56 he pervaded the country thus, setting forth the special bond of evangelical religion, uniting those different groups by the sacred seal of the bread and wine—who can doubt received with a profound and tremulous awe by lips to which the wafer had been hitherto the only symbol of that act of closest communion ?

This would seem to have been the chief work of Knox during the visit which, in the midst of his Geneva ministry, he paid to his native land : and it is easy to perceive that it was of supreme importance as identifying and separating the converts into a definite community, bound together by that sacrament of fealty, an oath more binding than any expressed only in words. Hitherto the preaching and teaching of the Word, which was itself a discovery, and came with all the freshness of a new revelation, had been the only sacred office carried on by the Reformers. The Sacraments were all in the hands of ecclesiastics, who had been for generations past losing the confidence and respect of the nation—though one cannot but believe there must still have been here and there a humble curate, a parish priest like Chaucer's Parsoune, to strengthen the hold of the accustomed ordinances upon men's minds, who, however strongly they might turn against

the miracle of transubstantiation, could not cast aside the
only means of partaking in the great mystery of the body
and blood of Christ.   To all such here was now the answer
set forth, and the hope—the holy Table, the communion of
saints, the bread and wine of the great and ceaseless commemoration.   It would be doing the greatest wrong to these
small devout assemblies, and to the fervent preacher, devoured
with eagerness to make them all, not almost but altogether
such men as himself, to call this an act of policy.   Yet that
it was so, and that a bond was thus established to consolidate
the party, more sacred, more binding, than any other, there
can be no reasonable doubt.

While travelling on this solemn mission from place to
place and house to house of the religious gentry of Scotland,
Knox would seem to have made Edinburgh his headquarters,
and preached there from time to time, not always secretly.
He had here " a greater audience than ever before " in " the
Bishop of Dunkeld's great lodging," that ancient habitation
from which Gawin Douglas, the poet-bishop, had watched and
waited while the fight went on within the gates of the Nether
Bow, and from which he rushed out to rescue the other prelate
whose corselet rang under his rochet.   Strange association,
yet not inappropriate ; for the mild Bishop of Dunkeld had
also found many potent words to say against the abuses of
the Church, though the new presbyter who now took his
place was rather of Beatoun's warlike mettle than of Douglas's.
The nobles who came thither to hear the preacher were so
" weill contented " with his doctrine—which is his own
moderate version of what was no doubt an enthusiasm of
grave approbation—that they seem to have imagined, in that
solemn simplicity which belongs to fresh conviction, that he
might perchance, could she but hear him, move the Regent
Queen herself, Mary of Guise, an unlikely convert no doubt.
He was accordingly exhorted by three gentlemen, specified
as the Earl of Glencairn, the Earl Marischal, and Harye
Drummond, to write a letter to the Queen, which Knox,
always eager for the pen, and full of matter boiling to have
utterance, immediately did.   It is difficult not to think of

the *sancta simplicitas,* which rarely belongs to such a group
of men, when we think of the grave trio of advisers, and the
still graver but fiery prophet-preacher, making this wonderful
appeal.   It was less wonderful in him who loved nothing so
much as to write when he could not be preaching, to set
forth those high-handed arraignments before the visionary
tribunal of the one true and only faith, of whomsoever he
could address, queen or peasant ; but it is strange that men
of the world, and of the society of their time, should have
thus thought it possible to convert a lady so full of policy
and cares of government, so entirely occupied with the most
important matters of statesmanship, not to say so determined
a Catholic, as the daughter of the Guises, the sister of the
Cardinal.

The attempt, as was natural, failed completely.   " Which
letter," resumes Knox, " when she had read within a day or
two she delivered it to the proud prelate, Beatoun, Bishop of
Glasgow, and said in mockage, ' Please you, my lord, to read
a pasquill ? ' "   It is against the perfection of the prophet, but
not the character of the man, that this scorn stung him as
no persecution could have done.   He made certain additions
to the letter, and published it in Geneva on his return there.
We are not told which part of the letter these additions are,
but what he tells us seems to indicate that the threatening
prophecies, of which he says in his Historie, " lett those very
flatterers see what hath failed," had been added to the
original text.   We forgive him his ready wrath, and even
the " threatenings " which he always considered himself at
liberty to launch at those who, in his own language, " withstood the truth " : but we could have wished that Knox had
been more magnanimous, and could have forgotten the
offence after the passage of years.   Mary's careless speech
would have been but " ane merry boord " had it been directed
against one of his enemies.

When Knox went back to Geneva after this winter's
work to resume his pastorate there, he left the growing cause
of Reform in Scotland with a constitution and organisation
sanctified by the most sacred rites of religion, an advantage

quite inestimable in the circumstances, and placing the cause
as in an ark of safety. And when he returned to Edinburgh
two years later, the scattered groups to whom in country
houses and castles he had administered the Lord's Supper
had become the Congregation, an army existing in all
quarters of Scotland, ready to rally to the aid of any
portion of the body, or eminent individual, who might be
attacked : and headed by a phalanx of Scots nobility, Lords
of the Congregation, the heads of a new party in the State,
as well as of a new Church, an altogether novel development
of national life. It would have been difficult to have spoken
more boldly than Knox had done in his letter to the Queen
Regent three years before, but the Congregation in its established position as a national party took stronger ground, and
pressed their claims to a hearing with the force of petitioners
too strong to be gainsaid. Knox had called upon Mary herself in her own person to hear the Word and abjure her errors,
but the body of Reformers asked for measures more compre-
hensive and still more subversive of the established order of
things. In their first address to Mary they upbraided themselves, with a manly penitence which must have been bewildering to royal ears, that they had permitted their brethren
in the faith to be destroyed by " faggot fyre and sword "
without resistance. "We acknowledge it," said these strange
petitioners, " to have been our bounden duty before God
either to have defended our brethren from those cruel
murtherers (seeing we are a part of that power which God
hath established in this realm) or else to have given open
testification of our faith with them." This, however, being
no longer in their power, they besought the Queen to make
such horrible accidents impossible in the future, and to grant
to them permission to establish their worship ; to meet
publicly or privately to make their common prayer, and read
the Scriptures in the vulgar tongue ; to have the assistance
of " qualified persons in knowledge " to expound to them
" any hard places of Scripture," and to have the Sacraments
administered " in the vulgar tongue," and the Lord's Supper
in both kinds. Last of all they desired of the Queen that

" the wicked, scandalous, and detestable life of prelates and of the State Ecclesiastical" should be reformed, stating at the same time their wish to have the case between themselves and the priests tried not only by the rules of the New Testament, but by the writings of the ancient Fathers. In all this there was no intolerance, but a wholly just and reasonable prayer, suggesting harm to no one, not even the persecutors from whom they had suffered ; altogether a claim of justice and native right magnanimously as well as forcibly made, with dignified recollection of their own position as " a part of that power which God hath established in this realm," to which it would have been difficult for any reasonable sovereign to return a discourteous or imperious answer.

Mary of Guise did no such thing. She did not receive the address of the Congregation as she had done the letter of Knox. But she did what was worse, she gave no answer at all save fair words and delay. It would have been perhaps too much to expect that even those moderate and manly petitioners should have taken into consideration the complicated circumstances by which she was surrounded, or the difficulties of her position, with the " State Ecclesiastical" so strong and wealthy, arbiters for the moment of her faith, and France and her kindred expectant of impossible things from her, and Rome itself regarding with a watchful eye what a Princess of so Catholic a family—defender of the faith in a distant but at this moment exceedingly important field—should do. Mary temporised, which was perhaps the best thing possible for the Reformers if not for herself, and promised to take order, to regulate matters for their advantage so soon as it was possible, when she should have concluded various matters of more importance that were in hand, such, for instance, as that of awarding the crown matrimonial to her daughter's husband the young King of France, to whom all earthly distinctions were soon to matter so little. During this period of delay the Reformers were left unmolested to multiply and mature, so that when her other business was despatched, and the Queen could no longer avoid some action in the matter, the Congregation had attained both numbers

and power. When the preachers were summoned to appear
before her to plead their own cause "it was concluded by the
whole brethren that the gentlemen of every country should
accompany their preachers to the day and place appointed."
This was a proceeding entirely sanctioned by Scotch custom,
of which there were many historical examples, but it was not
perhaps calculated to promote the ends of peaceful discussion ;
for the gentlemen thus described were accompanied by their
households at least, if not by a stout following of retainers,
and the result was the assemblage of "such a multitude"
that even the leaders considered it likely to have "given fear"
to the Queen, although this multitude was, as the record says,
with a gleam of grim humour, "without armour as peciable
men, minding only to give confession with their preachers."
Mary wisely interposed another period of delay when she
was warned what the "peaceable" escort was with which the
preachers were obeying her call.

It was, however, as little safe to let loose such an
army of confessors through the country which had to be
traversed before they could reach their homes, as to receive
them in Stirling where the appointment had been. For, mild
as was their purpose and godly their intentions, it proved too
much for the sense and moderation even of that religious
crowd when they found themselves on their way northward
masters of St. Johnstone (or Perth, as moderns call it) with
the fumes of a sermon of Knox's still in their brain, and a
report about that the Queen meant to put the preachers "to
the horn," for all so softly spoken as she was. Knox's sermon had been "vehement against idolatrie," though preached
in a church still wealthy and bright with all the adornments
of the ancient faith, and in which, as the crowd dispersed, a
priest appeared in his vestments to say his mass. It gives
us a curious impression of the chaos that reigned, to hear that
in the town, which was full to overflowing of this Protestant
crowd, and in the very church which still rang with the echoes
of Knox's vehement oratory, he who had no words strong
enough to denounce that idolatrous rite—there should come
forth in the calm of use and wont a nameless humble priest

with his acolyte to say the mass, which was his bounden
duty whatever obstacles might be in his way.   The manner
in which it is recorded, with the violent antagonism of the
time, is this—" That a priest in contempt would go to the
masse ; and to declare his malignant presumption he would
open up ane glorious tabernacle which stood upon the Hie
altar."   On the other side no doubt the tale would be, that
with the faith and courage of a holy martyr this venerable
confessor ascended the steps of the altar to give his life, if
needful, for the holy mysteries, and fulfil his sacred office
whoever might oppose.   And which was the more true version who can tell ?   On neither side would it be believed,
what was probably the fact, that it was a simple brother
taking little thought of the commotions round him, who, as
soon as the clamour of the preaching was over, concerned
with nothing but his mass which had to be said during
canonical hours, had come in without other intention to perform his daily duty.

But in any case, the sight of the glorious tabernacle filled
with a fury of excitement the dregs of the crowd who still
lingered there.   A child's outcry, more " malapert " than the
priest, called the attention of the lingerers, and before any
one knew, the passion of destruction had seized like a frenzy
upon the people.   They flung themselves upon the " glorious
tabernacle," and all the statues and adornments, and laid
them in swift and sudden ruin.   The rumour flew through
the town, along with the shouts and crash of metal and stone ;
and the remainder of the lately-dispersed multitude came
rushing back to the church which was the scene of the outbreak, a mob " not of the gentlemen, neither of them that
were earnest professors, but of the rasckall multitude," which
finding nothing to do in the stripped walls and chapels,
hurried on, led, no doubt, by the first of the iconoclasts, who
had become intoxicated with the frenzy of destruction, to the
convents of the Grey and the Black Friars.   Their violence
grew as they passed on, from one scene of destruction to
another, many of them finding substantial inducements in the
shape of booty, in the well-filled meal-girnels and puncheons

of salt beef in the larders of the monks. By the time they
came to these it may be presumed that the special rage
against idolatry had been assuaged ; but the demon of
destruction had taken its place. And when the excited
multitude reached the noble Charterhouse with all its picturesque buildings, " the fairest abbaye and best biggit of any
within the realm of Scotland," surrounded by pleasant
gardens and noble trees, every restraint was thrown aside.
It had been founded by James I., and there lay the remains
of his murdered body along with those of many other royal
victims of the stormy and tumultuous past. So much conscience was left that the terrified monks, or at least the Prior
who is specially mentioned, was allowed to take away with
him as much silver and gold as he was able to carry. The
rest was beaten down into indiscriminating ruin, and " within
two days these three great places, monuments of idolatrie,
to wit the Grey and Black thieves and Charterhouse monks (a
building of a wondrous cost and greatness), were so destroyed
that the walls only did remain of all these great edifications."

That this was in no way the doing of Knox and his
colleagues is evident ; but it is equally evident that they
treated it as a mere accident and outrage of the mob, without consequence so far as the greater question was concerned. When the Queen, exasperated, threatened in her
anger on the receipt of the news to destroy St. Johnstone,
and began to collect an army to march upon the offenders,
the Congregation assembled in Perth professed astonishment
and incredulity, treating her threats as the mere utterances
of passion, and thinking " such cruelty " impossible. There
is not a word in the letters to the Queen's Majestie, to the
Nobilitie of Scotland, and the fierce address to the priests in
which they afterwards stated their case, of any wrong on
their own side or provocation given. The Congregation
takes at once the highest tone. They declare that, faithful
servants of the realm as they have always been, if this unjust tyranny is carried out they will be constrained to take
up the sword of just defence, notifying at the same time
their innocence not only to " the King of France, to our

S

Mistress and to her husband, but also to the Princes and Council of everie Christian realm, declaring unto them that this cruel, unjust, and most tyrannical murther intended against towns and multitudes, was and is the only cause of our revolt from our accustomed obedience." Thus they treat the threatened attack throughout as wholly directed against their religion and religious freedom, without the least reference to the just cause of offence given by riots so alarming and destructive, and by the ruin of a national monument so important as the Charterhouse. All these are as completely ignored as if the population of St. John-stone had been the most tranquil and law-abiding in the world. And they do this with such evident good faith that it is impossible not to believe that what had happened was to themselves an unimportant incident : though it was something like what the destruction of Westminster Abbey would have been in England. In these respects, however, the state of feeling produced by the Reformation followed no ordinary laws ; the fervour of hatred and contempt which the priesthood called forth in Scotland being beyond all example or comparison, except, indeed, in some parts of France, where Farel and his followers had set the example of destruction.

The Queen, however, did little more than threaten. Before she could move at all, the Westland lords, who had gone home, had heard the news and turned back in hot haste to succour their brethren. Even without that rein-forcement the French general had hesitated to approach too near the town occupied by so many resolute men, no longer "peaceable," but determined to defend themselves. It is very apparent that Mary wished above all things to avoid bloodshed and any step which would precipitate the begin-ning of a civil war : and she sent embassy after embassy, selected sometimes from her own side, sometimes from that of the Reformers, to exhort them to submission. If her part in the matter was that of an anxious and in many ways considerate ruler, bent, so far as in her lay, upon keeping the peace, the attitude of the Congregation was, at the same

time, a perfectly manly and moderate one, granting their
dulness of conscience in respect to the real outrage. " If the
Queen's grace would suffer the religion then begun to proceed, and not trouble their brethren and sisters that had
professed Christ Jesus with them," they declared themselves
ready to submit in any way to the Queen's commandment ;
but without this promise they would not stir. Knox himself, however, who was the soul of the party, was, according
to his wont, less self-controlled. He considered it his duty
to make a special statement to Argyle and the Lord James,
the future Earl of Murray, who were the Queen's first envoys,
and to send a message to the Regent in his own name, with
a curious assumption of the prophet's office, which is exceedingly remarkable so near the beginning of his career, and is
at once an evidence of the enormous influence which he had
acquired, and of the astonishing confidence in his own
mission and powers which must have helped him to acquire
it. " Say to the Queen's Grace Regent," he required them,
" in my name, that we whom she in her blind rage doth
persecute are God's servants, faithful and obedient subjects
to the authority of this realm : that that religion which she
pretendeth to maintain by fire and sword is not the religion
of Christ Jesus, but is express contrarie to the same, ane
superstition devised by the brain of man : which I offer
myself to prove against all that within Scotland will maintain the contrarie—liberty of tongue being granted to me,
and God's written word being admitted for judge."

   Thus the preacher flung down his glove like a knight
of the old chivalry, with a fiery and eager hardihood which
we could the better admire had he done more justice to his
adversaries, especially the Queen, whose good intentions it
seems so difficult to misconstrue. He warns her also, in the
same high tone, that her enterprise will not succeed, and that
the end shall be her confusion, " onless betimes she repent
and desist," with all the stern certainty of an inspired
prophet. Whether the serious emissaries, who, though they
were Protestants, " had begun to muse," and perhaps could
not keep their eyes from remarking the smoke and dust of

the ruins behind the energetic figure of the Reformer, conveyed this message in full we may be permitted to doubt.
They were both young men, and it is unlikely they would
prejudice their own career by repeating to the Queen's Grace
anything about her blind rage or the confusion which would
follow. Lord Sempill, who accompanied them, and who was
of the Queen's party—"a man sold under sin," says Knox—
perhaps did more justice to the message ; but Knox's sole
desire was that it should be repeated word by word.

We need not, however, follow the advances and retreats,
the always imminent encounter for which the Congregation
was fully ready, but from which the Queen and her general
constantly retired at the last moment, before the gates of
Perth, on Cupar Muir, and other places, making agreement
after agreement of which nothing came. In the course of
this curious dance of the two powers confronting each other
much ink was shed, however, if no blood, and the representa-
tions, letters, bonds, and assurances must have kept the
scribes on either side in constant occupation. The Congregation was certainly the more argumentative and long-
winded of the correspondents, and never seems to have lost
an opportunity of a letter. They pervaded the country,
an ever-increasing band, which, whenever an emergency
occurred, was multiplied from every quarter at the raising of
a finger on the part of the reforming lords. That the
violent beginning made in Perth had given to the populace
a taste for the pleasures of destruction, however, is very
fully evident, and it soon became clear that when the
preachers and their protectors moved "to make reformation," the mob who followed them would leave nothing but
ruins behind. This and the method of it is very well set
forth in the case of Scone, a place of great historical interest,
where the ancient kings of Scotland had been crowned. It
would seem to have been a raid of private vengeance which
directed the operations, "four zealous men," irrestrainable, it
would seem, by the leaders, having set out from Perth, "to
take order with that place," considering how obstinately
proud and despiteful the Bishop of Murray had been. The

lords had already sent a letter of warning to the Bishop, who was housed in some abbey near, advertising him that unless he would come and join them they could neither spare nor save his place. But while the answer lingered the town of Dundee took up the quarrel and set forth to carry out the work.

" To stay them was first sent the Provost of Dundee and his brother Alexander Halliburton Capitain, who little prevailing was sent unto them John Knox; but before his coming they were entered to the pulling down of the idols and dortour (dormitory). And albeit the said Maister James Halliburton, Alexander his brother, and the said John, did what in them lay to have stayed the fury of the multitude, yet were they not able to put order universalie; and therefore they sent for the lords, Earl of Argyle and Lord James, who coming with all diligence laboured to have saved the palace and the kirk. But because the multitude had found buried in the kirk a great number of idols, hid of purpose to have reserved them for a better day (as the Papists speak) the towns of Dundee and St. Johnstone could not be satisfied till that the whole reparation and ornaments of the church (as they term it) were destroyed. And yet did the lords so travel that they saved the Bishop's palace with the church and place for that night; for the two lords did not depart till they brought with them the whole number of those who most sought the Bishop's displeasure. The Bishop, greatly offended that anything should have been enterprised in reformation of his place, asked of the lords his bond and handwriting, which not two hours before he had sent to them (this was a promise to come immediately to arrange for the safety of his see, and also to support them in Parliament in gratitude for the warning they had given him); Which delivered to his messenger, Sir Adam Brown, advertisement was given that if any further displeasure chanced unto him that he should not blame them. The Bishop's servants that same night began to fortify the place again, and began to do violence to some that were carrying away such baggage as they could come by. The Bishop's girnel was kept the first night by the labours of John Knox, who by exhortation removed such as would violentlie have made irruption. The morrow following, some of the poor in hope of spoil, and some of Dundee to consider what was done, passed up to the said Abbey of Scone; whereat the Bishop's servants offended began to threaten and speak proudly, and as it was constantly affirmed one of the Bishop's sons stogged through with a rapier one of Dundee because he was looking in at the girnel door. This bruit noised abroad, the town of Dundee was more enraged than before, who putting themselves in armour sent word to the inhabitants of St. Johnstone, 'That unless they should support them to avenge that injury, that they should never from that day concur with them in any action.' They, easilie inflambed, gave the alarm, and so was that abbey and palace appointed to the

saccage ; in doing whereof they took no long deliberation, but committed
the whole to the merriment of fire ; whereat no small number of us was
so offended, that patientlie we could not speak to any that were of
Dundee or Saint Johnstone."

The reader will see in this frank narrative how many
elements were conjoined to bring about the outrage.　Local
jealousy and despite, the rage against the Bishop and his
priests, the eagerness of the needy in hope of spoil, the
excitement of a fray in which the first blow had been struck
by the adversary with just the crown of a supposed religious
motive to give the courage of a great cause to the rioters :
while on the other hand the Bishop's rashness in taking the
defence upon himself and slighting the assistance offered
him is equally apparent.　It is evident enough, however,
that the lords themselves had no urgent interest in the
preservation of the ancient buildings, and that Knox cared
little for any of these things.　The watch of the preacher at
the door of the Bishop's girnel or storehouse, keeping back
the rioters by his exhortations, is a curious illustration of
this.　He would not have the people soil their souls with
thieving, with the bishop's meal and malt ; as for the
historical walls, the altar where the old kings had been
anointed or the sanctuary where their ashes lay, what were
they ?　Knox was too much intent on setting Scotland loose
from all previous traditions—from the past which was
idolatrous and corrupt, and in which till it reached to the
age of the Apostles he recognised no good thing—to be
concerned about the temples of Baal.　What he wanted was
to cut all these dark ages away, and affiliate himself and his
country direct to Judæa and Jerusalem, to the Jewish church,
not the Gothic or the papal, or any perverted image of what
he believed primitive Christianity to have been.　He served
himself heir to Peter and Paul, to Elijah and Ezekiel, and
perhaps in the strong prepossession of his soul against
contemporary monks and ecclesiastics did not even know
that the Church which was so corrupt, and the religious
orders which had fallen so low, had ever brought or preserved light and blessing to the world.　Scottish history,

Scottish art, were corrupted too, and woven about with associations of these hated priests and their system which was not true religion, but "devised by the brain of man"; and though he was himself the most complete incarnation of Scotch vehemence, dogmatism, national pride, and fiery feeling, he was indifferent to their national records. His pride was involved in making his country stand, alone if need was, or if not alone then first, in passionate perfection in the new order of things in the kingdom of Christ: not to keep her a place in the unity of nations by preserving the traces of an old civilisation and institutions as venerable and noteworthy as any in Christendom, but to make of her a chosen nation like that people, long ago dispersed by a sufficiently miserable catastrophe, to whom was given of old the mission of showing forth the will of God before the world. Whether what he gained for his country was not much more important than what he thus deliberately sacrificed is a question that will never be answered with any unanimity. He gained for his race a great freedom, which cannot be justly called religious freedom, because it was, in his intention at least, freedom to follow their own way, with none at all for those who differed from them. He set up a high standard of piety and probity, and for once made the business of the soul, the worship of God and study of His laws, the most absorbing of public interests. He thrilled the whole country through and through with the inspiration of a fervent spirit, uncompromising in its devotion to the truth, asking no indulgence if also, perhaps, giving none, serving God in his own way with a fidelity above every bribe, scornful of every compromise. But he cut Scotland adrift so far as in him lay from the brotherhood of habit and tradition, from the communion, if not of saints, yet of many saintly uses, and much that is beautiful in Christian life. He made his country eminent, and secured for her one great chapter in the history of the world; but he imprinted upon her a certain narrowness uncongenial to her character and to her past, which has undervalued her to many superficial observers, and done perhaps a little, but a permanent, harm to her

national ideal ever since. A small evil for so much good,
but yet not to be left unacknowledged.

More interesting in its human aspect is Knox's appearance in St. Andrews, whither the Congregation now crowded
to " make reformation," though doubtful if even the populace
were on their side. The Bishop, " hearing of reformation to
be made in his cathedral church, thought time to stir, or
else never "—which was very natural. He was accompanied
by a hundred spears, which must have meant a company at
least of four or five hundred armed men, while the Lords of
the Congregation had " their quiet households," no doubt a
very adequate escort. The Bishop threatened that if John
Knox showed his face in the cathedral he should be saluted
with a dozen of culverins, and the gentlemen with him
hesitated much to expose him to such a risk : but their
doubts were not shared by the preacher. He had himself
given forth, when in the galley labouring at the oar in sight
of the beloved town and sanctuary, a prophecy that he
should yet preach there, unlikely as it looked ; and to recoil
from any danger, when such an opportunity arose, was not
in him. " To delay to preach the morrow (unless the bodie
be violentlie witholden) I cannot," he said. He preached
upon the casting out of the money-changers from the Temple
—a very dangerous subject for such an occasion, and " applied
the corruption that was there to the corruption that is in
the Papestrie " so well that the magistrates of the town, and
also the commonalty " for the most part, did agree to remove
all monuments of idolatrie, which also they did with expedition." But it was not on that day that the great church
shining from afar on its rocky headland, a splendid land-
mark over the dangerous bay, was reduced to the condition in which it now remains, with a few forlorn but
graceful pinnacles rising against the misty blue of sea and
sky. No harm would seem to have been done except
to the altars and the decorations ; and according to
all evidence it is more to the careless brutality of the
eighteenth century, which found an excellent storehouse
of materials for building in the abandoned shrine, than

ST. ANDREWS

to any absolute outrage that its present state of utter ruin is due.

The Congregation set forth on its march to Stirling, and thence to Edinburgh in June, and so great was the commotion which had been raised by the rumour of the "reformation" wrought in the north in Scone and St. Johnstone that the mere news of their approach roused "the rasckall multitude" to the mood of destruction. They had cleared out and destroyed the convents in Stirling, and those of the Black and Grey Friars in Edinburgh, before the Reformers came—a result which Knox at least in no way pauses to deplore : they had left nothing, he says, "but bare walls, yea, not so much as door or windok : wherthrou we were the less troubled in putting order in such places." Thus the flood of Revolution, of Reformation, of fundamental, universal change flowed on. The victory was not assured, however, as perhaps they had hoped when they entered Edinburgh, for though for a time everything went well, and the preaching seems to have been followed by the greater part of the city, the Queen, ever active, though never striking any decisive blow, had received reinforcements from France, and to the great alarm of the Congregation had begun to fortify Leith, forming a strong garrison there of French soldiers, and making a new stronghold near enough to be a perpetual menace to Edinburgh almost at her door. The position of affairs at this moment was curious in the extreme. The Queen in Leith, surrounded by the newly arrived forces of France, with Frenchmen placed in all the great offices, fulminated forth decrees, commands, explanations, orders, from within the walls that were being quickly raised to make the fort a strong place, and from amidst the garrison of her own countrymen, in whose fidelity she could fully trust. In Edinburgh the Congregation were virtually supreme, but very uneasy ; their substantial adversaries quieted, but ever on the watch ; the populace ready to pull down and destroy at their indication, but not to change their life or character—an unstable support should trouble come ; while in the castle Lord Erskine sat impartial, a sort

of silent umpire, taking neither side, though ready to inter-
vene with a great gun on either as occasion moved him.
The fire of words which was kept up between the two
parties is one of the most amazing features of the conflict.
For every page the Queen's secretaries wrote, John Knox
was ready with ten to demonstrate her errors, her falsehood,
the impossibility that any good could come from an idolater
such as she.   Other persons take part in the great wrangle,
but he is clearly the scribe and moving spirit.   He writes
to her in his own person, in that of the Lord James, in that
of the Congregation.   She accuses them of rebellion and
treasonable intentions against herself—and they her of her
Frenchmen and her fortifications.   She summons them to
leave Edinburgh on peril of all the penalties that attend
high treason ; they demand from her that the Frenchmen
should be sent away and the proceedings stopped.   She
accuses the Duke of Chatelherault—the head of the Hamiltons, the next heir to the throne—of treasonable proceedings,
and he vindicates himself by sound of trumpet at the Cross
of Edinburgh.   The correspondence grows to such a pitch
that when she loses patience and bids them be gone before
a certain day, they meet in solemn conclave, to which the
preachers are called to give their advice, to discuss whether
it is lawful to depose her from her regency : and all consent
with one voice to her deprivation.   The excitement of this
continual exchange of correspondence, the messages coming
and going, from the Queen's side the Lyon King himself, all
glorious among his pursuivants, advancing from Leith with
his brief letter and his " credit " as spokesman, the others
replying and re-replying, scarcely ever without a response
or a denunciation to read over and talk over, must have
kept the nerves and intelligence of all at a perpetual strain.
At St. Giles's and the Tolbooth close by, which were the
double centre of life in the city, there was a perpetual alter-
nation of preachings, to which Lords and Commons would
crowd together to listen to Knox's trumpet peals of fiery
eloquence, always upon some appropriate text, always
instinct with the most vehement energy, and consultations

upon public affairs and how to promote the triumph of
religion ; the lords pondering and sometimes doubtful, the
preacher ever uncompromising and absolute.   A question
of public honesty had arisen in the midst of the struggle
for the faith, and the Reformers had seized the Mint to
prevent the coining of base money, which the Regent was
carrying on for her necessities, and which the Congregation, no
doubt justly, considered ruinous to the trade of the country :
and the determined struggle with the Queen in respect to
her scheme for fortifying Leith and establishing a French
garrison there,—a continual check upon and menace to the
freedom of the capital,—was at least as much a question of
politics as religion.

The Congregation, however, was not yet strong enough
to be able to meet the French forces, and when they
attempted to besiege Leith and put a forcible stop to the
building they were defeated with shame and loss.   A curious
sign of the inevitable " rift within the lute," which up to this
time had been avoided by the concentration of all men's
thoughts upon the first necessity of securing the freedom of
the preachings, becomes visible before this futile attempt at
a siege.   When the leaders of the Congregation, among
whom on this occasion the contingent from the towns, and
especially from Dundee, seems foremost, began to prepare
for their expedition, they chose St. Giles's Church as the
most convenient for the preparation of the scaling ladders,
a practical evidence that sacredness had departed from the
church as a building, not at all to the mind of the preachers,
who probably saw no logical succession between the hammers
of the destroyers pulling down the " glorious tabernacles "
and those of the craftsmen occupied with secular work.
They did not, indeed, put their objections on this ground,
but on that of the neglect of the " preaching," a name now
characteristically applied to the public worship of God.
" The Preachers spared not openly to say that they feared
the success of that enterpryse should not be prosperous
because the beginning appeyred to bring with it some contempt of God and of His word.   Other places, said they,

had been more apt for such preparations than where the
people convened to common prayer and unto preaching, and
they did not hesitate to affirm that God would not suffer
such contempt of His word." Whether these objections
stole the heart out of the fighting men, who had hitherto
felt themselves emphatically the soldiers of God, it is impossible to say. They had hitherto overawed the Queen's party
by their numbers, and had never outwardly made proof of
their powers or sustained the attack of regular soldiers.
And the assault of Leith ended in a disastrous defeat. The
expedition set out rashly without leaders, while the lords
and gentlemen "were gone to the preaching," and had consequently no accompanying cavalry, and few, if any, experienced soldiers. They were driven back with loss, and
pursued into the very Canongate, to the foot of Leith Wynd
—that is, into the cross-roads and narrow wynds which were
immediately outside the city walls. Argyle and the rest,
as soon as they were aware of what had happened, got
hastily to horse, and did all they could to stop the flight,
but even this turned to harm, since the horsemen coming
out to the aid of their friends proved an additional danger
to the fugitives, and "over-rode their poor brethren at the
entrance of the Nether Bow."

After this all was confusion and trouble in Edinburgh.
The castle fired one solitary gun, which stopped with a note
of sudden protest the French pursuit, coming with extraordinary dramatic effect into the always graphic and picturesque narrative, over the heads of the flying, discomfited
crowd which was struggling among the horses' hoofs at the
narrow gate, and the Frenchmen straggling behind, up all
the narrow passages into the Canongate, snatching a piece
of plunder where they could find it, "one a kietill, ane other
ane pettycoat, the third a pote or a pan." "Je pense que
vous l'avez acheté sans argent," the Queen is reported to
have said with a laugh as the pursuers came back to Leith
with their not very important booty. "This was the great
and motherlie care she took for the truth of the poor subjects
of this realm," says Knox bitterly ; and yet it was very

natural that she should have been overjoyed, after all these controversies, to feel herself the stronger, if not in argument at least in actual fight.

This defeat told greatly upon the spirits of the Congregation which had hitherto been kept together by success, and which was in fact a mere horde of men hastily collected, untrained in actual warfare, and in no position for taking the offensive though strong in defence of their rights. And money had failed. It was determined that each gentleman should give his plate to be made into coin to supply the needs of the Congregation, as they had the Mint in their hands : but the officials stole away with the " irons " and this was made impracticable. They then sent for a supply to the English envoys who were anxiously watching the progress of events at Berwick : but the sum sent to them in answer to their application was intercepted by the Earl of Bothwell—his first appearance in history, on which he was to leave thereafter such traces of disaster. And other encounters with the Frenchmen took the heart entirely out of the Congregation ; the party began to dissolve, stealing away on every side. " Our soldiers " (mercenaries it is to be supposed in distinction from the retainers of the lords and gentlemen) " could skarslie be dang out of the town " to meet a sally from Leith. In Edinburgh itself the rasckall multitude, which had been so ready to destroy and ravage, began to throw stones at the Reformers and call them traitors and heretics. Finally with hearts penetrated by disappointment and the misery of defeat the Congregation abandoned Edinburgh altogether and marched to Stirling with drooping arms and hearts.

" The said day at nine in the night," says a contemporary authority, " the Congregation departed forth of Edinburgh to Linlithgow and left their artillerie void upon the causeway lying, and the town desolate." It was November, and the darkness of the night could not have been more dark than the prospects and thoughts of that dejected band, a little while before so triumphant. As the tramp of the half-seen procession went heavily down the tortuous streets at the back of the castle, probably by the West Bow and West Port, diving down into the darkness under that black shadow where the garrison sat grimly impartial taking no part, the populace, perhaps frightened by the too great success of their own fickle and cruel desertion of the cause, and hoping little from the return of the priests, would seem to have beheld with silent dismay the departure of the Congregation. The guns which had done them so little service which they left on the road, as the preachers would have had them leave all the devices and aid of men, were gathered in by the soldiers from the castle with little demonstration, and the town was left desolate. The anonymous writer of the *Diurnal of Occurrents* is curiously impartial and puts down his brief records without any expression of feeling : but a certain thrill is in these words as of something too impressive and significant to be passed by.

It is at this miserable moment that John Knox shows himself at his best. Hitherto his vehemence, his fierce oratory, his interminable letters and addresses, though instinct with all the reality of a most vigorous, even restless nature, represent to us rather a man who would if he could have done everything,—the fighting and the protocolling as well as the preaching, a man to whom repose was impossible, ever ready to draw forth his pen, to mount his pulpit, to add his eager word to every consultation, and enjoying nothing so much as to press the most unpleasant truths upon his correspondents and hearers,—than one of sustaining power and wisdom. The uncompromising fidelity with which he pointed out the short-comings of those about him, and the terrible penalties laid up for them ; and the stern denunciations in his letters, even those which he intended to be conciliatory, make his appearance in general more alarming than reassuring. An instance which almost tempts a smile, grave as are all the circumstances and surroundings, is his letter (written some time before the point at which we have now arrived) to Cecil whom he had known in England, and whose favour he desired to secure and indeed was confident of securing. For once he had something to ask for himself, permission to land

in England on his way back to his native country; and
greatly desired that a favourable representation of his case
might be made to Queen Elizabeth, who was naturally
prejudiced against him by his famous Blast against the
Monstrous Regiment of Women. The following letter was
written from Dieppe in April 1559 with the hope of procuring these favours from the great statesman.

"As I have no pleasure with long writing to trouble you, Rycht
Honourable, whose mind I know to be occupied with most grave matters,
so mind I not greatly to labour by long preface to conciliate your favour,
which I suppose I have already (howsomever rumours bruit the contrarie) as it becometh one member of Christ's body to have of another.
The contents, therefore, of these my presents shall be absolved in two
points. In the former I purpose to discharge in brief words my conscience towards you, and in the other somewhat I must speik in my
own defence and in defence of that poor flock of lait assembled in the
most godly Reformed church and city of the world Geneva. To you
Sir, I say, that as from God ye have received life, wisdom, honours and
this present estate in which ye stand, so ought you wholly to employ the
same to the advancement of His glory, who only is the Author of life, the
fountain of wisdom, and who, most assuredly, doth and will honour those
that with simple hearts do glorify Him; which, alas, in times past ye
have not done; but being overcome with common iniquity ye have
followed the world in the way of perdition. For to the suppressing of
Christ's true Evangell, to the erecting of idolatrie, and to the shedding
of the blood of God's dear children, have you by silence consented and·
subscribed. This, your most horrible defection from the truth known
and once professed, hath God to this day mercifully spared; yea, to
man's judgement He hath utterly forgotten and pardoned the same.
He hath not entreated you as He hath done others (of like knowledge),
whom in His anger (but yet most justly according to their deserts) He
did shortly strike after their defection. But you, guilty in the same
offences, He hath fostered and preserved as it were in His own bosom.
As the benefit which ye have received is great, so must God's justice
require of you a thankful heart; for seeing that His mercy hath spared
you being traitor to His Majesty; seeing, further, that among your
enemies He hath preserved you; and last, seeing that although worthy
of Hell He hath promoted you to honour and dignity, of you must He
require (because He is just) earnest repentance for your former defection,
a heart mindful of His merciful providence, and a will so ready to
advance His glory that evidently it may appear that in vain ye have
not received these graces of God—to performance whereof of necessity
it is that carnal wisdom and worldly policy (to the which both ye are
bruited too much inclined) give place to God's simple and naked truth—
very love compelleth me to say that except the Spirit of God purge your

T

heart from that venom which your eyes have seen to be destruction to others, that ye shall not long escape the reward of dissemblers. Call to mind what you ever heard proclaimed in the chapel of Saint James, when this verse of the first Psalm was entreated, 'Not so, oh wicked, not so; but as the dust which the wind hath tossed, etc.' . . . And this is the conclusion of that which to yourself I say. Except that in the cause of Christ's Evangel ye be found simple, sincere, fervent and unfeigned, ye shall taste of the same cup which politic heads have drunken before you."

This manner of approaching a powerful statesman whose good offices might be of the uttermost consequence both to the writer and his party, is highly characteristic. There is something almost comic, if we dared to interpose such a view between two such personages, in the warning against " carnal wisdom and worldly policy to the which both ye are bruited too much inclined," addressed to the great Burleigh. It is difficult to imagine the outburst of a laugh between such a pair, yet grave Cecil surely must have smiled.

The man who wrote this epistle and many another, leagues of letters in no one of which does he ever mince matters, or refrain to deliver his conscience before conveying the message of State with which he is charged—is often wordy, sometimes tedious, now and then narrow as a village gossip, always supremely and absolutely dogmatic, seeing no way but his own and acknowledging no possibility of error ; and the extreme and perpetual movement of his ever-active mind, his high-blooded intolerance, the restless force about him which never pauses to take breath, is the chief impression produced upon the reader by his own unfolding of himself in his wonderful history. Though he is too great and important to be called a busybody, we still feel sympathetically something of the suppressed irritation and sense of hindrance and interruption with which the lords must have regarded this companion with his " devout imaginations," whom they dared not neglect, and who was sure to get the better in every argument, generally by reason, but at all events by the innate force of his persistence and daring. But when they came to Stirling, after " that dusk and dolorous night wherein all ye my lords with shame and fear left the town," the eager nervous form, the dark keen face of the preacher, rose before the melancholy bands like those of the hero-leader, the standard-bearer of God. It was Wednesday the 7th of November 1559 when the dispirited Congregation met for the preaching, and to consider afterwards "what was the next remedy in so desperate a case." Knox took for his text certain verses of the eightieth Psalm. "How long wilt thou be angry against the prayer of thy people? Thou hast fed us with the bread of tears; and hast given us tears to drink in great measure. O God of hosts, turn us again, make thy face to shine; and we shall be saved." He began by asking, Why were the people of God thus oppressed?

" Our faces are this day confounded, our enemies triumph, our hearts have quaked for fear, and yet they remain oppressed with sorrow and shame. But what shall we think to be the very cause that God hath thus dejected us? If I shall say our sins and former unthankfulness to God, I speak the truth. But yet I spake more generallie than necessity required : for when the sins of men are rebuked in general, seldom it is that man descendeth within himself, accusing and damning in himself that which most displeaseth God."

To this particular self-examination he then leads his hearers in order that they may not take refuge in generalities, but that each man may examine himself. " I will divide our whole company," he says, "into two sorts of men. The one, those who have been attached to the cause from the beginning; the other, recent converts."

" Let us begin at ourselves who longest has continued in this battle. When we were a few in number, in comparison with our enemies, when we had neither Erle nor Lord (a few excepted) to comfort us, we called upon God, we took Him for our protector, defence, and onlie refuge. Among us was heard no bragging of multitude or of our strength or policy, we did only sob to God, to have respect to the equity of our cause and to the cruel pursuit of the tyraneful enemy. But since that our number has been multiplied, and chiefly since my Lord Duke his Grace with his friends have been joined with us, there was nothing heard but ' This Lord will bring these many hundred spears : if this Earl be ours no man in such and such a bounds will trouble us.' And thus the best of us all, that before felt God's potent hand to be our defence, hath of late days put flesh to be our arm."

This proved, which was an evil he had struggled against

with might and main, forbidding all compromises, all conces-
sions that might have served to attract the help of the
powerful, and conciliate lukewarm supporters, he turns to the
other side.

"But wherein hath my Lord Duik his Grace and his friends offended ?
It may be that as we have trusted in them so have they put too much
confidence in their own strength.   But granting so be or not, I see a
cause most just why the duke and his friends should thus be confounded
among the rest of their brethren.   I have not yet forgotten what was the
dolour and anguish of my own heart when at St. Johnstone, Cupar Muir,
and Edinburgh Crags, those cruel murderers, that now hath put us to
this dishonour, threatened our present destruction.   My Lord Duke his
Grace, and his friends at all the three jornayes, was to them a great
comfort and unto us a great discourage ; for his name and authority did
more affray and astonish us, than did the force of the other : yea without
his assistance they would not have compelled us to appoint with the
Queen upon unequal conditions.   I am uncertain if my Lord's Grace
hath unfeignedly repented of his assistance to those murderers unjustly
pursuing us.   Yea, I am uncertain if he hath repented of that innocent
blood of Christ's blessed martyrs which was shed in his default.   But let
it be that so he hath done, as I hear that he hath confessed his offence
before the Lords and brethren of the Congregation, yet I am assured
that neither he, nor yet his friends, did feel before this time the anguish
and grieving of heart which we felt when they in their blind fury pursued
us.   And therefore hath God justly permitted both them and us to fall
in this confusion at once ; us for that we put our trust and confidence in
man, and them because that they should feel in their own hearts how
bitter was the cup which they had made others to drink before them.
Rests that both they and we turn to the Eternal, our God (who beats
down to death to the intent that He may raise up again, to leave the
remembrance of His wondrous deliverance to the praise of His own name),
which if we do unfeignedly, I no more doubt that this our dolour, confusion, and fear, shall be turned into joy, honour, and boldness, than
that I doubt that God gave the victory to the Israelites over the
Benjaminites after that twice with ignominy they were repulsed and dang
back.   Yea, whatsoever shall come of us and our mortal carcasses, I
doubt not but this cause in despite of Satan shall prevail in the realm of
Scotland.   For as it is the eternal truth of the eternal God, so shall it
once prevail, however for a time it may be hindered.   It may be that
God shall plague some, for that they delight not in the truth, albeit for
worldly respects they seem to favour it.   Yea, God may take some of
His devout children away before their eyes see greater troubles.   But
neither shall the one or the other so hinder this action but in the end it
shall triumph."

When the sermon was ended, Knox adds, " The minds

of men began wonderfully to be erected." " The voice of
one man," as Randolph afterwards said, was " able in an
hour to put more life in us than six hundred trumpets continually blustering in our ears." The boldness with which
Knox thus exposed that elation in their own temporary success,
and in the adhesion of the Duke of Hamilton, which had
led the leaders of the Congregation into self-confidence and
slackened their watchfulness, was made solemn and authoritative by the force with which he pressed his personal
responsibility into every man's bosom. No turn of fortune,
no evil fate, but God's check upon an army enlisted in His
name yet not serving Him with a true heart, was this
momentary downfall ; the cause of which was one that every
man could remove in his degree ; not inherent weakness or
hopeless fate, but a matter remediable, nay, which must be
remedied and cast from among them—a matter which might
quench their personal hopes and destroy them, but could not
affect the divine cause, which should surely triumph whatever
man or Satan might do. More than six hundred trumpets,
more than the tramp of a succouring army, it rang into
the men's hearts. Their spirit and their courage rose ; the
dolorous night, the fear and shame, dissolved and disappeared ;
and the question what to do was met not with dejection and
despair but with a rising of new hope.

The decision of the Congregation in the Senate which
was held after this stirring address was, in the first place, to
address an appeal for help to England, the sister-nation
which had already made reformation, though not in their
way, and to fight the matter out with full confidence in a
happy issue. About this appeal to England, however, there
were difficulties ; for Knox who suggested it, and whose
name could not but appear in the matter, had given forth,
as all the world and especially the persons chiefly attacked
were aware, a tremendous " blast " against the right of
women to reign, particularly well or ill timed in a generation
subject to so many queens ; and it was necessary for him to
excuse or defend himself to the greatest of the female sovereigns whom he had attacked. Of course it was easy for him

to say that he had no great Protestant Elizabeth in his eye
when he wrote, but only a bigoted and sanguinary Mary,
of whom no one knew at the time that her reign was to be
short, and her power of doing evil so small.   It is almost
impossible to discuss gravely nowadays a treatise which,
even in its name (which is all that most people know of it),
has the air of a whimsical ebullition of passion, leaning
towards the ridiculous, rather than a serious protest calculated
to move the minds of men.   But this was not the aspect
under which it appeared to the Queens who were assailed,
not as individuals, but as a class intolerable and not to be
suffered ; and it was considered necessary that Knox should
write to excuse himself, and apologise as much as was in
him to the Queen, who was now the only person on earth to
whom the Congregation could look for help.   Knox's letter
to Queen Elizabeth, whom he addressed indeed more as a
lesser prince, respectful but more or less equal, might do,
than as a private individual, is very characteristic.   He has
to apologise, but he will not withdraw from the position he
had taken.   "I cannot deny the writing," he says, "neither
yet am I minded to retreat or call back any principal point
or proposition of the same."   But he is surprised that subject
of offence should be found in it by her for whose accession
he renders thanks to God, declaring himself willing to be
judged by moderate and indifferent men which of the parties
do most harm to the liberty of England, he who affirms that
no woman may be exalted above any realm to make the
liberty of the same thrall to any stranger nation, "or they
that approve whatsoever pleaseth Princes for the time."
Leaving thus the ticklish argument which he cannot withdraw, but finds it impolitic to bring forward, he turns to the
Queen's individual behaviour in her position as being the
thing most important at the present moment, now that she
has effectively attained her unlawful elevation.

"Therefore, Madam, the only way to retain and keep those benefits of
God abundantly poured now of late days upon you and upon your realm,
is unfeignedly to render unto God, to His mercy and undeserved grace,
the glory of your exaltation.   Forget your birth, and all title which

thereupon doth hing: and consider deeply how for fear of your life ye did decline from God and bow till idolatrie. Let it not appear ane small offence in your eyes that ye have declined from Christ in the day of His battle. Neither would I that you should esteem that mercy to be vulgar and common which ye have received: to wit that God hath covered your former offence, hath preserved you when you were most unthankful, and in the end hath exalted and raised you up, not only from the dust, but also from the ports of death, to rule above His people for the comfort of His kirk. It appertaineth to you, therefore, to ground the justice of your authority, not upon that law which from year to year doth change, but upon the eternal providence of Him who contraire to nature and without your deserving hath thus exalted your head. If then, in God's presence ye humble yourself, as in my heart I glorify God for that rest granted to His afflicted flock within England under you a weik instrument: so will I with tongue and pen justify your authority and regiment as the Holy Ghost hath justified the same in Debora that blessed mother in Israel. But if the premisses (as God forbid) neglected, ye shall begin to brag of your birth and to build your authority and regiment upon your own law, flatter you who so list your felicity shall be short. Interpret my rude words in the best part as written by him who is no enemy to your Grace."

It must have been new to Queen Elizabeth to hear herself called "a weik instrument," and it is doubtful whether the first offence would be much softened by such an address. Neither was Elizabeth a person to be amused by the incongruity or impressed by the uncompromising boldness of the Reformer to whom the language of apology was so hard. Policy, however, has little to do with personal offences, although to some readers, as we confess to ourselves, it may be more interesting to see the prophet thus arrested, hampered by his own trumpet-blast, and making amends as much as he can permit himself to make, though so awkwardly and with so bold a return upon the original offence, to the offended Queen. It was far more easy for him to warn her of what would happen did she fail in her duty than to soothe the affront with gentle words; and his attempt at the latter is but halting and feeble. But when he promises with tongue and pen to justify her if she does well, Knox is once more on his own ground—that of a man whose office is superior to all the paltry distinctions of kingship or lordship, a servant of God commissioned to declare His divine will, endowed with an insight beyond that of ordinary men, and declaring with boundless certainty and confidence the things which are to be.

We may, however, pass very shortly over the coming struggle. The English army marched into Scotland in April 1560, and addressed itself at once to the siege of Leith, the headquarters of the French whom the Queen Regent had brought into Scotland, and whom it was the chief aim of the Congregation and of their allies to drive out of the country. The siege went on for about six weeks, during which little effect seems to have been made, though Knox bears testimony that " the patience and stout courage of the Englishmen, but principally of the horsemen, was worthy of all praise." These proceedings, however, were brought to a pause by an event which changed the position of affairs. The Queen Regent, who, for some time, had been in declining health, harassed and beaten down by many cares, had left Leith and taken up her abode in Edinburgh Castle while the Reformers were absent from the capital. In that fortress, held neutral by its captain, in the small rooms where, some seven years after, her daughter's child was to be born, Mary lingered out the early days of summer : and in June, while still the English guns were thundering against Leith, her new fortifications resisting with diminished strength, and her garrison in danger—died, escaping from her uneasy burden of royalty when everything looked dark for her policy and cause. Many anecdotes of her sayings and doings were current during her lingering illness, such as might easily be reported between the two camps with more or less truth. When she heard of the " Band " made by the leaders of the army before Leith for the expulsion of the strangers she is said to have called the maledictions of God upon them who counselled her to persecute the preachers and to refuse the petitions of the best part of the subjects of the realm. Shut out from the countrymen and advisers in whom she had trusted, with the hitherto impartial Lord Erskine alone at her ear, adding his word concerning the " unjust possessors " who were to be driven " forth of this land," and overcome by sickness, sadness, and loneliness, this

lady, who had done her best to hold the balance even and
to refrain from bloodshed, though she had little credit for it,
seems to have lost courage.   She saw from her altitude on
the castle rock the great fire in Leith, which probably
looked at first like the beginning of its destruction, and all
the martial bands of England, and the Scots lords and their
followers, lying between her and her friends.   After some
ineffectual efforts to communicate with them otherwise, she
sent for the Lords Argyle, Glencairn, and the Earl Marischal,
with the Lord James, who visited her separately, " not all
together, lest that some part of the Guysian practice had
lurked under the colour of friendship."   Knox's heart was
not softened by the illness and isolation, nor even by the
regrets and repentance, of the dying Queen.   She consented
to see John Willock, his colleague, and after hearing him
" openly confessed that there was no salvation but in and by
the death of Jesus Christ."   " But of the Mass we had not
her confession," says the implacable preacher.   She died on
the ninth of June, worsted, overthrown, all that she had aimed
at ending in failure, all her efforts foiled, leaving those who
had been her enemies triumphant, and the future fate of her
daughter's kingdom in the hands of " the auld enemy," the
ever-dangerous neighbour of Scotland.   " God, for His good
mercy's sake, rid us from the rest of the Guysian blood,"
was the prayer Knox made over her grave.

And yet, so far as can be judged, Mary of Guise was no
persecutor and no tyrant.   To all appearance she had
honestly intended to keep peace in the kingdom, to permit
as much as she could without committing herself to views
which she did not share.   And nothing could be more
touching than such an end to a life never too brilliant or
happy.   She had gone through many alternations of gladness and of despair, had stood bravely by her sensitive
husband when the infant sons who were his hope had been
taken one after another, had discharged, as faithfully as
circumstances and the accidents of a tremendous crisis would
let her, her duties as Regent.   Her death, lonely, desolate,
and defeated, with no one near whom she loved, to smooth

her passage to the grave, might have gained her a more gentle word of dismissal.

Within little more than a month after her death peace was signed ; the French forces departed, and the English army, not much more loved in its help than the others in their hostility, was escorted back to the Border and safely got rid of. On the 19th of July, all being thus happily settled, St. Giles's was once more filled with a crowd of eager worshippers, " the haill nobilitie and the greatest part of the Congregation,"—a number which must have tried the capacity of the great church, large as it is. Knox does not give his sermon on the occasion, but we have a very noble and devout prayer, or rather thanksgiving, which was used at this service, and in which, though there is one reference to " proud tyrants overthrown," the spirit of devout thankfulness is predominant. He tells us, however, that the subject of his discourses, delivered daily, were the prophecies of Haggai, which he found to be " proper for the time." Some of his hearers, he informs us, spoke jestingly of having now to " bear the barrow to build the house of God." " God be merciful to the speaker," cries the stern prophet, " for we fear he shall have experience that the building of his ain house, the house of God being despised, shall not be so prosperous or of such firmity as we desire it were "—so dangerous was it to jest in the presence of one so tremendously in earnest. The speaker referred to, of this, as of most of the other caustic sayings of the time, is said to have been Lethington.

The first thing done by the Parliament was the distribution of the handful of ministers then existing among the districts which most needed them ; the second, the verification and establishment of the Confession of Faith. No more curious scene could have been than this momentous ceremony. The Parliament consisted of all the nobility of Scotland, including among them the bishops and peers of the Church, and the delegates from the boroughs. The Confession was read article by article, and a vote taken upon each. Three only of the lords voted against it. The bishops said nothing. What their feelings must have been, as they

sat in their places looking on, while the long array of the
Congregation voted, it is vain to attempt to imagine.   There
was nothing the Reformers would have liked better than that
discussion to which Knox had vainly bidden his opponents,
throwing down his glove as to mortal combat.   " Some of
our ministers were present," he says, " standing upon their
feet ready to have answered in case any would have defended the Papistrie and impugned our affirmations."   But
no one of all the ecclesiastics present said a word.   The
Earl Marischal, when he rose in his turn to vote, commented
upon this remarkable abstinence with the straightforwardness
of a practical man.   " It is long since I have had some
favour to the truth," he said, " and since I have had a suspicion of the Papistical religion ; but I praise my God this
day has fully resolved me in the one and the other.   For,
seeing that my Lord Bishops here present, who for their
learning can, and for the zeal they should bear to the
veritie would, I suppose, gainsay anything that directly
repugns to the veritie of God, speaks nothing in the contraire
of the doctrine proposed, I cannot but hold it to be the very
truth of God."   Even this speech moved the bishops to no
reply.   They sat silent, perhaps too much astonished at such
an extraordinary revolution to say anything ; perhaps
alarmed at the strength of the party against them.   It might
be that there was little learning among them, though they
had the credit of it ; certainly the arguments which Knox
reports on several occasions are inconceivably feeble on the
side of the old faith.   But whatever was the meaning there
they sat dumb, and looked on bewildered, confounded, while
the new Confession was voted paragraph by paragraph, and
the whole scope of the Scottish constitution changed.

The next step was the abolition of the mass, an act by
which it was forbidden that any should either hear or say
that office " or be present thereat, under the pain of confisca-
tion of all their goods movable and immovable, and punishing
of their bodies at the discretion of the Magistrates."   Another
edict followed abolishing the jurisdiction of the Pope under
pain of " proscription, banishment, and never to brook honour,

office, or dignity within this realm." "These and other
things," says the Reformer, "were orderly done in lawful and
free Parliament," with the bishops and all spiritual lords in
their places sitting dumb and making no sign. The Queen
was at liberty to say afterwards, as was done, that a Parliament where she was not represented in any way, either by
viceroy or regent, where there was no exhibition of sceptre,
sword, or crown, and in short where the monarch was left
out altogether, was not a lawful Parliament. But the most
remarkable feature of this strange assembly amid all the
voting and "bruit" is the dramatic silence of the State
ecclesiastical. It is curious that no fervent brother should
have been found to maintain the cause of his faith. But
probably it was better policy to refrain. The extraordinary
absence of logic as well as toleration which made the
Reformers unable to see what a lame conclusion this was
after their own struggle for freedom, and that they were
exactly following the example of their adversaries, need not
be remarked. John Knox thought it a quite sufficient answer
to say that the mass was idolatry and his own ways of
thinking absolutely and certainly true ; but so of course has
the Roman Catholic Church done when the impulse of
persecution was strongest in her. There is one only thing
to be said in favour of the Reformers, and that is, that while
a number of good men had been sacrificed at the stake for
the Reformed doctrines, no one was burned for saying mass ;
the worst that happened, notwithstanding their fierce enactments, being the exposure in the pillory of a priest. Rotten
eggs and stones are bad arguments either in religion or
metaphysics, but not so violently bad as fire and flame.

Thus the Reformed religion was established in Scotland,
and Knox settled in St. Giles's for the remainder of his life.
Whether he was at once placed in the picturesque house with
its panelled rooms and old-fashioned comfort and gracefulness
which still bears his name, standing out in a far-seeing angle
from which he could contemplate the abounding life of the
High Street, the great parish in which half his life was spent,
is not certain ; but it was a most fit and natural lodging for

KNOX'S HOUSE, HIGH STREET

the minister of St. Giles's. And for the rest of his life, with very few intervals, all the stream of public life in Scotland flowed about this dwelling. His importance in every national question, the continual references made to him, the appeals addressed to him by monarch and noble, as well as by burghers and retainers, show better than any statement the unique position he held. He was at this time a man of fifty-five. His Marjory Bowes, never I think mentioned but by this name, the "weill belovit sister" who is associated with so much of his life without one trace of human identity ever stealing through the mist that envelops her, was dead ; disappearing noiseless into the grave, where it would seem her mother, Mrs. Bowes, the religious hypochondriac who had required so many solemn treatises in the shape of letters to comfort her, had preceded her daughter. Two boys, the sons of Marjory, were with their father in these panelled rooms. They both grew up, but not to any distinction ; he did not spare the rod as appears in an after statement, but loved not to see them in tears, and probably was a fond father enough. All these things, however, are too petty to find any record in what he says of himself.

CHAPTER II

UNDER QUEEN MARY

WHEN the Parliament which did these great things was over, the newly established Kirk began to labour at its own development, supplying as far as was possible ministers to the more important centres. There were but thirteen available in all according to the lists of those appointed to independent charges: and though they no doubt were supplemented by various of the laymen who had already been authorised to read prayers and preach in the absence of other qualified persons—one of whom, Erskine of Dun, became one of the superintendents of the new organisation—the clerical element must have been very small in comparison with the number of the faithful and the power and influence accorded to the preachers. When these indispensable arrangements had been made the chiefs of the Reformers began to draw up the Book of Discipline,—a compendium of the constitution of the Church establishing her internal order, the provisions to be made for her, her powers in dealing with the people in general, and special sinners in particular,—as the Confession of Faith was of her doctrines and belief. But this was a much harder morsel for the lords to swallow. Many a stout spirit of the Congregation had held manfully for the Reformed faith and escaped with delight from the exactions and corruptions of the Romish clergy who yet had not schooled his mind to give up the half of his living, the fat commendatorship or priory which had been obtained for him by the highest influence, and upon which he had calcu-

HOLYROOD PALACE AND ARTHUR'S SEAT

lated as a lawful provision for himself and his family. One
would have supposed that the meddling and keen supervision
of every act of life, which was involved in the Church's stern
claim of discipline, would also have alarmed and revolted a
body of men not all conformed to the purest models of
morality. But this seems to have troubled them little in
comparison with the necessity of giving up their share of
Church lands and ecclesiastical wealth generally, in order to
provide for the preachers, and the needs of education and
charity. " Everything that repugned to their corrupt affections
was termed in their mockage ' devout imaginations,' " says
Knox : and it was no doubt Lethington from whose quiver
this winged word came, with so many more.

A number of the lords, however, subscribed to the Book
of Discipline though with reluctance, but some, and among
them several of the most staunch supporters of the Reformation, held back. Knox had himself been placed in an
independent position by his congregation, the citizens of
Edinburgh, and he was therefore more free to press stipula-
tions which in no way could be supposed to be for his own
interest : but he evidently had not taken into account the
strong human disposition to keep what has been acquired and
the extreme practical difficulty of persuading men to a
sacrifice of property. In other matters too there were drawbacks not sufficiently realised. There can be no grander
ideal than that of a theocracy, a commonwealth entirely ruled
and guided by sacred law : but when it is brought to practice
even by the most enlightened, and men's lives are subjected
to the keen inspection of an ecclesiastical board new to its
functions, and eager for perfection, which does not disdain
the most minute detail, nor to listen to the wildest rumours,
the high ideal is apt to fall into the most intolerable petty
tyranny. And notwithstanding the high exaltation of many
minds, and the wonderful intellectual and emotional force
which was expended every day in that pulpit of St. Giles's,
swaying as with great blasts and currents of religious feeling
the minds of the great congregation that filled the aisles of
the cathedral, it is to be doubted whether Edinburgh was a

very agreeable habitation in those days of early fervour,
when the Congregation occupied the chief place everywhere,
and men's thoughts were not as yet distracted by the coming
of the Queen.   During this period there occurs a curious
and most significant story of an Edinburgh mob and riot,
which might be placed by the side of the famous Porteous
mob of later days, and which throws a somewhat lurid light
upon the record of this most triumphant moment of the early
Reformation.   The Papists and bishops, Knox says, had
stirred up the rasckall multitude to "make a Robin Hood."
We may remark that he never changes his name for the
mob, of which he is always sternly contemptuous.   When
it destroys convents and altars he flatters it (though he
acknowledges sometimes a certain ease in finding the matter
thus settled for him) with no better a title.   He was no
democrat though the most independent of citizens.   The
vulgar crowd had at no time any attraction for him.

It seems no very great offence to "make a Robin Hood":
but it is evident this popular festival had been always an
occasion of rioting and disorderly behaviour since it was
condemned by various acts of previous Parliaments.   It will
strike the reader, however, with dismay and horror to find
that one of the ringleaders having been taken, he was condemned to be hanged, and a gibbet erected near the Cross
to carry this sentence into execution.   The *Diurnal of
Occurrents* gives by far the fullest and most graphic account
of what followed.   The trades rose in anxious tumult, at
once angry and terrified.

"The craftsmen made great solicitations at the hands of the provost, John Knox minister, and the baillie, to have gotten him relieved,
promising that he would do anything possible to be done saving his
life—who would do nothing but have him hanged.   And when the
time of the poor man's hanging approached, and that the poor man
was come to the gibbet with the ladder upon which the said cordwainer
should have been hanged, the craftsman's children (apprentices ?) and
servants past to armour ; and first they housed Alexander Guthrie and
the provost and baillies in the said Alexander's writing booth, and syne
come down again to the Cross, and dang down the gibbet and brake
it in pieces, and thereafter past to the tolbooth which was then steekit :
and when they could not apprehend the keys thereof they brought

hammers and dang up the said tolbooth door perforce, the provost, baillies, and others looking thereupon ; and when the said door was broken up ane part of them passed in the same, and not only brought the said condemned cordwainer forth of the said tolbooth, but also all the remaining persons being thereintill : and this done they passed up the Hie gate, to have past forth at the Nether Bow."

The shutting up of the provost and bailie in the "writing booth"—one of the wooden structures, no doubt, which hung about St. Giles's, as round so many other cathedrals, where a crowd of little industries were collected about the skirts of the great church, the universal centre of life—has something grimly comic in it, worthy of an Edinburgh mob. Guthrie's booth must have been at the west end, facing the Tolbooth, and the impotence of the authorities, thus compelled to look on while the apprentices and young men in their leather aprons, armed with the long spears which were kept ready in all the shops for immediate use, broke down the prison doors with their hammers and let the prisoners go free—must have added a delightful zest to the triumph of the rebels, who had so lately pleaded humbly before them for the victim's life, but in vain. The provost was Archibald Douglas of Kilspindie, a name little suitable for such a dilemma. When the rude mob, with their shouts and cries, had turned their backs, the imprisoned authorities were able to break out and take shelter in the empty Tolbooth ; but when the crowd surged up again, finding the gates closed at the Nether Bow, into the High Street, a scuffle arose, a new " Clear the Causeway," though the defenders of order kept within the walls of the Tolbooth, and thence shot at the rioters, who returned their fire with hagbuts and stones—from three in the afternoon till eight o'clock in the evening, " and never ane man of the town stirred to defend their provost and baillies." Finally the Constable of the Castle was sent for, who made peace, the craftsmen only laying down their arms on condition not only of absolute immunity from punishment for the day's doings, but with an undertaking that all previous actions against them should be stopped, and their masters made to

receive them again without grudge or punishment—clearly
a complete victory for the rioters.   This extorted guarantee
was proclaimed at the Cross at nine o'clock on the lingering
July night, in the soft twilight which departs so unwillingly
from northern skies ; and a curious scene it must have been,
with the magistrates still cooped up behind the barred
windows of the Tolbooth, the triumph of the mob filling
the streets with uproar, and spectators no doubt at all the
windows, story upon story, looking on, glad, can we doubt ?
of something to see which was riot without being bloodshed.
John Knox adds an explanation of his conduct in his narrative of the occurrence, which somewhat softens our feeling
towards him.   He refused to ask for the life of the unlucky
reveller not without a reason, such as it was.

"Who did answer that he had so oft solicited in their favour that
his own conscience accused him that they used his labours for no other
end but to be a patron to their impiety.   For he had before made
intercession for William Harlow, James Fussell, and others that were
convict of the former tumult.   They proudly said 'that if it was not
stayed both he and the Baillies should repent it.'   Whereto he answered
'He would not hurt his conscience for any fear of man.'"

It was not perhaps the fault of Knox or his influence
that a man should be sentenced to be hanged for the rough
horseplay of a Robin Hood performance, or because he was
"Lord of Inobedience" or "Abbot of Unreason," like Adam
Woodcock ; but the extraordinary exaggeration of a society
which could think such a punishment reasonable is very
curious.

Equally curious is the incidental description of how "the
Papists" crowded into Edinburgh after this, apparently
swaggering about the streets, "and began to brag as that
they would have defaced the Protestants."   When the
Reformers perceived the audacity of their opponents, they
replied by a similar demonstration : "the brethren assembled together and went in such companies, and that in
peaceable manner, that the Bishops and their bands forsook
the causeway."   Many a strange sight must the spectators
at the high windows, the old women at their "stairheads,"

from which they inspected everything, have seen—the bishops one day, the ministers another, and John Knox, were it shade or shine, crossing the High Street with his staff every day to St. Giles's, and seeing everything, whatever occurred on either side of him, with those keen eyes.

This tumult, however, was almost the end of the undisturbed reign of the Congregation. In August, Mary Stewart, with all the pomp that her poor country could muster for her, arrived in a fog, as so many lesser people have done, on her native shores; and henceforward the balance of power was strangely disturbed. The gravest of the lords owned a certain divergence from the hitherto unbroken claims of religious duty, and a hundred softnesses and forbearances stole in, which were far from being according to the Reformer's views. The new reign began with a startling test of loyalty to conviction, which apparently had not been anticipated, and which came with a shock upon the feelings even of those who loved the Queen most. The first Sunday which Mary spent in Holyrood, preparations were made for mass in the chapel, probably with no foresight of the effect likely to be produced. Upon this a sudden tumult arose in the very ante-chambers. "Shall that idol be suffered again to take its place in this realm? It shall not," even the courtiers said to each other. The Master of Lindsay, that grim Lindsay of the Byres, so well known among Mary's adversaries, standing with some gentlemen of Fife in the courtyard, declared that "the idolatrous priests should die the death." In this situation of danger the Lord James, afterwards so well known as Murray, the Queen's brother, put himself in the breach. He "took upon him to keep the door of the chapel." There was no man in Scotland more true to the faith, and none more esteemed in the Congregation. He excused himself after for this act of true charity by saying that his object was to prevent any Scot from entering while the mass was proceeding: but Knox divined that it was to protect the priest, and preserve silence and sanctity for the service, though he disapproved it, that Murray thus intervened. The Reformers did not appreciate the good brother's devotion. Knox declared that he was more afraid of one mass than of ten thousand armed men, and the arches of St. Giles's rang with his alarm, his denunciation, his solemn warning. He recounts, however, how by degrees this feeling softened among those who frequented the Court. "There were Protestants found," he says, "that were not ashamed at tables and other open places to ask 'Why may not the Queen have her mass, and the form of her religion? What can that hurt us, or our religion?' until by degrees this indulgence rose to a warmer and stronger sentiment. 'The Queen's mass and her priests will we maintain: this hand and this rapier shall fight in their defence.'" One can well imagine the chivalrous youth or even the grave baron, with generous blood in his veins, who, with hand upon the hilt of the too ready sword, would dare even Knox's frown with this outcry; and in these days it is the champion of the Queen and of her conscience who secures our sympathy. But the Reformer had at least the cruel force of logic on his side, the severe logic which decreed the St. Bartholomew. To stamp out the previous faith was the only policy on either side.

Then, as now, we think, there are few even of those who are forced to believe that the after-accusations against Queen Mary were but too clearly proved, who will not look back with a compunctious tenderness upon that early and bright beginning of her career. So strong a sense of remorseful pity, and the intolerableness of such a fate, overcomes the spectator, that he who stands by and looks on, knowing all that is coming, can scarcely help feeling that even he, unborn, might send a shout from out the dim futurity to warn her. She came with so much hope, so eagerly, to her new kingdom, so full of pleasure and interest and readiness to hear and see, and to be pleased with everything—even John Knox, that pestilent preacher, of whom she must have heard so much; he who had written the book against women which naturally made every woman indignant yet curious, keenly desirous to see him, to question him, to put him on his defence. I think great injustice has been done to both in the repeated interviews in which the sentimentalist perceives nothing but a harsh priest upbraiding a lovely woman and making her weep ; and the sage of sterner mettle sees an almost sublime sight, a prophet unmoved by the meretricious charms of a queen of hearts.   Neither of these exaggerated views will survive, we believe, a simple reading of the interviews themselves, especially in Knox's account of them.   He is not merciless nor Mary silly.   One would almost fancy that she liked the encounter which matched her own quick wit against the tremendous old man with his "blast against women," his deep-set fiery eyes, his sovereign power to move and influence the people.   He was absolutely a novel personage to Mary : their conversations are like a quick glancing of polished weapons—his, too heavy for her young brilliancy of speech and nature, crushing with ponderous force the light-flashing darts of question ; but she, no way daunted, comprehending him, meeting full in the face the prodigious thrust.   A brave young creature of twenty confronting the great Reformer, in single combat so to speak, and retiring from the field, not triumphant indeed, but with all the honours of war, and a blessing half extorted from him at the end, she secures a sympathy which the weaker in such a fight does not always obtain, but which we cannot deny to her in her bright intelligence and brave defence of her faith.   When his friends asked him, after this first interview, what he thought of the Queen, he gave her credit for "a proud mind, a crafty wit, and an indurate heart."   But curiously enough, though the effect is not unprecedented, the faithfulness of genius baulks the prejudices of the writer, and there is nowhere a brighter or more genial representation of Mary than that which is to be found in a history full of abuse of her and vehement vituperation.   She is "mischievous Marie," a vile woman, a shameless deceiver ; every bad name that can be coined by a mediæval fancy, not unlearned in such violences ; but when he is face to face with this woman of sin it is not in Knox to give other than a true picture, and that—apart from the grudging acknowledgment of her qualities and indication of evil intentions divined—is almost always an attractive one.

He, too, shows far from badly in the encounter.   In this

case, as in so many others, the simple record denuded of all
gloss gives at once a much better and we do not doubt much
more true representation of the two remarkable persons involved, than when loaded with explanations, either from other
people or from themselves.   It cannot be said that Knox is
just to Mary in the opinions he expresses of her, as he is
in the involuntary picture which his inalienable truthfulness
to fact forces from him.   It must be remembered, however,
that his history was written after the disastrous story had
advanced nearly to its end, and when the stamp of crime (as
Knox and so many more believed) had thrown a sinister
shade upon all her previous life.   Looking back upon the
preliminaries which led to such wild confusion and misery, it
was not unnatural that a man so absolute in judgment
should perceive in the most innocent bygone details indications of depravity.   It is one (whether good or bad we will
not say) consequence of the use and practice of what may, to
use a modern word, be called society, that men are less disposed to believe in the existence of monstrous and hideous
evil, that they do not attach an undue importance to trifles
nor take levity for vice.   Knox had all the limitations of
mind natural to his humble origin, and his profession, and
the special disadvantage which must attach to the habit of
investigating by means of popular accusation and gossip,
problematical cases of immorality.   He was able to believe
that the Queen, when retired into her private apartments
with her ladies, indulged in "skipping not very comelie for
honest women," and that all kinds of brutal orgies went on
at Court—incidents certainly unnecessary to prove her after-
guilt, and entirely out of keeping with all the surrounding
associations, as if Holyrood had been a change-house in
"Christ Kirk on the Green."   It did not offend his sense of the
probable or likely that such insinuations should be made, and
he recorded them accordingly not as insinuations but as facts,
in a manner only possible to that conjoint force of ignorance
and scorn which continually makes people of one class mis-
conceive and condemn those of another.   Dancing was in
those days the most decorous of performances: but if Mary

had been proved to have danced a stately *pas seul* in a minuet, it was to Knox, who knew no better, as if she had indulged in the wildest bobbing of a country fair—nay, he would probably have thought the high-skipping rural performer by far the more innocent of the two.

This is but an instance of many similar misconceptions with which the colour of the picture is heightened. An impassioned spectator looking on with a foregone conclusion in his mind, never apparently able to convince himself that vice does not always wear her trappings, but is probably much more dangerous when she observes the ordinary modesties of outward life, is always apt to be misled in this way. The state of affairs in which a great body of public men, not only ministers, but noble men and worthy persons of every degree, could personally address the Queen, and that almost in the form of an accusation couched in the most vehement terms, because of a libertine raid made by a few young gallants in the night, on a house supposed to be inhabited by a woman of damaged character, is inconceivable to us—a certain parochial character, a pettiness as of a village, thus comes into the great national struggle. The Queen's uncle, who had accompanied her to Scotland, was one of the young men concerned, along with Earl Bothwell and another. "The horror of this fact and the raretie of it commoved all godlie hearts," said Knox—and yet there was no lack of scandals in that age notwithstanding the zeal of purification. When the courtiers, alarmed by this commination (in which every kind of spiritual vengeance upon the realm and its rulers was denounced), asked, "Who durst avow it?" the grim Lindsay replied, "A thousand gentlemen within Edinburgh." Yet if Edinburgh was free from disorders of this kind, it was certainly far from free of other contentions. The proclamations from the Cross during Mary's brief reign give us the impression of being almost ceaseless. The Queen's Majestie proclaimed by the heralds now one decree, now another, with a crowd hastily forming to every blast of the trumpet : and the little procession in their tabards, carrying a moving patch of bright colour and shining ornament up all the long picturesque line of street, both without and within the city gates, was of almost daily occurrence. It was some compensation at least for the evils of an uncertain rule to have that delightful pageant going on for ever. Sometimes there would arise a protest, and one of the lords, all splendid in his jewelled bonnet, would step forward to the Lord Lyon and "take instruments and crave extracts," according to the time-honoured jargon of law; while from his corner window perhaps John Knox looked out, his eager pen already drawn to answer, the tumultuous impassioned sentences rushing to his lips.

When it was found that no punishment was to follow that "enormitie and fearful attemptal," but that "nightly masking" and riotous behaviour continued, some of the lords took the matter in their own hands, and a great band known as "my Lord Duke his friends" took the causeway to keep order in the town. When the news was brought to Earl Bothwell that the Hamiltons were "upon the gait," there were vows made on his side that "the Hamiltons should be driven not only out of the town but out of the country." The result, however, of this sudden surging up of personal feud to strengthen the bitterness of the quarrel between licence and repression, was that the final authorities were roused to make the fray an affair of State; and Murray and Huntly were sent from the abbey with their companies to stop the impending struggle. These sudden night tumults, the din of the struggle and clashing of the swords, the gleaming torches of the force who came to keep order, were sights very familiar to Edinburgh. But this fray brings upon us, prominent in the midst of the nightly brawls, the dark and ominous figure whose trace in history is so black, so brief, and so disastrous—once only had he appeared clearly before, when he intercepted in the interest of the Queen Regent the money sent from England to the Congregation. Now it is in a very different guise. Bothwell, as probably the ringleader in the disorders of the young nobles, was apparently the only person punished. He was confined to his own lodging, and it was apparently

at this time that he sought the intervention of Knox, who
seems to have been the universal referee. Knox gladly
granted his prayer for an interview, which was brought him
by a citizen of Edinburgh, with whom the riotous Earl had
dealings. No doubt the Reformer expected a new convert ;
and indeed Bothwell had his preliminary shrift to make, and
confessed his repentance of his previous action against the
Congregation, which he said was done " by the entysements
of the Queen Regent." But the Earl's object was not entirely
of this pious kind. He informed Knox that he had offended
the Earl of Arran, and that he was most anxious to recover
that gentleman's favour, on the ground, apparently, that a
feud with so great a personage compelled him to maintain a
great retinue, " a number of wicked and unprofitable men, to
the utter destruction of my living."

Knox received with unusual favour this petition for his
intervention, and for (to the reader) an unexpected reason :
" Albeit to this hour," he said, " it hath not chanced me to
speak to your lordship face to face, yet have I borne a good
mind to your honour, and have been sorry in my heart of
the troubles that I have heard you to be involved in. For,
my lord, my grandfather, goodsire and father, have served
your lordship's predecessors, and some of them have died
under their standards ; and this is part of the obligation of
our Scottish kindness." He goes on naturally to exhort his
visitor to complete repentance and " perfyte reconciliation with
God ;" but ends by promising his good offices for the wished-
for reconciliation with man. In this mediation Knox was
successful : and as the extraordinary chance would have it,
it was at the Kirk of Field, doomed to such dismal association for ever with Bothwell's name, that the meeting with
Arran, under the auspices of Knox—strange conjunction !—
took place, and friendship was made between the two enemies.
Knox made them a little oration as they embraced each other,
exhorting them to " study that amitie may ensure all former
offences being forgotten."

This is strange enough when one remembers the terrible
tragedy which was soon to burst these walls asunder ; but

stranger still was to follow. The two adversaries thus reconciled came to the sermon together next day, and there was much rejoicing over the new penitent. But four days after, Arran, with a distracted countenance, followed Knox home after the preaching, and calling out "I am treacherously betrayed," burst into tears. He then narrated with many expressions of horror the cause of his distress. Bothwell had made a proposal to him to carry off the Queen and place her in Dunkeld Castle in Arran's hands (who was known to be half distraught with love of Mary), and to kill Murray, Lethington, and the others that now misguided her, so that he and Arran should rule alone. The agitation of the unfortunate young man, his wild looks, his conviction that he was himself ruined and shamed for ever, seem to have enlightened Knox at once as to the state of his mind. Arran sent letters all over the country— to his father, to the Queen, to Murray—repeating this strange tale, but soon betrayed by the endless delusions which took possession of him that his mind was entirely disordered. The story remains one of those historical puzzles which it is impossible to solve. Was there truth in it—a premature betrayal of the scheme which afterwards made Bothwell infamous? did this wild suggestion drive Arran's mind, never too strong, off the balance? or was it some strange insight of madness into the other's dark spirit? These are questions which no one will ever be able to answer. It seems to have caused much perturbation in the Court and its surroundings for the moment, but is not, strangely enough, ever referred to when events quicken and Bothwell shows himself as he was in the madman's dream.

The chief practical question on which Knox's mind and his vigorous pen were engaged during this early period of Mary's reign was the all-important question to the country and Church of the provision for the maintenance of ministers, for education, and for the poor—the revenues, in short, of the newly established Church, these three objects being conjoined together as belonging to the spiritual dominion. The proposal made in the Book of Discipline, ratified and confirmed by the subscription of the lords, was that the tithes and other revenues of the old Church, apart from all the tyrannical additions which had ground the poor (the Uppermost Cloth, Corpse present, Pasch offerings, etc.), should be given over to the Congregation for the combined uses above described. This in principle had been conceded, though in practice it was extremely hard to extract those revenues from the strong secular hands into which in many cases they had fallen, and which had not even ceased to exact the Corpse present, etc. The Reformers had strongly urged the necessity of having the Book of Discipline ratified by the Queen on her arrival ; but this suggestion had been set aside even by the severest of the lords as out of place for the moment. To such enlightened critics as Lethington the whole book was a devout imagination, a dream of theorists never to be realised. The Church, however, with Knox at her head, was bent upon securing this indispensable provision, though it may well be supposed that now, with not only the commendators and pensioners but the bishops themselves and other ecclesiastical functionaries, inspirited and encouraged by the Queen's favour, and hoping that the good old times might yet come back, it was more difficult than ever to get a hearing for their claim. And great as was the importance of a matter involving the very existence of the new ecclesiastical economy, it was, even in the opinion of the wisest, scarcely so exciting as the mass in the Queen's chapel, against which the ministers preached, and every careful burgher shook his head ; although the lords who came within the circle of the Court were greatly troubled, knowing not how to take her religious observances from the Queen, they who had just at the cost of years of conflict gained freedom for their own. On one occasion when a party of those who had so toiled and struggled together during all the troubled past were met in the house of one of the clerk registers, the question was discussed between them whether subjects might interfere to put down the idolatry of their prince—when all the nobles took one side, and John Knox, his colleagues, and a humble official or two were all that stood on the other. As a manner of reconciling the conflicting opinions Knox was commissioned to put the question to the Church of Geneva, and to ask what in the circumstances described the Church there would recommend to be done. But the question was never put, being transferred to Lethington's hands, then back again to those of Knox, perhaps a mere expedient to still an unprofitable discussion rather than a serious proposal.

While these questions were being hotly and angrily discussed on all sides, the preachers and their party growing more and more pertinacious, the lords impatient, angry, chafed and fretted beyond bearing by the ever-recurring question in which they were no doubt conscious, with an additional prick of irritation, that they were abandoning their own side, Mary, still fearing no evil, very conciliatory to all about her, and entirely convinced no doubt of winning the day, went lightly upon her way, hunting, hawking, riding, making long journeys about the kingdom, enjoying a life which, if more sombre and poor outwardly, was far more original, unusual, and diverting than the luxurious life of the French Court under the shadow of a malign and powerful mother-in-law. It did not seem perhaps of great importance to her that the preachers should breathe anathemas against every one who tolerated the mass in her private chapel, or that the lords and their most brilliant spokesman, her secretary Lethington, should threaten to stop the Assemblies of the Church in retaliation. The war of letters, addresses, proclamations, which arose once more between the contending parties is wonderful in an age which might have been thought more given to the sword than the pen. But it at last became evident that something must be done in one way or the other to stop the mouth of the indomitable Knox, with whom were all the central mass of the people, not high enough to be moved by the influences of the Court, not low enough to fluctuate with every fickle popular fancy. Finally it was decided that the Queen should issue a decree for a valuation of all ecclesiastical possessions in Scotland—a necessary preliminary measure, but turned into foolishness

by the stipulation that these possessions should be divided
into three parts, two to remain with the present possessors,
while the remaining portion should be divided between the
ministers and herself.   This proposed arrangement, with
which naturally every one was discontented, called forth a
flight of furious jests.   " Good-morrow, my lords of the Twa-
pairts," said Huntly to the array, spiritual and secular, who
were to retain the lion's share ; while, on the other hand,
Knox in the pulpit denounced the division.   " I see twa
parts partly given to the Devil, and the third maun be divided
between God and the Devil," he cried.   " Bear witness to
me that this day I say it : ere it be long the Devil shall have
three parts of the third ; and judge you then what God's
portion shall be."—" The Queen will not have enough for
a pair of shoes at the year's end after the ministers are
sustained," said Lethington ; and Knox records the " dicton
or proverb " which arose, as such sayings do, out of the
crowd, in respect to the official, the Comptroller, who had
charge of this hated partition—" The Laird of Pitarrow,"
cried the popular voice, " was ane earnest professor of Christ ;
but the meikle Deil receive the Controller."

About this time Knox had the opportunity he had long
coveted of a public disputation upon the mass ; but it was
held far from the centre of affairs, at the little town of May-
bole in Ayrshire, where Quentin Kennedy of the house of
Cassilis, Abbot of Crossraguel (upon whose death George
Buchanan secured his appointment as pensioner), announced
himself as ready to meet all comers on this subject.   Knox
would seem to have attached little importance to it, as he
does no more than mention it in his History ; but a full
report exists of the controversy, which has much more the
air of a personal wrangle than of a grave and solemn discussion.   " Ye said," cries the abbot, " ye did abhor all
chiding and railing, but nature passes nurture with you."
—" I will neither change nature nor nurture with you for all
the profits of Crossraguel," says the preacher.   These amenities belonged to the period.   But the arguments seem singularly feeble on both sides.   The plea of the abbot rested

upon the statement in the Old Testament that Melchizedec offered bread and wine to God. On the other side a simple denial of this, and reassertion that the mass is an idolatrous rite, seems to have sufficed for Knox. It is almost impossible to believe that they did not say something better worth remembering on both sides. What they seem to have done is to have completely wearied out their auditors, who sat for three days to listen to the altercation, and then broke up in disgust. It is curious that Knox, so unanswerable in personal controversy, should have been so little effectual (so far as we can judge) in this. There is a discussion in another part of the history upon baptism, in which he denounces the Romish ceremonies attached to that rite as unscriptural, precisely as if the Apostles had described in full the method to be employed.

It is probable that it was the progress of Knox through the West on this occasion which encouraged and stimulated the gentlemen of that district, always the most strenuous of Reformers, the descendants of the Lollards, the forefathers of the Whigs, to take the law into their own hands in respect to those wandering and dispossessed priests who, encouraged by the example and support of the Queen, began to appear here and there in half-ruined chapels or parish churches to set up a furtive altar and say a mass, at peril if not of their lives at least of their liberty. When Knox returned to Edinburgh the Queen was at Lochleven, not then a prison but a cheerful seclusion, with the air blowing fresh from the pleasant loch, and the plains of Kinross and Fife all broad and peaceful before her, for the open-air exercises in which she delighted. She sent for Knox to this retirement and threw herself upon his aid and charity to stop these proceedings. It was not the first time they had met. Two previous interviews had taken place, in the first of which Mary gaily encountered the stern author of the " Blast " upon that general subject, and won from him a blessing at the end of the brief duel in which there was no bitterness. The second had been on the occasion when Knox, in the pulpit, objected to the dancing and festivities of Holyrood ; but still was of no very formidable

character. I cannot doubt that Mary found something very
humorous and original in the obstinate and dauntless prophet
whom she desired to come to her and tell her privately when
he objected to her conduct, and not to make it the subject
of his sermons—a very natural and apparently gracious request : from which Knox excused himself, however, as having
no time to come to her chamber door and whisper in her ear.
" I cannot tell even what other men will judge of me," he
said, " that at this time of day am absent .from my buke, and
waiting upon the Court."—" Ye will not always be at your
buke," said the Queen. And it was on this second interview
that as he left the presence with a composed countenance
some foolish courtier remarked of Knox that he was not
afraid, and elicited the answer, noble and dignified if a little
truculent and exaggerated after an encounter not at all
solemn, " Why should the pleasing face of a gentlewoman
afray me ? I have looked in the faces of many angry men
and yet have not been affrayed above measour "—a most
characteristic reply.

Mary, however, had another purpose when she sent for
Knox to Lochleven, to help her in a strait. " She travailed
with him earnestly two hours before her supper that he would
be the instrument to persuade the people and principally the
gentlemen of the West not to put hands to punish (the
priests) any more for the using of themselves in their religion
as pleased them." The Reformer perceiving her intention
assured her that if she would herself punish these malefactors,
no one would interfere ; but he was immovable to any
argument founded on the patent fact that he and his party
had lately called that the persecution of God's saints which
now they termed the execution of the law. Mary did not
enter into this controversy ; she kept to her point—the vindi-
cation of her own authority. " Will you," she said, " allow
that they should take my sword in their hand ? " a question
to which Knox had his answer plain and very full, that the
sword was God's, and that Jezebel's priests were not spared
by Elijah nor Agag by Samuel because the royal authority
was in their favour. It would be difficult to conceive any-

thing more exasperating than such an immovable front of dogmatism; and it was a wonder of self-control that Mary should only have shown herself "somewhat offended" when

LOCHLEVEN

she broke off this hopeless argument, and withdrew to supper. The Reformer thought he was dismissed; but before sunrise next morning two several messengers came to his chamber to

bid him speak with the Queen before he took his departure.
It was a May morning, and no doubt there was soon much
cheerful commotion in the air, boats pushed forward to the
landing steps with all that tinklè of water and din and jar of
the oars which is so pleasant to those who love the lochs and
streams—for Mary was bound upon a hawking expedition,
and the preacher's second audience was to be upon the mainland.   The Queen must have been up betimes while the mists
still lay on the soft Lomonds, and the pearly gray of the
northern skies had scarcely turned to the glory of the day :
and probably the preacher who was growing old was little
disposed to join the gay party whose young voices and
laughter he could hear in his chamber, where he lay " before
the sun "— setting out for the farther shore with a day's
pleasure before them.   It would be interesting to penetrate
what were his thoughts as he was rowed across the loch at a
more reasonable hour, when the sunshine shone on every
ripple of the water, and the green hills lay basking in the
light.   Did he look with jealous eyes, and wonder whether
the gray walls among the trees on St. Serf's isle were giving
shelter to some idolatrous priest ? or was his heart invaded
by the beauty of the morning, the heavenly quiet, the murmur
of soft sound ?   His mind was heavy we know with cares for
the Church, fears for the stability of the Reformation itself,
forebodings of punishment and cursings more habitual to
his thoughts, and perhaps more congenial to the time, than
prosperity and blessing.   It might be even that a faint
apprehension (not fear, for in his own person Knox had little
occasion for fear even had he been of a timorous nature) of
further trouble with the Queen overclouded his aspect : and
if he caught a glimpse of the ladies and their cavaliers on
the mainland, the joyous cavalcade would rouse no sympathetic pleasure, so sure was he that their frolics and youthful
pleasure were leading to misery and doom—in which, alas !
he was too sooth a prophet.

But when Knox met the Queen's Majestie "be-west
Kinross," Mary all bright with exercise and pleasure had
forgotten, or else had no mind to remember, the offence of

the previous night. She began to talk to him of ordinary
matters, of Ruthven who had (save the mark !)—dark Ruthven
not many years removed from that dreadful scene in the
closet at Holyrood—offered her a ring, and other such lively
trifles. She then turned to more serious discourse, warning
Knox against Alexander Gordon, titular Bishop of Athens,
"who was most familiar with the said John in his house and
at his table," and whose professions of faith seemed so genuine
that he was about to be made Superintendent of Dumfries.
" If you knew him as well as I do, you would never promote
him to that office nor to any other within your Kirk," she
said. "Thereintil was not the Queen deceived," says Knox,
though without any acknowledgment of the service she did
the Church : for on her hint he caused further inquiries to be
made, and foiled the Bishop. Again, as so often, a picture
arises before our eyes most significant and full of interest.
Mary upon her horse, perhaps pausing now and then to glance
afar into the wide space, where her hawk hung suspended
a dark speck in the blue, or whirled and circled downward to
strike its prey, while the preacher on his hackney paused
reluctant, often essaying to take his leave, retained always by
a new subject. Suddenly she broached another and more
private matter, turning aside from the attendants to tell Knox
of the new troubles which had broken out in the house of
Argyle between the Earl and his wife, who was Mary's illegitimate sister. The Reformer had already settled a quarrel
between this pair, and the Queen begged him to interfere
again, to write to Argyle and smooth the matter over if
possible. Then, the time having now arrived when she must
dismiss him, the field waiting for her and the sport suspended,
Mary turned again for a parting word.

"And now," said she, "as touching our reasoning yesternight I promise to do as ye required. I sall cause summon the offenders, and ye
shall know that I shall minister justice."

"I am assured then," said he, "that ye shall please God and enjoy
rest and prosperity within your realm ; which to your Majesty is more
profitable than all the Pope's power can be."

We have heard enough and to spare about Mary's tears

QUEEN MARY'S BATH

and the severity of Knox—here is a scene in which for once there is no severity, but everything cheerful, radiant, and full of hope. Was there in all Christendom a more hopeful princess, more gifted, more understanding, more wise? for it was not only that she had the heart to take (or seem to take) in a very hard matter the advice of the exasperating Reformer, entirely inaccessible to reason on that point at least as he was—but to give it, and that in a matter of real use to himself and his party. Was it all dissembling as Knox believed? or was there any possibility of public service and national advantage, and as happy and prosperous a life as was possible to a queen, before her when she turned smiling upon the strand and waved her hand to him as he rode away? Who can tell? That little tower of Lochleven, that dark water between its pastoral hills, had soon so different a tale to tell.

Had Mary deserted her faith as it would have been such admirable policy to do; had she said, like the great Henry, that Scotland was well worth a mass or the sacrifice of a mass; had she turned round and persecuted the priests of her own Church as she now was about, for their safety and with a subterfuge excusable if ever subterfuge was, to pretend to do—would posterity have thought the better of her? Certainly it would not; but Knox would, and her path would have been a thousand times more clear. Only it has to be said at the end of all, that religion had little part in the woes of Mary. Had there been no Darnley or Bothwell in her path, had it been in her nature to take that wise resolution of Elizabeth's, wise for every woman who has great duties and position of her own, how wonderfully everything might have been changed! Such reflections, however, are very futile, though they are strangely fascinating.

Knox wrote to Argyle immediately after with that plain speaking in which he delighted, and made the Earl very angry. It might well have been part of Mary's "craft," knowing that he was sure to do this, to embroil him with her brother-in-law. And she prosecuted her bishops to save them from the Westland lords, and imprisoned them gently to keep them out of

harm's way.   Neither of these acts was very successful, and it
would seem that the mollifying impression that had been made
upon Knox soon died away ; for when the Queen opened the
next Parliament he speaks of her splendour and that of her
train in words more like those of a peevish scold than of a prophet and statesman.   " All things mislyking the preachers,"
he says with candour, " they spoke boldly against the tarjat-
ting of their tails, and against the rest of their vanity, which
they affirmed should provoke God's vengeance not only against
those foolish women, but against the whole Realm."   God's
vengeance was freely dealt out on all hands against those who
disagreed with the speakers ; but the silken trains that swept
the ground, the wonderful clear starching of the delicate ruffs,
the embroidered work of pearls and gems which the fashion
of the time demanded, were but slight causes to draw forth
the flaming sword.   And that Parliament was very unsatisfactory to Knox and his friends : they tried to bring in a
sumptuary law ; they endeavoured to have immorality recognised as crime, and subjected to penalties as such ; and above
all, they attempted to obtain the ratification of various
matters of discipline upon which Knox so pressed that the
quarrel rose high between him and Murray, and there ensued
a breach and lasting coolness—Murray being as unwilling to
press Queen Mary into measures she disliked, as Knox was
determined that only by doing so was God's vengeance to be
averted.   When the Parliament was over the preacher made
his usual commentary upon it in the pulpit, warning the lords
what miseries were sure to follow from their carelessness, and
discussing the chances of the Queen's marriage with much
freedom and boldness.   Once more, though with more reason,
was God's vengeance invoked.   " This, my lords, will I say
(note the day and bear witness after), whensoever the Nobili-
ties of Scotland, professing the Lord Jesus, consents that ane
infidel (and all Papists are infidels) shall be head to your
Soverane, ye do so far as in ye lieth to banish Christ Jesus
from this realm."   This sermon was reported to Mary with
aggravations, though it was offensive enough without any
aggravations ; and once more he was summoned to the pre-

sence. The Queen was "in a vehement furie," deeply offended, and in her nervous exasperation unable to refrain from tears, a penalty of weakness which is one of the most painful disabilities of women. "What have ye to do with my marriage?" she cried again and again, with that outburst which Knox describes somewhat brutally as "owling." His own bearing was manly though dogged. Naturally he did not withdraw an inch, but repeated to her the scope of his sermon with amplifications, while the gentler Erskine of Dun who accompanied him endeavoured to soothe the paroxysm of exasperated impatience and pain which Mary could not subdue, and for which no doubt she scorned herself.

> "The said John stood still without any alteration of countenance, while that the Queen gave place to her inordinate passion; and in the end he said, 'Madam, in God's presence I speak, I never delighted in the weeping of any of God's creatures; yea, I can scarcely well abide the tears of my own boys whom my own hand corrects, much less can I rejoice in your Majestie's weeping. But seeing that I have offered you no just occasion to be offended, but have spoken the truth as my vocation craves of me, I must sustain, albeit unwillingly, your Majesty's tears rather than I dare hurt my conscience or betray my Commonwealth through my silence.'"

He was ordered to withdraw after this, and retired proud and silent to the ante-room where he had immediate proof what it was to lose the royal favour. Hitherto he had been, it is clear, a not unwelcome visitor: to Mary an original, something new in prickly opposition and eloquence, holding head against all her seductions, yet haply, at Lochleven at least, not altogether unmoved by them, and always interesting to her quick wit and intelligence; and Maister John had many friends among the courtiers. But now while he waited the Queen's pleasure, not knowing perhaps if she might not send him to the Castle or the Tolbooth in her wrath, all his fine acquaintances forsook him. He stood, "the said John," for an hour in that bustling ante-room, "as one whom men had never seen," only Lord Ochiltree who had come to Holyrood with him, and whose daughter he was about to marry, giving any sign of acquaintance to the disgraced preacher. And Knox was human: he loved the cold shade

as little as any man, and the impertinences of all those butter-
fly courtiers moved him as such a man ought not to have
been moved.   He burst out suddenly upon the ladies who
sat and whispered and tittered among themselves (no doubt)
at his discomfiture.   He would not have us think even then
that his mind was disturbed ; he merely said—

"Oh fayr Ladies, how pleasant were this life of yours if it should
ever abide, and then in the end that we might pass to heaven with all
this gay gear !   But fie upon that Knave Death that will come whether we
will or not.   And when he has laid on his arrest the foul worms will be
busy with this flesh be it never so fayre and so tender, and the silly soul, I
fear, shall be so feeble that it can neither carry with it gold garnissing,
tarjetting, pearls, nor precious stones !"

Knox was never called to the royal presence more, nor
did Mary ever forgive him the exhibition of feminine weakness into which his severity had driven her.   It was intolerable, no doubt, to her pride to have been betrayed into
those tears, to have seen through them the same immovable
countenance which had yielded to none of her arguments
and cared nothing for her anger, and to have him finally
compare her to his own boys whom his own hands corrected—
the blubbering of schoolboys to the tears of a queen !   There
is perhaps always a mixture of the tragi-comic in every
such scene, and this humiliating comparison, obtusely intended
as a sort of blundering apology, but which brought the
Queen's exasperation and mortification to a climax, and
Knox's bitter assault upon the ladies in their fine dresses
outside, give a humiliating poignancy to the exasperated
feeling on both sides such as delights a cynic.   It was the
end of all personal encounter between the Queen and the
preacher.   She did not forgive him, and did her best to
punish : but in their last and only subsequent meeting, Knox
once more had the better of his royal adversary.

He had never been during all his career in such stormy
waters as now threatened to overwhelm him.   Hitherto his
bold proceedings had been justified by the support of the
first men in the kingdom.   The Lords of the Congregation,
as well as that Congregation itself, the statesmen and

"natural counsellors," as they call themselves, of Scotland, had been at his back : but now one by one they had fallen away. The Lord James, now called Murray, the greatest of all both in influence and character, had been the last to leave his side. The preachers, the great assembly that filled St. Giles's almost daily, the irreconcilables with whom it was a crime to temporise, and who would have all things settled their own way, formed, it is true, a large though much agitated backing ; but the solid force of men who knew the world better than those absolute spirits, had for the moment abandoned the impracticable prophet, and the party of the Queen was eagerly on the watch to find some opportunity of crushing him if possible. It was not long before this occurred. While Mary was absent on one of those journeys through the kingdom which had been the constant habit of Scottish monarchs, the usual mass was celebrated in the Chapel of Holyrood, the priests who officiated there evidently feeling themselves authorised to continue their usual service even in the Queen's absence, for whose sake alone it was tolerated. But they were interrupted by "a zealous brother," and some little tumult rose, just of importance enough to justify the seizure of two offenders, who were bound under sureties to "underlie the law" at a given date, within three weeks of the offence. In the excited state of feeling which existed in the town this arrest was magnified into something serious, and "the brethren," consulting over the matter with perhaps involuntary exaggeration, as if the two rioters were in danger of their lives, concluded that Knox should write a circular letter to the Congregation at a distance, as had been done with such effect in the early days under the Queen Regent, bidding them assemble in Edinburgh upon the day fixed for the trial. A copy of this letter was carried to the Court then at Stirling and afforded the very occasion required. Murray returned in haste from the north, and all the nobility were called to Edinburgh to inquire into this bold semi-royal summons issued to the Queen's lieges without her authority and in resistance to her will. "The Queen was not a little rejoiced," says Knox, "for she thought once to be revenged

of that her great enemy." And it was evident that Mary
did look forward to the satisfaction of crushing this arrogant

WEST DOORWAY, HOLYROOD CHAPEL

priest and achieving a final triumph over the man whom she
could neither awe nor charm out of his own determined way.

The commotion produced by these proceedings was

unexampled. One after another of the men who had by
Knox's side led the entire movement of the Reformation and
to whom he had been spokesman, secretary, and counsellor,
came with grave looks and anxious urgency to do what they
could to procure his submission. The Master of Maxwell,
hitherto his great friend, but who now broke off from him
entirely, was the first to appear. Then Speirs of Condie
(whom he convinced), then Murray and Lethington with whom
he held one of those long arguments which were of frequent
recurrence, and which are always highly dramatic — the
dour preacher holding his own like a stone wall before all
the assaults, light, brilliant, and varied, of the accomplished
secretary, whose smile of contempt at the unconquerable
personage before him and his " devout imaginations " is
often mingled with that same exasperation which drove
Mary to the womanish refuge of tears. But no one could
move him. And at last the day, or rather night, of the
trial came.

It was in December, the darkest moment of the year,
between six and seven in the evening, when the Lords assembled at Holyrood, and the formidable culprit was introduced
to their presence. The rumour had spread in the town that
Knox was to be put on his trial, and the whole Congregation
came with him down the Canongate, filling the court of Holyrood with a dark surging mass of men, who crowded the very
stairs towards the room in which the council was held. The
lords were " talking ane with another " in the preliminary
moment before the council was formed, when Knox entered
the room. They were then told to take their places, headed
on one side by " the Duke " Chatelherault, and on the other
by Argyle. Murray, Glencairn, Ruthven, the Earl Marischal,
Knox's tried companions in arms, who had stood with him
through many a dark day, took their seats with averted
looks, his judges now, and judges offended, repulsed, their
old sympathies aggravating the breach. Then came the
Queen " with no little worldly pomp," and took the chair
between those two rows of troubled counsellors, Lethington
at one side, Maxwell at the other. She gave an angry laugh

as she took her place. "Wat ye[1] whereat I laugh?" she said (or is reported to have said) to one of these intimate supporters. "Yon man gart me greit, and grat never tear himself: I will see if I can gar him greit."

The proceedings being opened, Knox's letter was read. It was not a conciliatory letter, being in reality a call if not to arms yet to that intervention of an army of resolute men which had overawed the authorities again and again in earlier times. It contained the usual vehement statements about that crime of saying mass which, or even to permit it, was the most desperate of public offences in Knox's eyes: and there is little doubt that it exaggerated the danger of the crisis, and contained at least one misleading statement as to matters of which there was no proof. When it was read a moment of silence ensued, and then Lethington spoke :—

"Maister Knox, are ye not sorry from your heart, and do ye not repent that sic ane letter has passed your pen, and from you is come to the knowledge of others?"

John Knox answered, "My Lord Secretaire, before I repent I must be taught my offence."

"Offence!" said Lethington; "if there were no more but the convocation of the Queen's lieges the offence cannot be denied."

"Remember yourself, my lord," said the other, "there is a difference between ane lawful convocation and ane unlawful. If I have been guilty in this, I have often offended since I came last in Scotland; for what convocation of the brethren has ever been to this day with which my pen served not? Before this no man laid it to my charge as a crime."

"Then was then," said Lethington, "and now is now. We have no need of such convocations as sometime we have had."

John Knox answered, "The time that has been is even now before my eyes; for I see the poor flock in no less danger now than it has been at any time before, except that the Devil has gotten a vissoure upon his face. Before he came in with his own face discovered by open tyranny, seeking the destruction of all that has refused idolatrie; and then I think ye will confess the brethren lawfully assembled themselves for defence of their lives. And now the Devil comes under the

---

[1] It would be curious to know what language Mary spoke when she is reported to have made these very characteristic utterances. It is one of the points in the discussion about the famous Casket letters that she could not write Scots. Did she make love and make war, and hold courts and councils of this grave description, in French or in a broken version of her native tongue? No one ever says so, and it is surely a thing that could not be passed without remark.

cloke of justice to do that which God would not suffer him to do by strength."

"What is this?" said the Queen. "Methinks ye trifle with him. Who gave him authoritie to make convocation of my lieges? Is not that treason?"

"Na, Madam," said the Lord Ruthven, "for he makes convocation of the people to hear prayer and sermon almost daily, and whatever your Grace or others will think thereof, we think it no treason."

"Hold your peace," said the Queen, "and let him answer for himself."

"I began, Madam," said John Knox, "to reason with the Secretare, whom I take to be ane far better dialectician than your Grace is, that all convocations are not unlawful; and now my Lord Ruthven has given the instance, which, if your Grace will deny, I shall address me for the proof."

"I will say nothing," said the Queen, "against your religion, nor against your convening to your sermons. But what authority have ye to convocate my subjects when you will, without my commandment?"

"I have no pleasure," said John Knox, "to decline from the former purpose. And yet, Madam, to satisfy your Grace's two questions I answer, that at my will I never convened four persons in Scotland; but at the order that the brethren has appointed I have given divers advertisements and great multitudes have assembled thereupon. And if your Grace complain that this was done without your Grace's commandment, I answer, so has all that God has blessed within this Realm, from the beginning of this action. And therefore, Madam, I must be convicted by ane just law, that I have done against the duties of God's messenger in writing this letter, before that either I be sorry or yet repent for the doing of it, as my Lord Secretare would persuade me; for what I have done I have done at the commandment of the general Kirk of this realm; and therefore I think I have done no wrong."

This detailed report is in the form of an addendum to Knox's original manuscript, written hurriedly as if from dictation, as though in the leisure of his later days the Reformer had thought it well to enrich the story with so lifelike and well-remembered a scene. Nothing could be more animated than the introduction of the different personages of this grave tribunal. The long argument with Lethington which might have been carried on indefinitely till now, the hasty interruption of the Queen, not disposed to be troubled with metaphysics, to bring it back to the practical question, the quibble of Ruthven of which Knox makes use, but only in passing, are all as real as though we had been present at the council. The Queen, with feminine

persistence holding to her question, is the only one of the
assembly who has any heart to the inquiry.   The heat of a
woman and a monarch personally offended is in all she
says, as well as a keen practical power of keeping to her
point.   It is she who refers to the *corpus delicti*, carrying
the question out of mere vague discussion distinctly to the
act complained of.   Knox had said in his letter that the
prosecution of the men who had interrupted the service at
Holyrood was the opening of a door "to execute cruelty
upon a greater multitude."   "So," said the Queen, "what
say ye to that?"   She received in full front the tremendous
charge which followed :—

"While many doubt what the said John should answer he said to
the Queen, 'Is it lawful for me, Madam, to answer for myself? Or
shall I be dampned before I be heard?'

'Say what ye can,' said she, 'for I think ye have enough ado.'

'I will first then desire this of your Grace, Madam, and of this maist
honourable audience, whether if your Grace knows not, that the obstinate
Papists are deadly enemies to all such as profess the evangel of Jesus
Christ, and that they most earnestly desire the extermination of them
and of the true doctrine that is taught in this realm?'

'The Queen held her peace ; but all the lords with common voice
said, 'God forbid that either the lives of the faithful or yet the staying
of the doctrine stood in the power of the Papists ; for just experience
tells us what cruelty lies in their hearts.' "

This sudden turn of opinion, coming from her council
itself, and which already constituted a startling verdict against
her, Mary seems to have sustained with the splendid courage
and self-control which she displayed on great occasions : no
tear now, no outburst of impatience.   She did not even
attempt to deny the tremendous indictment, but allowed
Knox to resume his pleading.   And when she spoke again
it was with a complete change of subject.   Apparently her
quick intelligence perceived that after that remarkable incident the less said to recall the first object of the council the
better.   She went back to her original grievance, accusing
Knox though he spoke fair before my lords (which indeed
it was a strain of forbearance to say) that he had caused her
"to weep many salt tears" at their previous meeting.   His
reply has much homely dignity.

" Madam," he said, " because now the second time your Grace has branded me with that crime I must answer, lest for my silence I be holden guilty.   If your Grace be ripely remembered, the Laird of Dun, yet living to testify the truth, was present at that time whereof your Grace complains.   Your Grace accused me that I had irreverently handled you in the pulpit ; that I denied.   Ye said, what ado had I with your marriage ?   What was I that I should mell with such matters ? I answered as touching nature I was ane worm of this earth, and ane subject of this Commonwealth, but as touching the office whereintil it has pleased God to place me, I was ane watchman both over the Realm, and over the Kirk of God gathered within the same, by reason whereof I was bound in conscience to blow the trumpet publicly as oft as ever I saw any upfall, any appearing danger either of the one or of the other. But so it was that ane certain bruit appeared that traffic of marriage was betwixt your Grace and the Spanish Ally ; whereunto I said that if your nobilitie and your Estates did agree, unless that both you and your husband shall be so directly bound that neither of you might hurt this Commonwealth nor yet the poor Kirk of God within the same, that in that case I would pronounce that the consenters were troublers of this Commonwealth and enemies to God and to His promise planted within the same.   At those words I grant your Grace stormed and burst forth into an unreasonable weeping.   What mitigation the Laird of Dun would have made I suppose your Grace has not forgot.   But while that nothing was able to stay your weeping I was compelled to say, I take God to witness that I never took pleasure to see any creature weep (yea, not my own children when my own hand bett them), meikle less can I rejoice to see your Grace make such regret.   But seeing I have offered your Grace no such occasion, I must rather suffer your Grace to take your own pleasure than that I dare to conceal the truth and so betray both the Kirk of God and my Commonwealth.   These were the most extreme words I said."

Having thus repeated his offence (even to the tears of the schoolboys) the Reformer's shrift was ended and he was told that he might return to his house " for that night."   No doubt what he himself said is more clearly set forth than what others replied, but that he distinctly carried the honours of the discussion with him, and that his mien and bearing, as were depicted, are manly, grave, and dignified as could be desired, will not be denied by any reasonable reader.   That they impressed the council in the same way is equally evident ; that council was composed of his ancient companions in arms, the comrades of many an anxious day and of many a triumphant moment.   That he had offended and broken with several of them would not affect the consideration that to condemn John Knox was not a light matter ; that through all the hours of that winter evening half Edinburgh had been filling the Court of Holyrood and keeping up a murmur of anxiety at its gates ; and that it was a dangerous crowd to whom my lords would have to give account if a hair of his head was touched. The conclusion apparently came with the force of a surprise upon the Queen's Majestie, and perhaps shook her certainty of the sway over her nobility, which she had been gradually acquiring, which was sufficient to make them defend her personal freedom and tolerate her faith, but not to pronounce a sentence which they felt to be unjust.

" John Knox being departed, the Table of the Lords, and others that were present were demanded every man by his vote, if John Knox had not offended the Queen's Majestie. The lords voted uniformly they could find no offence. The Queen had past to her cabinet, the flatterers of the Court, and Lethington principally, raged. The Queen was brought again and placed in her chair, and they commanded to vote over again, which thing highly offended the haill nobilitie so that they began to speak in open audience—' What ! shall the Laird of Lethington have power to control us ? or shall the presence of ane woman cause us to offend God and to dampen ane innocent, against our conscience for pleasure of any creature ? ' And so the haill nobilitie absolved John Knox again."

The Queen was naturally enraged at this decision, and taunted bitterly the Bishop of Ross, who joined in the acquittal, with following the multitude, to which he answered with much dignity, " Your Grace may consider that it is neither affection to the man nor yet love to his profession that moved me to absolve him, but the simple truth"—a noble answer, which shows that the entire body of prelates in Scotland were not deserving of the abuse which Knox everywhere and on all occasions pours upon them.

This was his last meeting with Mary. The part he played in public affairs was as great, and the standing quarrel with the Court, and all those who favoured it, more acrimonious than ever, every slanderous tale that came on the idle winds of gossip being taken for granted, and the

most hideous accusations made in the pulpit as well as in
private places against the Queen and her lighthearted company.   The principles, of such profound importance to the
nation, which were undoubtedly involved, are discredited by
the fierce denunciations and miserable personal gossip with
which they were mingled.   That judgment should follow
the exhibition of "tarjetted tails," *i.e.* embroidered or highly
decorated trains, and loom black over a Court ball ; and that
Scotland should be punished because the Queen and her
Maries loved dancing, were threats in no way inconsistent
with the temper of the time ; but they must have filled the
minds of reasonable men with many revoltings of impatience
and disgust.   It says much for the real soundness of purpose
and truth of intention among the exclusive Church party
that they did not permanently injure the great cause which
they had at bottom honestly at heart.

DOORWAY, HOLYROOD PALACE

CHAPTER III

THE TRIUMPH AND END

When the Assembly of the Church met in December shortly after these stirring incidents it was remarked that Knox took no part at first in the deliberations, an unexampled event. After the first burst of discussion, however, on the subject of the provision for the Church, he disclosed the reason of his unusual silence, which was that he had of late been accused of being a seditious man, and usurping power to himself—and that some had said of him, "What can the Pope do more than send forth his letters, and require them to be obeyed?" When one of the great officials present, no less a person than the Lord Justice-Clerk, took upon him to reply, Knox silenced him with a few emphatic words—"Of you I ask nothing," he said, "but if the Kirk that is here present do not either absolve me or else condemn me, never shall I, in public or in private, as ane public minister, open my mouth in doctrine or in reasoning." It is needless to say that the Kirk decided that it was his duty to advertise the brethren of danger whenever it might appear—but not without "long contention," probably moved by the party of the Court. At this period all the members of the nobility had been so universally acknowledged as having a right to be present at the Assembly sittings, that messengers were sent to advertise them of their guilt in absenting themselves when in the extremely strained character of the relations between Church and State they stayed away. There ensued, some time after, a singular conference between the leading ministers and

the lords upon various matters, chiefly touching the conduct of John Knox, whose constant attacks upon the mass,
his manner of praying for the Queen, and the views he had
advanced upon obedience to princes, had given great offence
not only at Court but among the moderate men who found
Mary's sway, so far, a gentle and just one. This conference
took the form of a sort of duel between Knox and Lethington, the only antagonist who was at all qualified to confront
the Reformer. The comparison we have already employed
returns involuntarily to our lips ; the assault of Lethington
is like that of a brilliant and chivalrous knight against some
immovable tower, from the strong walls of which he is perpetually thrown back, while they stand invulnerable, untouched
by the flashing sword which only turns and loses its edge
against those stones. His satire, his wit, his keen perception
of a weak point, are all lost upon the immovable preacher,
whose determined conviction that he himself is right in every
act and word is as a triple defence around him. This conviction keeps Knox from perceiving what he is by no means
incapable by nature of seeing, the grotesque conceit, for
instance, which is in his prayer for the Queen. During the
course of the controversy he repeats the form of prayer which
he is in the habit of using—being far too courageous a soul
to veil any supposed fault. And this is the *salvam fac*
employed by Knox :—

   "Oh Lord ! if Thy pleasure be, purge the heart of the Queen's
Majesty from the venom of idolatry, and deliver her from the bondage
and thraldom of Satan in the which she has been brought up and yet
remains, for the lack of true doctrine ; that she may avoid that eternal
damnation which abides all obstinate and impenitent unto the end, and
that this poor realm may also escape that plague and vengeance which
inevitably follow idolatrie maintained against Thy manifest Word and
the open light thereof." "This," Knox adds, "is the form of my
common prayer as yourselves were witness. Now what is worthy of
reprehension in it I would hear ?"

   "There are three things," said Lethington, "that never liked me ;
but the first is, 'To pray for the Queen's Majestie with ane condition
saying, "Illumine her heart if Thy good pleasure be," whereby it may
appear that ye doubt of her conversion.' Where have ye the example
of such prayer ?"

"Wheresoever the examples are," said the other, "I am assured of the rule which is this, 'If we ask anything according to His will He will hear us'; and our Maister Christ Jesus commanded us to pray unto our Father 'Thy will be done.'"

After this discussion has gone on for some time, Lethington, impatient, returns to the original question.

"But yet," said Lethington, "why pray ye not for her without moving any doubt?"

"Because," said the other, "I have learnt to pray in heaven. Now faith, as ye know, depends upon the words of God, and so it is that the word teaches me that prayers profit the sons and dochters of God's election, of which number whether she be ane or not I have just cause to doubt; and therefore I pray God illuminate her heart if His good pleasure be."

"But yet," said Lethington, "ye can produce the example of none that has so prayed before you."

"Thereto I have already answered," said John Knox, "but yet for further declaration I will demand ane question, which is this—Whether ye think that the Apostles prayed themselves as they commanded others to pray?"

"Who doubts of that?" said the haill company that were present.

"Weil then," said John Knox, "I am assured that Peter said these words to Simon Magus, 'Repent therefore of this thy wickedness, and pray to God that if it be possible the thought of your heart may be forgiven thee.' Here we may clearly see that Peter joins ane condition with his commandment."

With such extraordinary arguments, unconscious it would seem of the absolute incongruity of his illustrations, obtusely perverse in the dogmatism which destroys both Christian charity and sound perception, though he was as far from obtuse as ever man was by nature—the preacher stood immovable, nay, unassailable. The perception which defines and sets apart things that differ was as much beyond his great intellectual abilities, at least in those personal questions, as was the charity which thinketh no evil. The tongues of angels could not have convinced him that what was said to Simon Magus had no fitness to be applied to Mary Stewart. Such distinctions might be for the profane, they were not for him, to whom one example of Scripture was like another, always applicable, of equal authority in every case. It is not difficult to understand the exasperation of so modern a mind

as that of Lethington, while he attempted in vain to bring
this astounding debate to a conclusion.   For Knox always,
so to speak, proves his case.   Granting the twist in all his
logic, the confusion of things between which there was no
just comparison—and this twist and confusion belonged to
his period as well as to himself—his grotesque argument has
an appearance of reality which carried away those who agreed
with him, and confounded in their inability to come to any
ground of comprehension those who did not.

The debate was long and minute, and Knox was no
more shaken from his determination that the mass was
idolatry and that every idolater should die the death, than
from his conviction that he did his utmost for the Queen in
praying that God might convert her, if it were possible.   The
argument as to resisting princes is still longer and more
elaborate, but as it involves only large and general questions
is argued out with much more justice and perception.   It
was one of the subjects most continually under discussion
among all who held the Reformed faith, and Lethington himself and all his audience had both in profession and practice
held the popular view in the time of Mary of Guise.   It is
like enough, indeed, that somewhere among the crowd of
faces turned towards the disputants there was that long head
and saturnine countenance, still one of the best-known effigies
of his time, of the scholar who was at that period proud to
be Queen Mary's tutor, reading Livy with her in the afternoons, and who upon this question had views as clear as a
crystal, waiting for the moment when they could be set forth.
But George Buchanan, though he held office in the Assembly,
had no warrant to claim a hearing between such men as the
learned and lively Lord Secretary and the great prophet and
preacher John Knox.

The discussion ended in nothing, as may be supposed,
except a deepened offence on the part of the Court with the
impracticable Reformer, and an additional bitterness of
criticism on the part of the Congregation touching all that
went on at the abbey—the gaieties, and the beautiful dresses,
as well as the mass, and now and then a whisper of scandal,

unproved but taken for granted with that miserable eagerness which such opposition brings. Edinburgh, between
these two conflicting powers, was no doubt able, with the
wonderful impartiality of common life, to carry on its usual
existence much less affected than we could imagine possible
by any of the disorders, which almost reached the height of
civil war when Murray and the other lords were banished,
and the tide of Mary's fate began to rise darkly between the
unhappy fool she had chosen for her husband, and all the
wild conflicting elements which had been enough to tax her
strength without that aggravation. Even Knox acknowledges
that " the threatenings of the preachers were fearful," though
he himself had been the first to warn the people of national
judgments to be looked for because of the offences in costume
and other matters of their Queen. We lose, however, here
the picturesque and dramatic scenes which added so much
interest to the history during the brief period when she and
he were friends. The debate with Lethington, indeed, is the
conclusion of the brilliant and vivid piece of history in which
we have been made to see all that was going on in the
centre of Scottish life—the continual tumults, the great
gatherings in the Church, the sermons, daily orations full of
burning eloquence and earnestness in which every occurrence
of the moment was discussed, as well as the sacred subjects
which were familiar in the mouths of all. That vigorous
and trenchant pen falls from the hand of the preacher. The
fifth book of his History is prepared it is said from his notes
and under his eyes, but it is no longer the same as when
the very diction was his own, and his vivid memory, to which
all these incidents were present as when he acted in them,
was the storehouse upon which he drew. He himself appears
but on one occasion after the marriage of Mary. Darnley,
with perhaps an effort to hold the balance even and propitiate
the Church, attended the service at St. Giles's, or, as the
writer now calls it, the High Kirk of Edinburgh, where Knox
was preaching in his ordinary course unprepared for such an
honour. In the course of his sermon it chanced that he
characterised as one of the punishments with which God

follows national sins, that boys and women should rule over
the nations.   The young King (as he was called) was
passionately offended, and Knox was called next day to the
council to answer for himself, and at the same time forbidden
to preach for a stipulated time.   He replied that he had
spoken only according to his text, and that if the Church
commanded him to abstain from preaching he would obey.
This is all the formal record ; but the following marginal
note is added which gives a faint but not altogether ineffect-
ive glimpse of the Knox we know :—

"In answering he said more than he preached, for he added,
that as the King had, to pleasure the Queen, gone to mass and dishonoured the Lord God, so should God in His justice make her an
instrument of his ruin ; and so it fell out in a very short time ; but the
Queen being incensed with these words fell out in tears, and to please
her John Knox must abstain from preaching for a time."

As a matter of fact this penalty meant nothing.   Knox
was enjoined to silence as long only as the Queen and
Darnley were in Edinburgh ; and as they took their departure
that week, his work was scarcely interrupted at all.

During several eventful years after this Knox remained
in the shade, separated from his friends, the enemy of the
Court, and much denuded of his national importance.   It
was at this period that he married for the second time.   He
was nearly sixty, in shattered health and worn with many
fatigues, and it was scarcely wonderful that his enemies
should have said that nothing but witchcraft could have
induced a noble young lady, Lord Ochiltree's daughter, a
Stewart not far from the blood royal, to bestow her youth
upon the old preacher.   So it was, however, whether seemly
or not.   The lady must at least have known him well, for
her father had long been his faithful friend ; and no doubt
domestic comfort and care were doubly necessary to a man
whose labours were unending, and who had never spared
himself during his whole public life.

It is doubly unfortunate that we should have no record
from himself of the first chapter of that tragedy which was
soon to make Scotland the centre of curiosity and horror to

Christendom, and which came into the already troubled
national life like a thunderbolt.   Nothing, perhaps, will ever
fully clear up the dark death-scene of Rizzio, the darker
conspiracies and plots that led to it.   The fact that the
return of the banished lords was simultaneous with his
murder, and that Murray and the rest had bound themselves
in a covenant of duty and service to Darnley for his good
offices in procuring their recall, of the same date with the
other and darker bond which bound that wretched boy to
the executioners of the favourite, will always make it possible
for the partisans of the Queen to make out a certain case
against the lords.   And that Knox should have left Edinburgh suddenly and without a word when that dark deed
was accomplished is once more a painful presumption against
him.   But there seems no absolute evidence that either one
or the other were involved.   It is extremely possible, since
the English envoy knew beforehand of some such dark
purpose, that they too may have known.   But it is also
evident that so summary a conclusion to the matter was not
in the mind even of Ruthven when he first presented himself
like a ghost in the Queen's closet.   Persistent tradition will
have it still, in spite of demonstration to the contrary, that
Signor Davie was killed in Mary's presence at her feet ; but
the evidence would seem to prove that immediate execution
had not even been determined on, and that but for the fury
of the party among whom the struggling Italian was flung,
and who could not wait for their vengeance, there might
have been some pretence at legality, some sort of impeachment and condemnation, to justify the deed, in which proceedings had they been taken both Knox and Murray would
have concurred.   It is satisfactory, however, to see that Sir
James Melville, Mary's trusted and faithful friend, who was
in Holyrood during the night of the murder, and who had
previously urged upon the Queen, with all the zeal and
earnestness of a man who felt his mistress's dearest interests
to be at stake, to recall and pardon Murray (which had been
done also in the strongest terms by Sir N. Throgmorton, the
English envoy), had evidently not the slightest suspicion of

any complicity on his part, and even recorded the disappointment of Ruthven and the rest to find that the returned
exiles looked coldly on them.   Melville does not even
mention Knox, nor is there any further proof of guilt on his
part than is involved in the fact that he left Edinburgh on the
afternoon of the day which saw the flight, early in the morning, of Ruthven and his band.   This hurried departure must
always be to the prejudice of the Reformer ; for he had been in
circumstances more apparently dangerous before and had
never flinched.   He had the town of Edinburgh at his back
and all the Congregation.   Murray, with whom his friendship
had been renewed, was again in Edinburgh, and for the
moment at least in favour with the Queen, who had need of
all the supporters she could find.   Why should Knox have
fled ?   He promises in his History to write one day a full
account of the death of Davie, but never did so.   Evidence,
indeed, either of one kind or other, is entirely wanting ; but
why did he fly ?

Whatever was the reason, Knox at this period disappeared
entirely from the scene where so long he had occupied the
very foreground of affairs ; and until that cruel and terrible
chapter of history was completed, he was not again visible
in Scotland.   We cannot help feeling that though inexplicable on other grounds, this was well for his fame.   His
violent tongue and pen, no doubt, would have been in the
heat of the endless controversy.   As it is, he was not only
absent from the scene, but, what is still more singular, took
no part whatever in it.   The veil of age was falling over
the prophet, and the penalties of a weak constitution over-
strained.   Perhaps the comparative calm of England, where,
strangely enough, he chose this time to visit his boys (brought
up in a manner extraordinary for the sons of such a father, in
the obscure and comfortable quiet of English life, and evidently
quite insignificant—one of them dying unknown, a fellow of
his college, the other a country clergyman), had something
to do in taming his fiery spirit.   To see the two lads with
such blood in their veins in the tame security and insigni-
ficance of an existence so different from his own, looking at

their famous father with wonder, perhaps not unmixed with youthful disapproval, as a Presbyterian and a firebrand, must have given that absolute soul a curious lesson. And how strange is his appearance altogether, first and last, in the midst of that substantial, respectable county family of Bowes—carrying off the two ladies in his wild train : the mother to whom he was spiritual physician, director, and guide ; the gentle and silent daughter who was his wife ; flaming over the Continent and through all the troubles in Scotland with these incongruous followers behind him, then coming back to drop the two tame sparrows in the quiet nest which their mother had left for love of him ! All we know of them is that in their early childhood he did not spare the rod ; yet was grieved to see them weep. It would be strange if it were not a disappointment to him, if perhaps a relief as well, to find no sympathy in his sons for his own career. The daughters whom the young wife of his old age brought him lived to be like him ; which it is said is the only good fortune in paternity likely to so great a man.

When Knox emerged out of the silence which here falls so strangely upon his life (broken but by one energetic protest and appeal to the community against the re-erection of the bishopric of St. Andrews, which is full of all his old force) he was a weakened and ailing man, not less ready in spirit to perform all his ancient offices as standard-bearer and champion, but sadly unable in body to bear the fatigues and excitement of such an agitated life. He reappeared in public for the first time when the infant James was crowned in Stirling, preaching the sermon which preceded that melancholy ceremony. He then returned to Edinburgh, where for a brief period he saw the accomplishment of all his desires under the Regent Murray's government : the mass banished ; the Kirk re-established ; a provision, though still limited to a third of the old ecclesiastical property, securely settled for the maintenance of religion, and every precaution taken for the stability of the settlement. He was no longer able to take the part he had done in the affairs of the time and the guidance of the Assemblies, but

MORAY HOUSE, CANONGATE

he was still able to con-
duct, at least, the Sunday
services at St. Giles's, and
to give his strenuous
advice and help in all
the difficulties of government.   It must have seemed to
him that the light which comes at eventide had been fully
granted to his prayers.   But the death of Murray changed
all this like the end of a happy dream.   His sermon in St.
Giles's, after that terrible event, is a wail of impassioned
lamentation.   "He is at rest, O Lord! but we are left in
extreme misery," he cries, his grief redoubled by the thought

that it was he who had procured from Murray the pardon
of the assassin.   St. Giles's was full of the sound of weeping
when the old man, worn with labour and trouble, pronounced
those beautiful words which have breathed like the tone of
the silver trumpets over so many a grave : " Blessed are the
dead that die in the Lord."   It was one of the last of his
appearances in that great cathedral which he had made his
own, and to which he had given the only compensation and
adornment which could make up for its old sanctities and
decoration sacrificed—the prodigious crowd of eager and
sympathetic listeners, the great voice not without discords
and broken notes, but full of natural eloquence and high
religious feeling, of an orator and prophet.

A few months after Knox was prostrated by a fit of
apoplexy, it is said ; but it would rather seem of paralysis,
since his speech was affected.   He recovered and partially
resumed preaching, but never was the same again ; and the
renewed troubles into which Scotland and Edinburgh were
plunged found the old leader of the Church unequal to the
task of making head against them.   The curious complica-
tion of affairs which had already existed on several occasions
in the capital when the castle and its garrison were hostile
to the city at their feet, ready to discharge a gun into the
midst of the crowded streets or threaten a sally from
the gates which opened directly upon the very centre of the
town, was now accentuated to the highest degree by the
adoption of the Queen's cause by its Captain, Kirkaldy of
Grange.   We cannot pause now to give any sketch of that
misplaced hero and knight of romance, the Quixote of
Scotland, who took up Mary's quarrel when others deserted
her, and for much the same reasons, because, if not guilty,
she was at least supposed to be so, and at all events was
tragically unfortunate and in circumstances wellnigh hopeless.
These views brought him into desperate opposition to Knox,
once his friend and leader ; and though it is impossible to
believe that a man so chivalrous and honourable would
have injured the old Reformer, yet there were many
partisans of less repute who would no doubt have willingly

struck a blow at Knox under shelter of the Captain's name. As was natural to him, however, the preacher in these circumstances redoubled his boldness, and the more dangerous it was to denounce Mary under the guns of the fortress held in her name, was the more anxious with his enfeebled voice to proclaim, over and over again, his opinion of her, and of the punishment which, had there been justice in the world or faith in Zion, she must have undergone. Knox's failing life was assailed at this agitated period by a kind of persecution much more trying to him than anything he had undergone in the past. He was assailed by anonymous libels, placards affixed to the church doors, and thrown into the Assembly, charging him over again with railing against the Queen, refusing to pray for her, seeking the support of England against his native country, and so forth. These accusations had no doubt a foundation of truth. But whatever one may think of the matter as a question of fact, there can be no doubt that the very air must have rung with the old man's words when he got up under those lofty vaults of St. Giles's, and, with his gray hair streaming and his deep eyes, deeper sunk with age and care than nature, blazing from under their shaggy eyebrows, gave "the lie in his throat to him that either dare or will say that ever I sought support against my native country." "What I have been to my country," he went on, with a courage and dignity that calls forth all our sympathies, "albeit this unthankful age will not know, yet the ages to come will be compelled to bear witness to the truth. And thus I cease, requiring of all men that have to oppose anything against me that he will do it so plainly as I make myself and all my doings manifest to the world ; for to me it seems a thing most unreasonable that in my decrepit age I should be compelled to fight against shadows and howlets that dare not abide the light."

These flying accusations against him, to which, however, he was well accustomed, were followed, it is said, by more startling warnings, such as that of a musket ball which came through his window one evening, and had he been seated in

his usual place would have killed him ; a thing which might
have been accidental, though no one believed so. He was
persuaded at last to leave Edinburgh only by the representa-
tions of the citizens that were he attacked they were resolved
to defend him, and their blood would consequently be on his
head. On this argument he moved to St. Andrews, the
scene of his first ministry, and always a place beloved ; leaving
Edinburgh at the darkest moment of her history, the Church
silenced with him, and all the order and peace of ordinary
life suspended. At this crisis of the struggle, when Kirkaldy's
garrison was reinforced by all the party of the Hamiltons, and
the city lay, overawed and helpless, at the mercy of the
fortress, the life of the Edinburgh citizens underwent an extraordinary change. The churches were closed, and all the
pious habits of the time suspended : " neither was there any
sound of bell heard in the town, except the ringing of the
cannon." How strange this was among a population which
had crowded daily to the sermon and found the chief excitement of its life in the orations of the preacher, it is scarcely
necessary to point out.

The picture of Knox in St. Andrews, where he went in
May 1571, after all these agitations, is wonderfully soothing
and subdued. He was far from being without agitation even
there. The new institution of " Tulchan " bishops—called so
by the popular wit, men who bore the title alone of their
supposed bishopric, transferring the revenue to the lay patron,
and who officiated, it would appear, much as pleased them,
according to the old rule, or to the form of the Reformed
service—had just been invented ; and Knox was called upon
to instal the nominal bishop of St. Andrews, a thing which
he refused to do. He was in consequence accused by some
foolish person of himself desiring to have the bishopric (such
as it was), an accusation of which it is extraordinary that he
condescended to take any notice. But apart from these rags
and remnants of familiar conflict, his life in the little city by
the sea has a pleasant repose and calm. " He ever spoke
but sparingly against the mock bishop, because he loved the
man." This softer note is carried out in the two glimpses

of him which appear to us chiefly through the recollections
of the gentle James Melville, then a youth studying at St.

THE PENDS, ST. ANDREWS

Andrews.   The old man seems to have taken pleasure in the
sight of the boys about, who were carrying on their education

in the place where he himself had taught those "bairns," whom Wishart had sent him back to in his fervid manhood. " He would sometimes come in and repose him in our college yard, and call us scholars to him, and bless us and exhort us to know God and His work in our country, and stand by the good cause—to use our time well and learn the guid instructions and follow the guid examples of our maisters. Our haill college (St. Leonard's) maister and scholars were sound and zealous for the good cause, the other two colleges not so." Nor did he disdain the amusements of the young men, for when one of the professors made a play at the marriage of Mr. John Colvin, it was performed in Mr. Knox's presence. Alas! truth compels us to add that the subject of the play was grim and not so peaceful as the occasion, for it represented the imaginary siege and taking of the Castle of Edinburgh—then in full activity, and carrying fire and flame to the houses of the Edinburgh burghers—and "the Captain with ane or twa with him hanged in effigies." It would seem, however, that Knox loved the young scholars better than their instructors, for in one of his few letters written from St. Andrews, to the Assembly meeting at Perth, he charges the brethren above all things "to preserve the Kirke from the bondage of Universities," neither to subject the pulpit to them, nor to exempt them from its jurisdiction.

Knox was lodged in the abbey of which there now remains nothing but a portion of the enclosing wall, and it was but an old man's saunter in the sunny morning, with his staff and his servant's arm, through the noble gateway of the Pends to where St. Leonard's stood, looking away to the East Neuk over the ripening fields. St. Leonard's, however, has shared the fate of the abbey and exists no more.

Still more characteristic is the description given by the same pen of Knox's public appearances. It was young Melville's greatest privilege, the best of all the benefits he received during that year, to hear " that maist notable prophet and apostle of our nation preach."

" I had my pen and my little book and took away such things as I could comprehend. In the opening of his text he was moderate for the space of half an hour, but when he entered to application he made me so to grew and tremble that I could not hold a pen to write. In St. Andrews he was very weak. I saw him every day of his doctrine go hulie and fear (hooley and fairly, gently and with caution), with a furring of martins about his neck, a staff in the ane hand, and gude godlie Richart Ballenden holding up the other oxter, from the Abbey to the Parish Kirk ; and by the same Richart and another servant lifted up to the pulpit, where he behoved to lean at his first entry ; but ere he had done his sermon, he was sae active and vigorous that he was like to ding the pulpit in blads and flie out of it."

Melville says much, as indeed most of the narratives of the time do, of Knox's prophecies, especially in respect to the Castle of Edinburgh, which he said would run like a sand-glass—a prediction supposed to be fulfilled by a shower of sand pouring from some portion of the rock ; and its Captain, Kirkaldy, who was to escape over the walls, but to be taken and to hang against the sun. All of which things, and many more, occurred precisely as the seer said, after his death, striking great awe to the hearts of those to whom the predictions were made. The special prophecy in respect to Grange was softened by the announcement that " God assures me there is mercy for his soul." And it is at once pathetic and impressive to read of the consolation which this assurance gave to the chivalrous Kirkaldy on the verge of the scaffold ; and the awe-inspiring spectacle presented to the believers, who after his execution saw his body slowly turn and hang against the western sun, as it poured over the Churchyard of St. Giles's, " west, about off the northward neuk of the steeple." But this was after the prophet himself had passed into the unseen.

Knox returned to Edinburgh in 1572, in August, the horrors of the struggle between the Queen's party and the King's, as it was called, or Regent's, being for the moment quieted, and the banished citizens returning, although no permanent pacification had yet taken place. He had but a few months remaining of life, and was very weary of the long struggle and longing for rest. " Weary of the world, and daily looking for the resolution of this my earthly taber-nacle," he says. And in his last publication dated from St.

Andrews, whither the printer Lekprevik had followed him, he heartily salutes and takes good-night of all the faithful, earnestly desiring the assistance of their prayers, "that without any notable scandal to the evangel of Jesus Christ I may end my battle ; for," he adds, "as the world is weary of me, so am I of it." He lived long enough to welcome his successor in St. Giles's, to whom, to hasten his arrival, he wrote the following touching letter, one of the last compositions of his life :—

"All worldlie strength, yea even in things spiritual, decayes, and yet shall never the work of God decay. Belovit brother, seeing that God of His mercy, far above my expectation, has callit me over again to Edinburgh, and yet that I feel nature so decayed, and daylie to decay, that I look not for a long continuance of my battle, I would gladly ance discharge my conscience into your bosom, and into the bosom of others in whom I think the fear of God remains. Gif I had the abilitie of bodie, I suld not have put you to the pain to the whilk I now requyre you, that is, ance to visit me that we may confer together on heavenly things ; for into earth there is no stability except the Kirk of Jesus Christ, ever fighting under the cross ; to whose myghtie protection I heartilie commit you. Of Edinburgh the VII. of September 1572.   JHONE KNOX.
"Haist lest ye come too lait."

He lived to induct this successor, and to hear the terrible news of that massacre in France, which horrified all Christendom, but was of signal good to Scotland by procuring the almost instantaneous collapse of the party which fought for the Queen, and held the restoration of Roman Catholic worship to be still possible. That hope died out with the first sound of the terrible news which proved so abundantly Knox's old assertion that in the hands of the Papists there was no safety for his life, or the life of any who believed with him. Almost, however, before this grain of good in the midst of so much evil became apparent the prophet had taken his departure from this world. After the simple ceremonial at which he had officiated, of his successor's installation, John Knox returned home in the light of the brief November day, as Melville had seen him, supported by the arm of his faithful servant. The crowd which had filled St. Giles's hurrying out before him lined the street, and watched the old man as he crept along down the hill to his house,

INTERIOR OF ST. GILES'S

with many a shaken head and many a murmured blessing. In this last scene all were unanimous ; there was no one to cast a gibe or an unkindly look upon that slow aged progress from the scene of his greatest labours to the death-bed which awaited him. When the spectators saw him disappear within his own door, they all knew that it was for the last time. He lay for about a fortnight dying, seeing everybody, leaving a charge with one, a prophecy with another, with a certain dignified consciousness that his death should not be merely as other men's, and that to show the reverential company of friends who went and came how to die was the one part of his mission which had yet to be accomplished. He ended his career on the 24th November 1572, having thus held a sort of court of death in his chamber and said everything he had to say—dying a teacher and prophet to men, as he had lived.

No man has been more splendidly applauded, and none more bitterly dispraised. It is in one sense the misfortune of our age that it is little able to do either. If steadfast adherence to what he thought the perfect way, if the most earnest purpose, the most unwearying labour, the profoundest devotion to his God and his country are enough to constitute greatness, John Knox is great. He was at the same time a man all faults, bristling with prejudices, violent in speech, often merciless in judgment, narrow, dogmatic, fiercely in-tolerant. He was incapable of that crowning grace of the imagination and heart which enables a man to put himself in another's place and do as he would be done by. But even this we must take with a qualification ; for Knox would no doubt have replied to such an objection that had he been a miserable idolater, as he considered the upholders of the mass to be, he could not but have been grateful to any man who had dragged him by whatever means from that superstition. He was so strong in the certainty of being right that he was incapable even of considering the possibility that he might be wrong. And there were in him none of those reluctances to give pain, none of those softening expedients of charity which veil such a harsh conviction and make men hesitate to condemn. He knew not what hesitation was, and scorned a compromise as if it had been a lie, nor would he suffer that others should do what was impossible to himself. His determination to have his own way was indeed justified by the conviction that it was the way of God, but his incapability of waiting or having patience, or considering the wishes and convictions of others, or contenting himself with a gradual advance and progression, have no such excuse.

These were, however, of the very essence of his character. A perfectly dauntless nature fearing nothing, the self-confidence of an inspired prophet, the high tyrannical impulse of a swift and fiery genius impatient of lesser spirits, were all in him, making of him the imperative, absolute, arrogant autocrat he was ; but yet no higher ambition, no more noble purpose, ever inspired a man. He desired for his countrymen that they should be a chosen people like those of old whom God had selected to receive His revelation ; his ambition was to make Scotland the most pure, the most godlike, of all countries of the earth. In many things he was intolerable, in some he was wrong and self-deceived. He was too eager, too restless, too intent upon doing everything, forcing the wheels of the great universe and clutching at his aim whatever conditions of nature might oppose—to be wholly heroic. Yet there are none of the smoother or even more lovable figures of history whom it would be less possible to strike from off the list of heroes. The impression which he left upon the religion and character of Scotland remains to this day ; and if we think, as many have done during all these ages, that that development of national life is the highest that could be aimed at, John Knox was one of the greatest of men. But if he transmitted many great qualities to his country, he also transmitted the defects of these qualities. He cut Scotland adrift in many respects from the community of Christendom. He cut her off from her ancestors and from those hallowing traditions of many ages which are the inheritance of the universal Church. He taught her to exult in that disruption, not to regret it ; and he left an almost ineradicable conviction of self-superiority to a world lying in wickedness, in the innermost heart of the nation. It is a wonderful testimony to a man that he should have thus been able to imprint his own characteristics upon his race : and no doubt it is because he was himself of the very quintessence of its national character to start with, that he has maintained this prodigious power through these three hundred years.

He lies, it is thought, if not within the walls of St. Giles's under the flags between the Cathedral and the Parliament House, with all the busy life of modern Edinburgh, the feet of generations of men treading out the hours and years over his head ; a more appropriate bed for him than green mound or marble monument. That stony square is consecrated ground blessed near a thousand years ago by ancient priests who cared little more for Rome than do their modern successors now. But little heeded Knox for priestly blessing or consecrated soil. " The earth is the Lord's and the fulness thereof " was the only consecration of which he thought.

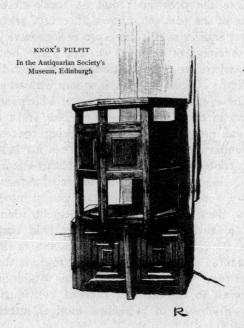

KNOX'S PULPIT
In the Antiquarian Society's
Museum, Edinburgh

CHAPTER IV

THE SCHOLAR OF THE REFORMATION

THE age of Mary Stewart is in many ways the climax of Scottish national history, as well as one of the most interesting and exciting chapters in the history of the world. The Stewarts of Scotland had been up to this point a native race entirely Scots in training as in birth, and bent above all things upon the progress and consolidation of their own ancient kingdom, the poor but proud ; a speck all but lost in the distance of the seas, yet known all over Christendom wherever errant squires or chivalrous pretensions were known. But the new sovereign of Scotland was one whose heart and pride were elsewhere, whose favourite ambitions were directed beyond the limits of that ancient kingdom with which she had none of the associations of youth, and to which she came a stranger from another Court far more dazzling and splendid, with hopes and prospects incapable of being concentrated within the boundary of the Tweed. There is no indication that the much-contested history of Mary Stewart has lost any of its interest during the progress of the intermediate centuries ; on the contrary, some of its questions are almost more hotly contested now than they were at the moment when they arose. Her chivalrous defenders are more bold than once they were, and though the tone of her assailants is subdued, it is from a natural softening of sentiment towards the past, and still more from the fashion of our time, which finds an absorbing interest in the manifestations of individual character and the discussion of individual motives, rather than from any change of opinion. I do not venture to enter into that long-continued conflict, or to attempt to decide for the hundredth time whether a woman so gifted and unfortunate was more or less guilty. Both parties have gone, and still go, too far in that discussion ; and Mary would not have thanked (I imagine) those partisans who would prove her innocence at the cost of all those vigorous and splendid qualities which made her remarkable. She could scarcely be at once an unoffending victim and one of the ablest women of her time.

As this is the most interesting of all the epochs of Scottish history—and that not for Mary's sake alone, but for the wonderful conflict going on apart from her, and in which her tragic career is but an episode—so it is the most exciting and picturesque period in the records of Edinburgh, which was then in its fullest splendour of architectural beauty and social life ; its noble streets more crowded, more gay, more tumultuous and tragical ; its inhabitants more characteristic and individual ; the scenes taking place within it more dramatic and exciting than at any other part of its history. Fine foreign ambassadors, grave English diplomates trained in the school of the great Cecil, and bound to the subtle and tortuous policy of the powerful Elizabeth ; besides a new unusual crowd of lighter import but not less difficult governance, the foreign artists, musicians, courtiers of all kinds, who hung about the palace, had come in to add a hundred complicating interests and pursuits to the simpler if fiercer contentions of feudal lords and protesting citizens : not to speak of the greatest change of all, the substitution for the ambitious Churchman of old, with a coat of mail under his rochet, of the absolute and impracticable preacher who gave no dispensations or indulgences, and permitted no compromise. All these new elements, complicated by the tremendous question of the English succession, and the introduction of many problems of foreign politics into a crisis bristling with difficulties of its own, made the epoch extraordinary ; while the very streets were continually filled by exciting spectacles, by processions, by sudden fights and deadly struggles, by pageants and splen-

dours, one succeeding another, in which the whole population
had their share.   The decree of the town council that " lang
weapons," spears, lances, and Jedburgh axes, should be provided in every shop—so that when the town bell rang every
man might be ready to throw down his tools or his merchandise and grip the ready weapon—affords the most
striking suggestion of those sudden tumults which might rise
in a moment, and which were too common to demand any
special record, but kept the town in perpetual agitation and
excitement—an agitation, it is true, by no means peculiar to
Edinburgh.   No painter has ever done justice to the scene
which must have been common as the day, when the beautiful young Queen, so little accustomed to the restraints and
comparative poverty of her northern kingdom, and able to
surround herself with the splendour she loved out of her
French dowry, rode out in all her bravery up the Canongate, where every outside stair and high window would be
crowded with spectators, and through the turreted and
battlemented gate to the grim fortress on the crown of the
hill, making everything splendid with the glitter of her
cortege and her own smiles and unrivalled charm.   Sadder
spectacles that same beautiful Queen provided too—miserable journeys up and down from the unhappy palace, sometimes through a stern suppressed tumult of hostile faces,
sometimes stealthily under cover of night which alone could
protect her.   Everything in Edinburgh is associated more or
less with Mary's name.   There is scarcely an old house
existing, with any authentic traces of antiquity, in which she
is not reported to have taken refuge in her trouble or visited
in her pleasure.   The more vulgar enthusiasts of the cause-
ways are content to abolish all the other associations of old
Edinburgh for Mary's name.

But I will not attempt to revive those pageants either of
joy or sorrow.   There are other recollections which may be
evoked with less historical responsibility and at least a little
more freshness and novelty.   No figure can be introduced
out of that age who has not some connection one way or
other with the Queen ; and the great scholar, whose reputa-

tion has remained unique in Scotland, had some share in her earlier and happier life, as well as a link, supposed of treachery, with her later career. George Buchanan was the Queen's reader and master in her studies when all was well with her. He is considered by some of her defenders to be the forger of the wonderful letters which, if true, are the most undeniable proof of her guilt. But these things were but incidents in his career, and he is in himself one of the most illustrious and memorable figures among the throngs that surrounded her in that brief period of sovereignty which has taken more hold of the imagination of Scotland, and indeed of the world, than many a longer and, in point of fact, more important reign.

It is difficult to understand how it is that in later days, and when established peace and tranquillity of living might have been supposed to give greater encouragement to study, accurate and fine scholarship should have ceased to be prized or cultivated in Scotland. Perhaps, however, the very advantages upon which we have plumed ourselves so long, the general diffusion of education and higher standard of knowledge, is one of the causes of this failure—not only the poverty of Scotch universities and want of endowments, but the broader and simpler scale on which our educational systems were founded, and which have made it more important to train men for the practical uses of teaching than permit to them the waywardness and independence of a scholar. These results show the "*défauts de nos qualités*," though we are not very willing to admit the fact. But in the earlier centuries no such reproach rested upon us. Although perhaps, then as now, the Scotch intelligence had a special leaning towards philosophy, there was still many a learned Scot whose reputation was in all the universities, whose Latinity was unexceptionable, and his erudition immense, and to whom verses were addressed and books dedicated in every centre of letters. One of the most distinguished of these scholars was George Buchanan, and there could be no better type of the man of letters of his time, in whom the liberality of the cosmopolitan was united with the exclusiveness of the member of a very strait and limited caste. He had his correspondents in all the cities of the Continent, and at home his closest associates were among the highest in his own land. Yet he was the son of a very poor man, born almost a peasant and dying nearly as poor as he was born. From wandering scholar and pedagogue he became the preceptor of a King and the associate of princes ; but he was not less independent, and he was scarcely more rich in the one position than the other. His pride was not in the high consultations he shared or the national move-ments in which he had his part, but in his fine Latinity and the elegant turn of those classical lines which all his learned compeers admired and applauded. The part that he played in history has been made to look odious by skilled critics ; and the great book in which he recorded the deeds of his contemporaries and predecessors has been assailed violently and bitterly as prejudiced, partial, and untrue. But nobody has been able to attack his Latin or impair the renown of his scholarship ; and perhaps had he himself chosen the foundation on which to build his fame, this is what he would have preferred above all. History may come and politics go, and the principles of both may change with the genera-tions, but Latin verse goes on for ever : no false ingenuity of criticism can pick holes in the deathless structure of an art with which living principles have had nothing to do for a thousand years and more.

Buchanan was born in a farmhouse, " a lowly cottage thatched with straw," in the year 1506, in Killearn in the county of Stirling ; but not without gentle blood in his veins, the gentility so much prized in Scotland, which makes a traceable descent even from the roughest of country lairds a matter of distinction. His mother was a Heriot, and one wonders whether there might not be some connection between the great scholar and the worthy goldsmith of the next generation, who did so much for the boys of Edinburgh. Buchanan's best and most trustworthy biographer, Dr. Irving,[1]

---

[1] I must explain that this chapter was written before the publication of the recent, and I believe excellent, biography of Buchanan by Mr. P. Hume Brown.

pictures to his readers the sturdy young rustic trudging two
miles in all weathers to the parish school, with his "piece" in
his pocket, and already the sonorous harmonies of the great
classic tongues beginning to sound in his ears—a familiar

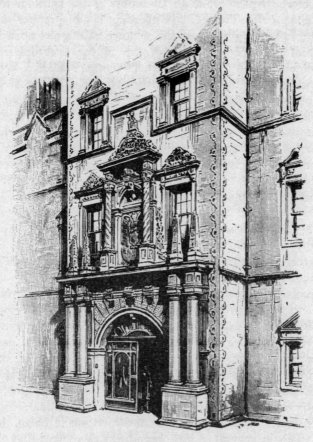

NORTH DOORWAY, HERIOT'S HOSPITAL

picture which so many country lads born to a more modest
fame have emulated. In the parish school of Killearn, in
that ancient far-away Scotland before the Reformation, which
it is hard to realise, so different must it have been from the
characteristic Scotch school of all our traditions, the founda-

2 A

tions of Buchanan's great scholarship and power were laid. His father died while he was still a mere child, and the future man of letters had plenty of rough rustic work, helping his mother about the farm on the holidays, which must have been more frequent while all the saints of the calendar were still honoured.   Trees of his planting, his biographer says, writing in the beginning of this century, still grow upon the banks of the little stream which runs by the beautiful ruins of Dunblane, and which watered his mother's fields.   When he had reached the age of fourteen an uncle Heriot seeing his aptitude for study sent him off, it would seem alone, in all his rusticity and homeliness, to Paris——a curious sign of the close connection between Scotland and France——where he carried on his studies or, a phrase more appropriate to his age, learned his lessons amid the throngs of the French schools.   Before he was sixteen, however, his uncle died, leaving him desolate and unprovided for amongst strangers ; and the boy had to make his way home as best he could, half begging, half working his passage, stopping perhaps here and there to help a schoolboy or to write a letter for the unlearned, and earning a bed and a meal as poor scholars were used to do.   He remained a year in his mother's house, but probably was no longer wanted for the uses of the farm, since his next move was to the wars.   He himself informs us in the sketch of his life which he wrote in his old age that he was "moved with a desire to study military matters," a desire by no means unusual at seventeen.   These were the days when the fantastic French Albany was at the head of affairs in Scotland, during the childhood of James V, and the country was in great disorder, torn with private quarrels and dissensions.   It is evident that, the kind uncle being dead and affairs in general so little propitious, there would be little chance in the resources of the farm of securing further university training for the boy who had his own way to make somehow in the world ; and perhaps his experience of Paris and possession of the French language (no inconsiderable advantage when there were so many French adventurers and hangers on about the court) might be expected to give him chances of promotion; while his service perhaps exempted an elder brother, of more use than he upon the farm, from needful service, when his feudal lord called out his men on the summons of the Regent.

George Buchanan accordingly followed the Laird's flag upon one of the wildest and most fruitless of Albany's expeditions to the Border, for the siege of Wark. The great Border stronghold, the size and wonderful proportions of which astonished the Scots army, stands forth again, clear as when it first struck his boyish imagination, in the description which Buchanan gives of it nearly half a century later in his history of that time—where the reader can still see the discomfited army with its distracted captains and councils, and futile leader, straggling back through the deep snow, each gloomy band finding its way as best it could to its own district. Buchanan would seem to have had enough of fighting; and perhaps he had succeeded in proving to his relatives that neither arms nor agriculture were his vocation ; for we next find him on his way to St. Andrews, "to hear John Major who was then teaching dialectics or rather sophistry." Here he would seem to have studied for two years ; taking his degree in 1525 at the age of nineteen. After this he followed Major to France, whether for love of his master, or with the idea that Major's interest as a doctor of the Sorbonne might help him to find employment in Paris, we are not told. One of the many stories to his prejudice which were current in his after-career describes Buchanan as dependent on Major and ungrateful to him, repaying with a cruel epigram the kindness shown him. But there seems absolutely no foundation for this accusation which was probably suggested to after-detractors anxious for evidence that ingratitude, as one of them says, "was the great and unpardonable blemish of his life"—by the epigram in question, in which he distinguishes his professor as "solo cognomine Major." It might very well be, however, that Buchanan expected a kind recommendation from his St. Andrews master, such as the habit of the kindly Scots was apt to give, and some help perhaps in procuring employment, and that the failure of any aid of this description betrayed the youth into the national tendency to harshness of speech and the bitter jeer at one who was great only in his name.

A stranger with nothing but his learning and his Latin epigrams (though these last were a more marketable commodity then than now) would no doubt be forlorn enough, struggling to find himself standing-ground and a living, subsisting hardly on what chance employment might fall in his way, and reflecting, as most adventurers are apt to do, how easy it would be for his prosperous countryman to befriend him. Paris, always full of stir and commotion, had at this moment a new source of agitation in the rising force of the Reformation principles or, as Buchanan calls it, " the Lutheran controversy, which was already spreading far and wide," and into the midst of which he fell on his return. Whether his interest in the new creed did him harm in his search for an establishment we are not told : and probably the "struggle with adverse fortune for about two years" which he records was merely the difficulty in making himself known which affects every young man. At the end of that time he got an appointment in the College of St. Barbe as Professor of Grammar, and was henceforward exempted at least from the heart-sickening conflict with absolute poverty.

Buchanan would seem to have had already high ambitions and a certainty that he was fit for something better than the post of schoolmaster in a French college—for notwithstanding his eagerness to get this post we soon find him lamenting, in the abstract indeed, but in a manner too particular to be without special meaning, the small profit of intellectual labour and the weariness of a continual toil which was so little rewarded. His plaint of the long night's work, the burning of the midnight oil, the hunt through dusty and rotting manuscripts, seems touched with a tone of bitterness unusual in the student's murmurs over a lot which after all brings him as much pleasure as weariness. The ambitious lad was already, it is evident, longing for more brilliant scenes.

" Pervigil in lucem lecta atque relecta revolves
Et putri excuties scripta sepulta situ :
Sæpe caput scalpes, et vivos roseris ungues,
Irata feries pulpita sæpe manu."

At St. Barbe, however, he secured a noble young pupil
of his own country, the future Earl of Cassilis, who opened
to him a brighter way, and finally led him back to his own
country and for a time to higher fortune.   When young
King James came to Paris to meet Magdalen of France—
with the sudden pathetic result of a hasty romantic marriage
soon followed by the poor young lady's death—young
Cassilis was still there with his tutor, who was himself but
little advanced in life beyond his patron.   And it was presumably in the train of the royal pair that the young men
returned home.   In that case Buchanan must have witnessed
the touching scene that took place at the poor young Queen's
disembarkation when she kissed the soil of her new country,
the land which was to afford her only a grave.   Whether
dreams of Court favour and advancement were beginning to
germinate in the young scholar's brain as he was thus suddenly
swept into the train of royalty there is nothing to say ; but
at all events he observed everything with keen attentive
eyes, unconsciously collecting the best materials for the history he was yet to write.   And it is clear that this accidental
connection with the King bore after-fruit.   Buchanan went
to Ayrshire with his young patron who had come of age, and
whose studies were over it is to be supposed : and in the
leisure of that relaxation from former duties amused himself
with compositions of various sorts, and in particular with the
Somnium, a lively poetical satire upon the Franciscans.   The
monks, who had been the favourite butt of all the ages, were
more than ever open to the assaults of the wits now that the
general sentiment had turned so strongly against them, and
Buchanan said no more than Dunbar with full permission,
before any controversy arose, had said, nor half so much as
David Lindsay was privileged to say.   And Lord Cassilis'
tutor had all the freedom of a private individual responsible
to no one while he lingered at his young patron's castle,

pleased to make as many as comprehended his Latin laugh, though probably there were few capable of appreciating its classical beauty. This, however, was but a pastime, and his mind again began to turn towards Paris, where alone perhaps there was to be found the kind of work for which he was most fit and the literary applause and emulation which were dear to his soul.

He was about to set out when the King, who doubtless had owed some entertainment to Buchanan on the lingering homeward journey, and who must have been well aware of his character and gifts, made him pause by offering him the tutorship of his illegitimate son, one among several for whom James, so young as he was, not more than twenty-five, was already responsible, another James Stewart, though not the notable James who was afterwards the Regent Murray. This appointment brought Buchanan at once within the charmed circle of the Court, and probably prepared the way for all his after-honours. But his career in Edinburgh at this moment was not especially glorious. Delighted by the *Somnium*, which had been read to him and applauded by all the obsequious audience round, James, who though a good Catholic liked a clever assault upon the priests as much as any one, recommended the new member of his household to resume the subject. It is supposed that the Grey Friars from their great lodgment so near the Court had found fault with the appointment of Buchanan and assailed himself as a profane and scoffing heretic. It was certainly strange that a man who had adopted the heresies of Luther should be appointed to the care of the son of a Catholic King, but Buchanan it is probable kept his religious opinions to himself, and it was not necessary to be a Protestant to give vent to the broadest satires against the monks and friars who had been for so long the least defensible portion of the Catholic establishment. Buchanan, however, was not bold enough to fall upon his enemies as Sir David Lindsay did. A poor man and a dependant, had he the highest spirit in the world, must still bear traces of the yoke to which circumstances have accustomed him, and a scholar is not necessarily brave.

He shrank from encountering the great and powerful community of the Grey Friars in the eye of day, and instead of the lively assault expected from him, temporised and wrote something which was neither satisfactory to the King who wanted a laugh at the expense of the monks, nor to the monks who were more enraged by the covert character of a satire which could be read both ways, than they would have been by straightforward abuse. The dissatisfaction of James moved Buchanan to bolder measures, and after his half-hearted attempt to compromise himself as little as possible, he was goaded into the most virulent use of his pen, and cut down his adversaries with the sharp shafts of his *Franciscanus* with a vigour and malice which left nothing to be desired. The Court had its laugh which was resounding and long, but neither King nor courtiers had any penalty to pay for the pranks which the classical Samson wrought for their pleasure.

Though they were thus mocked in high places, the Churchmen, however, had lost none of their power, and even the protection of the royal household did not avail the audacious poet. In the raid upon heretics which was made in the beginning of the year 1539 Buchanan's name was included among the guilty. He himself tells us that "Cardinal Beatoun bought his life from the King with money" : making it probably the price of some concession that this audacious assailant should be delivered into the hands of the Church. At all events the terrified scholar had no confidence in the power or will of his Sovereign to protect him, and, scared by the flames of various burnings which had taken place throughout the kingdom, directed his best wits to finding a way of safety. He escaped through a window while his keepers were asleep, some say from the Castle of St. Andrews, some from that of Edinburgh. His own account is more simple and goes into no detail. "He made his way into England, eluding the guards set for him." But England was not more secure than Scotland. The quick-witted fugitive found Henry VIII impartially burning victims from both sides, on the same day at the same stake, and considered this sublime indifference as still more dangerous

than the strife of Scotch affairs. " His old familiarity with
the French, and the singular hospitality of that nation," led
him back to the city which was then the favourite resort of
all the Muses.   When, however, Buchanan arrived in Paris
he found that his special enemy, Cardinal Beatoun, had preceded him there as ambassador from King James, and,
alarmed by so dangerous a vicinity, he accepted at once an
offer made to him by Andrew Govra, one of his colleagues
of former times, who had been appointed to the charge of a
college in Bordeaux, and removed thither with the greatest
expedition before his foe could be made aware of his presence
in Paris.

This was in the end of the year 1539, when Buchanan
had attained the age of thirty-three.   His residence in the
capital of the famous province of Gascony seems to have
been active and happy.   He was Professor of Latin in the
college ; perhaps the terms would be more just if we said
he was Latin master in one of the most flourishing and
successful of French schools ; but our neighbours still prefer
the more high-sounding nomenclature.   The great Garonne
was not full of ships and trade at that period as it is now ;
but Bordeaux was one of the old capital cities of France,
possessing a rank which now belongs to no French provincial
town, and had its own characteristic society, its scholars and
provincial statesmen.   But the most important and notable
human being of all whom Buchanan found in his new sphere
was a certain small seigneur of Gascony, six years old, and
already an accomplished Latinist, having learned no other
language from his cradle, bearing the name of Michel de
Montaigne and already a little philosopher as well as scholar.
The great essayist speaks afterwards of " George Buchanan,
the celebrated Scotch poet," as one of his masters, but he
does not say whether Buchanan was the enlightened pedagogue who connived at his endless reading and let him off
as much as was possible from other less congenial studies.

Buchanan, however, must have found the cheerful southern
city, with its Parliament and its colleges, and all the teeming
life and restless energies of the Gascon race, not unlike a

kind of warmer and more brilliant Scotland, full of national
brag and gallantry, a congenial sphere. He had been for a
long time shedding complimentary verses, sonnets, dedications, about him after the manner of the time, serving out to
everybody who was kind to him a little immortality in the
shape of classic thanks or compliment : but in Bordeaux he
began to produce works of more apparent importance, " four
tragedies " intended primarily for the use of his college,
where it was the custom to represent yearly a play, generally
of an allegorical character—one of the fantastical miracle
plays which delighted the time, and which were often as
profane in reality as they were religious in pretence. The
great classicist considered his boys to be wasting their
faculties in representing such inferior performances, but
humoured the prevailing taste so much as to choose two
Scriptural subjects, Jephthah and John the Baptist, alternately
with the Medea and Alcestis. He "was successful beyond
his hopes," he says, in these efforts. In all of the plays the
little Montaigne was one of the chief performers. "Before a
fit age, *Alter ab undecimo tum me vix ceperat annus,*" says that
great writer, " I sustained the first parts in the Latin tragedies
of Buchanan, which were played in our College de Guienne,
with dignity." The little scene is pleasant to think of, not
too long out of date to recall the scholastic pastimes of to-day,
though there is no Buchanan to produce plays for Eton or
Harrow, and probably no young Montaigne to play the hero.
The learned Scot, with his peasant breeding no doubt making
him still more conscious of the strain of gentle blood in his
veins, a little rough, irascible, and impatient in nature, notwithstanding the elegance of his Latin speech, and the little
noble, gentilhomme to his fingers' end, half respectful, half
contemptuous of the pedagogue, make a picturesque contrast.

Buchanan, however, did not feel himself safe even in
Bordeaux, where he remained only three years. It is said
that Cardinal Beatoun wrote to the Archbishop recom-
mending his arrest, and the Franciscan community in the
Gascon city, which had heard from their brethren of his
offences against the Order, kept an unfriendly eye upon him,

ready to take advantage of any hostile opportunity. He
therefore returned to Paris, where in a similar but apparently
more obscure position he spent some years. In 1547 he
was very glad to accompany Govra, who had brought him
to Bordeaux, and whom Montaigne describes as "beyond
comparison the greatest Principal in France," to his native
country Portugal, whither his King had summoned him in
order that his talents might be of use to his own nation as
the head of the new University of Coimbra. It would seem
that Govra carried his whole staff along with him to Portugal.
"Most of them," Buchanan says, "were men bound to him
(Buchanan) for many years in the ties of closest friendship,
men who were renowned for their works all over the world,"
and in whose society the Scottish scholar felt that he would
be not among strangers but among kinsmen and friends.
A still stronger inducement was, that while all Europe was
ablaze with wars and religious controversies, that one little
kingdom was at peace. The band of scholars thus removed
together to their new sphere, like a hive of bees, and at first
all went well with them; but they had not been long in
Portugal when Govra died, leaving them without any powerful patronage or protection, a band of strangers, no doubt
appearing in the aspect of supplanters of native talent to
many hostile lookers-on. Men of their pursuits and modes
of thought, aliens in an unknown country, perhaps sufficiently
free of speech to alarm the narrow-minded, no great observers
of ritual or ceremony, were too likely under any circumstances
to attract the notice of the Inquisition in a place so wholly
given over to its sway.

Buchanan was probably the most distinguished among
this band of scholars; and a vague report that he had
written something against the Franciscans attached to him
a special prejudice. As nobody knew what this work was,
it could not be brought formally against him, but lesser
crimes were found, such as that of eating meat in Lent and
speaking disrespectfully of monks, sins which even in Portugal
most people were more or less guilty of. Buchanan, however, had no very dreadful penalty to bear. He was

imprisoned for some months in a monastery, that he might
be brought by the monks' instruction to a better way of
thinking. The prisoner was fair enough to admit that he
found his jailors by no means bad men or unkindly in their
treatment of him—an acknowledgment which is greatly to
his credit, since prejudice was equally strong on both sides
and a persecuted scholar was as little apt to see the good
qualities of his persecutors as they were to accept his satires.
It would be interesting to know what the homely fathers
thought of him, this dreadful freethinker and satirist committed to their care for instruction. He found them
" entirely ignorant of religious questions," though evidently
so much less hostile than he had expected, and occupied his
enforced leisure in making his translation of the Psalms, a
monument of elegant verse and fine Latinity, for which the
quiet of the convent and the absence of interruptions must
have been most favourable. He would seem to have
corrected the bad impression he had at first made, by these
devout studies and his behaviour generally ; for when he
was released the King would not let him go, but gave him
a daily allowance for his expenses until some fit position
could be found for him. But there was evidently nothing
in Lisbon which tempted Buchanan to stay. He languished
in the little capital separated from all congenial society, and
sighed for his beloved Paris which he addressed as his
mistress, writing a poem, *Desiderium Lutetiæ*, in praise of
and longing for the presence of that nymph whom so many
have wooed.

At last he contrived to escape in a ship bound for
England, which, however, he found as little congenial as
Portugal, and with as short a delay as possible he returned
to that Lutetia which he loved. Arrived there, he would
seem to have resumed his old work as schoolmaster in
one of the colleges, no way advanced, despite his fame and
adventures, from the first post he had held when little more
than a boy, though he was now between forty and fifty, and
one of the best-known scholars of his time. A few years
later he became a member of the household of the Maréchal

de Brissac as tutor to his son, and with him spent five years, partly in Italy in the province of Liguria where the Maréchal was governor. For the first time he would seem to have been treated with honour, and his advice taken in affairs of state and public business generally, and here he tells us he devoted much of his time to the study of sacred literature, so that he might be able to form a matured judgment as to the controversies which were tearing the world asunder. In the year 1560, his services being no longer required by his pupil, Buchanan at last decided upon returning to his native country. "The despotism of the Guises," he says, "was over, and the religious excitement had begun to calm down." It would appear that though his convictions had so long been on the side of the Reform, he had not yet publicly made himself known as a member of that party. And his return to Scotland was made with the full intention so to do.

Such was the wandering and uncertain career of the scholar and man of letters of the sixteenth century. Perhaps Buchanan's temper was less compliant, his character less easily adaptable to the society in which he found himself, than most ; but it may be doubted whether this was the cause of the very small advancement in life to which he had come, since he was complaisant enough to indite many fine verses in praise of people who gave him a banquet or a shelter, and he seems to have gone nowhere without making friends. He had got abundant reputation, however, if not much else, and was known wherever he went as the celebrated poet, which doubtless was agreeable to him if not very profitable. But it gives us a certain insight into the life of the literary class in his time to see so notable a man wandering from one place to another, professor or regent or private tutor as it happened, never well off, never secure, often in the position of a dependant. When Milton speaks of the "others," poets whom he thus adopts into a kind of equality, who "use"

> " To sport with Amaryllis in the shade,
>   Or with the tangles of Neæra's hair,"

it is supposed to be Buchanan whom he refers to, which is
perhaps honour enough for a modern classicist; though
Amaryllis, the critics say, was no more individual a love
than the Lutetia before mentioned, for whom he pined.
Yet though all the scholars of his time admired and followed
him, he had to return again and again to his Latin grammar,
and to small boys not so wonderful as Michel of Montaigne;
and when he returned to Edinburgh at the age of fifty-five
his worldly position was scarcely better than when he got
his first appointment at twenty-one to the College of St.
Barbe. His life was now, however, to take another form.

Buchanan's return to Scotland " after the despotism of the
Guises was over" corresponded very nearly with the return of
Queen Mary. It is surmised that he may have travelled in
the suite of "the Lord James," the future Earl of Murray,
who paid his sister a visit very soon after the death of
her husband, King Francis : certainly nothing could be more
probable than that the Scotch scholar, seeking an opportunity
to return to his native country, should have joined himself to
the train of the prince, who probably had been acquainted in his
childhood with his brother's tutor, and who was himself a man
of education and a patron of literature.   If this guess should
be correct it would account for Buchanan's rapid promotion to
Court favour.   Edinburgh was in a state of happy expectation
when the poet came back.   What was virtually a new reign,
though Mary had been the nominal possessor of the throne
from her birth, was about to begin ; the fame of the young
Queen had no doubt been blown far and wide about the
country on every breeze—that fame of beauty, sweetness,
and grace which is the most universally attractive of all
reputations, and which made the proud Scots prouder still
in the possession of such a prodigy.   That there were graver
thoughts among the very serious and important party, who
felt the safety of their newly-established and severely-reformed
Church to be in doubt if not in danger, and who hated and
feared "the mass" and the priests who performed it as they
did the devil (with whom indeed they were more amiably
familiar), does not alter the fact that the anticipation of

Mary's return was a happy one, and her welcome cordial
and without drawback. Nobody knew that there had been
a project of a landing at Aberdeen, where Huntly and the
other northern lords had proposed to meet her with twenty
thousand men, thus enabling her to march upon her capital
as a conquering heroine of the old faith, putting Satan, in
the shape of John Knox, under her feet. Had she accepted
this proposal how strangely might the face of history have
been changed! But there is no reason to suppose that
Mary desired to come to Scotland with fire and flame, any
more than there is that her destruction was a foregone conclusion. She came with many prognostics of success, though
also with a continual possibility that "terrible tragedies"
might come of it; and for some time it would appear that
her Court was as seemly and pleasant as any Court could be,
full of youthful pleasure and delight as became her years and
the gay youthful company that surrounded her, but also of
graver matters and thoughts and purposes becoming a noble
Queen.

The first notice we have of Buchanan after his return to
Scotland is conveyed in a letter from Randolph, the English
envoy in Edinburgh, in which the question, "Who is fittest
to be sent from this Queen to attende upon the Queen's
Majesty (Elizabeth) for the better continuance of intelligence
with her Highness?" is discussed. "Of any that I know,"
says the representative of England, "David Forrest is
likeliest, and most desireth it. There is with the Queen one
called Mr. George Buchanan, a Scottishe man very well
learned that was schollemaster unto Monsieur de Brissac's
son, very godly and honest, whom I have always judged
fitter than any other I know." This was written in January
1562, and shows that Buchanan was at that time about the
Court and in the way of employment, though he was not
then chosen as confidential messenger between the two
queens. A little later he is visible in the exercise of his old
vocation as the tutor of Mary herself. "The Queen readeth
daily after her dinner," says the same careful narrator,
"instructed by a learned man, Mr. George Buchanan, some-

what of Lyvie." These few words set before us a curious
scene. Mary at the height of her good resolutions and good
beginning, keeping up her literature as well as all her pleasures, her hunting her riding, her music, her embroideries,
all the accomplishments of her royal training—makes a
delightful picture. She had the habit of working with her
needle like any innocent lady in her bower, while the lords
of her Council, grim lords whom it is strange to associate with
this pretty pose of royal simplicity, discussed around her the
troublous affairs of the most turbulent kingdom in Christendom : and after her dinner, in the languor of the afternoon,
one wonders if the lovely lady was diligent over her Livy or
rather seduced her preceptor to talk about Paris, that much-
desired Lutetia which he had so longed for, as no doubt in
the bottom of her heart she too was sometimes doing. The
two so unlike each other—the beautiful young princess not
quite twenty, the old scholar and schoolmaster though a
poet withal, drawing near the extreme boundaries of middle
age, and worn with much struggling against the world and
poverty—would yet find a subject and mutual interest far
apart from the book, which made endless conversation
possible, and many a pleasant comparison of experiences so
different. Buchanan had dedicated a book to one of those
fair and famous Margarets who adorned Paris at that epoch,
and presumably knew her or something of her state, and
could understand her Majesty of Scotland's allusions, and
knew something of the gossip of the Court, or at least could
pretend to do so, as a man who was aware what was expected
of a courtier. It is possible indeed that Mary was truly
studious, and liked her Livy as her contemporary did, the
gentle Lady Jane who had so sad a fate ; but it is much
more likely, we think, that the big volume lay open, while the
scholar's eyes glowed and shone with cherished reminiscences
of that enchanting city in which his best days had flown,
and Mary Stewart responded to his recollections with all her
gay wit and charm of pleasant speech. Many are the
tragic associations of Holyrood : it is well to note that other
companions more sober than Signor Davie, more calm than

Chastelar, shared now and then the Queen's leisure. Grave commentators conclude that it spoke well for her Majesty's latinity that Buchanan put her on Livy ; for my part I have no doubt that these two unlikely gossips, after perhaps a sentence or two, forgot about Livy, and talked of their Paris all the time.

Buchanan took the opportunity of this quiet and prosperous period, when all was hopeful in the nation as well as in his own prospects, to publish the poetical version of the Psalms which had occupied his enforced leisure in the Portuguese monastery years before. They had not yet seen the light in a complete form, although several of them had been included by the well-known printer Etienne, or Stephanus as he is more generally called, in a collection of similar translations by several learned hands, among which he gives in a flattering preface by far the highest place to Buchanan. The terms of laudation in which he speaks, and which it was the fashion of the time to employ, may be judged from the following extracts quoted by Irving. After commenting upon the general excellence of his friend's work, superior to all others, he adds,—

"There is nothing more honourable, nothing more splendid, than after excelling all others, at length to excel one's self ; so in my judgment you have most happily attained to this praise in your version of these psalms. For in translating the other odes of this sacred poet, you have been Buchanan, that is, you have been as conspicuous among the other paraphrasists as the moon among the smaller luminaries ; but when you come to the hundred and fourth psalm you surpass Buchanan ; so that you do not now shine like the moon among the lesser luminaries but like the sun you seem to obscure all the stars by your brilliant rays."

The community of letters in those days was in the habit of expressing the intensest mutual admiration, except when a contrary feeling not less strong animated their minds and pens. Buchanan dedicated his psalms to his beautiful pupil and patron in terms as highflown but more elegant, and with a justifiable wealth of hyperbolical adulation. It would be an undue demand upon humanity to require nothing more than plain fact in a poetical address to a young Sovereign so gracious, so accomplished, and so fair. And yet in the extraordinary circumstances, so soon to be swallowed up in the abyss of a catastrophe still more extraordinary, there is little extravagance in Buchanan's address, of which we shall attempt a translation though most unworthy.

> " Lady, who bears the sceptre of this land
>   By endless forefathers transmitted down,
> Whose worth exceeds thy fortune far, as stand
>   Thy virtues o'er thy years, and the renown
> Of noble gifts over thy noble line,
>   And spirit o'er thy sex :—without a frown
> Accept in this poor Latin garb of mine
>   The noble songs of Israel's prophet king.
> Far from Parnassus and the classic shore,
>   From under northern stars my gift I bring ;
>   Nor had I ventured such an ill-born thing
> To lay before thee, but for fearing more
> To miss the little chance of pleasing thee,
> Whose understanding gives a merit not in me."

Buchanan followed this publication by various others, and strangely enough, while still enjoying the royal favour brought out his *Franciscanus,* his *Fratres Fraterrimi,* and other satires specially directed against the monks : which, however, seem to have done him no harm, for he talks in 1567 of "the occupations of a court," which kept him from bestowing the time and trouble he wished on the preparation of his various books for the press. Whether the readings from Livy went on all this time we have no record ; but when Queen Mary married Darnley, and when her son was born, Buchanan would still seem to have occupied the position of Court poet, and celebrated both events by copies of verses as flattering, as well as elegant, as the dedication. From the first of these we may quote the lines in which Buchanan proves, notwithstanding his long absence and cosmopolitan training, that the native brag of the Scot was as strong in him as if he had never left his native shores. It could scarcely be to flatter either of the bridal pair that he burst forth into this celebration of " the ancient Kingdom."

> " For herein lies the glory of the Scot,
>   To fill the woods with clamour of the chase ;
>   To swim the stream, and cold and heat defy,

> And hunger and fatigue.   To guard their land
> Not with deep trench or wall, but with the force
> Of arms, contemning life for honour's sake ;
> To keep their troth, to reverence the bonds
> Of friendship, to love virtue and not gifts.
> Such acts as these secured throughout the land
> Freedom and peace, when war raged o'er the world,
> And every other nation was constrained
> To change its native laws for foreign yoke,
> The fury of the Goth stopped here ; the onslaught fierce
> Of the strong Saxon, and the tribes more strong,
> The Dane and Norman, who had conquered him,
> Nay, in our ancient annals live the tales
> Of Roman victory stayed—the Latin tide
> Which neither south wind checked, nor Parthia bleak,
> Nor waves of Meroi, nor the rushing Rhine,
> Was here arrested by this only race
> Before whose face the Roman paused and held
> The frontier of his empire, not by lines
> Of hill and river, but by walls and towns,
> By Caledonian axes oft assailed,
> Laying all hope of further gain aside."

In the meantime, while these poetical performances went on, and the scholar occupied his leisure in preparing for publication his scattered works—an occupation which of itself proved the quiet and good hope in which he was living— more serious labours also occupied his mind.   Notwithstanding his tutorship at Court, Buchanan took advantage of the moment to declare himself an adherent of the newly formed and very belligerent Church, now settled and accepted on the basis of the Reformation, but with little favour at Court as has been seen.   He not only put himself and his erudition at once on that side in the most open and public way, but sat in the General Assembly, or at least in one of the Assemblies which preceded the formal creation of that great ecclesiastical parliament, in 1563, less than two years after his arrival in Scotland.   Nor was his position that of a simple member taking part in the debates ; he seems to have sat upon various special committees, and to have been entrusted, along with several others, to revise the Book of Discipline, the standard of order and governance : and this while he was still a courtier, Mary's tutor and gossip, holding his place in her presence, and celebrating the events of the time in courtly and scholarly verse—a curious instance of toleration in a time which scarcely knew its name.

To recompense Buchanan's services Queen Mary granted him, in the year 1564, an allowance from the forfeited Church property, making him pensioner of the Abbey of Crossraguel, with an income of five hundred pounds Scots—a sum very different, it need not be said, from the same sum in English money. The abbey had been held by a Kennedy, the brother of Buchanan's first pupil, the Earl of Cassilis, and very probably he had thus some knowledge of and connection with the locality, where he had gone with Cassilis many years before. The grant would seem for some years to have profited him little, the then Earl of Cassilis, son of his gentler Gilbert, having little inclination to let go his hold of the rents which his uncle had drawn, either in favour of a new abbot or of the pensioner ; and the cruelties with which this fierce Ayrshire lord treated the functionary who succeeded his uncle seem incredible to hear of. George Buchanan kept out of his clutches ; but it was not till some years afterwards that we find the local tyrant bound over in sureties to leave the two lawful proprietors of these funds alone. So far as can be made out, Mary's grant to Buchanan was almost identical in date with the publication of the Psalms and the sonnet which he placed at their head : a graceful and royal return for the compliment, quite in harmony with the customs of the time. Both events occurred, as would appear, in the year 1564, when all was still well with the unfortunate Queen.

Buchanan has been accused of great ingratitude to Mary, because at one time he served and flattered her, and received as a recompense for the incense he offered, a substantial benefit : but afterwards turned from her party to that of her brother, and condemned her with unsparing blame in his History, as well as acted against her after her downfall. But the ingratitude is quite incapable of proof. To be devoted to a royal personage in his or her youth, and to maintain unbroken, however he or she may change, this early devotion through evil and through good report, is a romantic grace which is given to few.   It was given to very few of those who received with enthusiasm the young Queen of Scotland, when she came unsullied, with all her natural fascination and charm, into the country which hoped everything from her, yet knew nothing of her.   After the half-dozen years of disaster and tragedy, of which a much greater number of her people believed her the guilty cause than the innocent victim, there were few indeed who maintained their faith.   And Buchanan was neither romantic nor young ; he had none of the elements of an enthusiast in him.   A caustic man of the world, a self-absorbed scholar without domestic ties or usage in the art of loving, it would have been wonderful indeed had he constituted himself the champion of his beautiful pupil in her terrible adversity because she had shown him a little favour and he had laid poetical homages at her feet in a brighter time.   It would be hard indeed if such a passage of mutual good offices were to bind a man's judgment for ever, and prevent him from exercising the right of choosing whom he will serve to all time.   Mary's bounty would suffice to give to her tutor the independence which he had struggled for all his life, if it had been paid ; but it was not paid for several years ; and it was a bounty which cost the giver nothing, so that the claim for eternal gratitude is overweening in any case.

At the same time, both then and ever, Buchanan's patron and backer was the Lord James, a man with whom he was very much more likely to find himself in sympathy than with the young Queen.   A grave temper and some learning, and also the charm of early association, would naturally attract the elderly scholar more than Mary's feminine gifts, however great their charm.   It was Murray, no doubt, who presented him to the Queen, and procured him his position at Court ; and just as the tragic moment approached, when Mary's brilliant life was about to plunge into darkness, Murray bestowed on Buchanan the place of all others best suited for him, and to which his whole previous existence tended—that of Principal of the College of St. Leonard's in the University of St. Andrews.   A more fit position, as the best field for his

great gifts and dignified retirement for his old age, could not
be imagined. Buchanan was sixty ; he was of all the scholars
of his time *facile princeps*, according to the opinion of the
great French printer and scholar, whose expressions were
adopted in the register of the University as describing the
qualifications of the new Principal. It might well have been
supposed that in the reconstitution and improvement of that
old University, in the supervision of his students, in the peri-
odical visit to Edinburgh for Church matters or educational
duties, which has afforded the necessary relaxation to many
a succeeding principal, the peaceful days of the greatest
scholar in Europe would now have passed tranquilly, until he
found his resting-place, like so many others, under the soft
green mantle of the turf which, broken only by solemn
mounds—the last traces of individuality—encircled the great
Cathedral of St. Andrews as it now encircles the ruins of that
once splendid shrine.

The events of the time, however, permitted no such dignified and calm conclusion. One can imagine the horror and
dismay with which the little community at St. Andrews heard
the dreadful news, carried far and wide on every breeze, with
every kind of whispered comment and suggestion—soon to
be no longer whispered with pale face and bated breath, but
proclaimed from the housetops — of Darnley's murder.
Buchanan had poured forth his celebrations of Mary's
marriage and of the birth of the heir while still a member
of her household. And no doubt he had become aware of
the dissensions in that royal house, of Darnley's ingratitude
and folly and the Queen's impatience, before he escaped from
all the talk and endless gossip to the quiet of his college.
But it would seem equally clear that when the action of the
sombre tragedy quickened he was absent from the scene and
knew of it only by the rumours and reports that came across
the Firth. First Rizzio's murder, which the distant spectators would discuss, no doubt, with a thrill not entirely of
horror, a stern sense that justice had been done, a satisfied
prejudice—and no doubt some patriotic, if still prejudiced,
hope that now the Italian was removed there would be less

of foreign policy, and a more entire regard for the welfare of affairs at home. Then would come the rumours of the Queen's vengeance, lightly held at first, of Bothwell always in the foreground, her chief supporter and partisan—Bothwell who, though loved by nobody, was yet a Protestant, and therefore not altogether beyond hope. And then with ever-quickening haste event after event—the murder of the King, for whom no one would have mourned much had it been attended by circumstances less terrible ; the mad proceedings of the Queen, whether constrained or free, her captivity, out-rage, or conspiracy, whichever it was, her insane and incom-prehensible marriage, which no force or persuasion could account for. As the posts arrived at uncertain intervals, delayed by weather, strong winds and heavy seas, by break-ing down of conveyances, by the very agitations and tumults in the capital which made them so terribly interesting, the eager spectators in Fife must have congregated to await their arrival with an intensity of excitement, of which, with our endless sources of information and constant communica-tion, we can form little idea now.

And there would seem to be no doubt of the strong immediate feeling which arose against the Queen, the instant conclusion of the bystanders as to her guilt. There have been no greater fluctuations in historical opinion than those that have arisen around the facts of Mary's life. Historians of the eighteenth century considered it as a test of a man's moral sanity whether he persisted in believing in Mary's innocence or not. Among her contemporaries the progress of time which softened impression, and the many pathetic situations of her later history, the terrible misfortunes under which she fell, her endless miseries and troubles, and the brave spirit with which she met them, turned some hearts again towards her, an ever-troubled but ever-devoted body of partisans. But at the moment when these terrible events occurred there can be little doubt that the horror and condemnation were almost unanimous. No reasoning could explain away those wild and mad acts, no discussion of probability come in. The mob in Edinburgh which raged against her was checked in its fierceness and subdued to pity at sight of the wretched lady in her despair, at that awful moment when she appeared at the window of the Provost's lodging in the High Street, and made her wild appeal, in all the force of impassioned and terrible emotion, to the overawed and excited crowd.   They saw her in the carelessness of misery half-dressed, unadorned, disenchanted, and delivered from the maddening delusion which had carried her away, recognising in its full extent the horrors of the result—and their hearts were rent with pity.   But notwithstanding that pity and all the innate chivalry which her sufferings called forth, Edinburgh and Scotland, the whole alarmed and terrified nation, believed at first the evidence of their senses. There seems nothing more distinct than this fact throughout all the trouble and tumult of the moment.   It is not to be taken as an absolute proof of Mary's guilt.   Such impressions have existed in other though less conspicuous cases and have been proved untrue.   But that it did exist universally there can be little doubt.

The scene at the window of the Provost's lodging where the unfortunate Queen was lodged, near the Nether Bow of Edinburgh, when brought back from Dunbar after the flight of Bothwell by the angry lords, with the mob clamouring underneath, and her enemies holding her fate in their hands, seems to me one of the most significant in her history.   No woman was ever in circumstances more terrible.   The situation is stronger if we suppose her guilt, and that what we see before us is a great spirit carried away by passion—that something beyond reason, beyond all human power to restrain, which sometimes binds an angelic woman to a villain, and sometimes a man of the highest power and wisdom to a lovely trifler or a fool.   It seems to me as at once more consistent with the facts and with human nature to realise the position of the unhappy Queen as transported by that overwhelming senti-ment, and wrought on the other side to an impatience almost maddening, by the injuries, follies, treacheries, and universal provocation of her unworthy husband, until the force of the bewildering current carried her in a disastrous moment over

a precipice worse than any Niagara, in a headlong course of
mingled misery, exasperation, love, and despair.   Before she
had even accomplished the terrible circle of events, and
become Bothwell's wife, it requires no strong effort of the
imagination to perceive that the despair might well have
come uppermost, and that Mary fully recognised, not only
the horror, but the futility and wretched failure into which
she had plunged.   We do not pretend to believe that there
was much to cause remorse in the mind of such a woman in
such an age in the death, however brought about, of the
miserable Darnley.   Mary could have brushed him from her
memory like a fly, had that been all.   But the rage of
despair and failure was in her soul when she raved like a
caged lion from door to window, imprisoned, trapped, and
betrayed, expressing her incoherent transport of pain to the
mob which would have had her blood, but which, overcome
by the spectacle of that supreme and awful passion, became
silent with awe or hushed by a spasm of pity and tears.

So it has remained, a spectacle to all the earth, which
the fiercest assailant and the most rigid judge cannot long
contemplate without yielding to a painful compassion which
rends the heart.   Why should all that faculty and force, all
that wonderful being, with every capacity for happiness and
making happy, for wise action and beneficent dealing, for
boundless influence and power—why such youth, such
strength, such spirit, equal to every enterprise, should they
have been swept away by that remorseless fate?   We can
still see the trapped and ruined Queen—exasperated still
further by the consciousness that many of the men now
holding her in bonds were at least as guilty as she, guilty of
Darnley's blood, guilty if not of favouring yet of fearing
Bothwell and yielding their countenance to his plans—pacing
that chamber, appearing at that window, her loveliness, her
adornments, and all the wiles of triumphant beauty forgotten,
throwing forth to the earth that was as brass and the skies
that were as iron, like a wild animal in its torment, her
hoarse inarticulate cry.   And, whatever we may think of
her merits, that terrible spectacle is more than flesh and

blood can bear. Pity takes the place of wrath and indignation that she alone should suffer : why not Lethington,
Huntly, Athole, and the rest, all those stern peers who
counselled with her upon the most effectual way of having
Darnley removed, the thankless fool who disturbed every
man's peace—why were not they tried along with her, they
who took such high ground as her judges ? Why should she
bear the brunt of all ? Even Bothwell had escaped, and
Mary stood at the bar of the world alone.

But such thoughts would not seem to have moved the
first spectators, to whom all that damning sequence of events,
one precipitated on the heels of another, came fresh as they
occurred day by day. As for Buchanan, he would be less
prone to doubt than any. He knew something of the Court
of France and of the atmosphere in which Mary had received
her training. He was acquainted with many a royal scandal,
and had much experience of a world in which vice was the
rule and good behaviour a mere exception, due to a cold
temperament, or a wariness uncongenial to generous youth.
Such an old man of the world is slow to believe in innocence
at all, and it is very likely that to him who knew her so
well it was impossible to conceive of Mary as an example of
weak but spotless virtue. The Principal of St. Leonard's
went over to Edinburgh a few days after the completion of
that tragic chapter, when Mary had been consigned to Lochleven, and Murray had assumed the Regency. The city
was still agitated by much discussion of the dreadful questions which occupied all minds yet was slowly calming down
like an angry sea, with long seethings and swellings of
excitement. The object of Buchanan's visit was not curiosity
or desire to be in the centre of that excitement, but a simpler
matter, which has drawn many a Principal of St. Andrews
since to the capital of Scotland, an Assembly of the Church,
which opened "in the Nether Tolbooth" on the 25th of
June. Of this Assembly he, though a layman, was appointed
Moderator "for eschewing of confusion in reasoning"—a
curious motive, which proves at least that his contemporaries
had great confidence in his judgment, and also that the

passion of this excited and tumultuous time ran so high in
the Church that a stronger authority than usual was wanted
to keep it within bounds.   The sentiment of the Church, or
at least of the dominant party in it, would seem to have been
rather satisfaction that the Sovereign, foreign alike in training
and religion, had been set aside than any distress at the
cause.   The Assembly congratulates itself that " this present
has offered some better occasion than in times bygane, and
has begun to tread down Satan under foot," which is not a
very amiable deliverance : but kindness and charity were not
the Christian virtues most approved in those days.

From this time Buchanan took up with vehemence, and
indeed with violence, the prosecution of Mary, acting often
as her accuser, and always as an active agent, secretary, or
commissioner, in the conduct of the indictment against her.
He has been subject on this account to very hard treatment,
especially from the recent defenders of the Queen.   Mr.
Hosack, in his able book *Mary Queen of Scots and her
Accusers*, denounces him as having offered verses and adula-
tions to the Queen at a time when, according to his own
after-statement, everybody knew her to be living in shameless vice and corruption.   This, however, is not at all a
necessary inference.   It might, on the contrary, very well
have lent bitterness to Buchanan's historical record, written
after the dreadful catastrophe which so many accepted as a
revelation of Mary's real character, that he had himself been
one of the deceived, who for years had entertained no
suspicion, but accepted the fair seeming as truth.   Such a
sentiment is one of the most common in human nature.
The friend deceived becomes the bitterest enemy ; and he
who has been seduced into undeserved approval is apt to go
farther than the fiercest adversary when he learns that his
own utterances have helped to veil the crime which he had
never suspected the existence of.   This motive is enough, we
think, to account for the special virulence with which
Buchanan certainly does assail the Queen, and the passion
which thrills through the *Detectio*, a sort of fury and abhorrence which makes every paragraph tingle.   She had done

nothing to Buchanan to rouse any desire for individual vengeance ; and it is more rational, certainly, to believe that the
horror of the discovery inspired with a sort of rage the bosom
of the scholar—rage which was perfectly genuine in its beginning, though it might, no doubt, be raised to whiter heat
by the continually increasing fervour of partisanship.   The
curious description of him given by Sir James Melville (the
courtier, not the divine) that "he was easily abused, and so
facile that he was led with any company that he haunted for
the time, which made him factious in his old days; for he spoke
and writ as they that were about him for the time informed
him," would, if accepted, give a still easier solution to this question.   But it is a little difficult to accept such a character of
Buchanan, who does not seem to have been a man easily put
off from his own way, especially when taken in conjunction
with the Assembly's minute, recording his election as president "for eschewing of confusion in reasoning."   It is more
easy to believe the statement that he was "extreme vengeable
against any man that offended him, which was his greatest
fault."

The much darker accusation against Buchanan, that he
was a party to, or indeed the most active agent in, the
forging of certain letters reported to have been sent by Mary
to Bothwell before Darnley's murder, and known far and wide
as the Casket Letters, seems to rest upon nothing but conjecture.   He was one of the few members of the party who
possessed the literary gift, the only one, perhaps, except
Lethington, whom Mr. Skelton has presented to us as not
only a very enlightened statesman, but at all times the faithful servant of Mary, but who is accused by earlier writers
of much tergiversation and falsehood.   He it was, according
to Chalmers, who was the forger, reaching the summit of
wickedness "in forging his mistress's handwriting for the
odious purpose of convicting her of the crime of aggravated
murder."   Chalmers was as sturdy a champion of Mary's
innocence in the eighteenth as Mr. Skelton is in the nineteenth century, but the conduct of historical research has very
much altered in the meantime.   The changes have been rung

between Lethington and Buchanan by various critics, but the
last light upon the subject seems to be that there is none,
and that if the letters were forged the forger at least cannot
be identified by any art known to history.

It is unnecessary to pursue the question, or to bring
further arguments to prove that nothing else in Buchanan's
writings indicates the possession of such dramatic and con-
structive power as would be necessary for the production of
such a letter as that professedly written from Glasgow, which
is by far the most important of the contents of the Casket.
A woman's distracted soul, divided between passion and
shame, the very exaltation of guilty self-abandonment and
the horror of conscious depravity and despair, is not a thing
which can be imagined or embodied by the first ready pen,
or even able intellect. No one of all the tumultuous band
that directed affairs in Scotland has given us any reason to
suppose that he was capable of it. Its very contradictions,
those changes of mood and feeling which the most ignorant
reader can perceive, are quite beyond the mark of ordinary
invention. Mr. Froude has said that only Shakespeare or
Mary Stewart could have written it—at all events the writer,
supposing it to be forged, must have been of unquestionable
imaginative genius. It is one of the most wonderful compositions ever given to the world. We look on with awe
while those dark secrets of the heart are unfolded. The revelation is too tremendous, too overwhelming, and far too
true to nature, to call forth mere horror and condemnation.
It is a proof of the often-repeated statement that could we
but see into the heart of the greatest criminal pity would
mingle with our judgment. Nothing could be more criminal
and horrible than the acts therein anticipated, yet we think
it would be impossible for any unbiassed mind to read this
letter for the first time without an increase at least of interest
in the writer, so transported by her love, ready almost to
brag of the falsehood and treachery into which it leads her,
till sick shame and horror of herself breathes over her changing mood, and she feels that even he for whose love all is
undertaken must loathe her as she loathes herself. To ima-

gine Buchanan, an old man of the world, somewhat coarse, fond of a rough jest, little used to women, and past the age of passion, as producing that tragical and terrible revelation, is almost more than impossible, it is an insult to the reader's intelligence. And accordingly the latest writers on this subject have relinquished that accusation ; they no longer charge the old pedagogue with such an effort of genius ; they confine themselves to accusing him of ingratitude towards his benefactress, which is as much as to say that a little personal favour, even when well earned, is to compel a man to shut his eyes henceforward to the character and conduct of the person who has conferred it, and that both patriotic feeling and political policy are to be quenched by a pension, which is a strange view.

There can be no doubt, however, that Buchanan made out the case against the Queen with all the rhetorical force of which he was capable ; that the accusation was bitter, as of a man who had been personally deceived and injured, as indeed it is quite possible that he may have felt himself to be ; and that there was no pity, no mercy, nor compunction towards her, such as arose in many men's bosoms after a little time, and have been rife ever since both in writers and readers. The *Detection* is without ruth, and assumes the most criminal and degrading motives throughout. Its intention clearly is to convince Scotland, England, and the world of Mary's utter depravity, and the impossibility of any excuse for her or argument in her favour. The strong and fiery indignation in it is indeed lessened in effect, at least to us in these latter days, by the over strength of the indictment ; and the reader who turns from the perusal of the Glasgow letter—which damns indeed yet rouses a world of conflicting feelings, awe and terror and pity for the lost soul thus tragically self-condemned—to the historical document in which the charges against the Queen are authoritatively set forth, cannot fail to be struck by the difference. It is far from being simple abhorrence with which we regard the revelation of the one, but in the other there is no light ; the picture is inhuman and impossible in its utter blackness, the guilt imputed to the Queen is systematic, unimpassioned, the mere commonplace of an utterly depraved nature. The wild emotion and terrible impulse in her becomes mere vulgar vice in her accuser's hands. In this there is nothing wonderful, nothing out of the common course of nature, which is prone to make every indictment more bitter than the facts that prove it.

But it may well be believed that it was something of a fierce consolation to the high-tempered and strong-speaking Scots, in the rush of universal popular condemnation, to believe and assert that the Queen, who had so disappointed and disenchanted all her well-wishers, had been bad through and through, indecent and shameless. The inclination, almost the wish, to think the worst of every fallen idol has not died out with the generation which condemned Mary Stewart ; and Buchanan was the spokesman, the advocate of the other party, whose conduct could only be justified by the establishment of her guilt. If she were not guilty, they were traitors. If all the proof against her was but a mass of distorted facts and false swearing, nothing in the way of punishment was too bad for her unfaithful subjects. A mistake was impossible, the struggle was one of life and death. The spokesman in such a tremendous issue, the narrator and setter forth of the terrible question, especially if he is a person whose trade it is to write, and who can be accused of doing his work for hire, is always at a disadvantage. It can never be proved to the vulgar mind that he has not formed his opinions to order, that he does not give them out to the world according as they may best benefit and satisfy his employers. His masters may be hated, but he is both hated and despised. If it could be proved that Murray was solely actuated by ambition and the hope of getting the throne for himself, he would still be a belligerent with the honours of war due to him ; but the scribe, the hireling who is employed to state the whole matter, has no position but that of a venal dependant ready to set forth whatever is for his master's interests. Thus the historian of a party, who makes money by his work, the literary advocate whose office it is to make the strongest statement possible of his employer's case, is subject—or at least was subject in more primitive times—to the worst reproaches. His testimony was seldom taken as conscientious or true.

Buchanan's *Detection* was peculiarly subject to this reproach. It was written for the purpose of proving the case of the lords by demolishing entirely that of the Queen —before England and the commissioners of England first, seated in session to investigate the subject, and after them before the world in general. The inquiry which was opened at York in October 1568, six months after Mary's escape to England, was the most like a trial of anything in which her history was discussed. She was represented by commissioners, while Murray and several of his colleagues were present in person, along with Buchanan and other secretaries or minor commissioners. It was at this inquiry that the Casket Letters were first produced under, we are bound to say, if we judge by the rules of a period of settled law and order like our own, very suspicious circumstances. Even the question of the language in which they were written is a very difficult one. All through, indeed, this question is difficult, though it is never formally discussed until that tragical occasion. In what language did Mary and Knox hold their discussions? Could it be always in French that this accomplished Queen wrote and spoke? When she is reported to have said, as recorded in a previous chapter, " That man gar't me greet sore, and grat never tear," is this expression, so distinctively and strongly Scots, a translation from some more elegant murmur in another language? She who had so many tongues, had she left out that in which she had been born, the language of her childhood and of her country? This problem is only considered by the historians when it is required to prove that a letter must be forged because it is apparently first written in Scots. There is also a very great point made of the difference between Scots and English, which seems to have been very slight indeed, a difference of spelling more than anything else, nothing that could confuse any but the most ignorant reader.

The following sentences from Buchanan's " *Admonition direct to the Trew Lordis, maintaineris of justice* " will throw some light on the latter question, the difference between the written speech of the two different kingdoms, which one writer tells us would have made it easier for Queen Elizabeth to read letters in French than Scots :—

" It may seme to zour lordshippis," says Buchanan, " yat I, melling with heich materis of governing of comoun welthis do pass myne estait, being of sa meane qualitie, or forgetting my dewtie geveing counsal to ye wysest of yis realme. Not the les seeing the miserie sa greit appeiring, and the calamitie sa neir approching, I thocht it les fault to incur the cryme of surmounting my private estait than the blame of neglecting the publict danger."

From this the reader will be able to judge what extraordinary difficulty there was in the Scotch to an English reader of those days. The use of z instead of y, of y instead of th, are matters very easily mastered ; and it is surely the utmost folly to suppose that Queen Elizabeth could have found the slightest difficulty in deciphering this northern version of the common tongue.

The document quoted above is a very powerful and no doubt also violent assault upon the Hamiltons, especially called forth by the murder of the Regent Murray, the slackness of the succeeding Government in the punishment of his assassin, and the powerful reasons there were for destroying —a measure which Buchanan thought imperative both for the safety of the realm and the child-king—that powerful family, the head of which was next in succession to the Scotch Crown, and had been popularly believed to be ready for any crime to obtain it. Now that there was nothing but the life of a child between the Hamiltons and this elevation, Buchanan lifted up his testimony against the supineness which left the race undisturbed to carry out its evil designs. Murray had been murdered in the beginning of 1570, and the *Admonition* was printed at Stirling a few months later. In the same year Buchanan wrote that curious tract called the *Chameleon*, a satirical attack upon Lethington, which is not very brilliant either in language or conception, and fails altogether in the incisive bitterness which characterises most of Buchanan's other political papers. " It is at least equal in vigour and elegance to that of most compositions in the ancient Scottish language," says Buchanan's biographer, but few modern readers will agree in this verdict. Buchanan's hand had not the lightness necessary for such a performance. The guilt of Mary and the death of Murray furnished him with more emphatic motives than the iniquities of Maitland, and he was evidently stronger in assault and invective than in the lighter methods of composition.

It might have been supposed that his hopes of preferment would have been seriously injured by Murray's death. But it was after this event that he was selected for the greatest office which Scotland could bestow upon a scholar—the education of the young King. Buchanan's services were no doubt well worthy of such a reward : at the same time it may be allowed that a scholar so renowned, the first of contemporary poets according to the judgment of his class, and the greatest of lettered Scotsmen beyond all question, could not be passed over. During the intervening time he had retained the appointment of Principal of St. Leonard's College, his frequent absences being made possible by the fact that though he had much to do with the government and regulation of the University of St. Andrews, he was not actively employed in giving instruction. But after this we float at once into a halcyon time. It was in the end of 1569 or beginning of 1570 that he was appointed the governor of the King, and in this capacity and amid peaceful surroundings more appropriate to his character than the rage of politics, the old scholar becomes more distinctly visible than it was possible he could be in the midst of contention and under the shadow of greater men. He was about sixty-four at the time he entered upon the active duties of the office. " A man of notable endowments for his knowledge of Latin poesie— much honoured in other countries, pleasant in conversation, rehearsing on all occasions moralities short and instructive, whereof he had abundance, inventing when he wanted," says Sir James Melville. *Sandford and Merton* had not been

STIRLING CASTLE

written for the advantage of schoolboys in Melville's days, yet the picture is that of an antiquated Mr. Barlow never forgetting the art of instruction. The particular anecdotes, however, told of Buchanan, do not recall Mr. Barlow or his " moralities " at all.

The little King James, a precocious and clever child like all the infantile monarchs of the house of Stewart, had been established at Stirling, always a favourite residence of the Scotch kings, where he held his baby Court in peace while his mother pined in England, and the Scotch lords struggled for the mastery, and succeeded each other as Regents at home. The troubles of the world outside seem to have been kept far from the surroundings of the boy, to whom both the kingdoms looked as their heir, the child in whom the glories of his race came to a climax, and the union of the warring kingdoms was at last secured. Personally, he was by far the least distinguished of his name, but no one as yet suspected this fact or thought of Buchanan's pupil as less hopeful than any of the gallant Jameses who had preceded him. The little Court at Stirling was presided over at this early period by the Lady Mar, a dignified matron who was "wise and sharp and kept the king in great awe," although at the same time very tender of the child and respectful of his royal dignity. Almost all James's immediate surroundings seem to have belonged to this powerful race. The master of the household was a certain Laird of Drumwhasel, to whom no other name is given, and who is described as ambitious and greedy, a man whose "greatest care was to advance himself and his friends." Alexander Erskine, another member of the household, calls forth something like enthusiasm in the courtly narrative as "a gallant, well-nurtured gentleman, loved and honoured by all men for his good qualities and great discretion, no ways factious nor envious, a lover of all honest men, desiring to see men of good conversation about the prince rather than his own nearest friends if he found them not so meet." In addition to this official household were the tutors charged with James's education, two of them being members of the Erskine family, abbots of Cambuskenneth and Dryburgh, though those titles were no doubt merely fictitious, meaning only that the "temporalities," the endowments of the extinct monasteries, were in their hands. The other and principal masters of James were Sir Peter Young and Mr. George Buchanan. Young was "gentle, loth to offend the king at any time, carrying himself warily as a man who had a mind to his own weal by keeping of his majesty's favour"—"but Mr. George," adds the historian, "was a Stoick philosopher who looked not far before him." He "held the king in great awe," so that James "even trembled," as he himself says elsewhere, "at his approach," and did not spare either rod or word in the interests of his pupil. Some of the anecdotes of this severe impartiality are amusing enough. At one time annoyed by the noise which the King and his playfellows were making, Buchanan bade them be silent under certain penalties if the offence were repeated, and provoked by a childish impertinence from James, took up the little culprit and whipped him with exemplary impartiality, notwithstanding that his companion, the little Master of Mar, stood by, on whom vicarious chastisement might have been applied. Lady Mar, rushing to the scene of action at the sound of "the wailing which ensued," took the child from his master's hands and consoled him in her motherly arms, asking Buchanan indignantly how he dared to touch the Lord's anointed. The incident is very natural and amusing in its homely simplicity ; the child crying, the lady soothing him, the sardonic old master in his furred night-gown and velvet cap, looking on unmoved, bidding her kiss the place to make it well. The Master of Mar no doubt would cry too for sympathy, and the old gentleman take up his big book and move off to seek a quieter place for study. On another occasion, when the little King tried to get a sparrow from his companion and crushed the bird in the struggle, Buchanan rated him as himself a bird out of a bloody nest. He was an old man and alone in the world, indifferent to future favours from a king whose reign he would probably not live to see, and treating him with impartial justice.

There was, however, no indifference to James's education in this austere simplicity : indeed it would seem that Buchanan, like other preceptors of monarchs, had some hope of forming an ideal prince out of the boy. A few years after his appointment to his office, and when James was still too young to profit by it, he began to write his famous treatise, in the form of a dialogue, upon the laws of the kingdom, the duty respectively of kings and subjects. The *De Jure Regni*, published when the King was about twelve, was dedicated to him in a grave and dignified letter in which Buchanan describes his work as an attempt to expound the prerogatives

of the Scottish Crown, " in which," he says, " I endeavoured
to explain from their very cradle, so to speak, the reciprocal
rights and privileges of kings and their subjects." He goes
on to say that the book was written in the midst of the public
troubles with a view to enlightening the disturbers of the
commonwealth as to their duties : but that peace beginning
to be established he had sacrificed his argument for the sake
of public tranquillity. Now, however, that it may be useful
to the development of the King he brings it forth again.
The direct address to James is full of that curious self-decep-
tion or defective insight which is so common among those
who have the training of a pupil of great importance in the
world. The boy had grown beyond the age of personal
chastisement ; he had reached that in which the precocious
facility of comprehension, which is so strongly fostered by the
circumstances of such a position as his, looks to the dazzled
pedagogues and attendants like genius, and there seems no
prognostic too happy or too brilliant for the new career in
which at last there is about to be fulfilled all that men have
dreamed of a king.

" Many circumstances tend to convince me that my present exertions
will not prove fruitless, especially your age, yet uncorrupted by perverse
opinions ; a disposition beyond your years, spontaneously urging you to
every noble pursuit ; a facility in obeying not only your preceptors, but
all prudent monitors ; a judgment and dexterity in disquisition which
prevent you from paying much regard to authority, unless it be confirmed by solid argument. I likewise perceive that by a kind of
natural instinct, you so dislike flattery, the nurse of tyranny, and the
most grievous pest of a legitimate monarchy, that you as heartily hate
the courtly solecisms and barbarisms as they are relished and affected
by those who consider themselves as the arbiters of every elegance, and
who, by way of seasoning their conversation, are perpetually sprinkling it
with majesties, lordships, excellencies, and, if possible, with other expressions still more nauseous. Although the bounty of nature and the
instruction of your governors may at present secure you against this
error, yet am I compelled to entertain some slight degree of suspicion
lest evil communication, the alluring nurse of the vices, should lend an
unhappy impulse to your still tender mind, especially as I am not
ignorant with what facility the external senses yield to seduction. I
have therefore sent you this treatise, not only as a monitor, but even as
an importunate and sometimes impudent dun, who in this turn of life
may convoy you beyond the rocks of adulation ; and may not merely

offer you advice, but confine you to the path which you have entered, and if you should chance to deviate may reprehend you and recall your steps. If you obey this monitor you will ensure tranquillity to yourself and your family, and will transmit your glory to the most distant posterity."

That James VI should be described as disliking flattery and despising authority, if not enforced by solid argument, is strange to hear ; and that he should be so boldly called upon to consider a plea for national freedom and a constitutional rule, as the chief guarantee of tranquillity and honour, is still more remarkable.   Certainly it was not from Buchanan that he got those high pretensions of divine right, which had never flourished in Scotland ; although by a not uncommon paradox the most faithful partisans of the family which was brought to ruin by these pretensions were found in the northern kingdom.   Very different were the doctrines upon which Buchanan nourished the royal child.   James acknowledged afterwards not ungracefully the distinction of his instructor in letters.   "All the world," he says, "knows that my master George Buchanan was a great master in that faculty."   But his opinions in politics found no favour in his pupil's eyes when James emerged from his youthful subjection and began to show his native mettle.   At twelve, individuality in that respect would scarcely be developed, and a reverence for his tutor's sharp tongue and ready hand would keep the King from premature opposition.

While this work was going on in the comparative quiet of Stirling, Scotland was lost in the turmoil of one of the most wild and terrible portions of her history.   It is indeed rather from the glimpse we have of the little royal household in the foreground of all that strife and bloodshed, the Lady Mar in her matronly dignity, Buchanan in his furred gown among his books, and the clamour and laughter of the two boys interrupting the quiet, that we can believe in any semblance of peace or domestic life at all in the distracted country.   The Regent Lennox, the King's grandfather, was killed under the very rocks of the castle where James learned his lessons.   His young companion's father, the Earl of Mar, was taken from the family at Stirling and

raised to a brief and agitated Regency, through all of which
a civil war was raging.   And till from beyond the seas there
came the still more horrible news of that French massacre
which convulsed the world, and made an end of Mary's
party, nothing was secure from one day to another in Scotland.   It was in the midst of that very tumult and endless
miserable conflict, in which Mary's followers had at last set
up the doctrine of her irresponsibility and divine right to
retain her position as Queen whatever might be her guilt as
Mary Stewart—that the scholar set himself to compose his
work upon the rights of the kingdom and the duties of
kings.   His high temper, his strong partisanship, his stern
logic, would find an incitement and inspiration in those
specious arguments on the other side which were so new to
Scotland, and had been contradicted over and over again in
her troublous history, where no one was so certain to be
brought to book for his offences as the erring or unsuccessful
monarch.   It must be difficult for a great classicist to be at
the same time a believer in the divine right of kings ; and
it was a new idea for the mediæval Scot accustomed to
reverence the name, but to criticise in the sharpest practical
way the acts of his sovereign.   And we may imagine that
the old scholar, who could not but hear from his window the
shouts of the warfare between the Queen's party and the
King's, would have a grim satisfaction as he sat high above
them, protected more or less by the royal name, in forging
at his leisure those links of remorseless argument which,
though they had no effect upon the pupil to whom they
were dedicated, had their share in regulating that great
rebellion which had so important an effect upon the after-
history of the two kingdoms.

During this period, however, Buchanan had other
occupations besides his tutorship and his literary work.   He
was made "director of the Chancery," whatever that may
mean, and in 1570 was elevated to the post of Keeper of
the Privy Seal, in which capacity he served in various Parliaments : and was also a member of the Privy Council.   When
the conspiracy arose against the Regent Morton which ended

in his temporary deprivation of the Regency, Buchanan seems to have taken part against him, though on what argument we are not told : for it was Morton's power which had brought about the re-establishment of peace and order to which he refers in the dedication of his book. And it is a feasible conjecture that it was by his crafty suggestion that the Regent's fictitious plaints of being weary of his high office and desiring nothing more than that the King's Majesty should take the government into his own hand, were ingeniously twisted so as to give his dismissal the air of a gracious consent to Morton's own wishes. An old man like Buchanan, well acquainted with the wiles of logic and the pretexts of state, was more likely to use an advantage in which there is a certain grim humour, and to take the adversary in his own toils, than such an inexperienced politician as young Mar, or any of the undistinguished nobles who carried out that stratagem. Whether Buchanan supported his old pupil, Mar, in his attempt to seize the governorship of the castle and the King's person out of the hands of his uncle, or in what aspect he was regarded when Morton returned to the head of affairs, we have no means of knowing. Whatever his influence might be at the King's ear or amid the secret meetings of the malcontents, neither as Lord Privy Seal nor as King James's tutor did he come in public collision with any public authority. His action, whenever he appears publicly, is perfectly characteristic of his real position and faculties. He took part in a commission for the establishment of a system of municipal law : he was one of the Church's commissioners on two occasions in determining her policy and discipline. When the reform of the Universities of Scotland, so often taken up since then, and so slow to be accomplished, was brought under the consideration of Parliament, Buchanan was one of the chief of the commissioners appointed to consider it. He is reported to have been the author of a scheme of reconstruction to be employed in the University of St. Andrews ; and it is interesting to find in this new system that special attention was enjoined to be given to Greek, and that the study of Hebrew was also re-

commended to the students.   The latter language, we believe,
still remains an established part of the studies of young men
in preparation for the ministry in the Church of Scotland.
Buchanan desired that the Principal of his own College,
St. Leonard's, should lecture on Plato.   And he made a
present of a number of Greek books, still carefully preserved,
to Glasgow University, though why he should have chosen
to send them there, instead of to his own smaller and
poorer University, we have nothing to show.   It is thus
apparent that in his active public work Buchanan's chief
attention was given to his own proper subjects.   There is
no evidence that he did more than was indispensable to his
official character in matters more exclusively political.

His old age thus passed, in a certain learned leisure
which it is very difficult to imagine as existing in so tumultuous a period and amid so many violent changes and vicissitudes.   He had many learned correspondents throughout
the world, almost all the great scholars of the time being
numbered among his friends ; and the letters which he
received from all quarters implied a considerable amount of
letter-writing on his side.   He sent copies of his books to
his friends as if he had been the most modern of novelists,
and it is curious to think of the big laborious volume of
solemn Latin dramas, or that thin but weighty tome, instinct
with another and more living kind of interest, which set forth
the rights of nations—sent by some trusty messenger, a
young scholar finding in the packet entrusted to his charge
the best introduction to one of the lights of learning on the
Continent, or some adventurer making his way to a commission in the Scottish Archers or other service of arms more
profitable for a younger son than the frays and feuds of
Scotland.   The learned doctors of the Sorbonne, the scholars
of Geneva, and the printers of Holland, replied on their side
not only with elaborate thanks and eulogies, but with re-
sponsive presents, treatises or translations of their own, some
of them dedicated to the royal boy who was the pupil of
their friend, and of whom he gave so wonderful a description.
" I have been guilty of trifling with a sacred subject," wrote

Berger with his volume of poems, "and I have dedicated my trifles to a king." Another learned correspondent sends a Plato which he has edited, one volume of which he had also inscribed to James, begging that his friend would present it to his Majesty. They would seem to have shared Buchanan's satisfaction in his princely pupil, and it is chiefly by way of reflection, through these responses, that we perceive what his opinion of the young King was, and how much proud delight, expressed no doubt in the most classical language, he took in the boy's aptitude and promise. The following letter, however, which is not classical at all, but written in choice Scots and addressed to Queen Elizabeth's envoy, Sir Thomas Randolph, gives a less dignified but very graphic description of his own circumstances and occupations. It is written from Stirling during Morton's Regency, when peace prevailed and even prosperity had returned in some measure to the distracted kingdom.

"To Maister Randolph, Squiar, Maister of Postes to the Queen's Grace of England.

"Maister, I haif rescevit diverse letters frome you, and yit I haif answerit to nane of them—of the quhilk albeit I haif mony excuses such as age, forgetfulness, business, and disease, yet I will use nane as now, except my sweirness (reluctance) and your gentleness : and gif ye think nane of them sufficient, content you with ane confession of the falt without fear of punition to follow on my onkindness. As for the present I am occupied in writyng of our historie, being assured to content few, and to displease many therethrow. As to the end of it if ye gett it not or (before) this winter bepassit lippen (trust) not for it, no nane other writyngs from me. The rest of my occupation is with the gout quhilk halds me busy both day and night. And quhair ye say ye have not lang to lyif I trust to God to go before you, albeit I be on foot, and ye ryd *the post* : praying you also not to *dispost* my hoste at Newark, Jone of Kelsterne. This I pray you partly for his awyn sake quhame I tho't ane gude fellow, and partly at request of such as I dare not refuse. And thus I take my lief shortly at you now, and my lang lief when God pleases, committing you to the protection of the Almighty. At Stirling, xxv. day of August, 1577.—Yours to command with service,

"G. BUCHANAN."

The mild, aged jest about preceding his friend out of life though he must go on foot and Randolph had the advantage of commanding the Post, and his recommendation of the

erring postmaster at Newark, who was a good fellow, throw
a pleasant light of kindly humour into this letter.   And we
thus hear for the first time of the History, the greatest work
of his life, which he seems to have begun in the tranquillity
of the palace-castle, notwithstanding the hostile influence of
gout and years——hostile above all to so great a piece of work.
He was now over seventy, and the end of his career seemed
near at hand, although he had but recently taken in hand so
great an enterprise.   Buchanan's History is not, more than
other great histories which have succeeded it, an absolutely
impartial work ; but it is, throughout all his own stirring and
momentous age, the record of a bystander with abundant
means of knowledge and a keen apprehension of all the controversies and struggles of his time.   If he may perhaps
glorify too much the character of his patron and friend the
Regent Murray, and take the darkest view of Mary, we can
only say that he would have been more angel than man had
he kept himself absolutely without bias in that hot and still
unexhausted debate.   And there was nothing angelical about
the old scholar who had taken a part in so many historical
events, from the siege of Wark Castle, where he was present
as a boy, to the Conferences at York and Westminster, which
were matters of yesterday.   The science of history has so
much developed since his time that it may almost be said to
have made a new beginning ; and much that was considered
authoritative and convincing then has fallen into the limbo
of uncertainty, when not rejected altogether.   The many
differing motives and agencies which can only be fully esti-
mated when the period of discussion is past, have come to
occupy a far greater space in the mind of the historian than
had been dreamed of in Buchanan's days ; and the careful
examination of evidence with which we are now familiar was
unknown either in the study of the writer or the courts of
law during a time which has left endless questions from both
to be debated and re-debated by succeeding generations.
But yet Buchanan's History remains the most important and
dignified record of the national existence up to his time ; and
no one would now venture to treat the story of ancient

Scotland, the chronicles of her kings, or even the still un-
decided questions of Mary Stewart's life and reign, without
the guidance more or less of this great authority.   It was a
bold step to dedicate to King James a record in which his
mother's life was denounced and condemned with such unsparing freedom ; but the astonishing absence of sympathy
or human understanding shown in this was shared by the
greater part of Buchanan's contemporaries, who evidently felt
the facts of the mother's guilt to be too abundantly demonstrated and universally consented to, to demand any delicacy
of statement as addressed to her son.   No one, we think, can
entertain any doubt of the historian's own strong conviction
on this subject.   Among the many fables current about
Buchanan, there was one circumstantial and oft-repeated, of
his repentance on his deathbed of his judgment of the Queen ;
but this is entirely set at rest by the affecting record which
we shall quote farther on of a last visit paid to him by certain
of his friends who had taken fright at the boldness of his
statements, and feared that the King, now grown up and developing his own individual sentiments, might stop the issue
of the book when he saw these uncompromising records.

We must add one pretty story of Buchanan's kindness to
his brethren in scholarship and literature which shows the
sharp and cautious scholar in a very pleasant light.   A certain Thomas Jack, a schoolmaster in Glasgow, had composed
in Latin verse a little book upon the ancient poets, called the
Onomasticon Poeticum, and encouraged by the friendship
already, as he says, shown to him by Buchanan, carried the
book to him for revision.

" I found him in the royal palace of Stirling, diligently engaged in
writing his History of Scotland.   He was so far from being displeased by
the interruption that he cheerfully took my work from my hands, and
after reading two or three pages of it, collected together his own papers
which were scattered on the table, and said, ' I will desist from my work
till I have done what you wish.'   This promise he accurately fulfilled ;
and within a few days gave me a paper written with his own hand, and
containing such corrections as he thought necessary."

One can imagine the old scholar seated with his documents before him in the light of a broad window, perhaps

arrived at some knotty point which wanted consideration, and turning from the crabbed papers, which would not fit themselves in, with that delight in a lawful interruption and temptation to idleness which only hard-working students know.   Much has been said about the misery of such interruptions to the absorbed writer, but no one has pointed out the occasional relief and comfort which they bring.   Buchanan must have hailed this occasion of evading for a moment his legitimate work with all the pleasure of an old critic and connoisseur suddenly appealed to with such a congenial demand.   Even in our ashes live their wonted fires, and where is the scholar who does not turn with delight from his history or his sermon to criticise a copy of verses, to *savourer* a fine latinism or dig his pen through a false quantity as if he were cutting down an enemy ?   Thomas Jack has departed into oblivion along with his *Onomasticon* : but this record of the friendly reception he and his book met with affords a delightful gleam of light upon the historian's waning days.

It is more remarkable when we find another witness describing our somewhat irascible and sharp philosopher as growing young again in the boys who surrounded him, and adapting his mind to all ages and classes of men.   Probably by the time he came to be the King's preceptor Buchanan had ceased to be so compliant, or very probably conceived it appropriate, on principle, to be less indulgent to a pupil whose danger it would be to have too many flatteries and caresses.

We have no very clear record when it was that the tutelage of James was supposed to be over, or if Buchanan was ever formally freed from his office.   Informally the King would have seemed to be more or less his own master at the end of Morton's Regency, when, though subject to "raids" like that of Gowrie and the contending influence of one party after another, there was no longer any Regent thought of, and the business of the country was conducted formally in the King's name.   It would seem, however, from the dedication of the History, that Buchanan had ceased for some time before its publication to take an active part in James's education. He speaks in this of "the incurable illness" which made him incapable of "discharging the office entrusted to me of cultivating the genius" of the young King; and presents the book as making up in some degree for that personal failure. The History ends with the death of the Regent Lennox, he who was killed in Stirling almost under the historian's eyes, and when Scotland was still distracted between two parties, and in a state of civil warfare. It has been made a subject of reproach to Buchanan that he stopped his chronicle before the beginning of the Regency of Morton, because of his personal hatred to that brave and able personage—a singular charge, seeing that Buchanan lived only a few months after the last Regent of Scotland; and he has expressly mentioned in one of his dedications the increased tranquillity which was the result of Morton's government.

It is in Edinburgh we find the old man of letters in the last scene of his long and laborious life. In September 1581 he was visited by three gentlemen from St. Andrews, one of whom gives us the most lifelike and interesting account of this last interview. It would have been still more interesting had they afforded some indication where they found him, whether he had some pleasant room granted to him in Holyrood, after so many years with the King, a suitable retreat for his old age; or if he had retired to some private lodging in the Canongate to end his days. His visitors make no mention of such unimportant circumstances, but they leave us a most touching and faithful picture of the end of his life. These visitors were the famous Andrew Melville, Principal of the New College at St. Andrews, a scholar almost as distinguished as himself, who had at an earlier period been Buchanan's pupil, and who had acquired his great knowledge in the same way, in the famous schools of the continent; James Melville, his nephew, minister of Kilrenny on the shores of Fife; and Thomas Buchanan, the cousin of the dying historian. James Melville relates this last visit as follows :—

"That September in time of vacans, my uncle Mr. Andrew, Mr. Thomas Buchanan and I, hearing that Mr. George Buchanan was weak, and his Historie under the press, past over to Edinbruck annes errand (expressly) to visit him and see the work.   When we came to his chalmer we found him sitting in his chair, teaching his young man that servit him in his chalmer, to spell a, b, ab, and e, b, eb, etc.   Efter salutation Mr. Andro says, ' I see, sir, ye are not idle.'—' Better this,' quoth he, ' nor stealing sheep—or sitting idle which is as ill.'   Thereafter he shew us the Epistle Dedicatorie to the King, the which when Mr. Andro had read he told him that it was obscure in some places, and wanted certain words to perfeyt the sentence.   Sayes he, ' I may do na mair for thinking on another matter.'—' What is that ? ' sayes Mr. Andro.   ' To die,' quoth he ; ' but I leave that and manie more things for you to help.'

"We went from him to the printer's workhouse, whom we found at the end of the 17 book of his Cornicle at a place which we thought verie hard for the tyme, which might be an occasion for staying the haill work, anent the burial of Davie.   Therefore staying the printer from proceeding, we came to Mr. George again, and fand him bedfast by his custom, and asking him how he did, ' Ever going the way of weilfare,' says he.   Mr. Thomas, his cousin, shawes him of the hardness of that part of his Storie, that the King would be offendit with it, and it might stay all the work.   ' Tell me, man,' says he, ' gif I have told the truth ? '—' Yes,' says Mr. Thomas, ' Sir, I think so.'—' I will bide his feud and all his kin's then ; ' quoth he.   ' Pray, pray to God for me, and let Him direct all.'   So by the printing of his Cornicle was endit, that maist learned, wyse, and godly man endit this mortal life."

He was a pedagogue, perhaps something of a pedant, a hot partisan, a special pleader ; but few lives can show a more dignified and noble end.   If it was the truth he had written this old man cared for nothing else, not even for that fame which is the last infirmity of noble minds.   The King might keep back the great work of his life, but he could not silence the lips in which no fear of man was. Whatever might happen afterwards, Buchanan's record was clear ; to have told the truth was all with which he had anything to do.

There is a touch of what for want of a better word we must call cynicism in the humorous indifference with which the old philosopher is said to have discussed his own burial. Finding, as the story goes, that there was not money enough in the house for the last expenses, he ordered what there was to be given to the poor, declaring that he was not

concerned as to what was to become of his remains.   If
they did not choose to bury him they might let him lie, he

GREYFRIARS CHURCHYARD

said in grim jest.   He was, however, reverently buried by
the authorities of Edinburgh, in the historical churchyard of

the Greyfriars, attended by " a great company of the faithful,"
though no stone seems ever to have been placed to indicate
the spot where he was laid.   Thus in some unknown corner
he rests, like so many other illustrious persons—a man who
never rested in his life, and carried down his labours to
the very verge of the grave.   It is a curious satire upon
human justice that his name should have been kept green
in Scotland by the rough jests of an imaginary Geordie
Buchanan, commonly supposed to have been the King's
fool, as extraordinary a travesty as it is possible to conceive.
It is almost as strange a twist of all the facts and meaning
of life that the only money of which he could be supposed
to be possessed at his death should have been one hundred
pounds (Scots, no doubt), *arrears* of the pension due to him
from the Abbey of Crossraguel, given by Queen Mary to
that learned pupil of the Sorbonne and lover of Lutetia
with whom she read Latin at Holyrood in the early days
before trouble came.

PART IV

THE MODERN CITY

CHAPTER I

A BURGHER POET

AFTER the extraordinary climax of dramatic interest which brought the history of Edinburgh and of Scotland to the knowledge of the whole world, and which has continued ever since to form one of the most exciting chapters in general history, it was inevitable that when that fated Court dispersed, and the lady who was its charm and head disappeared also under the tragic waves which had been rising to engulf her, there should fall a sudden blank into the record, a chill of dulness and tedium, the charm departed and the story done. In fact, it was not at all so, and the metropolis of Scotland continued to seethe with contending elements, and to witness a continued struggle, emphasised by many a martyrdom and deed of blood, and many a desperate battle both hand to hand and head to head in the streets and in the council chambers, all with more or less the religious question involved, and all helping to work out the final settlement. When that final settlement came after all the tumults and blood it had cost, it is scarcely possible not to feel the downfall from those historical commotions to the dead level of a certain humdrum good attained, which was by no means the perfect state hoped for, yet which permitted peace and moderate comfort and the growth of national wellbeing. The little

EDINBURGH: GENERAL VIEW

homely church towers of the Revolution, as they are to be
seen, for instance, along the coast of Fife, are not more unlike the Gothic spires and pinnacles of the older ages, than
was the limited rustical provision of the Kirk, its restricted
standing and lowered pretensions, unlike the ideal of Knox,
the theocracy of the Congregation and the Covenant.
Denuded not only of the wealth of the old communion, but of
those beautiful dwelling-places which the passion of the mob
destroyed and which the policy of the Reformers did not do
too much to preserve—deprived of the interest of that long
struggle during which each contending presbyter had something of the halo of possible martyrdom about his head—the
Church of the Revolution Settlement lost in her established
safety, if not as much as she gained, yet something which it
was not well to lose.   And the kingdom in general dropped
in something like the same way into a sort of prose of existence, with most of the picturesque and dramatic elements
gone.   Romance died out along with the actual or possible
tragedies of public life, and Humour came in, in the
development most opposed to romance, a humour full of
mockery and jest, less tender than keen-sighted, picking out
every false pretence with a sharp gibe and roar of laughter
often rude enough, not much considerate of other people's
feelings.   Perhaps there was something in the sudden cessa-
tion of the tragic character which had always hitherto distinguished her history, which produced in Scotland this reign
of rough wit and somewhat cynical, satirical, audacious mirth,
and which in its turn helped the iconoclasts of the previous
age, and originated that curious hatred of show, ceremony,
and demonstration, which has become part of the Scottish
character.   The scathing sarcasm—unanswerable, yet false as
well as true—which scorned the " little Saint Geilie," the
sacred image, as a mere " painted bradd," came down to
every detail of life; the rough jokes of the Parliament House
at every trope as well as at every pretence of superior virtue ;
the grim disdain of the burgher for every rite ; the rude
criticism of the fields, which checked even family tendernesses
and caresses as shows and pretences of a feeling which ought

to be beyond the need of demonstration, were all connected
one with another. Nowhere has love been more strong
or devotion more absolute ; but nowhere else, perhaps,
has sentiment been so restrained, or the keen gleam of
a neighbour's eye seeing through the possible too-much,
held so strictly in check all exhibitions of feeling. Jeanie
Deans, that impersonation of national character, would no
more have greeted her delivered sister with a transport of
kisses and rapture than she would have borne false testimony
to save her. There is no evidence that this extreme self-
restraint existed from the beginning of the national history,
but rather everything to show that to pageants and fine sights,
to dress and decoration, the Scots were as much addicted
as their neighbours. But the natural pleasure in all such
exhibitions would seem to have received a shock, with which
the swift and summary overthrow of Mary's empire of beauty
and gaiety, like the moral of a fable, had as much to do as
the scornful destruction of religious image and altar. The
succeeding generations indemnified themselves with a laugh
and a gibe for the loss of that fair surface both of Church
and Court : and the nation has never given up the keen
criticism of every sham and seeming which exaggerated
the absolutism of its natural character, and along with the
destruction of false sentiment imposed a proud restraint and
restriction upon much also that was true.

To come down from the age when Mary still reigned in
Holyrood and Knox in St. Giles's—and Edinburgh saw every
phase of passion and tragedy, wild love, hatred, revenge, and
despair, with scarcely less impassioned devotion, zeal, and
fury of Reformation, and all the clang of opposed factions,
feuds, and frays in her streets—to the age when the Parliament House and its law courts were the centre of Edinburgh,
when Holyrood was the debtors' sanctuary, and St. Giles's a
cluster of parish churches, even its distinctive name no
longer used : and when the citizens clustered about the Cross
of afternoons no longer to see the heralds in their tabards
and hear the royal proclamations, but to tell and spread the
news from London and discuss the wars in the Low Countries,

and many a witty scandal, gibes from the Bench and repartees
from the Bar, the humours of the old lords and ladies in
their "Lodging" in the Canongate, and the witticisms of the

ALLAN RAMSAY'S SHOP

favourite changehouse—is as great a leap as if a whole world
came between.   The Court at St. Germains retained the devotion of many, but Anne Stewart was on the throne, and
rebellion was not thought of, while everything was still full

of hope for the old dynasty, so that Edinburgh was at full leisure to talk and jeer and gossip and make encounter of wits, with nothing more exciting in hand. In this tranquil period, his apprenticeship being finished, a certain young man from the west, by the name of Allan Ramsay, opened a shop in the High Street " opposite Niddry's Wynd " as a " weeg-maker "—perhaps, if truth were known, a barber's shop, in all ages known as the centre of gossip wherever it appears. It is odd, by the way, that a place so entirely dedicated to the service of the male portion of the population, and where women have no place, should have this general reputation ; but so it has always been. He had spent his early years as a shepherd on Crawford Moor in the Upper Ward of Clydesdale, and no doubt had there learned every song that floated about the country-side. " Honest Allan " was in every respect a model of the well-doing and prosperous Edinburgh shopkeeper of his time—a character not too entirely engrossed by business, always ready for a frolic, a song, a decorous bout of drinking, and known in all the haunts of the cheerful townsmen : tolerant in morals yet always respectable, fond of gossip, fond of fun, and if not fond of money yet judiciously disposed to gain as much as he could make, or as his apprentices and careful wife could make for him : and gradually progressing from a smaller to a larger shop, from a less to a more " genteel " business, and finally to a comfortable retirement.

In such a life there was plenty of room for enjoyment, for relaxation, and no want of leisure to tell a good story or compose a string of couplets where that gift existed, even when most busy. We may imagine that he did not sit much at his block, but rather in the front of the shop amusing his customers, while their periwigs were curled or fitted, with Edinburgh gossip and wit in the familiarity of common citizenship, or with anecdotes which enlightened the country gentlemen, especially those from the west, the last *bon mot* of the Parliament House, or the Lord Advocate's latest deliverance. And his clubs were as numerous as those of a young man of fashion. The " Easy Club " was composed of " young anti-unionists," which indicates the politics

which the wigmaker mildly held in cheerful subjection to
the powers that were. No doubt he would have gone
to the death (in verse) for the privileges of Edinburgh :
but the anti-unionism or sentimental Jacobitism of his
class was not of a kind to trouble any Government. And
except the question of the Union, which was settled early in
his career, politics do not seem to have been of an exciting
character in Edinburgh. Local matters, always the most
interesting of any to the inhabitants of a town not great
enough to be cosmopolitan but full of distinct and striking
individuality, furnished the poetical wigmaker with his first
themes. It would seem that he only learned to rhyme from
the necessity of taking his part in the high jinks of the club ;
at least all his early productions were intended for its
diversion. An " Elegy on Maggie Johnston," mistress of a
convenient " public " at Morningside, then described as " a
mile and a half west from Edinburgh," a suburb on " the
south side," though now a part of the town—which would lie
in the way of the members when they took their walks
abroad, and no doubt formed the end of many a Sabbath
day's ramble—was almost the first of his known productions :
and we may well believe that the jovial shopkeepers were
delighted with the sensation of possessing a poet of their own,
and held many a discussion upon the new verses—brimful
of local allusions and circumstances which everybody knew
—over their ale as they rested in the village changehouse,
or among the fumes of their punch in their evening
assemblies. Verses warm from the poet's brain have a
certain intoxicating quality akin to the toddy, and no doubt
the citizens slapped their thighs and snapped their fingers
with delight when some well-known name appeared, the
incidents of some story they knew by heart, or the features of
some familiar character. The satisfaction of finding in what
they would call poetry a host of local allusions about which
there was no ambiguity, which they understood like their
ABC, would rouse the first hearers to noisy enthusiasm. And
thus encouraged, the cheerful bard (as he was called in those
days) went on till his fame penetrated beyond the club.

Another elegy of a more serious description was so highly
thought of that it was printed and given to the world by the
club itself.   That world meant Edinburgh, its many tradesmen, the crowded inhabitants of all the lofty "lands" about
that centre of busy social life where the Cross still stood, and
the old Tolbooth gloomed over the street, cut in two by its
big bulk and the fabric of the Luckenbooths, a sort of
island of masonry which divided what is now the broad and
airy High Street opposite St. Giles's into two narrow straits.
The writers and the advocates, the professors and the clergy,
Councillor Pleydell and his kind, were not the first to discover
that Ramsay the wigmaker had something in him more
than the other rough wits of the shops and markets.   And
by and by the goodwives in their high lodgings, floor over
floor, ever glad of something new, learnt to send one of the
bairns with a penny to the wigmaker's shop in the afternoon
to see if Allan Ramsay had printed a new poem : and received with rapture the damp broadsheet brought in fresh from
the press, with a fable or a song in "gude braid Scots," or a
witty letter to some answering rhymester full of local names
and things.   There was no evening paper in those days,
and had there been it was very unlikely it would have
penetrated into all the common stairs and crowded tenements.   But Allan's songs, of which Jean or Peggy would
"ken the tune," and the stories that would delight the
bairns, were better worth the penny than news from distant
London, which was altogether foreign and unknown to that
humble audience.

This no doubt was the sort of fame and widespread
popular appreciation which made the statesman of that
day—was it Fletcher of Saltoun or Duncan Forbes the
great Lord President ?—bid who would make the laws so
long as he might make the songs of the people.   He had in
all likelihood learnt Allan's widely flying, largely read verses,
which every *gamin* of the streets knew by heart, in his childhood.   And though they might not be in general of a very
ennobling quality, there are glimpses of a higher poetry to
come in some of these productions, and a great deal of

cheerful self-assertive content and local patriotism, as well
as of rough fun and jest.   If it were not for the very unnecessary introduction of Apollo as the god to whom "the
bard" addresses his wishes, there would be something not
unworthy of Burns in the following lines.   The poet has of
course introduced first, as a needful contrast, "the master o' a
guid estate that can ilk thing afford," and who is much
"dawted (petted) by the gods."——

> "For me, I can be weel content
>   To eat my bannock on the bent,
>   And kitchen't wi' fresh air ;
> O' lang-kail I can make a feast
> And cantily haud up my crest,
>   And laugh at dishes rare.
> Nought frae Apollo I demand,
>   But through a lengthened life,
> My outer fabric firm may stand,
>   And saul clear without strife.
>   May he then, but gi'e then,
>   Those blessings for my share ;
>   I'll fairly, and squarely,
>   Quit a', and seek nae mair."

It was no doubt after he had achieved this reputation of
the streets—a thing more difficult than greater fame—that his
imagination developed in more continuous and refined effort.
Whether he himself printed his penny broadsheet as well as
sold it we are not informed, but as he began after a while
to combine bookselling with wigmaking we may be allowed
to imagine that the press which produced these flying leaves
was either in or near his shop.   It is difficult to realise the
swarming of life and inhabitation within the high houses of
the old town in an age when comfort was little understood :
and even the concentration within so small a space, of business, work, interest, idleness, and pleasure, is hard to comprehend by people who have been used to appropriate a
separate centre to each of the great occupations or exercises
of mankind.   When London was comparatively a small
town it had still its professional distinctions—the Court,
the Temple, the City, the place where law was administered

and where money was made, where society had its abode and poverty found a shelter. But in old Edinburgh all were piled one on the top of another—the Parliament House within sight of the shops, the great official and the poor artificer under the same roof: and round that historical spot over which St. Giles's crown rose like the standard of the city, the whole community crowded, stalls and booths of every kind encumbering the street, while special pleaders and learned judges picked their steps in their dainty buckled shoes through the mud and refuse of the most crowded noisy market-place, and all the great personages of Edinburgh paced the "plainstanes" close by at certain hours, unheeding either smell or garbage or the resounding cries of the street.

CROWN OF ST. GILES'S

In such a crowded centre the sheets that were being read so eagerly, laughed over by the very cadgers at their booths, conned by the women at the stairheads, lying on every counter, where Allan's new verses would be pulled to pieces by brother wits who had known him to do better, or heard a livelier witticism from his lips no farther gone than yestreen, must very soon have come to the notice of the westland lads at the college, and from them to the learned professors, and still more directly to the lively groups that went and came to the Parliament House. Already the wigmaker's shop had thriven and prospered ; the little man, short and fat and jovial, who had begun to lay out books in his window under the shadow of the curled and powdered peri-wigs, found the results of his double traffic more satisfactory than poets use. He boasts in one of his rhymed addresses that he thatches the outside and lines the inside of many a douce citizen, "and baithways gathers in the cash." He adds—

"And fain would prove to ilka Scot,
That poortith's no the poet's lot."

It must have been altogether an odd little establishment —the wigs set out upon their blocks, perhaps, who knows, the barber's humbler craft being plied behind backs ; the books multiplying daily on shelves and in windows, and the ragged boys with their pennies waiting to see if there was a new piece by Allan Ramsay ; while perhaps in the corner, where lay the lists of the new circulating library—the first in Scotland—Miss Lydia Languish with her maid, or my lady's gentlewoman from some fine house in the Canongate, had come in to ask for the last new novel from London, the Scotch capital having not yet begun to produce that article for itself.

One may be sure that Allan, rotund and smiling, was always ready for a crack with the ladies, and to recommend the brand new *Pamela*, the support of virtue, or some contemporary work of lesser genius. Though the general costume was like that worn in the other parts of the island, perhaps a little behind London fashions, the fair visitors would still be veiled with the plaid, the fine woven screen of varied tartan which covered the head like a hood and could on occasion conceal the face more effectually than Spanish lace or Indian muslin—a singular peculiarity not ancient and scarcely to be called national, since the tartan came from the still-despised Highlands, and these were Lowland ladies who

wore the plaid. This fashion would seem to have begun to
be shaken by Ramsay's time, for he pleads its cause with all
the fervour of a poetical advocate. There is something
grotesque in the arguments, and still more grotesque in the
names by which he distinguishes the wearers of the plaid.

> " Light as the pinions of the airy fry
> Of larks and linnets who traverse the sky,
> Is the Tartana, spun so very fine
> Its weight can never make the fair repine ;
> Nor does it move beyond its proper sphere,
> But lets the gown in all its shape appear ;
> Nor is the straightness of her waist denied
> To be by every ravished eye surveyed ;
> For this the hoop may stand at largest bend,
> It comes not nigh, nor can its weight offend.
>
> .   .   .   .   .
>
> " If shining red Campbella's cheeks adorn,
> Our fancies straight conceive the blushing morn,
> Beneath whose dawn the sun of beauty lies,
> Nor need we light but from Campbella's eyes.
> If lined with green Stuarta's plaid we view,
> Or thine, Ramseia, edged around with blue,
> One shews the spring when nature is most kind,
> The other heaven whose spangles lift the mind."

The description of the manner in which this engaging
garment is worn has all the more reason to be quoted that
it was not only a new piece by Allan Ramsay, but affords a
glimpse of the feminine figures that were to be seen in the
High Street of Edinburgh going to kirk and market in the
beginning of the eighteenth century. There is, too, a
pleasant touch of individuality in the musical street cry that
wakes the morn.

> " From when the cock proclaims the rising day,
> And milkmaids sing around *sweet curds and whey*,
> Till grey-eyed twilight, harbinger of night,
> Pursues o'er silver mountains sinking light,
> I can unwearied from my casements view
> The Plaid, with something still about it new.
> How are we pleased when, with a handsome air,
> We see Hepburna walk with easy care !
> One arm half circles round her slender waist,
> The other like an ivory pillar placed,

To hold her plaid around her modest face,
Which saves her blushes with the gayest grace ;
If in white kids her slender fingers move,
Or, unconfined, jet through the sable glove.

" With what a pretty action Keitha holds
Her plaid, and varies oft its airy folds !
How does that naked space the spirits move,
Between the ruffled lawn and envious glove !
We by the sample, though no more be seen,
Imagine all that's fair within the screen.

" Thus belles in plaids veil and display their charms,
The love-sick youth thus bright Humea warms,
And with her graceful mien her rivals all alarms."

The fair Hepburna, Humea, Campbella, and the rest may tempt the reader to a smile ; but the picture has its value, and is a detail of importance in the realisation of that animated and crowded scene. By this time probably Ramsay had removed his shop to the end of the Luckenbooths, which faced "east" to the unencumbered portion of the High Street, where the City Cross stood, and where all the notable persons made their daily promenade. It was here that he was visited by a kindred spirit, the poet Gay, who had been brought to Edinburgh by his patroness the Duchess of Queensberry, and soon formed acquaintance with the local poet. The two little roundabout bards used to stand together at the door of the shop to watch the crowd, in which no doubt Ramsay would be gratified by a friendly nod from the Lord President, and swell with civic and with personal pride to point out to the English visitor that distinguished Scotsman the loyal and the learned Forbes. The Cross, round which this genteel and witty crowd assembled daily, stood then, according to the plans of the period, in the centre of the High Street, where it had been removed for the advantage of greater space in the previous century. And the view from Ramsay's shop—from which by this time the wigs had entirely disappeared, and which was now a refined and cultured bookseller's, adorned outside with medallions of two poets, Scotch and English, Ben Jonson and Drummond of Hawthornden— was bounded by the gate of the Netherbow with its picturesque

tower, and glimpses through the open roadway, of the Canongate beyond, and the cross lines of busy traffic leading to
Leith.   It was thus a wide space between the lines of high
houses, more like a Place than a street, upon which the two
gossips gazed, no doubt with a complacent thought that their
living presence underneath carried out the symbol of the two
heads above—the poets of England and of Scotland—and
that in the teeming street below them were many who pointed
out to each other this new and delightful combination. They
were not great poets, either of these round, fat, oily men of
verse.   And yet the association was pleasant.   Perhaps the
duchess's coach-and-six, in which the English bard had been
conveyed from London, might drive through the open port,
as the two stood delighted, watching the pedestrians hurry
out of the way and the great lawyers and officials preparing
to pay their devoirs to her Grace as she drew up before the
bookshop.   No doubt they thought it a scene to be remembered in the history of letters.   She was at Penicuik House
on a visit to the Clerks, who were friends and patrons of
Allan, and no doubt had supped or drunk a dish of tea at
New Hall, where the Lord President (who was only the Lord
Advocate in those days) often took his ease in his cousin's
house, where Ramsay was a familiar and frequent guest.
When Allan made wigs no longer, when all his occupations
were about books, and everybody in Edinburgh, gentle and
simple, knew him as the poet, he would be still more free to
make his jokes and his compliments to all those fine people.
But at no time was the genial little poet " blate," as he would
himself have said.   There was no shyness in him.   He " braw'd
it," as he says, with no doubt the finest of periwigs, long before
he had ceased to be a skull-thatcher, and swaggered through
the wynds and about the Cross with the best.   The Edinburgh shopkeeper has never been " blate."   He has always
maintained a freedom of independence which has nothing of
the obsequiousness of more common traders, and which gave
the greater value to the sly compliment which he would
insinuate between two jests.   No doubt Campbella and
Hamilla would laugh at the little man's compliments, his

bows and admiring glances, yet would not object to his ex-
position of the tartan screen, the delicate silken plaid under
which they shielded their radiant complexions and golden
locks.

Allan must have seen many curious sights from those
windows. The riding of the Parliament, when in gallant
order two by two—the commissioners of the boroughs and the
counties leading the way, the peers following, through the
guards on either side who lined the streets—they rode up
solemnly from Holyrood to the Parliament House, with
crown and sword and sceptre borne before them, the old in-
signia, without which the Acts of the ancient Parliaments
of Scotland were not considered valid—marching for the
last time to their place of meeting to give up their trust
—would be one of the most remarkable. The commoners had each two lackeys to attend him, the barons
three, the earls four, a blue-coated brigade, relic of the old
days when no gentleman moved abroad without a following;
and Lyon King-at-arms in his finery to direct the line. With
lamentation and humiliation was the session closed; even wise
men who upheld the Union consenting to the general pang
with which the last Scots Parliament went its way. And the
glare of the fire must have lighted up the poet's rooms, and
angry sparks fallen, and hoarse roar of voices drowned all
domestic sounds, when the Porteous Mob turned Edinburgh
streets into a fierce scene of tragedy for one exciting night.
It would be vain indeed to describe again what Scott has set
before us in the most vivid brilliant narrative. Such a scene
breaking into the burgher quietude—the decent households
which had all retired into decorous darkness for the night
waking up again with lights flitting from story to story, the
axes crashing against the doors of the Tolbooth, the wild
procession whirling down the tortuous gloom of the West
Bow—was such an interruption of monotonous life as few
towns in the eighteenth century could have equalled ; and it
is curious to remember the intense national feeling and keen
patriotic understanding of how far the populace would or
could endure interference, which made Duncan Forbes in his

place in Parliament stand up as almost the defender of that
wild outburst of lawlessness, and John of Argyle turn from
the Royal presence to prepare his hounds, as he said, against
the Queen's threat of turning the rebellious country into a
desert. These proud Scotsmen had supported the Union :
they had perceived its necessity and its use : but there was a
point at which all their susceptibilities took fire, and Whig
lords and politicians were at one with every high-handed
Tory of the early times.

Allan Ramsay must also have seen, though he says
nothing of it, the brief occupation of Edinburgh by the unfortunate Prince Charles Edward, and at a distance the
pathetic little Court in Holyrood, the Jacobite ladies in their
brief glory, the fated captains of that wild little army, in
which the old world of tradition and romance made its last
outbreak upon modern prose and the possibilities of life.
One would imagine that for a man who had lived through
that episode in the heart of the old kingdom of the Stewarts,
and whose house lay half-way between the artillery of the
castle, where a hostile garrison sat grimly watching the invaders below, and the camp at Holyrood—there would have
been nothing in his life so exciting, nothing of which the
record would have been more distinct. But human nature,
which has so many eccentricities, is in nothing so wonderful
as this, that the most remarkable historical scenes make no
impression upon its profound everyday calm, and are less
important to memory than the smallest individual incident.
The swarm of the wild Highlanders that took sudden possession of street and changehouse, the boom of the cannon
overhead vainly attempting to disperse a group here and
there or kill a rebel, and the consciousness which one would
think must have thrilled through the very air, that under
those turrets in the valley was the most interesting young
adventurer of modern times, the heir of the ancient Scots
kings, their undoubted representative—how could these
things fail to affect the mind even of the most steady-going
citizen ? But they did, though we cannot comprehend it.
Allan has a word for every little domestic event in town or

SMOLLETT'S HOUSE

suburbs, but there is not a syllable said either by himself or his biographers to intimate that he knew what was going on under his eyes at that brief and sudden moment, the "one crowded hour of glorious life," which cost so much blood of brave men, and which the hapless Prince paid for afterwards in the disenchanted tedium of many a dreary year.

It was before this time, however, that Ramsay reached the height of his fame and of his productions in *The Gentle Shepherd*. He had written some years before "A Pastoral Dialogue between Patie and Roger," published as usual in a sheet for a penny, and no doubt affording much pleasure to the great popular audience to whom the "new piece" was as the daily *feuilleton*, that friendly dole of fiction which sweetens existence. It was evidently so successful that after a while the poet composed a pendant—a dialogue between Jenny and Peggy. These two fragments pleased the fancy of both the learned and the simple, and no doubt called forth many a flattering inquiry after the two rustic pairs and demands for the rest of their simple history, which inspired the author to weave the lovers into the web of a continuous story, adding the rural background, so fresh and true to nature, and the rustic and humorous characters which were wanted for the perfection of the pastoral drama. Few poems ever have attained so great and so immediate a success. It went from end to end of Scotland, everywhere welcomed, read, conned over, got by heart. Such a fame would be indeed worth living for. The fat little citizen in his shop became at once the poet of his country, as he had been of the Edinburgh streets. It was nearly two centuries since Dunbar and Davie Lyndsay had celebrated their romantic town : and though the name of the latter was still a household word (" You'll no find that in Davie Lyndsay " being the popular scornful dismissal of any incredible tale), yet their works had fallen into forgetfulness. The new poet was received accordingly with acclamation. People did not talk of sales and profits in those days, and we have no information as to the numbers issued, or the time they took to find a home in every cottage, as well as to receive the distinction of illustration and critical discussion, which proved that it was not only the people who interested themselves in the new poet, but a more highly trained and difficult audience as well. We have before us two goodly octavos in which the little rustical comedy is enshrined in hundreds of pages of notes ; and where the argument as to its localities, identifying every spot, occupies chapter after chapter of earnest discussion, proving exactly where every cottage is situated, and that New Hall, the home of the Forbeses, was the mansion of the poem, with its little farm-steading round. Shakspeare could not have been more closely followed, and we doubt if the localities which he has made famous were ever discussed at such length. I can remember nearly fifty years ago investigating, with the eagerness of a child to whom books were the most precious objects in existence, the little shelf high on the wall at the bedhead, where a very old woman, an old nurse in her retirement, kept her treasures, and mounted high upon a chair, finding a much-thumbed unbound copy of *The Gentle Shepherd* in the dim twilight, ruddy with the glimmer of the fire, of the cottage room. In such places it was never absent ; it was the one book which held its ground by the side of the Bible and perhaps a volume of old-world devotion, *The Crook in the Lot*, or *The Saint's Rest*. Such a distinction is a far more true and genuine triumph than the sale of many editions. It went straight into the heart of the peasant, who understood and appreciated every scene and line. And it was discussed by all the Edinburgh clubs, and by the literati who knew their Theocritus and could write dissertations on pastoral poetry. The greatest poet could have hoped for no more.

And pastoral poetry was the fashion of the time. Ramsay himself had made various other attempts before he lighted upon this quite legitimate strain. We read with a shudder of comic horror a dialogue "On the Death of Mr. Addison," in which the interlocutors are " Richy and Sandy," to wit, Sir Richard Steele and Mr. Alexander Pope! who bewail their loss, which is far worse than misfortune to their flocks, or the scorn of their lasses, being no less than this, that " Addie, that

played and sang so sweet, is dead "! The poet received, indeed, a complimentary copy of verses upon this production, in
which he is thus addressed—

> "Well fare thee, Allan, who in mother tongue
> So sweetly hath of breathless Addy sung :
> His endless fame thy nat'ral genius fired,
> And thou hast written as if he inspired.
> ' Richy and Sandy,' who do him survive,
> Long as thy rural stanzas last, shall live."

The grotesque in poetry could scarcely go farther. Mr.
Burchett, who addressed good Allan in these rhymes, was
the refined gentleman who put the wigmaker's poems into
English. " Richy and Sandy " was contained in a volume
which Ramsay published by subscription, and which brought
him in, to the immense admiration of his biographer, four
hundred guineas sterling, which no doubt was a very admirable recompense indeed for so many foolish verses. This
volume contained, among other things, Ramsay's bold continuation of " Christ's Kirk on the Green," which the same
biographer describes as " King James the First's ludicrous
poem," in which the poet of the High Street skilfully turns
the poet-monarch's rustic revel into a vulgar village debauch.
But these pieces of presumption and non-comprehension are
happily all dead and gone, and Ramsay's reputation rests
upon a happier basis. It is not a small matter to have pervaded a whole country with the simple measures of a rural
idyll—a poem in which there are not perhaps five lines of
poetry, but which is fragrant of the moors and fields, full of
rustic good sense and feeling, and as free of harm or offence
as the most severe moralist could desire. This latter quality
is all the more remarkable as it belongs to an age not at all
squeamish in these matters, and to which the frankest
assaults upon a heroine's virtue were supposed to be quite
adapted for the treatment of fiction. But there is no Lovelace
in *The Gentle Shepherd* ; the rustic love-making is ardent, but
simple and without guile. The swains respect as much as
they admire their nymphs : the nymphs are confident in
their frank innocence, and fear no evil ; the old fathers

sit cheerful and sagacious at their doors and indulge in their cracks, not less pleased with themselves and their share of life than are the young ones with their livelier pleasures : the cows breathe balmy breath into the wild freshness of the pastoral scenery. There is scarcely anything affected, false, or even stilted in the poetical dialogues which, with a little license for the verse and something for the sentiment, come naturally and simply from the wholesome, genial young shepherds and their sweethearts. To say this is to say as much as the most fastidious critic could desire from such a composition.

Nor is it spoiled by classic models or similes. How Ramsay succeeded in keeping Venus and Cupid out of it, in forgetting all eclogues and pastorals, Virgil or Theocritus, and indulging in nothing that was out of place in Scotland, it is hard to tell. The Mantuan bard, the oaten reed, Philomela and her songs, Hymen, Ganymede, Bacchus, and all the Olympian band disport themselves in his other verses : but *The Gentle Shepherd* is void of those necessary adjuncts of the eighteenth-century muse. The wimpling burn is never called Helicon nor the heathery braes Parnassus, and nothing can be more genuine, more natural, and familiar than the simple scenery of Habbie's Howe—in which the eager critics identified every scene, and the sensible poet enhanced his art by a perfect truth to nature. *The Gentle Shepherd* is perhaps the only so-called Pastoral of which this can be said, and it must have required no small amount of self-denial to dispense with all those accustomed auxiliaries. Even the sentiments are not too highflown for the locality. If they are perhaps more completely purified from everything gross or fleshly than would have been the case in fact, the poet has not been afraid to temper passion with those considerations which naturally rise to the mind of the young farmer in choosing his mate. His Peggy, though she has beauty enough to make up for every deficiency, has also " with innocence the wale of sense."

> " In better sense without a flaw,
>   As in her beauty, far excels them a'."

She, on her part, anticipates not raptures and blisses in her marriage, but the hallowed usages of life.

> " I'll employ with pleasure all my art
> To keep him cheerful, and secure his heart.
> At e'en, when he comes weary frae the hill,
> I'll have a' things made ready to his will :
> In winter when he toils through wind and rain,
> A bleezin' ingle, and a clean hearth-stane ;
> And soon as he's flung by his plaid and staff,
> The seething pot's be ready to tak' aff."

Ramsay's sobriety here shines in comparison with all the fables and idylls of his age. It is entirely natural, living, and of his time. Patie plays upon a flute of " plum-tree made with ivory virls round," which he bought from the proceeds of " sax good fat lambs " sold at the West Port, instead of the rustic pipe or oaten reed, which in his heart of hearts no doubt our wigmaker thought much finer. Thus he secured his audience, who knew nothing about oaten reeds, and instead of the plaudits of the dilettanti secured the true fame of popular comprehension and knowledge. Burns was far higher and nobler in genius, and the worship awarded to him by his countrymen is one of the favourite subjects of gibe and jest among writers on the other side of the Tweed. But even Burns had not the universal acceptance, the absolute command of his audience, which belonged to honest Allan. There were politicians and there were ecclesiastics, and good people neither one nor the other, who shook their troubled heads over the ploughman who would not confine himself to the daisy of the field or the Saturday night's observances of the Cottar, but was capable of Holy Willie and the Holy Fair. But Ramsay had no gainsayer, and *The Gentle Shepherd* was the first of books in most Lowland homes. Its construction, its language and sentiments, are all as commonplace as could be imagined, but it is a wholesome, natural, pure, and unvarnished tale, and the mind that brought it forth (well aware of what pleased his public) and the public who relished and bought it, give us a better view of the honest tastes and morals of the period

than anything else which has come to us from that time.
There has always been a good deal of drinking, and other
vices still less consistent with purity of heart, in Scotland.
Now and then we are frightened by statistics that give
us a very ill name : but it is difficult to believe that if the
national heart had been corrupt *The Gentle Shepherd* could
have afforded it such universal and wholesome delight.

It is curious to find two very ordinary and prosaic
tradesmen thus in the front of popular literature in the
beginning of the eighteenth century.   There is no comparison between Allan Ramsay and Samuel Richardson in
respect to genius.   That humdrum old bookseller evoked by
some miraculous art the most delicate and lovely of creations
out of the midst of revolting and disgusting circumstances.
Fielding was a far finer gentleman, a much more accomplished
writer, even a greater genius ; but there are none of his
women who are fit to tie the shoes of Clarissa Harlowe, to
whom indeed there exists no fit companion out of Shakspeare.   Our good-humoured Allan had no such gift, but he
had the art of producing one spotless and lifelike tale,
absolutely true to nature and within the power of verification
by any reader, which was accepted by a whole country
with enthusiasm as the best rendering of its rural life.   We
doubt if there ever was a greater literary triumph.

Ramsay would not have been the true man he was to
every tradition and inheritance of his class had he not shown
a modest complacency in his own success.   He was assailed,
we are told, by nameless critics, who put forth " A Block for
Allan Ramsay's Wigs," " Remarks on Ramsay's Writings,"
and so forth—and retaliated, not without dignity : " Dull
foes," he says, " nought at my hand deserve."

> " The blundering fellows ne'er forget,
>   About my trade to sport their fancies,
>   As if, forsooth, I would look blate,
>   At what my honour most advances.

> " Auld Homer sang for's daily bread ;
>   Surprising Shakspeare fin'd the wool ;
>   Great Virgil creels and baskets made ;
>   And famous Ben employed the trowel.

> "Yet Dorset, Lansdown, Lauderdale,
>   Bucks, Stirling, and the son of Angus,
> Even monarchs, and o' men the wale,
>   Were proud to be enrolled amang us."

It is true that Homer and Shakspeare might be sur-prised to find themselves rubbing elbows with the wigmaker of the High Street. Still, he shows a fine spirit, and his very strut is respectable.

In the end of his life, when the author of *The Gentle Shepherd* by all his trades, both as poet and shopkeeper, had amassed a fortune, he built himself a house in the most glorious position which poet could have chosen. It is on the crest of the hill, a little way below the castle, and is still to be seen from Princes Street—a distinct feature in the picturesque and varied line of building. He is said, though on what authority we are not told, to have applied to the Crown for ground enough to build a cage for *his burd*, meaning his wife : which is supposed to be the reason why he built his house in an octagonal shape like a cage : his wife, however, did not live long enough to inhabit it. Additions and emenda-tions have been made, so that there is no great peculiarity in the form of the old square house on the summit of the green slope, just clear of the rocks of the castle, as it is visible to-day. When it was built the new town of Edin-burgh was not yet dreamed of, and nothing disturbed the panorama of green fields that lay between Edinburgh and the Firth. The town wall was falling into ruin, yet still existed in fragmentary towers and ramparts here and there, and low down in the depths of the descent, which was not so precipitous there as under the castle, the high houses and green braes were reflected in the quiet waters of the North Loch. From thence the fields and scattered farmhouses, the Calton Hill in unadorned greenness, a church spire and a cluster of village roofs here and there, led the eye to the shining of the Scottish sea, the great water with its islands, the coast of Fife with its dotted line of little fishing towns, the two green Lomonds standing softly distinct against the misty line of more distant hills. It was the same view

that moved Fitz-Eustace to ecstasy, still but little changed
in the eighteenth century from what it had been in the
sixteenth.   And picturesque as Edinburgh still continues to

ALLAN RAMSAY'S HOUSE

be in spite of many modern dis-
advantages, it was no doubt
infinitely   more   picturesque
then, crowning the rocky ridge,
with straggling lanes and wynds
dropping steeply down into
the valley—opening here and there a glimpse of the green
country and the shimmer of the Firth—while on the edge of
the hill, from all the high windows, the wide landscape softened
into distance on every side, into the far-off broken ranges
of mountains and cloudy rolling vapours, and the far-
retiring sweep of a horizon traversed by all the lights and
all the storms—a wide world of air and space and infinite
variety. The life of our busy modern world had scarcely
yet invaded that city on the hill. It stood isolated on the
height of its rock, reigning from that domination over all the

tranquil country : while within its lines still thronged and
clamoured an active noisy population cooped up and packed
together as if it were still unsafe to stray away out of shelter
of the walls, all the faculties and trades, all the wit and
the wealth, one above another, with the concentration, the
picturesqueness, the universal acquaintance and familiarity of
a mediæval town.   And beautiful as the prospect must have
been from those high-built houses, it could scarcely have
exceeded the sight of the old Edinburgh of the kings from
without, standing high above the level of the soil, with the
open crown of St. Giles's rising over its grey heights, its
walls broken down by careless peace and wellbeing, its tall
tenements standing up like a line of castles.   And in the
night with its glimmer of household lights at every window
hanging high in mid air, repeated with a gleam in the waters
beneath and in the stars above, which sparkled keen out of
the northern blue, and the mist of habitation, the smoke of the
fires and the lamps hanging over all—confusing outlines, yet
revealing all the more brightly a higher and a higher altitude
of human lights—what a wonderful sight rising sheer out of
the green and silent champaign below !

Such was royal Edinburgh still, when the shopkeeper-
poet, with his jokes and his quips, and his good-humoured
self-esteem, and certainty of his own power, settled down in
Ramsay Lodge.   It would be well if all poets had as prosperous and as fair a retirement for their old age.   He lived
for some time in his quaint self-contained (according to the
equally quaint Scotch phraseology) birdcage upon the top of
the hill, and enjoyed his celebrity and his ease and the pleasant conviction that " I the best and fairest please."   His
only son, the second Allan Ramsay, was a painter of some
reputation, and he had daughters to care for him and keep
his home cheerful as long as he lived.   A man more satisfied with his lot could not be.   His chirrup of self-satisfaction,
the flattery, yet familiarity, of his address to all the noble
lords and lairds, the judges and advocates, his laugh of
jovial optimism and personal content, belong perfectly to the
character of the comfortable citizen, " in fair round belly

with good capon lined," and the shopkeeper's rather than the poet's desire to please. One can better fancy him at the door of his shop looking down the High Street jocose and beaming, with a joke for the Lord President and for the Cadie alike, hand in glove with all the Town Council, with a compliment for every fair lady or smiling lass that tripped by under her tartan screen, delighted with himself and all around him—than retired in his garden on the Castle Hill, though with all the variations of the heavens and magnificence of the landscape before his eyes. He had no doubt the admiration of that landscape which is never wanting to an Edinburgh citizen, a part of the creed to which he is born ; but the homely limits of the green glens and knowes, the wimpling burn, the washing-green, the laird's hospitable house behind, were more in Allan's way when he wanted any relaxation from the even more attractive town. The High Street and Habbie's Howe are the true centres of his soul.

It would be wrong not to note the collections of songs which made his name dear to all the pleasant singers both of drawing-room and cottage. It is a strange peculiarity in a nation possessing a characteristic and melodious popular music of its own like Scotland, to find how little place music as a science, or even in its more serious developments, has ever had in the country. Nothing can be more sweet, more touching, more tender, than the native growth of Scottish song—nothing more full of fun and spirit than the brilliant dance music which, like the song, seems to have sprung spontaneous from the soil. And no country has ever more loved both songs and strathspeys, or clung to them with greater devotion. It would be perhaps impossible for the most learned to decide between the rival claims of Scotland and Ireland in respect to the airs which seem native to both ; but Ireland has always laboured under the disadvantage of being far less homogeneous than Scotland, and certainly, before the time of Moore at least, her native songs did not belong to all classes as in the sister country. And Scotland has always through all ages (previous to the present age) preferred her own songs to every other. During the

eighteenth century, when Edinburgh was almost more completely the centre of society than ever before, the old tunes
were sung by ladies as much as by maid-servants, and the
delicate old spinets performed a soft accompaniment to
ballads of the "Ewebuchting" and of the "Corn Rigs," and
prolonged the pathetic notes of "Waly, waly" and the
trembling wail of the "Flowers of the Forest" in the finest
houses as in the humblest. Music, more properly so called,
the art which has gradually made its way from being a
modest handmaiden of poetry to full rivalship, if not a half-
implied superiority, was already a scientific pursuit in England ; and though the Italian opera aroused a violent
opposition, and Tweedledum and Tweedledee called forth the
gibes of the wits, there existed a vigorous English school of
learned musicians, and Handel and Haydn found an
audience not incapable of appreciating their best works.
But while this development went on in London, Scotland
still sang her ancient simple melodies, and contemned everything else with that audacious superiority which is born of
ignorance. One might almost imagine that this was the
penalty of a national inheritance so ample and so sweet, and
that the comparative absence of traditionary music in
England opened the heart of the country to strains more
ambitious and classical. However it came about, there is no
denying that so it was. If there was any Scottish composer
at all, his productions were only imitations or modifications
of the old airs. Music continued to be represented by the
songs of immemorial attraction, the woodnotes wild of
nameless minstrels, pure utterance of the soil. Perhaps the
absence of music, except in the kindred shape of psalm tunes,
which was but another form of popular song, in the Church,
was one great prevailing cause of the national insensibility
to all more lavish and elaborate strains. But this peculiarity
and insensibility had at least one advantage—they kept in
constant cultivation a distinct branch of national literature,
and one that is always attractive and delightful. I do not
think it is too strong an utterance of national partiality to
say that the songwriters of Scotland are beyond comparison

with those of either of the other united kingdoms. The
simplest of the old ditties brought out of the ancient poets
contain a grace of genuine poetry and real feeling far above
the unmeaning jingle of verse which is the most common
utterance of popular song; and the cultivation of this
delightful gift has called forth the most tender and artless
poems from gentle writers whom nothing but that inspiration
could have made to produce what was in them. The pathetic
wail of the poor lady who found to her cost that

> " Love is bonnie, a little time when it is new,"

but that

> " When love's auld it waxeth cauld,
> And fades away like morning dew ";

and that touching lullaby in which the mother hushes the
babe whose

> " Father wrought her great annoy,"

with its tender and simple refrain—

> " It grieves me sore to hear thee weep,"

breathe out of the ancient depths of human trouble with a
reserve and simplicity of feeling that seem almost personal.
But the kindred inspiration which called forth the two ver-
sions of the " Flowers of the Forest " and the ballad of " Auld
Robin Gray," along with many more, shows how warm was
the impulse to this expression of feelings, which were at once
intensified and drawn out of the sphere of revelations too individual by the breath of the melody which carried them forth.

Allan Ramsay has the merit of being the first collector
of Scottish song. He was remorseless, like his century, and
made the wildest havoc with some of his originals, cutting
and slashing as suited his fancy, and adding of his own whenever it pleased him so to do. But with the exception of a
number of Strephons and Chloes, not always ungraceful, in
the newer fashion, and a sprinkling of ruder verses in which
there is more indecency than immorality, the first two volumes
of the *Tea-table Miscellany* are full of merit, and include many
delightful simple lyrics, songs which compare most advan-

tageously with the insipid "words" which at this present advanced age are used as a sort of necessary evil to serve the purpose of the music. " Say that our way is only an harmonious speaking of many witty or soft thoughts after the poet has dressed them in four or five stanzas," says Ramsay, with the apology which is a veiled assertion of higher aims, " yet undoubtedly these must relish best with people who have not bestowed much of their time in acquiring a taste for that downright perfect music which requires none or very little of the poet's assistance." And he tells us in the same preface of a letter he has had from America informing him that there too his manual of song has gone, and that his

> " Soft verse made to a Scottish air
> Is often sung by our Virginian fair."

The book is dedicated to the ladies—the *Donne qui hanno intelletto d'amore*, long supposed to be the final critics and judges of such productions : and is confidently recommended to these "fair singers" for whose "modest eyes and ears," according to the poet (but with notable exceptions, as has been said), they were prepared. The third volume consisted almost exclusively of English songs, among which are many classic verses. If it were but as a stepping-stone to those perfect lyrics, so full of natural truth and feeling, with which Burns afterwards brought to a climax the songs of his country, the *Tea-table Miscellany* would have a merit of its own.

Ramsay died in 1758, when the troubles of the country were over, the last seeds of insurrection stamped out, and the powerful revolution begun which made the clans loyal to Government and Scotch politicians faithful to the Union. He was buried in the Greyfriars Churchyard, where so many of the most notable of the citizens of Edinburgh were laid. A hundred years or so after, the enlightened community placed his statue in the gardens that lie between the old town and the new. And thus the poet's career was run ; it was a prosperous one, full of the success that was most sweet to him ; comfort and competence and reputation, at once that

2 F

of a warm and well-to-do citizen and that of a poet. Few
poets have lived to see their productions so popular. *The
Gentle Shepherd* may be said to have been in every cottage
in Scotland in its author's lifetime, and his songs were sung
by everybody. Nor did this fame interfere with the citizen's
well-earned and more substantial reward. The shop in which
he began his prosperous career, and which was crowded so
continually by eager messengers with their pennies in search
of Allan Ramsay's last new piece—the most immediate and
one of the most pleasant evidences of success—still exists,
with its high steps and broad low windows, in the heart of
the old town with which his name is so completely associated ; and the quaint square house in which his later days
of ease and retirement were spent still keeps its place on the
east of the Castle Hill, surveying from its windows the
enriched and amplified yet unalterable panorama so dear and
beautiful to all Scottish eyes.

ALLAN RAMSAY'S MONUMENT

DOORWAY, LADY STAIR'S CLOSE

CHAPTER II

THE GUEST OF EDINBURGH

ROYAL Edinburgh, the city of the Scots kings and Parliament, the capital of the ancient kingdom, would seem to have become weary somewhere in the eighteenth century of dwelling alone upon her rock. There were, to be sure, reasons more prosaic for the construction of the New Town, the partner and companion of the old historical city. The population had increased, the desire for comfort and space, and many luxuries unknown to the early citizens of Edinburgh, had developed among the new. It was no longer agreeable to the lawyers and philosophers to be crowded up with the other inhabitants of a common stair, to have the din of street cries and commotion ever in their ears, and the lowest of the population always about their feet, as was inevitable when gentle and simple were piled together in the High Street and Canongate. The old houses might be noble houses when they were finally got at, through many drawbacks and abominations—though in those days there was little appreciation even of the stately beauty of old masonry and ornament—but their surroundings became daily more and more intolerable. And it was an anachronism to coop up a learned, elegant, and refined class, living under the Hanoverian Georges in peace and loyalty, within the circle of walls now broken down and useless, which had been adapted to protect the subjects of the old Scottish Jameses from continual attacks.

Happily the nature of the situation prevented any amalgamation or loss of the old boundaries and picturesque features of the ancient city, in the new. There was no question of continuation or enlargement. Another Edinburgh rose at the feet of the first, a sober, respectable, modern, and square-toed town, with wide streets and buildings solid and strong, not without pretensions to a certain stateliness of size and design, but in strong contrast with the architecture and fashion native to the soil—the high gables and turreted stairs of the past. The old town had to throw a drawbridge, permanent and massive, over the hollow at her feet before she could even reach the terraced valley on which the first lines of habitation were drawn, and which, rounding over its steep slope, descended towards another and yet another terrace before it stood complete, a new-born partner and companion in life of the former capital, lavish in space as the other was confined, leisurely and serious as the other was animated—a new town of great houses, of big churches—dull, as only the eighteenth century was capable of making them—of comfort and sober wealth and intellectual progress. The architects who adorned the Modern Athens with Roman domes and Greek temples, and placed fictitious ruins on the breezy hill which possessed a fatal likeness to the Acropolis, would have scoffed at the idea of finding models in the erections of the fourteenth century—that so-called dark age—or recognising a superior harmony and fitness in native principles of construction.

Yet though the public taste has now returned more or less intelligently to the earlier canons, it would be foolish not to recognise that there is a certain advantage even in the difference of the new town from the old. It is not the historical Edinburgh, the fierce, tumultuous, mediæval city, the stern but not more quiet capital of the Reformers, the noisy, dirty, whimsical, mirth-loving town, full of broad jest and witty epigram, of the eighteenth century. The new town has a character of its own. It is the modern, not supplanting or effacing, but standing by the old. Those who built it considered it an extraordinary improvement upon all that Gothic antiquity had framed. They were far more proud of these broad streets and massive houses than of anything their fathers had left to them, and flung down without remorse a great deal of the antiquated building after which it is now the fashion to inquire with so much regret. Notwithstanding the change of taste since that time, the New Town of Edinburgh still regards the old with a little condescension and patronage ; but there is no opposition between the two. They stand by each other in a curious peacefulness of union, each with a certain independence yet mutual reliance. London and Paris have rubbed off all their old angles and made themselves, notwithstanding the existence of Gothic corners here and there, all modern, to the extinction of most of the characteristic features of their former living. But happy peculiarities of situation have saved our northern capital from any such self-obliteration. Edinburgh has been fortunate enough to preserve both sides— the ancient picturesque grace, the modern comfort and ease. And though Mr. Ruskin has spoken very severely of the new town, we will not throw a stone at a place so well adapted to the necessities of modern life. Those bland fronts of polished stone would have been more kindly and more congenial to the soil had they cut the air with high-stepped gables and encased their stairs in the rounded turrets which give a simple distinctive character to so many Scottish houses ; and a little colour, whether of the brick which Scotch builders despise or the delightful washes [1] which their forefathers loved, would be a godsend even now. But still, for a sober domestic partner, the new town is no ill companion to the ancient city on the hill.

This adjunct to the elder Edinburgh had come into being between the time when Allan Ramsay's career ended in the octagon house on the Castle Hill, and another poet, very different from Ramsay, appeared in the Scotch capital. In the meantime many persons of note had left the old town and migrated towards the new. The old gentry of whom so many stories have been told, especially those old ladies who held a little court, like Mrs. Bethune Balliol, or made their bold criticism of all things both new and old, like those who flourish in Lord Cockburn's lively pages—continued to live in the ancestral houses which still kept their old-fashioned perfection within, though they had to be approached through all the squalor and misery which had already found refuge outside in the desecrated Canongate ; but society in the Scotch metropolis was now rapidly tending across the lately erected bridge towards the new great houses which contemplated old Edinburgh across the little valley, where the Nor' Loch glimmered no longer and where fields lay green where marsh and water had been. The North Bridge was a noble structure, and the newly built Register House at the other end one of the finest buildings of modern times to the admiring chroniclers of Edinburgh. And the historians and philosophers, the great doctors, the great lawyers, the elegant critics, for whom it was more and more necessary that the ways of access between the old town and the new might be made more easy, presided over and criticised all those wonderful new buildings of classic style and unbroken regularity, and watched the progress of the

---

[1] In this respect I venture to think all Scotland errs. Many houses throughout the country, built roughly with a rude and irregular but solid mason-work, were made points of light in the landscape by these washes of colour which poor dwellings retain. There is a yellow which I remember on many old houses in which the stains of time and weather produced varieties of tone almost as agreeable as the mellowing of marble under the same influences, which are now stripped into native roughness and rise in sombre grey, sometimes almost black, abstracting a much-needed warmth from the aspect of the country round.

Earthen Mound, a bold and picturesque expedient which filled up the hollow and made a winding walk between, with interest as warm as that which they took in the lectures and students, the books and researches, which were making their city one of the intellectual centres of the world.

This is a position to which Scotland has always aspired, and the pride of the ambitious city and country was never more fully satisfied than in the end of last and the beginning of the present century.   Edinburgh had never been so rich in the literary element, and the band of young men full of genius and high spirit who were to advance her still one step farther to the climax of fame in that particular, were growing up to take the places of their fathers.   A place in which Walter Scott was just emerging from his delightful child-hood, in which Jeffrey was a mischievous boy and Henry Brougham a child, could not but be overflowing with hope, especially when we remember all the good company there already—Dugald Stewart, bringing so many fine young gentlemen from England to wonder at the little Scotch capital, and a crowd of Erskines, Hunters, Gregories, Monroes, and Dr. Blair and Dr. Blacklock, and the Man of Feeling — not to speak of those wild and witty old ladies in the Canongate, and the duchesses who still recog-nised the claims of Edinburgh in its season.   To all this excellent company, whose fame and whose talk hung about both the old Edinburgh and the new like the smoke over their roofs, there arrived one spring day a wonderful visitor, in appearance like nothing so much as an honest hill farmer, travelling on foot, his robust shoulders a little bowed with the habit of the plough, his eyes shining, as no other eyes in Scotland shone, with youth and genius and hope.   He knew nobody in Edinburgh save an Ayrshire lad like himself, like what everybody up to this time had sup-posed Robert Burns to be.   The difference was that the stranger a little while before had put forth by the aid of a country printer at Kilmarnock a little volume of rustic poetry upon the most unambitious subjects, in Westland Scotch, the record of a ploughman's loves and frolics and

thoughts. It is something to know that these credentials
were enough to rouse the whole of that witty, learned, clever,
and all-discerning community, and that this visitor from the
hills and fields in a moment found every door open to him,
and Modern Athens, never unconscious of its own superiority
and at this moment more deeply aware than usual that it was
one of the lights of the earth, at his feet.

Burns was but a visitor, the lion of a season, and therefore
we are not called upon to associate with Edinburgh the whole
tragic story of his life. And yet his appearance was one of
the most remarkable that has distinguished the ancient town.
He arrived among all the professors, the men of letters, the
cultured classes who held an almost ideal pre-eminence, more
like what a young author hopes than is generally to be
met with among men—his heart beating with a sense of the
great venture on which he was bound, and a proud determination to quit himself like a man whatever were the
magnitudes among which he should have to stand. Mere
Society so called, with all its bustle of gaiety and endless
occupation about nothing, might have exercised upon him
something of the fascination which fine names and fine
houses and the sweep and whirl of hurried life certainly
possess ; but he who expresses almost with bitterness his
disgust to see a blockhead of rank received by one of his
noble patrons with as much, nay more, consideration than is
given to himself, would probably have had very little toleration for the butterflies of fashion : whereas Edinburgh society
impressed him greatly, as of that ideal kind of which the
young and inexperienced dream, where the best and brightest
are at the head of everything, where poetry is a passport to
the innermost sanctuary and conversation is like the talk of
the gods. They were all distinguished for one literary gift
or grace or another, philosophers golden-mouthed, poets of
the most polished sort : their knowledge, their culture, their
intellectual powers, were the foundation upon which their
little world was built. The great people who were to be
found among them were proud to know these scholars and
sages—it was they, and not an occasional family of rank, or

LADY STAIR'S CLOSE

still more rare man of wealth, who gave character and
meaning to Edinburgh. To be received in such society was
the highest privilege which a young poet could desire ;
and it was worthy to receive and foster and encourage that
new light that came from heaven.

On their side the heads of society in Edinburgh were
much interested in this young man. There had been an
article in the *Lounger*, fondly deemed a Scotch *Spectator*, an
elegant literary paper widely read not only in Scotland
but even beyond the Border, upon him and his works.
" The Ayrshire Ploughman " was the title of the article,
and it set forth all the imperfections of his breeding, his
want of education, his ignorance both of books and of
the world, and yet the amazing verses he had produced,
which, though disguised in a dialect supposed to be
unknown to the elegant reader, and for which Henry
Mackenzie, the Man of Feeling, supplied a glossary—living,
he himself, in an old-fashioned house in the South Back of the
Canongate and within the easiest reach of those wonderful old
ladies who spoke broad Scotch, and left no one in any doubt
as to the strong opinions expressed therein—were certified
to be worthy the perusal of the most fastidious critic. Lord
Monboddo, who was the author of speculations which forestalled Darwin and who considered a tail to be an appendage
of which men had not long got rid, on the one side, and the
metaphysicians and philosophers on the other, would no
doubt prick up their ears to hear of this absolutely new
being in whom there might be seen some traces of primeval
man. We forget which of the early Jameses it was who is
said to have shut up two infants with a dumb nurse in one
of the islands of the Firth to ascertain what kind of language
they would speak when thus left to the teaching of nature.
The experiment was triumphantly successful, for the heaven-
taught babies babbled, the chroniclers tell us, a kind of
Hebrew, thus proving beyond doubt that the language of
the Old Testament was the original tongue of man. The
Edinburgh savants must have received Burns with something of the same feeling : for here was a new soul which

had been shut up amid the primeval elements, and the language it spoke was Poetry! yet poetry disguised in imperfect dialect which might yet be trained and educated into elegance. They asked him to dinner as a first step, and gathered round him to hear what he would have to say ; to observe the effect produced by the sight of learning, criticism, knowledge; to enjoy his awe, and note the improvement that could not but ensue. This curiosity was full of kindness ; their hearts were a little touched by the ploughman, by his glowing eyes, and by the strange sight of him there among them in the midst of their high civilisation, a rustic clown who knew nothing better than a thatched cottage and a clay floor. No doubt they had the sincerest desire that he should be made to understand how much he was deficient, what a great deal he had to learn, and be taught to use fine language, and turn his attention to higher subjects, and be altogether elevated and brought on in the world. The situation is very curious and full of human interest, even had the stranger been less in importance than he was. It is wonderfully enlightening in any circumstances to see such an encounter from both sides, to perceive the light in which it appears to them, and the very different light in which it is seen by *him*. There was the usual great divergence between the views of the visitor and the highly-cultured community to which he came. For he indeed did not come there at all to be enlightened and trained and put in the way he should go. He came full of delightful hope that he was coming among his own kind, that he was for the first time to meet his own species, and recognise in other human faces the light that shone about his own path, but in none of the other muddy ways of the country-side ; to make friends with his natural brethren, and be understood of them as no one yet had been found to understand him. In his high anticipations, in his warm enthusiasm of hope, he himself figured dimly as a sort of noble exile coming back to his father's house. So does every child of fancy regard the world of which he knows nothing, the world of the great and famous, where to dazzled fancy all the beautiful things, words, and thoughts for which he has been sighing all his life are to be found.

They met, and they were, if not mutually disappointed, yet strangely astonished and perplexed. Burns would seem to have been always on his guard, too much on his guard we should be disposed to say, suspicious of the intention to guide, to chasten, to educate and refine, which was indeed in the kindest way at the bottom of everybody's thoughts. He was determined to be astonished by nothing, to keep his head so that no one should ever be able to say that it was turned by his new experiences—an attitude which altogether bewildered the good people, who were willing to give him every kind of education, to excuse any rudeness or rough-ness or imperfection, but not to see a man at his ease, appearing among them as if he were of them, requiring no allowance to be made for him, holding his head high as any man he met. All the accounts we have of his appearance in Edinburgh agree in this. He was neither abashed nor embarrassed ; no rustic presumption or vulgarity, but quite as little any timidity or awkwardness, was in the Ayrshire ploughman. His shoulders a little bent with the work to which he had been accustomed, his dress like a countryman, a rougher cloth perhaps, a pair of good woollen stockings rig and fur, his mother's knitting, instead of the silk which covered limbs probably not half so robust—but so far as manners went, nothing to apologise for or smile at. The accounts all agree in this. If he never put himself forward too much, he never withdrew with any unworthy shyness from his modest share in the conversation. Sometimes he would be roused to eloquent speech, and then the admiring ladies said he carried them " off their feet " in the contagion of his enthusiasm and emotion. But this was a very strange phenomenon for the Edinburgh professors and men of letters to deal with : a novice who had not come humbly to be taught, but one who had come to take up his share of the inheritance, to sit down among the great, as in his natural place. He was not perhaps altogether unmoved by their insane advices to him, one of the greatest of lyrical poets, a

singer above all—to write a tragedy, to give up the language
he knew and write his poetry in the high English which,
alas! he uses in his letters.   Not unmoved, and seriously
inclining to a more lofty measure, he compounded addresses
to Edinburgh :

> " Edina, Scotia's darling seat ! "

and other such intolerable effusions.   One can imagine him
roaming through the fields between the old town and the
new, and looking up to the " rude rough fortress," and on
the other side to the brand-new regular lines of building,
where

> " Architecture's noble pride
> Bids elegance and splendour rise,"

and musing in his mind how to celebrate them in polished
verse so that even the critics may be satisfied—

> " Thy sons, Edina ! social, kind,
>   With open arms the stranger hail;
> Their views enlarged, their liberal mind,
>   Above the narrow, rural vale ;
> Attentive still to sorrow's wail,
>   Or modest merit's silent claim ;
> And never may their sources fail !
>   And never envy blot their name ! "

One wonders what the gentlemen said to this in the old
town and the new—whether it did not confuse them still
further, as well intended perhaps, but not after all like the
"Epistle to Davie," though they had all advised him to amend
that rustic style.   A very confusing business altogether—
difficult for the kind advisers as well as for the poet, and
with no outlet that any one could see.

We have, however, a more agreeable picture of the
visitor on another occasion when he walked out into the
country with Dugald Stewart in a spring morning to the
hills of Braid and talked that gentle philosopher's heart
away, not now about Edina's palaces and towers.   " He told
me . . . that the sight of so many smoking cottages gave
a pleasure to his mind which none could understand who
had not witnessed like himself the happiness and worth

DUGALD STEWART'S MONUMENT

2 G

which they contained." It is more pleasant to think of the poet's dark eyes lighting up as he said this than to watch him proud and self-possessed in the drawing-rooms holding his own, taking such good care that nobody should divine how his heart was beating and his nerves athrill.

But after all there is no such account given of this wonderful visitor to Edinburgh as that we have from the after-recollections of a certain "lameter" boy who was once present in a house where Burns was a guest. The Scott boys from George Square had been admitted to the party which they were too young to join in an ordinary way, in order that they might see this wonder of the world, the ploughman-poet who was not afraid, but behaved as well as any of the gentlemen. And it befell by the happiest chance that Burns inquired who was the author of certain verses inscribed upon a print which he had been looking at. No one knew but young Walter, who we may be sure had not lost a look or a word of the stranger, and who had read everything in his invalid childhood. The boy was not bold enough to answer the question loud out, but he whispered it to some older friend, who told the poet, no doubt with an indication of the blushing and eager lad from whom it came, which procured him a word and a look never forgotten. But there passed at the same time a thought through young Walter's mind, the swift reflection of that never-failing criticism of youth which pierces unaware through all wrappings and veils of the soul. "I remember I thought Burns's acquaintance with English poetry was rather limited ; and also that having twenty times the ability of Allan Ramsay and of Fergusson, he talked of them with too much humility as his models." The much-read boy was a little shocked, no doubt disturbed in his secret soul that the poet—so far above any other poet that was to be seen about the world in those days—should not have known that verse : though indeed men better read than Burns might have been excused for their want of acquaintance with a minor poet like Langhorne ; but how true was the indignant observation, half angry, that with "twenty times the ability" it was Allan Ramsay and the

still less important unfortunate young Fergusson to whom
Burns looked up! Did the boy wonder perhaps, though too
loyal to say it—for criticism at his age is always keen—whether
there might be a something not quite real in that devotion,
and ask in the recesses of his mind whether it was possible
for such a man to be so self-deceived?

There were no doubt various affectations about Burns, as
when he talks big in his diary of observing character and
finding this pursuit the greatest entertainment of his life in
Edinburgh, with a pretension very general among half-
educated persons : but there is no reason to believe that he
was not quite genuine about his predecessors. A poet is not
necessarily a critic ; and Allan Ramsay's 'fame had been
exactly of the popular kind which would attract a son
of the soil, whereas Fergusson was the object of Burns's
especial tenderness, pity, and regard. And it is touching to
recollect that the only sign he left of himself in Edinburgh,
where for the first time he learned what it was to mix in fine
company and to feel the freedom of money in his pocket,
from which he could afford a luxury, was to place a stone
over the grave of Fergusson in the Canongate Churchyard,
where he lay unknown. His application to the Kirk-Session
for leave to do this is still kept upon the books—a curious
interruption amid the minutes of church discipline and
economics. One wonders if that homely memorial is kept
as it ought to be. It is a memorial not only of the admiration of one poet for another, but of Burns's poignant pity—a
wellnigh intolerable pang—for a young soul who preceded
himself in the way of poetry and despair, one whose life,
destined to better and brighter things, had been flung
away like a weed on the dismal strand. Only twenty-three
years of poetry and folly had sufficed that other reckless boy
to destroy himself and shatter his little lamp of light. Burns
was only a few years older, and perhaps, though on the
heights of triumph, felt something of that horrible tide
already catching his own feet to sweep him too into the
abyss. There are few things in the world more pathetic
than this tribute of his to the victim who had gone before him.

I may perhaps venture to say, with an apology for recurring to a subject dealt with in another book, that this poetic visit to Edinburgh reminds me of the visit of another poet in every way very different from Burns to another city which cannot be supposed to resemble Edinburgh except in the wonderful charm and attraction for devotees which she possesses. There is indeed no just comparison between Petrarch at Venice and Burns at Edinburgh, nothing but the fantastic link, often too subtle to be traced, which makes the mind glide or leap over innumerable distances and diversities from one thing to another. The Italian poet came conferring glory, great as a prince, and attended by much the same honours and privileges, though he was but a half priest, the son of an exile, in an age and place where birth and family were of infinitely more importance than they are now. He was the perfection and flower of learning and high culture, and a fame which had reached the point which is high-fantastical, and can mount no farther—and he came to a palace allotted to him by the Government, and every distinction which it was in their power to bestow, and demeaned himself *en bon prince*, adorning with skilful eloquent touches of description the glorious scene beneath his windows, the pageants at which he was an honoured spectator. Nothing could be more unlike the young, shy, proud, yet genial-hearted rustic, holding firmly by that magic wand of poetry which was his sole right to consideration, and facing the curious, puzzled, patronising world with a certain suspicion, a certain defiance, as of one whom no craft or wile could betray or pretension daunt—yet ready to melt into an enthusiasm almost extravagant when a lovely young woman or a noble youth pushed open with a touch the door always ajar, or at least unfastened, of his heart.

> " The mother may forget the child
>   That smiles sae sweetly on her knee ;
> But I'll remember thee, Glencairn,
>   And a' that thou hast done for me ! "

What Glencairn had done was nothing but kindness, a warm reception which not even the poet's susceptibility could think condescending : but he is repaid with an exuberant, extravagant gratitude. Such was the man ; ever afraid to compromise his dignity, but with no measure for the over-flowings of his heart. Petrarch, so much more assured in his eminence and superiority to all living poets, was driven from his palace on the Riva and all his delights by the impertinent gibes of some foolish young men. But Burns was flattered and caressed to the top of his bent, and—forgotten, or at least dropped, and no more thought of. He returned to Edinburgh only to find that, the gloss of novelty having worn off, his friends were no longer ready to move heaven and earth in order to bring him to their parties, though probably had he chosen he might have worked himself back "into society" in a slower but more permanent fashion. This, however, he did not choose, but fell back among the convivial middle class, the undistinguished and over merry, where nobody thought it too great humility to refer to Allan Ramsay and Fergusson as his models. It must be recollected, however, that his second visit to Edinburgh, and what seems in the telling a foolish and almost vulgar flirtation, produced one of the most impassioned and exquisite songs of love and despair which has ever been written in any language.

> "Ae fond kiss, and then we sever ;
> Ae farewell, alas ! for ever !"

There is a stillness of exhausted feeling in this wonderful utterance which is the very soul of despair.

There has been no more remarkable moment in the experience of the town which has known so many strange and striking scenes, though its interest has little to do with history or even with national feeling. It is pure humanity in an unusual development, an episode in the life of the poet such as has many less important parallels, but scarcely any so fully representative and typical. It discloses to us suddenly, as by a flash of light striking into the darkness, the persons, the entertainments, the sentiments of a hundred years ago. We make improvements daily in external matters, but society—we had almost said humanity—rarely

BURNS'S MONUMENT

learns.   There is not the smallest hope that in Edinburgh
or elsewhere a young man of genius in Burns's position would
now be either more wisely noticed or more truly benefited
by such a period of close contact with people who ought by
experience and knowledge to know better than he.   The
only thing that is probable is a falling-off, not an advance.
I think it highly doubtful whether a ploughman from Ayrshire, however superlative his genius, would now be received
at all in " the best houses " and by the first men and women
in Edinburgh ; and if not in Edinburgh, surely nowhere else
would such a reception as that given to Burns await the
untutored poet.   The world has seldom another chance
permitted to it, and in this case I cannot but think it would
be worse and not better used.

CHAPTER III

THE SHAKSPEARE OF SCOTLAND

THERE are many variations in degree of the greatest human gifts, but they are few in kind. The name we have ventured to place at the head of this chapter is one not so great as that of Shakspeare, not so all-embracing—though widely-embracing beyond any other second—not so ideal, not so profound. Walter Scott penetrated with a luminous revelation all that was within his scope, the most different kinds and classes of men, those whom he loved (and he loved all whom it was possible to love) and the few whom he hated, with the same comprehension and power of disclosure. But Shakspeare was not restrained by the limits of any personal scope or knowledge. He knew Lear and Macbeth, and Hamlet and Prospero, though they were beings only of his own creation. He could embody the loftiest passion in true flesh and blood, and show us how a man can be moved by jealousy or ambition in the highest superlative degree and yet be a man with all the claims upon our understanding and pity that are possessed by any brother of our own. Nothing like Lear ever came in our Scott's way : that extraordinary embodiment of human passion and weakness, the forlorn and awful strength of the aged and miserable, did not present itself to his large and genial gaze. It would not have occurred to him perhaps had he lived to the age of Methuselah. He knew not those horrors and dreadful depths of humanity that could make such tragic passion possible. But he had his revenge in one way even upon

ST. GILES'S FROM PRINCES STREET

Shakspeare.   Dogberry and Verges, as types of the muddle-headed old watch—pompous, confused, and self-important—are always diverting ; but they would have been men not all ridiculous had Scott taken them in hand—real creatures of flesh and blood, not watchmen in the abstract.   Our greater poet did not take trouble enough to make them individual, his fancy carrying him otherwhere, and leaving him scarce the time to put his jotting down.   To Shakspeare the great ideals whom he almost alone has been able to make into flesh and blood ; to Scott all the surrounding world, the men as we meet them about the common thorough-fares of life.   He knows no Rosalind nor Imogen, but on the other hand Jeanie Deans and Jenny Headrigg would have been impossible to his great predecessor.   Both, we may remark, are incapable of a young hero—the Claudios and the Bertrams being if anything a trifle worse than Henry Morton and Young Lovel.   But whereas Shakspeare is greatest above that line of the conventional ideal, it is below that Sir Walter is famous.   The one has no restriction, however high he may soar ; the other finds nothing so common that he cannot make it immortal.

It is, however, especially in the breadth and largeness of a humanity which has scarcely any limit to its sympathy and understanding that the great romancist of Scotland resembles the greatest of English poets.   They are both so great, so broad, so little restrained by any individual limitations, that a perverse criticism has made this catholic and all-comprehending nature a kind of reproach to both, as though that great and limpid mirror of their minds, in which all nature was reflected, was less noble than the sharp face of a stone which can catch but one ray.   They were both subject to political prejudices and prepossessions.   Shakspeare has made of many a youth of the nineteenth century an ardent Lancastrian, ready to pluck a red rose with Somerset and die for Margaret and her prince ; and Scott in like manner has made many a Jacobite, though in the latter case our novelist is too full of sense even in the midst of his own inclinations to become ever an out-and-out partisan.   But, except these

prepossessions, they have no *parti pris*. Every faction
renders up its soul of meaning, the most diverse figures
unclose themselves side by side. The wit, the scholar, the
true soldier, the braggart and thief, the Jew and the
Christian, the Hamlet, hero of all time, and Shallow and
Slender from the fat pastures of English rural life, come all
together, each as true as if on him alone the poet's eye had
fixed. And Scott is like him, setting before us with unerring
pencil the old superstitious despot of mediæval France, the
bustling pedant of St. James's, the ploughmen and shepherds, the churchmen, the Border reivers and Highland
caterans, the broad country lying under a natural illumination,
without strain or effort, large and temperate as the day.
Neither in the greatest poet nor the great romancer is
there any force put upon the natural fulness of life to twist
its record into a narrow circle with one motive only. It is
the round world and all that it inhabits, the grandeur and
divinity of a universe, that delights them. Their view is
large as the vision of God, or as nearly so as is given to
mortal eyes. It is in this, above all, that they resemble
each other. In degree Shakspeare, it need not be said, is
all-transcendent, reaching heights such as no other man has
reached in delineation and creation : but Scott is of his
splendid species, one of his kind, the only one among all
the many sons of genius with whom this island has been
blessed, for whom the boldest could make such a claim.

Walter Scott belongs to all Scotland. He was, no
man more, a lover of the woods and fields, of mountain-sides
and pastoral braes, of the river and forest, Ettrick and
Tweed and Yarrow, and Perthshire—that princely district,
half Highland, half Lowland—and the chain of silvery lochs
that pierce the mountain shadows through Stirling and
Argyle : every league of the fair country he loved. From the
Western Isles and the Orkneys to the very fringe of debat-
able land which parts the northern and the southern half of
Great Britain—is his, and has tokens to show of his presence.
When he came home to die at the end of almost the most
tragic yet most noble chapter of individual history which our

century has known, it was the longing of his sick heart above all other that he should not be so unblest as to lay his bones far from the Tweed.

But yet, above all other places, it was to Edinburgh that Scott belonged. His birth, his growth, the familiar scenes of his youth, his education and training, the business and work of his life, were all associated with the ancient capital. George Square—with its homely and comfortable old - fashion, which has nothing to do with antiquity, the first breaking out of the Edinburgh citizens into large space and air outside the strait boundaries of the city, with the Meadows and their trees beyond, and all the sunshine of the south side to warm the deep *corps de logis*, the substantial and solid mansions which are so grey without yet so full of warmth and comfort within—was the first home he knew, and his residence up to manhood.   No boy could be more an Edinburgh boy.   Lame though he was, he climbed every dangerous point upon the hills, and knew the recesses of Arthur's Seat and Salisbury Crags by heart before he knew his Latin grammar.   His schoolboy fights, his snow-balling, the little armies of urchins set in battle array, the friendly feuds of gentle and simple (sometimes attended by hard knocks, as among his own Liddesdale farmers), fill the streets with amusing recollections.   And when he was promoted in due time to the Parliament House and to all the frolics of the youthful Bar, and his proud father steps forth in the snuff-coloured suit which Mr. Saunders Fairford wore after him, to tell his friends that "my son Walter passed his private Scots law examination with good approbation," and on Friday "puts on the gown and gives a bit chack of dinner to his friends and acquaintances, as is the custom," how familiar and kindly is the scene, how the sober house lights up, and the good wine about which we have known all our lives comes out of the cellar and the jokes fly round—Parliament House pleasantries and recollections of the witticisms of the Bench gradually giving place to the sallies of the wild young wits, the shaft from the new-bent bow of the young advocate himself.   Nothing can be more true and

simple than he is through all the tale, or more real than
the Edinburgh atmosphere ; the fun that is mostly in the
foreground ; the work that is pushed into corners yet always
gets done, though it has not the air of being important
except to the excellent father whose steps on the stair are
the signal for the disappearance of a chess-board into a
drawer or a romance under the papers,— well - known
tricks of youth which we have all been guilty of. There is a
curious evidence, however, in Lockhart's *Life*, less known
than the usual tales of frolic and apparent idleness, of the
professional trick of Scott's handwriting, which showed how
steadily he must have laboured even in his delightful, easy,
innocently irregular youth. " I allude particularly to a sort
of flourish at the bottom of the page, originally, I presume,
adopted in engrossing as a safeguard against the intrusion
of a forged line between the legitimate text and the attest-
ing signature. He was quite sensible," adds his biographer,
" that this ornament might as well be dispensed with ; and
his family often heard him mutter after involuntarily per-
forming it, ' There goes the old shop again ! ' " Which of
us now could see that flourish without the water coming
into our eyes ?

It is impossible to eradicate, from the minds of youthful
students at least, the admiration which always attends the
performances of the young man who gains his successes
without apparently working for them. As a matter of
fact, it is the work which we ought to respect rather than
that apparently fortuitous accidental result : but nothing will
ever cure us of our native delight in an effect which appears
to have no vulgar cause, and great has been the misery produced by this prejudice to many a youth who has begun
with the tradition of easy triumph and presumed upon it to
the loss of all his after-life. But when there shows in the
apparent idler a sign like this of many a long hour's labour
ignored and lightly thought of, covered over with a pleasant
veil of fun and ease and happy leisure, the combination is
one that no heart can resist.

Scott had read everything he could lay his hands on

THE UNIVERSITY OF EDINBURGH

2 H

while he was still a child, and boasted himself a virtuoso, that is, according to his explanation, at six years old, "one who wishes and will know everything;" but his boyish tastes and triumphs became more and more athletic as he gained a firmer use of his bodily powers. No diseased consciousness of disability in respect to his lameness, like that which embittered Byron, could find a place in the rough wholesome atmosphere of the Edinburgh High School and playgrounds, where nobody was too delicate about reminding him of his infirmity, and the stout-hearted little hero took it like a man, offering "to fight mounted," and being tied upon a board accordingly for his first combat. "You may take him for a poor lameter," said one of the Eldin Clerks, a sailor, with equal friendly frankness to a party of strangers, "but he is the first to begin a row, and the last to end it." To such a youth the imperfection was a virtue the more. When the jovial band strolled forth upon long walks the cheerful "lameter" bargained for three miles an hour, and kept up with the best. They would start at five in the morning, beguiling the way with endless pranks, on one occasion at least without a single sixpence in all their youthful pockets with which to refresh themselves during a thirty miles' round. "We asked every now and then at a cottage door for a drink of water; and one or two of the goodwives, observing our worn-out looks, brought forth milk instead of water, so with that and hips and haws we came in little the worse." Little they cared for fatigue and inconvenience; they were things to laugh over when the lads got back. Scott only wished he had been a player on the flute, like George Primrose in the *Vicar of Wakefield*, and his father shook his head and doubted the boy was born "for nae better than a gangrel scrapegut" —reproach of little gravity, as the expedition so poorly provisioned was of little harm. Thus the young gentlemen bore cheerfully what would have been hardship to a ploughman, and gibed even at each other's weaknesses without a spark of unkindness, which made the weakness itself into a robust matter of fact not to be brooded over. High susceptibility might have suffered from the treatment, but high susceptibility generally means egotism and inordinate self-esteem, qualities which it is the very best use of public school and college to conjure away.

Nothing indeed more cheerful, more full of endless frolic and enjoyment, fresh air and fun and feeling, ever existed than the young manhood of Walter Scott. Talk of Scotch gravity and seriousness! The houses in which they were received as they roamed about—farmers' or lairds', it was all the same to the merry lads—were only too uproarious in their mirth; with songs and laughter they made the welkin ring. At home in Edinburgh the fun might be less noisy, but it was not less sincere. In the very Parliament House itself the young men clustered in their corner, telling each other the last good things, and with much ado to keep their young laughter within the bounds of decorum. The judge on the Bench, the Lord President himself, greatest potentate of all, was not more safe from the audacious wits than poor Peter Peebles. There was nothing they did not laugh at, themselves and each other as much as Lord Braxfield, and all the humours of a town more full of anecdote and jest, laughable eccentricity and keen satire and amusing comment, than any town in literature. The best joke of all perhaps was Sydney Smith's famous *bon mot* about the surgical operation, which no doubt he meant as an excellent joke in the midst of that laughing community, where the fun was only too fast and furious. Nowadays, when life is more temperate and the world in general has mended its manners, the habits of that period fill us with dismay; but perhaps after all there was less harm done than appears, and not more of the fearful tribute of young life which our fated race is always paying than is still exacted amid a population much less generally addicted to excess. But that of course increased rather than diminished the jovial aspect of Edinburgh life when Walter Scott was young, and when the few cares he had in hand, the occasional bit of work, interfered very little with the warm and lively social life in the midst of which he had been born. He dwelt, in every sense of the word, among his own people, his friends, the sons of his father's friends, his associates all belonging to families like his own, of good if modest rank and lineage, the "kent folk" of whom Scotland loves to keep up the record. This, which is perhaps one of the greatest advantages with which a young man can enter on life, was his from his infancy. He and his companions had been at school together, together in the college classes, in frequent social meetings, on the floor of the Parliament House. Familiar faces and kind greetings were round him wherever he went. No doubt these circumstances, so genial, so friendly and favourable, helped to perfect the most kind, the most generous and sunshiny of natures. And thus no man could be more completely at once the best product and most complete representative of his native soil.

His life too was as prosperous and full of good fortune and happiness as a man could desire. He married at twenty-six, and a few years later received the appointment of Sheriff-Depute of Selkirkshire, which rendered him independent of the precarious incomings of his profession, and made the pleasure he always took in roaming the country into a necessary part of his life's work. He had begun a playful and pleasurable authorship some time before with some translations from the German, Bürger's *Lenore* and Goethe's *Götz von Berlichingen*—the first of which was hastily made into a little book, daintily printed and bound, in order to help his suit with an early love, so easy, so little premeditated, was this beginning. With equal simplicity and absence of intention he slid into the Border Minstrelsy, which he intended not for the beginning of a long literary career, but in the first place for "a job" to Ballantyne the printer, whom he had persuaded to establish himself in Edinburgh—the best of printers and the most attached of faithful and humble friends—and for fun and the pleasure of scouring the country in pursuit of ballads, which was a search he had already entered upon to his great enjoyment. From this nothing was so easy as to float into original poetry, inspired by the same impulse and inspiration as his ballads. One of the ladies of the house of Buccleuch told him the story of the elfin page, and begged him to make a ballad of it ; and from this suggestion the *Lay of the Last Minstrel* arose. The time was ripe for giving forth all that had been unconsciously stirring in his teeming fertile imagination. It came at once like a sudden bursting into flower, with a splendid *éclosion*, outbursting, involuntary, unlaborious, delightful to himself as to mankind. From henceforward his name stood in one of the highest places of literature and his fame was assured.

Nothing could be more unintentional, more spontaneous, almost careless ; a thing done for his pleasure far more than with any serious purpose ; nothing—except the later beginning, equally unintentional, of a still more important stream of production. The poems of Scott will always be open to much criticism ; even those who love them most—and there are many whose love for this fresh, free, spontaneous, delightful fountain of song is strong enough to repress every impulse of criticism and transport it beyond the reach of comment to a romantic enchanted land of its own, where it flows in native sunshine and delight for ever—declining to pronounce any definite judgment as to their greatness. But to Scott in his after-work we are inclined to say no man worthy of expressing an opinion can give any but the highest place. It is true, and the fact has to be admitted with astonishment and regret, that one great writer, his countryman, speaking the same language and in every way capable of pronouncing judgment, has failed to appreciate Sir Walter. We cannot tell why, nor pretend to solve that amazing question. Perhaps it was the universal acclaim, the consent of every voice, that awoke the germ of perversity that was in Thomas Carlyle : an impulse of contradiction, especially in face of an opinion too unanimous, which is one of our national characteristics : perhaps one of those prejudices pertinacious as the rugged peasant nature itself, which sometimes warps the clearest judgment ; perhaps, but this we find it difficult to believe, a narrower intensity and passion of meaning in himself which found little reflection in the great limpid mirror which Scott held up to nature. The beginning of Scott's chief and greatest work was as fortuitous, as accidental (if we may use the word), as the poetry. He took up by some passing impulse the idea of a prose story on the events of the 'forty-five, which perhaps he considered too recent to be treated in poetry ; wrote (everybody knows the

PLAYFAIR'S MONUMENT, CALTON HILL

story) half a volume, read it to a trusted critic, who probably considered it foolish for a man who had risen to the heights of fame by one kind of composition to risk himself now with another. It is very likely that Scott himself was easily

moved to the same opinion.   He tossed the MS. into a
drawer, and gave it up.   There had been no special motive
in the effort, and it cost him nothing to put it aside, to
whistle for his dogs, and go out for a long round by wood
and hill, or to take his gun or rod, or to entertain his
visitors—all of which were more rational, more entertaining,
and altogether important things to do than the writing
of a dull story, which after all was not his line.   For years
the beginning chapters of *Waverley* lay there unknown.
They lay very quietly, we may well believe, not bursting the
dull enclosure as they might have done had the Baron of
Bradwardine been yet born ; but that good young Waverley
was always a little dull, and might have slept till doomsday
had nothing occurred to disturb his rest.   One day, however,
some fishing tackle was wanted for the use of one of Scott's
perpetual visitors at Ashiestiel—not even for himself, for
some chance man taking advantage of the Shirra's open
house.   Visitor arriving in a good hour ! fortunate sorner,
to be thereafter blessed of all men !   Let us hope he got just
the lines he wanted and had a good day's sport.   For in
his search Scott's eyes lighted upon the bundle of written
pages.   " Hallo ! " he must have said to himself, " there they
are !   Let's see if they're as bad as Willie Erskine thought."
In his candid soul he did not think they were very good, unless it was perhaps the description of Waverley Honour, a
great mild English mansion which he would admire all the
more that it was so unlike Tully Veolan.   Perhaps it was the
contrast which brought into his teeming brain a sudden
vision of that " Scottish manor-house sixty years since,"
which he went off straightway and built in his eighth chapter
with the baron and all his surroundings, which must have
been awaiting impatient that happy moment to burst into
life.

And thus by spontaneous accident, by delightful, careless
chance, so to speak, the thing was done.   One wonders by
what equally, nay more fortunate unthought-of haphazard
it was, that the country rogue Shakspeare, his bright eyes
shining with mock penitence for the wildness of his wood-

land career, and the air and the accent of the fields still on his honeyed lips, first found out that he could string a story together for the theatre and make the old knights and the fair ladies live again. Of this there is no record, but only enough presumption, we think, to make it sufficiently clear that the discovery which has ever since been one of the chief glories of the English name, and added the most wonderful immortal inhabitants to the population, was made, like Scott's, by what seems a divine chance, without apparent preparation or likelihood. In our day much more importance is given to a development which the scientific thinker would fondly hope to be traceable by all the leadings of race and inheritance into an evolution purely natural and to be expected ; while, on the other hand, there is nothing which appears more splendid and dignified to others than the aspect of a life devoted to poetry, in which the man becomes but a kind of solemn incubator of his own thoughts. It will always be, however, an additional delight to the greater part of the human race to see how here and there the greatest of all heavenly tools is found unawares by the happy hand that can wield it, no one knowing who has put it there ready for his triumphant grasp when the fated moment comes.

Everybody will remember as a pendant—but one so much more grave that we hesitate to cite it, though the coincidence is curious—the pause made by Dante in the beginning of the *Inferno*, which resembles so exactly the pause in Scott's career. The great Florentine had written seven cantos of his wonderful poem when the rush of his affairs carried him away from all such tranquil work and left the Latin fragment, among other more vulgar papers, shovelled hastily into some big cassone in the house in Florence from which he was a banished man. It was found there after five years by a nephew who would fain have tried his prentice hand upon the poem, yet finally took the better part of sending it to its author—who immediately resumed *Io dico sequitando*, in a burst of satisfaction to have recovered what he must have begun with far more zeal and intention than Scott. The resemblance, however, which is so curiously exact, the seven cantos and the seven chapters, the five years' interval, the satisfaction of the work resumed, is, different as are the men and their work, one of those fantastic parallels which are delightful to the fantastic soul. Nothing could be more unlike than that dark and splendid poem to Scott's sunshiny and kindly art ; nothing less resembling than the proud embittered exile with his hand against every man, and the genial romancer whose heart overflowed with the milk of human kindness. Yet this strange occurrence in both lives takes an enhanced interest from the curious dissimilarity which makes the repetition of the fact more curious still.

The sudden burst into light and publicity of a gift which had been growing through all the changes of private life, of the wonderful stream of knowledge, recollection, divination, boundless acquaintance with and affection for human nature, which had gladdened the Edinburgh streets, the Musselburgh sands, the Southland moors and river-sides, since ever Walter Scott had begun to roam among them, with his cheerful band of friends, his good stories, his kind and gentle thoughts—was received by the world with a burst of delighted recognition to which we know no parallel. We do not know, alas ! what happened when the audience in the Globe Theatre made a similar discovery. Perhaps the greater gift, by its very splendour, would be less easily perceived in the dazzling of a glory hitherto unknown, and obscured it may be by jealousies of actors and their inaptitude to do justice to the wonderful poetry put into their hands. But of that we know nothing. We know, however, that there were no two opinions about *Waverley*. It took the world by storm, which had had no such new sensation and no such delightful amusement for many a day. It was not only the beginning of a new and wonderful school in romance, a fresh chapter in literature, but the revelation of a region and a race unknown. Scotland had begun to glow in the sunshine of poetry, in glimpses of Burns's westland hills and fields, of Scott's moss-troopers and romantic landscapes, visions of battle and old tradition : but the wider horizon of a life more familiar, of a

broad country full of nature, full of character, running over
with fun and pawky humour, thrilling with high enthusiasm
and devotion, where men were still ready to risk everything
in life for a falling cause, and other men not unwilling to
pick up the spoils, was a discovery and surprise more
delightful than anything that had happened to the generation. The books flew through the island like magic, penetrating to corners unthought of, uniting gentle and simple in
an enthusiasm beyond parallel. How the multitude got at
them at all it is difficult to understand, for those were the days
of really high prices, before the actual cost of a book got modified by one-half as now, and when there were as yet no
cheap editions. *Waverley* was printed in three small volumes
at the cost of a guinea. We believe that to buy books was
more usual then than now, and there were circulating
libraries everywhere, conveying perhaps the stream of literature more evenly over the country than can be attained by
one gigantic Mudie. At all events, by whatever means it
was procured, *Waverley* and its successors were read everywhere, not only in great houses but in small, wherever there
was intelligence and a taste for books ; and the interest, the
curiosity, the eagerness, were everywhere overwhelming. I
have heard of girls in a dressmaker's workroom who kept
the last volume in a drawer, from whence it was read aloud
by one to the rest, the drawer being closed hurriedly whenever the mistress came that way. From this humble scene
to the highest in the land, where the Prince Regent sat—

> " His table spread with tea and toast,
>   Death-warrants, and the *Morning Post*,"

these volumes went everywhere. One of them lies before
me now in rough boards of paper, with the " blue back " of
which one of Scott's correspondents talks, not a prepossessing
volume, but independent of externals and all things else
except its own native excellence and power.

    For fifteen years after, this stream of living literature
poured forth in the largest generous volume like a great river,
through every region where English was spoken or known.

His work was as the march of a battalion, always increasing,
new detachments appearing suddenly, now an individual, now
a group, to join the line.   The Baron of Bradwardine with
his attendant bailie ; Vich Ian Vohr and noble Evan Dhu,
and all the clan ; the family at Ellangowan and that at
Charlieshope, good Dandie and all his delightful belongings ;
Jock Jabos and the rest; Monkbarns and Edie Ochiltree,
and all the pathos of the Mucklebackits ; Bailie Nicol Jarvie
and the Dougal Cratur ; humours of the clachan and the
hillside ; Jeanie Deans in her perfect humbleness and truth.
It would be vain to attempt to name the new inhabitants of
Scotland who appeared out of the unseen wherever Scott
moved.   Neither to himself nor to his audience could it
seem that these friends of all were new created, invented by
any man.   Scott, who alone could do it, withdrew the veil
that had concealed them.   He opened up an entire country,
a full world of men and women, so living, so various, with
their natural garb of fitting language, and their heart of
natural sentiment, and the thoughts which they must have
been thinking, by inalienable right of their humanity.   There
might have been better plots or more carefully constructed
stories ; as indeed in life, heaven knows, all our stories
might be much better constructed ; but could we conceive
it possible that these, our country-folk and friends, could be
dismissed again off the face of the earth, how impoverished,
how diminished, would Scotland be !   The want of them is
more than we could contemplate, and we can well understand how our country must have appeared to the world
a poor little turbulent country, without warmth or wealth,
before these representatives of a robust and manifold race
were born.

Yet, amid the delightful enrichment of these productions to the nation and the world, the man himself who
produced them was perhaps the finest revelation of all.
And here he transcends for once the larger kindred genius of
whom we do not know, yet believe, that he was such a man
as Scott, though better off in one way and less well in others.
Shakspeare must have been somewhat oppressed with noble

patrons, which Scott never was—patrons to whom his own
splendid courtesy and the magnifying glamour in his poetic
eyes must sometimes have made him more flattering than
was needful, overwhelming them with magnificent words ;
but on the other hand he had not those modern drawbacks
under which Scott's great career was so bitterly burdened,
the strain for money, the constant combat with debt and
liability.   To bear the first yoke must have taken much of
a man's strength and tired him exceedingly : but to bear the
second is perhaps the severest test to which any buoyant
spirit can be put.   And from the very beginning of his
career as a novelist Scott had this burden upon his shoulders.
He bore the chains very lightly at first with a hundred hair-
breadth 'scapes which made the struggle—as even that
struggle can be made while the sufferer is strong and young
— almost exhilarating, with a glee in the relief and the
power to surmount every difficulty, and a faith strengthened
by numberless examples of the certainty—however dark
things might seem up to the very last moment—of bursting
through, with an exquisite sensation of success, the hardest
coil of circumstance.   But as Scott grew older these
obstacles grew stronger ; he could not put sense or prudence
into the heads of his colleagues, and it was hard to teach
himself, the most liberal, the most hospitable and princely of
entertainers, those habits of frugality which are never harder
to learn than by a Scots gentleman of the ancient strain
accustomed to keep open house.   I do not think it has ever
been acknowledged that there is in this desperate struggle
to keep afloat a certain intoxication of its own.   To foil your
pursuers, your enemies, whether they take the form of armed
assailants or of pressing creditors, by ever another and
another daring combination, by sudden reliefs unthought of,
by a bold *coup* executed at the very moment when the
crisis seems inevitable, by all the happy yet desperate
chances of warfare, has a fascination in it which no one
could conceive as attending a sordid struggle for money.
The pursuit becomes exciting, breathless, in proportion as it
becomes desperate.   Sometimes, when all the stars in their

courses have seemed to be fighting against the combatant, a
sudden aid like the very interposition of heaven will bring him
safety ; and a confidence in this interposition takes possession
of him.   He does not see how deliverance can come, but it
will come.   His labouring breast strains, his brain whirls, he
is at his last gasp : when all at once the heart leaps up in his
bosom, the wheels in his head stand still, a flash of satisfaction
comes over him.   Once more and once more, again and
again, at the last gasp of the struggle he is saved.

No doubt something of this was in the long and desperate
fight which Scott waged with the creditors of the Ballantynes,
who were also his own.   The worst of the struggle is that it
almost legalises a prodigality which to men always fixed on
solid ground would be impossible.   The conviction that the
money will come somehow, added to the still more intoxicating conviction that this somehow depends oftenest upon
your own unrivalled power of work, and the confidence
which all men have in you, permits, almost sanctions, a
yielding to personal temptations, and the indulgence of a
little taste and inclination of your own in the midst of so
many burdens for others.   Thus Abbotsford grew, of which
all the critics have talked as if its, alas ! somewhat sham
antiquity and its few acres had been the cause of all the
trouble.   One could have wished that Scott's taste had been
more true, that he had so dearly bought and so fondly
collected curiosities more worthy, that he should have had
a genuine old house, a direct and happy lineage, son and
son's son, to bear his name—not to posterity, with whom it
was safe, but on Tweedside among the other Scotts,—a kindly
and not ignoble ambition.   But he has himself forestalled the
criticisms of the antiquarians by that delightful record of
good Monkbarns's mistakes and deceptions which would make
us forgive him for any " lang ladle " or fictitious relic ; and
it would be a hard heart that would be otherwise than
thankful that he had so much as Abbotsford to indemnify
him for his labours and trials.   As the time approached
when he was no longer able to maintain that gallant struggle,
and the power of labour failed and confidence was lost, the

position of the man becomes more tragical than the spectator can well bear to look upon. Who can read unmoved the story of the time when his faithful friends (though it was their necessities that had pulled him down to the ground of this bitter failure) had to come and tell him that his last romance was scarcely worth paper and print? who could refrain from going down on his knees to kiss that failing hand which could now only bring forth Count Robert of Paris where once it had set out in glorious array of battle Sir Kenneth of Scotland, and the stout old Constable of Chester, and Front de Bœuf, and the Scottish archers—and which still could not be inactive, but would struggle on, on—to pay that miserable money and leave behind a spotless name!

There is one melancholy and almost terrible consolation in such a heartbreaking record, terrible from the light it throws upon the constitution of human nature and the conditions of that supreme sympathy which is the noblest kind of fame. Had Sir Walter been able to throw his burdens from him, had he loosed the millstone from his neck and retired in full credit and comfort to his Abbotsford to pass the conclusion of peaceful and glorious days on the banks of the Tweed—had we known him only as the greatest romancist of the world, the next to Shakspeare in large creation and revelation of mankind, proud had every Scotsman been of his name, and fondly had the nation cherished his memory. But when his brilliant and wonderful life fell under the shadow of all these tragical clouds, when its course was arrested by obstacles which are usually unsurmountable, before which any other man must have broken down, when he stood in the face of fate, in the face of every misfortune, broken in health, in hope, in power, a lonely man where he had been the centre of every joy in life, an enchanter with his magic wand broken and his witchery gone—then, and then only, does Scott attain his highest greatness and give the world most noble assurance of a man. His diary as his life dwindles away, that life once so splendid and so full, is like the noblest poem—its broken and falling sentences go direct to the heart. *Fuimus* was never written

more grandly, with more noble patience and valour. Without
this downfall his triumph might have been but as the other
triumphs—the tragedy of the conclusion is a sight for men
and angels. Lockhart, who preserves the record for us,
becomes for the time the greatest, with a subject more
moving, more noble, than any that his hero had selected
from the records of the ages. The pity and anguish grow
too much for the spectator. We are spectators no longer,
but mournful and devoted retainers standing about, all
hushed and silent, scarcely able either to shed or to restrain
the choking tears.

One asks one's self, Is this the cost of supreme human
power? is it to be bought by nothing but the agony in
which failure, real or apparent, is a part, and in which all
the exquisite tenement of reputation, happiness, and delight-
some life seems to crumble down like a house of cards before
our eyes? Dread question for the genius of the future, sad
yet sublime problem of the past! At all events it was so
in the life of Scott, which in all its greatness was never so
great, so touching, so secure of love and honour, as in the
moment when his weapons fell from his hands and his
genius and being alike failed, breaking down in a last
supreme struggle for justice and honour and fair dealing,
to avoid what he thought disgrace and the intolerable
stigma of having done any man wrong.

It is a penalty of such greatness, especially in the midst
of an enthusiastic and unanimous country, that it becomes
more or less a thing to trade upon, the subject of vague
patriotic vapourings, and much froth of foolish talk from
uninstructed lips in the following generations. As Strat-
ford-on-Avon is in respect to Shakspeare all Scotland is in
respect to Burns and Scott. It has even become a mark of
culture and superiority among certain fine spirits in consequence to pretend to despise the former of these names—
perhaps really to despise it, for there is no fathom that can
sound the depths of human foolishness even in the learned
and wise. The vulgarity of fame when it becomes the cry
of the most prosaic is, however, calculated justly to alarm

the literary soul, and in the excess of Scott monuments, and wooden quaighs, and tartan paper-knives, there is a damping and depressing quality which we must all acknowledge.

SIR WALTER SCOTT'S HOUSE

We need not, however, in these follies forget the illuminating presence of Scott in the midst of all the picturesque scenes of what he has proudly called " mine

2 I

own romantic town." From the High School Yards and "the kittle nine steps," from George Square, lying cosy but grey in the hollow amid the enlarged and beautiful openings of the Meadows, to the Parliament House, withdrawn in the square, once blocked by the old Tolbooth, now confronted solely by an embellished and restored cathedral, and to the sober street on the other side of the hollow, where to 39 North Castle Street he took his bride and set up his independent home, there is no corner of Edinburgh where his step and voice have not been. And some of the most characteristic scenes which we can call to mind in recent history rise before us in his narrative as if we had been there. The Porteous Mob riots in our ears, the flare of the sudden fire at the gates of the Tolbooth, the blinding smoke, the tramp of the crowd, the sudden concentrated force of that many-headed multitude stilled by stern resolve into unity and action, are as visible as if they had happened yesterday. And after ransacking all the serious volumes that tell the story and picture the aspect of old Edinburgh, we turn back to that tale, and for the first time see the tortuous passage between the church and the Tolbooth, the dark old prison with its lofty turrets, the Luckenbooths linked on to its dark shadow, oppressing the now wide thoroughfare of the High Street, where these buildings have left no trace. No topographical record or painstaking print comes within a hundred miles of that picture, dashed in boldly by the way, to the entrancing tale. I cannot refrain from placing here one or two vignettes, which I have no doubt the artist himself will allow to surpass his best efforts, and which set the landscape before us with a distinct yet ideal and poetical grace which pencil and graver can very seldom equal. The first is of the exterior aspect of Edinburgh.

" Marching in this manner they speedily reached an eminence, from which they could view Edinburgh stretching along the ridgy hill which slopes eastward from the Castle. The latter, being in a state of siege, or rather of blockade, by the northern insurgents, who had already occupied the town for two or three days, fired at intervals upon such parties of Highlanders as exposed themselves, either on the main street, or elsewhere in the vicinity of the fortress.   The morning being calm and fair, the effect of this dropping fire was to invest the Castle in wreaths of smoke, the edges of which dissipated slowly in the air, while the central veil was darkened ever and anon by fresh clouds poured forth from the battlements; the whole giving, by the partial concealment, an appearance of grandeur and gloom, rendered more terrific when Waverley reflected on the cause by which it was produced, and that each explosion might ring some brave man's knell."

The second introduces us to the interior of the city.

"Under the guidance of his trusty attendant, Colonel Mannering, after threading a dark lane or two, reached the High Street, then clanging with the voices of oyster-women and the bells of pie-men, for it had, as his guide assured him, just 'chappit eight upon the Tron.'   It was long since Mannering had been in the street of a crowded metropolis, which, with its noise and clamour, its sounds of trade, of revelry and of license, its variety of lights, and the eternally changing bustle of its hundred groups, offers, by night especially, a spectacle which, though composed of the most vulgar materials when they are separately considered, has, when they are combined, a striking and powerful effect on the imagination.   The extraordinary height of the houses was marked by lights, which, glimmering irregularly along their front, ascended so high among the attics, that they seemed at length to twinkle in the middle sky.   This *coup d'œil*, which still subsists in a certain degree, was then more imposing, owing to the uninterrupted range of buildings on each side, which, broken only at the space where the North Bridge joins the main street, formed a superb and uniform Place, extending from the front of the Luckenbooths to the head of the Canongate, and corresponding in breadth and length to the uncommon height of the buildings on either side."

Since then this great Place has become more majestic, as well as more open, by the clearing away of the Luckenbooths : but nothing can be finer than the touch of the graphic yet reticent pencil which sets down before us the glimmering of the irregular lights which seemed at last to twinkle in the middle sky.   This was how the main street of Edinburgh still appeared when Scott himself was a boy, and no doubt he must have caught the aspect of the previous sketch on some king's birthday or other public holiday, the 4th of June perhaps, that familiar festival in other regions, when the guns of the Castle were saluting and the smoke hanging about those heights like a veil.

It was one of the privations of Scott's life as it began to fall into its last subdued and suffering stage that he had to give up his Edinburgh house and the cheerful company which had so long made his winters pleasant. He loved the country and his home there at all seasons, as the readers of the poetical chapters of friendly dedication and communing addressed to different friends between the cantos of *Marmion* will well remember : but yet the yearly change, the natural transfer of life in the short days to the cheerful surroundings of town, the twinkling of those very lights, the assembling of bright faces, the meeting of old friends, were always dear to him, and this sacrifice was not one of the least which he made during the tremendous struggle of his waning years.

With no other name could we so fitly close the story of our ancient capital, a story fitfully told with many breaks and omissions, yet offering some thread of connection to link together the different eras of a picturesque and characteristic national life. Had space and knowledge permitted, there is, in the records of Scottish law alone, much that is interesting, along with a still larger contribution of wit and humour and individual character, to the elucidation of the period which passed between the end of the history of Edinburgh under her native kings and the beginning of her brilliant record under the modern reign of literature and poetry. This book, however, does not pretend to set forth the Edinburgh of the Kirk or the Parliament House, each of which has an existing record of its own. Seated on the rocks which are more old than any history, though those precipices are now veiled with verdure and softness, and the iron way of triumphant modern science runs at their feet ; with her crown of sacred architecture hanging over her among the mists, and the little primeval shrine mounted upon her highest ridge ; with her palace, all too small for the requirements of an enlarged and splendid royalty, and the great crouched and dormant sentinel of nature watching over her through all the centuries ; with her partner, sober and ample, like a comely matron, attended by all the modern arts and comforts, seated at the old mother's feet,—

GEORGE STREET, EDINBURGH

Edinburgh can never be less than royal, one of the crowned and queenly cities of the world.   It does not need for this distinction that there should be millions of inhabitants within her walls, or all the great threads of industry and wealth gathered in her hands. The pathos of much that is past and over for ever, the awe of many tragedies, a recollection almost more true than any reality of the present, of ages and glories gone—add a charm which the wealthiest and greatest interests of to-day cannot give, to the city, always living, always stirring, where she stands amid traditionary smoke and mist, the grey metropolis of the North, the Edinburgh of a thousand fond associations,

Our Own Romantic Town.

THE END